Version 3.0

Contemporary Asian American Plays

Edited by Chay Yew

Theatre Communications Group
New York
2011

LIBRARY OF CONGRESS CATALOGING-IN-PUBLICATION DATA
Version 3.0 : contemporary Asian American plays / edited by Chay Yew.
p. cm.
ISBN 978-1-55936-363-1
1. American drama—Asian American authors. 2. American drama—20th century. 3. American drama—21st century. 4. Asian Americans—Drama. I. Yew, Chay. II. Title: Version three point zero.
PS628.A85V47   2011
812.008'0895073—dc23   2011019971

Book design and composition by Lisa Govan
Cover art and design by Bob Stern

First Edition, June 2011

Version 3.0

Version 3.0 is for David, Frank, Philip, Wakako and many other Asian American playwrights on whose shoulders we all stand, and for Asian American theatre companies which always gave us a place to call home.

This anthology is also dedicated to Gordon Davidson, the Founding Artistic Director of Mark Taper Forum in Los Angeles, who passionately supported the Asian Theatre Workshop (ATW) for ten years, from 1995–2005. The Workshop gave opportunities to many third-wave playwrights so that they could write, develop and produce their own work. Some of which you find in this anthology.

During that fervent decade, ATW was fueled by the encouragement and work of my fellow artists and colleagues at the Taper: Luis Alfaro, John Belluso, Anthony Byrnes, Dolores Chavez, Robert Egan, Brian Freeman, Nancy Hereford, Victoria Lewis, Phyllis Moberly, Lisa Peterson, Lee Richardson and Annie Weissman.

Contents

Contents

Foreword

By David Henry Hwang

In 1979, when my first play *FOB* was presented at the Eugene O'Neill National Playwrights Conference in Waterford, Connecticut, the idea of an Asian American play was relatively new. I remember overhearing the sound designer, not knowing I was within earshot, ask the stage manager, "So what are we going to use for this? Chink music?"

Since then, Asian American theatre has come a long way, and now includes many of America's indispensable theatre artists. As usual, one can see the glass as half full or half empty. On the one hand, works by Asian American playwrights have been produced in some of this country's most prestigious not-for-profit theatres, including New York's Public Theater and Los Angeles's Center Theater Group. Moreover, Asian American theatre companies have blossomed across the country. The invaluable *Asian American Theatre Revue* (www.aatrevue.com), at last count, lists more than ninety professional and community groups in North America.

The glass looks less full, however, when we consider that productions of Asian American plays by mainstream theatres remain relatively rare, particularly outside New York City or the west coast. Producers worry that they won't be able to cast these plays, or that audiences may not relate to the stories. As for the Asian American companies, many produce infrequently, and their ongoing futures are uncertain. San Francisco's seminal Asian American Theater Company, for instance, has struggled in recent years to survive.

Still, Asian American theatre continues to grow. I've been particularly impressed by this genre's capacity for change. The term "Asian American," first applied primarily to those with ancestry from a handful of East Asian nations, has itself expanded over the past decades. Similarly, Asian American plays have repeatedly broken new ground to remain relevant and bold.

As a kid in 1960s Los Angeles, when I knew a particular TV show or movie was going to feature an Asian character or storyline, I went out of my way *not* to watch it. It was safe to assume that whatever I saw would make me feel "icky." In those days, Asians and Asian Americans in pop culture could be "good," such as Charlie Chan; or "bad," such as Fu Manchu and various Chinese, Korean and Vietnamese soldiers. They rarely, however, resembled actual human beings. Instead, they were one- and two-dimensional figures, poorly written—literally alien. They were, in a word, inhuman.

In 1965, when the nation's first Asian American theatre, East West Players, was founded in Los Angeles, Asians constituted only about 0.5% of the U.S. population, as opposed to 5% in 2007. Since relatively few Americans came into contact with actual Asians, their primary frame of reference was popular imagery. They assumed that we all lived in, well, Asia, a land about which they knew very little, except that American kids should clean their plates because there were starving kids in China.

The so-called "first wave" of Asian American dramatists, emerging mostly in the 1960s and 1970s, sought to claim cultural space for works neither white American nor foreign-Asian. East West Players, originally envisioned as a showcase for Asian American actors, stepped up to the challenge when its founding artistic director, Mako, realized that the theatre's mission would not be achieved if it did not produce a body of new dramatic work.

In 1968, during East West Player's third season, my mother, Dorothy Hwang, served as the rehearsal pianist for a production of Menotti's operetta *The Medium*, reset in postwar Japan. I was ten years old, with no particular interest in theatre. Given the choice, however, of going to rehearsals or being babysat at my aunt's house, I chose the former. We rehearsed in the basement of a church in the Silver Lake district of Los Angeles. Looking back, I realize I was privileged to have seen Asian Americans as actors, artists and theatrical leaders, and to have witnessed Mako directing one of his first shows.

During the late 1970s, when I started trying to write plays in college, I was inspired by the work of first-wave dramatists such as Frank Chin, C. Y. Lee, Momoko lko and Wakako Yamauchi. I put together an Asian American arts series at my university, bringing artists to campus. In those pre-internet days, you had to ask around to find out who was doing interesting work. I was told of a singer-songwriter named Philip Kan Gotanda, and called him up to meet. Turned out, we were both interested in writing plays and, since I happened to play electric violin, we also formed a band together. Philip and I became part of Asian American playwriting's "second wave," as did R. A. Shiomi, a Japanese Canadian who brought us up to Vancouver to give a concert. Work, art and friendships blossomed in this underground scene. We never expected that what we were creating would one day be studied in schools, let alone penetrate mainstream American culture.

As a "second-wave" playwright, I found myself writing about identity, as did many of my peers. Once we tore down the stereotypes that mainstream America had imposed on us, what was left behind? Asian America itself was a uniquely *American* construct. In Asia, Chinese people do not see themselves as having a great deal in common with the Japanese or Filipinos. The term, invented in the late 1960s, was in many ways a convenience, unifying Asian people to broaden our political influence. It also, however, reflected the reality that, as a Chinese American, my life experiences were more similar to those of, say, a Japanese American, than to a Chinese person living in Shanghai.

Second-wave writers often searched for the holy grail of authenticity. Freeing ourselves from the racist images that mainstream America had imposed on us, we reasoned, would reveal our true selves. But which truth? Battles raged, with authors and scholars accusing each other of "reinforcing stereotypes" and writing "fake" stories.

Second-wave Asian American dramatists were not a particularly diverse group. We argued that the term "Asian" should replace the colonialist and geographically vague "Orient." However, we did not conceptualize ourselves as coming from the whole of Asia. Rather, the majority of us were of Japanese, Chinese and Filipino descent— in short, that same geographically vague area formerly known as the "Orient." As for mixed-race Asians, we remained a little uncertain about their place in the movement. The playwright Velina Hasu Houston, for instance, whose ancestries encompass Japan, Africa, Cuba and Native American Indians, has written about sometimes having felt excluded.

"Third-wave" playwrights, many of whom are represented in this volume, have expanded the world of Asian American theatre.

My generation, so close to the birth of Asian America, sometimes saw it as the key to the riddle of our identity: I am Asian American, therefore I am. Third-wave writers, who grew up taking the idea for granted, regard ethnicity as simply one piece in a much more complicated mosaic of identity. Their plays explore a wide variety of concerns: from family dramas like *Durango* and *Last of the Suns* to the pop culture/digital dreamscape of *wAve*.

Third-wave writers have largely abandoned the quest for the holy grail of authenticity, since Asian America is neither monolithic nor uniform. No single writer can represent an entire culture; only a community of writers can do that. Moreover, the genre now includes writers whose backgrounds span much more of Asia's actual geography. South Asian, Vietnamese and Korean American dramatists, for instance, are among today's most exciting. Furthermore, with about 14% of Asian Americans self-identifying as multiracial in the 2000 census, our theatre now embraces stories and artists of mixed ancestry.

Second-wave writers were determined to define ourselves as American, not foreigners. Third-wave writers grew up in a shrinking world, with national borders becoming ever less relevant. The immigration story of *Swoony Planet*, for instance, is more fluid than the similar stories of an earlier era; author Han Ong has described his play as a "frequent-flier narrative." Asian American theatre continues to push boundaries.

I am inspired by the writers in this volume, who have questioned assumptions and expanded the palate of our nation's dramatic literature. According to traditional thinking, children learn from their elders. In art, however, it is often the elders who have much to learn from the next generation. *Version 3.0* playwrights have kept Asian American theatre vital. On a personal level, seeing and reading their plays has kept me young.

May 2011
Brooklyn, New York

David Henry Hwang's plays include *M. Butterfly*, *Yellow Face*, *Golden Child* and *FOB*. He is a Tony Award-winner and three-time nominee, a three-time Obie Award-winner, and has twice been a finalist for the Pulitzer Prize.

Introduction

By Chay Yew

There is no single Asian theatre.

There are, however, myriad theatrical forms in Asia—Sanskrit drama in India; Beijing opera in China; Wayang Kulit in Indonesia; Kabuki, Bunraku and Noh in Japan; Talchum and Pansori in Korea, just to name a few.

Although they share several common characteristics, each theatrical form is different. Some are rarely spoken, instead they are sung, danced, mimed and chanted. Others are visual and evocative, and others, poetical and literary. These works are also loosely plotted; despite an emphasis on storytelling, the Western dramaturgy of escalating incidents, plot reversals and climaxes are largely absent. Much of these works are highly stylized; performance techniques require formal training and are passed on from generation to generation. The stories in these performances are rooted in tradition, religion and history; stories, small and epic, that were told three- or four-hundred years ago are still presented to a modern audience. Indian Sanskrit drama dates back to the eighth-century BCE, long before the birth of classical Greek tragedy. These works are some of the earliest theatrical texts.[1] The *Ramayana* and *Mahabharata* are still being performed in the streets of Mumbai or in festivals in Bali.

From the 1200s through the 1840s, the image of Far East Asia had been evolving for centuries in the minds of Westerners. From the Middle Ages to the early Renaissance, contacts between Europe and Asia were relatively sporadic. Stories of China were brought back by a handful of explorers, merchants and missionaries. Marco Polo's image of China also fueled Westerners' imaginations with the opulent, majestic East. Attracted by the wealth of the Far East, the Dutch and Portuguese began to sail to China; followed by the English and French. When they arrived, they learned that the country's resources could be exploited for financial gain. Soon, Europeans craved tea, spices and wares, such as Chinese silk, ivory, lacquer, collectively known as "chinoiserie."[2]

Given the curiosity and hunger for all things "Oriental," it wasn't long before stories about the Chinese appeared on European stages. The first known play to be performed in Europe was *The Orphan of China*. Originally written in 1330 by Chi Chun-Hsiang, the piece was often considered a minor work. More than four centuries after its completion, Father Prémare, a French Jesuit priest in China, conferred distinction on the work by making it the first Chinese play to be printed in any European language. In Father Prémare's version, informed by his knowledge of French Neoclassicism, he excised what he considered repetitive portions of the play and many allusions to classical Chinese literature. Moreover, French dramatic conventions did not allow characters to suddenly burst into song, so, all songs were cut.

In 1735, Prémare's play appeared in an anthology of Chinese works compiled by another French Jesuit, Du Halde, who had never visited China. For the next twenty years, *The Orphan of China* was translated into Italian and English, but the most important subsequent work was Voltaire's *L'Orphelin de la Chine* which opened at the Comédie-Française in August 1755 to acclaim. Voltaire altered the piece by adding a philosophical significance missing from Prémare's version and the Chinese original: he rewrote the story to accommodate the Confucian virtues of refinement and pacifism (the same virtues he saw in himself and his culture), which he greatly admired in the Chinese culture.[3]

The next noteworthy adaptation was Arthur Murphy's, the form in which was performed at London's Drury Lane in 1759, with David Garrick as the lead; it eventually opened before pre-Colonial American audiences at the Southwark Theatre in Philadelphia on January 16, 1767. Murphy's version presented prevailing Western attitudes about the Chinese, who they considered inferior, bloodthirsty, passionate and uncivilized.[4] This was the first representation of the Chinese on American stages and, for decades, it remained the only dramatic portrayal of Asians in America.

In the mid-nineteenth century, Chinese immigrants arrived in the United States to work as laborers, particularly on the transcontinental railroad and in the mining industry. While industrial employers were eager for new and cheap labor, the white public resented the presence of what would eventually become known as the "yellow peril." Despite the provisions for equal treatment of Chinese immigrants in the 1868 Burlingame Treaty, political and labor organizations rallied against the immigration of cheap Chinese labor. Newspapers condemned the policies of employers, and even church leaders denounced the entrance of these aliens into what was regarded as a land for whites only.

Given the growing presence of the Chinese population in the nineteenth-century United States, it wasn't long before they found themselves represented in other plays, such as Mark Twain and Brett Harte's play *Ah Sin*. The play opened at Daly's Fifth Avenue Theatre in New York City on July 31, 1877. One would assume that a Chinese character in a title role suggested the assimilation of the Chinese into American life. This was not the case. A stock character, Ah Sin, served only as a plot-advancing device between the machinations of the white villain Broderick and hero Plunkett. As Broderick's servant, Ah Sin was a simple buffoon who spoke broken English; throughout the play, he is called by other characters "a slanted-eye son of yellow jaunders," "moral cancer, you unsolvable political problem," "poor dumb animal" and a host of other disparaging descriptions.[5]

If the Chinese character was used sparingly as a comic foil and a plot device in *Ah Sin*, Chinese characters were antagonists that drove almost every scene in Henry Grimm's *The Chinese Must Go*. Here the Chinese are portrayed as sinister, greedy and duplicitous; they exhort and threaten the Blaine family for unpaid services; the Blaines (as with every other white family, Grimm warned) have long been too dependent on the Chinese for domestic services. Throughout the piece, the Chinese talk of white slavery, addicting white women to opium and the trafficking of Chinese prostitutes to America. At the top of the play, one Chinese character, Ah Coy, complains about white Americans while smoking on an opium pipe:

> I tellee you, white man big fools; eatee too muchee, drinkee too muchee and talkee too muchee . . . By and by, white man catchee no money; Chinaman catchee heap money; Chinaman workee cheap, plenty work; white man workee dear, no work . . . By and by, no more white working man in California; all Chinaman—sabee?[6]

With the white American cast as victim, the drama plays to the predominant fears of audiences that the Chinese were a menace needing to be contained and deported. Often at the most inappropriate moments of the play, the white character Frank repeats the phrase: "The Chinese Must Go!" This script was most likely performed by amateur actors in meetings held at "anti-coolie" clubs. The audience would have applauded because the play would have reflected its own racist and populist sentiments. In 1879, a small advertisement appeared in a major San Francisco newspaper offering the play to theatre managers. No records exist of a performance at any established theatre, but it was, however, later performed at a theatre in Tucson, Arizona, where it was a great success.[7]

As hostility against the Chinese grew, the United States Congress passed the Chinese Exclusion Act in 1882, which prohibited immigration from China for the next ten years. The Chinese Exclusion Act was the first U.S. law ever to prevent immigration and naturalization on the basis of race. This law was then extended by the Geary Act in 1892. The Geary Act also made it mandatory for Chinese residents of the U.S. to carry a resident permit; failure to carry the permit at all times was punishable by deportation or a year of hard labor. In addition, Chinese residents were not allowed to bear witness in court, nor could they receive bail in habeas corpus proceedings. Versions of the law actually remained in effect until the Immigration Act of 1965. These laws not only prevented new immigration but also prevented the reunion of the families of thousands of Chinese men already living in the U.S. who had left China without their wives and children; anti-miscegenation laws in many states also prohibited Chinese men from marrying white women.

Despite their anger at the "yellow peril," Americans continued to be fascinated by all things "Oriental" at the turn of the twentieth century. When Asian-themed plays were brought to the stage, such as *San Toy, The Daughter of Heaven, Sultan of Sulu* and *The Yellow Jacket,* one would find an exotic China still filled with historical inaccuracies and stereotypes; all characters, of course, were played by white actors.

One interesting exception was perhaps Eugene O'Neill's treatment of Marco Polo in *Marco Millions*, which appeared on Broadway in 1928. *Marco Millions* is a parody of Western attitudes of both the Far East and the Arab world, places where Christian moral attitudes and the European way of life and colonialism were never quite embraced, either in 1271 or later in 1928.[8] Here, O'Neill treated his Chinese characters "positively" and seriously and did not make them speak pidgin English.[9]

In 1934, Lindsay and Crouse's musical, *Anything Goes,* threw in two Chinese ninnies, Ching and Ling, as embarrassing comic relief, squawking and screeching in broken English.

After the repeal of prohibition in 1933, an Asian American night-club scene, commonly known as the "Chop Suey Circuit," emerged in clubs and restaurants in the Chinatowns of New York, Chicago, Seattle and several other cities. The most famous was the Forbidden City nightclub in San Francisco. Two or more shows were presented nightly to a Caucasian tourist trade attracted to the supposed exoticism of all-Asian revues. Singers and dancers mimicked popular white American acts; magicians, jugglers, acrobats and contortionists usually wore traditional flamboyant Asian costumes to evoke the mysterious Far East.[10] These supper clubs provided opportunities for Asian American entertainers to earn their living.

After World War II, Asians continued to appear as stereotypes—a ruthless polygamist barbaric king, an Oriental prostitute with a heart of gold and simple-minded postwar Japanese villagers in need of lessons in democracy—in *The King and I, The World of Suzy Wong* and *Teahouse of the August Moon.* These two-dimensional portrayals were not only found in the theatre but in movies and on television.

In 1958, a landmark Broadway musical featured Asian Americans as characters: Rodgers and Hammerstein's *Flower Drum Song,* adapted from C. Y. Lee's novel about a multigenerational conflict set in San Francisco's Chinatown (though the original production had many non-Asians in the leading roles). Despite a stronger presence of Asians and Asian Americans on stage, none of the above works were written by Asian Americans; playwright David Henry Hwang would later adapt the Oscar Hammerstein II and Joseph Fields book for *Flower Drum Song* for another Broadway outing in 2002, this time featuring an all Asian American cast of actors and singers.

The first signs of significant change came in 1965 when a group of actors founded East West Players in Los Angeles as a means to fight racism in Hollywood by creating nonstereotypical roles for Asian Americans. Led by an actor, Mako, the actors at East West envisioned theatre as a platform to showcase their talent for the television and film industries. By the early 1970s, the theatre began to actively encourage Asian American writers to adapt their short stories and novels into plays and to write original scripts.

In 1971, Frank Chin's *The Chickencoop Chinaman* shared this development slot with Momoko Iko's *The Gold Watch.* A year later, in May 1972, *The Chickencoop Chinaman* premiered at the

American Place Theatre, becoming the first Asian American play to be produced in New York City.

Chin later founded the Asian American Theatre Workshop in San Francisco to nurture original playwriting by Asian Americans (the theatre was later renamed Asian American Theatre Company). At this time, Asian American theatre began to flourish. Theatrical Ensemble of Asians began in 1974 on the campus of the University of Washington in Seattle (later becoming the Asian Exclusion Act, then changing its name to Northwest Asian American Theatre). In addition to acting and playwriting, the theatre emphasized community activism and became a cultural center for Asian Americans in the Pacific Northwest. Pan Asian Repertory Theatre emerged as part of Off-Off-Broadway theatre in 1978. Founded by Tisa Chang, Pan Asian Rep became the representative Asian American theatre company in New York City and introduced Asian American plays to East Coast audiences.

The first wave of Asian American playwrights included Wakako Yamauchi (*And the Souls Shall Dance*), Rick Shiomi (*Yellow Fever*), Momoko Iko (*Flowers and Household Gods*), Edward *Sakamoto* (*Yellow Is My Favorite Color*) and Frank Chin (*The Year of the Dragon*). Common themes in plays by first-wave writers included Asian American history and immigration, generational and familial conflict, cultural identity and nationalism.

The first commercially successful Asian American play was David Henry Hwang's *M. Butterfly*. Produced in 1988, it was the first Asian American play to be produced on Broadway, and went on to win the Tony Award for Best Play. The success of *M. Butterfly* created a countrywide interest in Asian American plays, and regional theatre companies around the country began to produce plays by Hwang and other second-wave playwrights, such as Philip Kan Gotanda (*The Wash, Yankee Dawg You Die*) and Velina Hasu Houston (*Tea*). These playwrights were interested in writing plays that bridged and straddled the old world with the new.[11]

Beginning in the late 1980s, a new crop of Asian American theatres flourished in cities across the country. These companies' artistic agendas expanded greatly from the original Asian theatres in aesthetics, mission and styles. As with the original four Asian American theatre companies, Ma-Yi Theater Company, Second Generation and Silk Road Theatre Project produced only new and original plays, while National Asian American Theatre Company focused on producing Western classical plays featuring all Asian casts; Pangea World Theater presented socio-geopolitical, multidisciplinary theatre; and Mu Performing Arts fused Asian theatrical aesthetics to specifically cater to local audiences.

In the late 1990s, Asian American plays further increased their presence in theatres around the country with works by third-wave playwrights. While these playwrights continue to wrestle with the same issues of the first two generations of writers, they feel that race and ethnicity are mere jumping-off points in addressing multifaceted experiences of being an Asian American; they are also interested in exploring their often complex relationships with other communities and people outside of Asian America.

Whereas the first two waves of playwrights were mainly Chinese and Japanese Americans, the third wave included Asians of Filipino, Indian, Korean and Vietnamese descent. This generation of playwrights also wrote less realistic plays and pushed theatrical and aesthetical borders further than the first two waves. Some of these playwrights include Prince Gomolvilas (*The Theory of Everything*), Naomi Iizuka (*36 Views*) and Elizabeth Wong (*Kimchee and Chitlins*).

The other third-wave playwrights are represented in this anthology *Version 3.0*. As no anthology could cover everything, this particular compendium hopes to capture the landscape that defines the third wave of Asian American plays. I see these plays not so much as a record of a specific generation of Asian American playwriting, but the cumulative legacy of Hwang, Gotanda, Chin and Yamauchi.

I did not like my work. But I did it. Every little thing have to be put into computer. Make a report and another report and another. All day long, every day, day after day . . . I did. And if I didn't get laid off, I would still be there, doing. And I would feel . . . lucky. Lucky to have some place to go every day. But why? Why did I want so little? Where did I learn to want so little for myself?

In Julia Cho's achingly haunting drama *Durango*, Boo-Seng Lee, a middle-aged Korean immigrant, sits poolside at a motel with a fellow guest, and describes the twenty-year office job from which he has just been laid off: "Where did I learn to want so little for myself?" That is the question that haunts the three-member Lee family: Boo-Seng, shackled for years in an arranged marriage, now a widowed father of two boys; Isaac, his twenty-one-year-old musician slacker son; and thirteen-year-old Jimmy, an overachieving swimming prodigy. All of them are trapped in lives of quiet desperation, and each yearn for something they think is unattainable. Their first, last and only chance for happiness is symbolized by a road trip to Durango, one that turns into a journey of self-discovery and acceptance. Julia Cho is a master witness to the complexities of the human heart; she exposes the brutal and honest feelings of her characters not in her dialogue but between the spaces of words and in the wells of pauses and silences. Early in the play, Isaac explains to Jimmy the enduring popularity of the Marvel comic book superhero Wolverine: "He was made to suffer. That's what his gift is. And because he suffers, because he feels pain, we see in him the truest expression of what we, as humans, experience." Those same words apply to the men of *Durango*. They exemplify, in some way, what we all go through every day.[12]

––––––

> We'll just go point A to point B. Then back to A and back to B and back and forth. Always in between. Living nowhere.

Sunil Kuruvilla's *Rice Boy* is a luscious, quietly moving, coming-of-age drama that explores the difficulties of migration with respect to a South Asian Canadian family. Tommy, a twelve-year-old boy, returns with his father to his parents' native Kerala, India, for the first time since his mother's tragic drowning there ten years earlier. Accustomed only to life in Canada, Tommy has a difficult time adjusting to India. He soon develops an endearing relationship with his sixteen-year-old cousin, Tina, a housebound paraplegic who is learning the ancient art of *kolam* (the creation of elaborate patterns with rice powder) from her grandmother in preparation for her arranged marriage to a man she has never met. As Tommy shows Tina the world beyond her front porch, he begins to see India with new eyes. This enchanting interwoven, cross-cultural narrative also situates the importance of disability aesthetics in the play, and this makes us consider questions of agency and independence in relation to the modern Indian woman who still faces constrictions of tradition.

––––––

> I'm not telling you this isn't your country / I'm telling you: / Know your cage . . . Know your cage well / memorize its dimensions / its distinguishing traits / so that when you go to bed / in the instant before you pitch into black that's what you see the clearest and / you'll know / if you run or / if you kill or / if you— What do you do.

The first play of his *Suitcase Trilogy*, Han Ong's *Swoony Planet* is an intimate epic about how immigration is changing the face of America. This gritty and poetic play tells of Kirtana, a single, Indian woman, who searches for her runaway son Farouk. Jessica, a Filipina who has adjusted to life in the Midwest, aids her search, leading Kirtana to an unimaginable world no child should experience. Artie, Jessica's son, races to find the father who abandoned him sixteen years ago. Each of them, longing for wholeness and the chance to "swoon," takes on an unforgettable, compromising journey into self and country. "In *Swoony Planet,* the immigrant narrative is a frequent-flier narrative," Ong says. "It's been flown so often, it's bleached dry of any significance. America almost desperately needs the mirror of the outsider. I don't think there is such a thing as the American Dream, personally. My characters have certain notions of it, such as the dream of being away from where you are, or were. Like the disillusion of all dreams, it's a journey from generic to specific— from the fuzziness of cotton and pink and the wide, blue expanse of sky to more specific details, like being spat on at a street corner. In my plays it's a journey from up to down, an inverted triangle. It's the limitless possibilities of coming to America and the disparity between its myth and reality."[13]

> I despise your petty desires, your dick stuck between countries. Your silly grasp towards a deeper identity. "Who Am I?" you ask in that whining voice. WHO THE FUCK CARES? Nobody. I renounce you as I would one of the Japanese soldiers taking my father to one of the work camps. Taking my mother to be a comfort woman. Face it. You're no more American than a bowl of kimchee stew, hot and fermented, opening your nostrils to the pigmented pigskin of your fucked up identity crisis.

Sung Rno sets his rollercoaster of a play, *wAve,* "somewhere between *M*A*S*H* and Margaret Cho, between the 38th Parallel, between two centuries, between McDonald's and Burger King."[14] Loosely inspired by Euripides' *Medea* and with a chorus of comic characters, this wildly inventive pop satire focuses on a dysfunctional love story that careens from madcap farce to tragedy, as an isolated Korean immigrant's dream of a perfect life as an American housewife turns deadly. In his own version of the classical myth, Sung Rno has called one of his leading characters M, and given her a husband named

Jason, who is having an affair with a digitized Marilyn Monroe while he's starring in a film version of *Miss Saigon* re-dubbed *Mister Phnom Penh*. Meanwhile, M, who betrayed her family on Jason's behalf, sits alone watching *The Chinky and Gooky Show*, featuring two film critics whose rating system runs along the lines of: "Moo goo gai PAN" and "Chicken kung PAO." The result is a passionately remixed, exhilaratingly lyrical work exploring the collision of cultures, love, immigration and contemporary American culture.

———

A meteorite. A chip off of some billion-year-old comet that came crashing through here to let out all the ghosts, all the stories, all the history . . . To let us know . . . we can make up the words ourselves.

In Diana Son's witty, wisely observed and unflinchingly explosive *Satellites*, her biting and urban characters inhabit a constantly shifting world where racial, social, economic and sexual borders have become so permeable that they never quite know who or where they are at any given moment. Korean American architect Nina and her African American husband, Miles, and their baby Hannah find themselves marooned in their new home—an uninhabited brownstone fixer-upper in a gentrifying Brooklyn. Amidst the couple's financial troubles, sexual inadequacies and Miles's unemployment, a brick is hurled through the couple's window—a literal wake-up call. Given Nina and Miles's own distance from their respective cultural identities, they wish for Hannah, a better connection. Nina, assimilated away from her Korean heritage, hires a nanny who's able to sing Korean lullabies to the baby and "basically do what a Korean mother would do," says Son. For Miles, the fact that his African American identity was sublimated by his adoption into a Caucasian family is made more evident by the visit of his adoptive, white brother. "Miles grew up in a white neighborhood and knew what it was like to stand on your front lawn and be called a nigger," Son adds. "I titled the play *Satellites* because all of the characters are free-floating . . . A satellite is an entity that orbits around a larger entity; all of the characters lack a defining thing within their lives, so they end up colliding into each other."[15]

———

Sometimes, Twila, sometimes you must go back to the first, the FIRST time, the beginner time when everything was new, and closer to true nature. Remember it . . . remember.

Alice Tuan's first play, *Last of the Suns,* centers on Yeh Yeh, a Chinese Nationalist army general, shriveling away under the harsh California sun as his failed ice-skating champion granddaughter, Twila, comes to visit him on his one-hundredth birthday. *Last of the Suns* is an acrobatically lyrical, perversely intelligent piece of theatre. Here, Tuan reinvents and deconstructs the Asian American play: bordering between the real and fantastical, she fuses Chinese mythology, her personal family history, her wicked sense of humor and American kitchen-sink drama in an amalgamated triumph that assaults every one of the five senses. She uses streetwise and theatrical language to blend Chinese folklore with the banalities of American consumerism. Says Tuan, "My grandfather, who was a lieutenant general in Chiang Kai-Shek's Nationalist army, lived with us in his later years. I woke to the sound of beeping one morning . . . beep beep beep, endlessly . . . and found my grandpaps bent over the microwave, pressing numbers, trying to warm his tea. He could not find the start button, and my screamed explanation to the ninety-three-year-old man sparked a moment of the past trying to start 'fire by buttons' in the modern world. This literally was the first scene I ever wrote. I think playwriting was a way to try and fuse contradictions, old/new, East/West, male/female power, which has led me to a synthesis point in which my drama thinking stems from, always striving for that point above the original plane of conception."[16]

I was one of these real American patriots then. Back then, I was all American . . . At the time, I was ashamed of being Japanese. I think many Japanese Americans felt the same way . . . That sort of changed while I was in the camp. I hated the war, because it wasn't just between the governments. It went down to the people, and it nurtured hate. The evacuation showed us that even though there is a constitution, constitutional rights could be taken away very easily.

In the wake of America's entry into World War II, more than 120,000 Americans of Japanese ancestry were forced to leave their homes, possessions and communities, and report to relocation centers and internment camps. This federal action, authorized by President Franklin Delano Roosevelt on February 19, 1942, through Executive Order 9066, led to the suspension of many civil rights of Japanese Americans. One lasting legacy of the internment experience was the so-called "loyalty questionnaire," which was designed to test the loyalty of the incarcerated Japanese Americans. Two questions: #27 (willingness to serve in the U.S. Armed Forces) and #28 (willingness to swear unqualified allegiance to the U.S. and forswear allegiance to any other nation or government), were both disturbing and confusing to the internees.

Using these questions as a focal point to reveal the unfair treatment of the internees, I wrote *Question 27, Question 28* to bring to life not only the experiences of the imprisoned Japanese Americans, but also of their non-Japanese contemporaries and how some of them reacted to this violation of civil rights. Told exclusively through the perspectives of women, this documentary play is based on verbatim excerpts from oral histories and interviews. When I was younger, I had little patience for historical dramas based on internment camps. I thought I could walk away from history and create my own, but history has a way of tapping you on the back as you're running toward the future. History came tapping after September 11, 2001, and made the relevance of the internment camps obvious to me and many others. Incidents quickly came to light in which law-abiding Arab Americans, or people who just looked as if they might be from the Middle East, suffered abuse ranging from suspicious stares to beatings. Civil liberty issues became ongoing news. Post–September 11 restrictions have not touched what befell the Japanese American community after December 7, 1941. But, I felt freedom's fragility in the face of a national crisis, and saw the story of the Japanese American internment as a cautionary tale worth repeating.[17]

———

> You know . . . has it ever occurred to you—that even a work written by someone who's one-hundred-percent non-Asian might be authentic? Or, that one written by a full-blooded Asian might not be? What if the book by the non-Asian was better? . . . What does "authentic" mean anyway? For instance, let's just say—what if we weren't real people, what if we were fictional characters, would we be authentic?

When I founded Asian Theatre Workshop at the Mark Taper Forum in 1995, my first priority was to commission established and emerging playwrights in American theatre to address the relationships between Asian Americans and non–Asian Americans in a single theatrical piece. *The Square* came to life one day through a conversation with Lisa Peterson, then resident director at the Taper. Riffing on an article about an environmental performance staged in a park by Peter Handke in Germany, we started conceiving a play set in a fictitious setting based on Columbus Park in Manhattan's Chinatown. Asian Theatre Workshop then commissioned eight Asian American and eight non–Asian American playwrights to create a theatrical forum of perceptions, experiences and relationships of the Asian American community with non–Asian Americans in a ten-minute piece that used the park and its environs as its setting. *The Square* stages the relationships of Asian Americans with other communities and enacts our contemporary dilemmas around issues of race and power. Like any collective identity, Asian American is intersected by multiple forces: diaspora, sexuality, class, gender, among others. And historical and demographic changes—interracial marriage, children of mixed race, post-1965 immigration—create an increasingly complicated, multiracial landscape. The playwrights voice these complexities and articulate visions of both danger and promise. Indeed, *The Square* contains the promise of our futures in its own structure. The product of interracial collaboration, it is alive with unexpected connections, startling contrasts and vibrant multiplicity.[18]

———

I encourage you to seek out other Asian American playwrights who are not featured in *Version 3.0*; discover, too, the other plays that make up the diverse body of work of each playwright included in this anthology. A wonderful online resource for Asian American plays and playwrights is the Asian American Theatre Revue (www.aatrevue.com), passionately maintained by Roger Tang.

I have not included theatre work by Asian American solo performers who exist alongside the third-wave playwrights. They are an integral part of our Asian American theatre ecology and have existed mainly in the fringe scene. The writings and performances of Alison M. de la Cruz (*Naturally Graceful*), Jude Narita (*Coming into Passion/Song for a Sansei*), Dan Kwong (*Monkhood in 3 Easy Lessons*), Sandra Tsing Loh (*Aliens in America*), Kristina Wong (*Wong Flew Over the Cuckoo's Nest*), Denise Uyehara (*Maps of City and Body*), to name a few, are provocative and political, as they are witty and poignant. They are not to be missed.

As I'm writing this, there has already been a fourth wave of Asian American playwrights emerging in the recent years. They include Rajiv Joseph (*Bengal Tiger at the Baghdad Zoo*), Young Jean Lee (*Songs of Dragons Flying to Heaven*), Michael Lew (*Microcrisis*), Kenneth Lin (*Po Boy Tango*), Qui Nguyen (*Trial by Water*), Lloyd

Suh (*American Hwangap*), Lauren Yee (*Ching Chong Chinaman*) and many others. The playwrights of this new generation do not always identify as Asian American, nor do they write plays with Asian American characters. Even third-wave playwright Julia Cho admitted, "What I was trying to articulate in a lot of these plays is what it is to be Asian American . . . But I think I might be getting to the end of that exploration."[19]

Since no single definable Asian theatre exists, no single Asian American theatre does either. These plays are as evocative as they are visual. Poetical and literary, these works are performed in a multitude of theatrical aesthetics: in traditional and experimental forms of drama, comedy, performance and musical theatre. Yet every play (epic or intimate) uniquely tells of a collective and varied experience of diaspora, immigration and citizenship. And these stories can only be born in the U.S. For Asian American's plays are undeniably American experiences, and our stories belong as part of American history and the American theatre canon.

Will a fifth or seventh wave of Asian American playwrights emerge in the future? Or will we be able to finally shed "Asian" and just be "American"? Will we have all assimilated into an increasingly diverse America? Shall we look to the history of Yiddish theatre or even perhaps gay theatre as examples? Once these theatres served a specific community and told stories that reflected their audiences. Now their voices can be heard from Broadway to storefront theatres around the country, without cultural or racial markers. Is this the result of assimilation? Will the plays in this anthology become historical artifacts of a time when race was differentiated? Or will we suddenly be cast as different, as Asian Americans, as foreign again, should another threatening national incident occur in the future, putting us back into similar situations as the internment camps in World War II or the Exclusion Act?

What plays will we write then? What plays will we return to? Will we see ourselves?

Time will tell.

May 2011
New York City

Notes

1. Edwin Wilson and Alvin Goldfarb, *Theatre: The Lively Art* (New York: McGraw-Hill, 2009).
2. Dave Williams, *Misreading the Chinese Character: Images of the Chinese in Euroamerican Drama to 1925* (New York: Peter Lang Publishing, 2000).
3. Ibid., p. 26.
4. Ibid., p. 33.
5. James S. Moy, *Marginal Sights: Staging the Chinese in America* (Iowa City: University of Iowa Press, 1993).
6. Dave Williams, *The Chinese Other: 1850–1925* (Lanham: University Press of America, Inc., 1997).
7. Ibid., p. 97.
8. Scott Harrah, "O'Neill's 'Marco Millions' Is Still on the Money," *The Villager*, August 16–22, 2006.
9. Moy, pp. 96, 101.
10. Frank Cullen, Florence Hackman and Donald McNeilly, *Vaudeville Old and New: An Encyclopedia of Variety Performers in America* (New York: Routledge, 2007), pp. 223–224.
11. Karen Wada, "If Not Broadway, Where?" *Los Angeles Times*, October 13, 2002.
12. Michael Criscuolo, review of *Durango*, by Julia Cho, November 16, 2006, http://www.nytheatre.com/showpage.aspx?s=dura4447.
13. John Heilpern, "Voices from the Edge: From West Hollywood to the East Village, a Bold New Generation of American Playwrights Is Speaking Out," *Vogue*, November 1993.
14. Terry Hong, "Sung Rno Particle and Wave: Nurtured on Physics and Cultural Dissonance, a Playwright Defies Categorization," *American Theatre*, February 1, 2004.
15. Dan Bacalzo, "Satellites Dish: Playwright Diana Son Discusses the World Premiere of Her Play at the Public Theater," June 5, 2006, http://www.theatermania.com/off-broadway/news/06-2006/satellites-dish_8370.html.
16. Adam Szymkowicz, "I Interview Playwrights Part 199: Alice Tuan," June 20, 2010, http://aszym.blogspot.com/2010/06/i-interview-playwrights-part-199-alice.html.
17. Mike Boehm, "Repeating the History: Playwright Chay Yew Thought the Story of the Japanese Internment of World War II Needed No More Telling. Then Came 9/11," *Los Angeles Times*, February 20, 2004.
18. Dorinne Kondo, "*The Square*: Program Notes," Mark Taper Forum, 2000.
19. Anita Gates, "An Asian American Playwright Turns a New Page," *New York Times*, September 24, 2006.

Question 27,
Question 28

Chay Yew

Author's Statement

Early in my career in the mid-1990s, I was quoted for saying I was tired of internment camp plays. It was a naïve and arrogant statement to make.

While I respected and benefited from numerous historical contributions that Asian Americans made, I was more interested in writing about the lives and issues of Asians living in America, how we related with others in the world, in the here and now.

Years and plays later, I came to the realization that most issues and concerns of today's Asian Americans invariably find their roots in Asian American histories, histories that I have chosen to ignore. In an effort to better understand the legacy I was given, I embarked on creating Asian American documentary pieces. *Question 27, Question 28* is one such project.

I began working on *Question 27, Question 28* for the Mark Taper Forum's Asian Theatre Workshop in 2003. When Pamela Wu approached me with the opportunity to develop this project with them, I immediately accepted and was excited to collaborate with Asian American Theatre Company in San Francisco again.

Oral history projects can never completely represent everyone's personal experience. I hope *Question 27, Question 28* will offer a small but truthful window into these brave women who fought, endured and lived through this dark period of world history.

Question 27, Question 28 and all internment camp stories belong to the Japanese Americans as they belong to non-Japanese Americans in a post-9/11 world. As much as we celebrate the adversity of these remarkable Americans, we must also be vigilant and proactive when this history revisits us, especially in this time in American history.

Production History

Question 27, Question 28 was originally commissioned by Asian American Theater Company in San Francisco (Pamela Wu, Executive Director).

The world premiere of *Question 27, Question 28* was produced by the Mark Taper Forum in association with the Japanese American National Museum in Los Angeles, California in February 2004. This production then transferred to the East West Players in March 2004. It was directed by Chay Yew. The play was performed by the following:

Shannon Holt
Dian Kobayashi
Emily Kuroda
Tamlyn Tomita

Question 27, Question 28 was performed in February 2006 at the National Museum of American History, Behring Center in Washington, D.C. It was directed by Chay Yew. The play was performed by the following:

Shannon Holt
Dian Kobayashi
Emily Kuroda
Tamlyn Tomita

Characters

Four women. Three Asian women and one Caucasian woman of varying ages.

Setting

This play should be staged simply as a play reading, with actors sitting on chairs, their scripts on music stands.

If slides cannot be employed in the production, an actor can simply announce the slide titles.

Note

Question 27, Question 28 uses and incorporates interviews, transcripts and testimonials taken from books, archives, newspapers and magazine journals.

Act One

Prologue

EMILY: Yuri Kochiyama.
DIAN: Haruko Niwa.
SHANNON: Kiyo Sato.
TAMLYN: Monica Sone.
EMILY: Chizu Iiyama.
DIAN: Mine Okubo.
SHANNON: Elaine Black Yoneda.
TAMLYN: Mary Tsukamoto.
EMILY (*Overlapping*): Miyo Senzaki—
DIAN (*Overlapping*): Emi Somekawa—
SHANNON (*Overlapping*): Eleanor Gerard Sekerak—
TAMLYN (*Overlapping*): Amy Uno Iishi—
EMILY (*Overlapping*): Masako Saito—
DIAN (*Overlapping*): Yoshiko Uchida—
SHANNON (*Overlapping*): Ada Endo—
TAMLYN (*Overlapping*): Haruko Hurt—
EMILY (*Overlapping*): Noriko Sawada Bridges—
DIAN (*Overlapping*): Helen Murao—
SHANNON (*Overlapping*): Mabel Ota—
TAMLYN (*Overlapping*): Nobu Miyoshi—

1.

Slide: Before Sunday

TAMLYN: Mary Tsukamoto.

EMILY: I was born in San Francisco. My parents came from Okinawa and had the Capitol Laundry on Geary Street, where I lived when I was very little. Then my father moved to Turlock.

When I was ten, he moved his family to Florin to raise strawberries, and became one of the biggest strawberry farmers there.

SHANNON: Haruko Niwa.

DIAN: My birthplace is Japan. I was born in 1906 in the city of Ueda. I graduate high school there, and then I went to Tokyo. I came here in 1923.

After I graduate from two years in business college in Tokyo, my father, who was in San Francisco with my brother, invite me for just one year, for just visit, but I stayed instead.

I like San Francisco and the United States and living in United States very much. It's very attractive.

And then, I married Mr. Niwa. I married and had two children.

EMILY: Amy Uno Iishi.

TAMLYN: I was born in Salt Lake City, Utah, on December 11, 1920. I'm the fifth of ten children.

My father and mother were both born and raised in Japan. My parents met a lot of hardship and discrimination in Japan because of the fact that they were Christians. Those days—the 1800s—very few Japanese were Christians; there were more Buddhists.

My father was chased and beaten by children in the neighborhood. He also told of other specific instances where he was discriminated against because he was Christian. He was encouraged to come to America by the missionaries. They told him—

SHANNON: "America is the land of the free and the home of the brave. Money grows on the orange trees in your backyard. The land is vast, not like Japan."

TAMLYN: They told him—

SHANNON: "With your intellect, your knowledge of history, and your ability in handing the English language—"

TAMLYN: (Even to the degree that he did at that time, which I guess was considered quite a bit)—

SHANNON: "You will go far in America. So go to America. Go to America."

TAMLYN: He arrived here in 1906 and worked on the railroad gang.

EMILY: Mary Gillespie.

SHANNON: I lived in this area most of my life, since 1909. My parents homesteaded here. We came from Ohio. My father's health was bad and he came here. That's how we happened to come here.

DIAN: Helen Murao.

TAMLYN: I was born in Portland, Oregon in 1926. My parents died within three years of each other in the mid-thirties, my mother dying first. I was still in grammar school when that happened, and we became wards of the state. I had an older sister, Mary, who died after this. So I was the oldest of three of us, me and my two younger brothers.

The Japanese community was very fearful and very reluctant to take us into their homes because Mary had had tuberculosis. There was nothing more fearful to them than that disease. So they did not offer their homes to us—even our very close family friends. It was with Caucasian people that we made our homes.

During those years it was very hard for me to come to grips with the realization that the Japanese people forsook us. They didn't want to have anything to do with us. Just out of fear for their health.

SHANNON: Mary Tsukamoto.

EMILY: I remember we had an annual oratorical contest sponsored by the Native Sons and Daughters, and I ended up one of the nine qualifying competitors. Then the principal and the teacher called me in and told me that I couldn't be in it because of my ancestry.

I was relieved I didn't have to do another oration, but the teacher didn't let me forget. She was upset and so discouraged that the Native Sons wouldn't change their position. That they would discriminate me made her very angry. But she couldn't do anything about it.

She was the one responsible for getting me to college because of that experience—to the College of the Pacific. That teacher was poor herself. But before my dad knew anything about it, she had arranged to get me a one-hundred-and-fifty dollar scholarship.

She even had to go and ask Dad if he would let me go and not help at home. You see, every child was needed for the strawberries at that time. Every child and everybody in the family worked together to eke out a living.

My dad was so deeply touched. Of course, he let me go.

TAMLYN: Pauline Miller.

SHANNON: Lone Pine? I thought it was a godforsaken country.

But after we were here for a while—because I came from Los Angeles and missed all my friends, you know, to come to a little town like this—we weren't here very long before we became acquainted and we liked it very much. I was thirty-five at the time. My husband bought an automobile dealership and a gasoline station.

DIAN: Amy Uno Iishi.

TAMLYN: I was twelve years old when I left home. But it was a different way of leaving home.

I sat down and talked to my mother and said, "Look, this is 1932 and I'm in junior high school now, the seventh grade. You're having a hard time feeding all these mouths, putting shoes on the feet, and putting patch upon patch on the clothes. So, would it help any if I moved out of the house and worked as a domestic? If I worked in a home and went to school away from here, I would come and see you on my days off."

Tears just rolled down my mother's cheeks and she said—

DIAN: "It would really help. If it's one less mouth to feed, one less person to have to clothe and worry about, it would help so much."

TAMLYN: So I said, "Then I will look for a job."

SHANNON: Masako Saito.

DIAN: We were all told we had to study hard, you have to be good, not do anything to shame the family. It was pounded into us. There was favoritism. My sister above me was very smart. We were always told to be as smart as Kiyo.

My mother wouldn't let Kiyo do a lot of things—

EMILY: "Let her study because she's the smart one!"

DIAN: And I was the dumb one. So I had to do a lot of things—running around, helping them, take the wash up to the roof, four floors, and hang it up.

My parents managed to send us to piano lessons, and we had to go to Japanese school. But we think, in spite of it all, we managed to turn out pretty well adjusted.

SHANNON: Yuri Kochiyama.

EMILY: I was red, white and blue when I was growing up. I taught Sunday school, and was very, very American.

I got a job at a department store. But for us back then, it was a big thing, because I don't think they had ever hired an Asian in a department store before.

It was hard for Asians. Even for Japanese, the best jobs they felt they could get were in Chinatown. Most Japanese were either in some aspect of fishing, such as in the canneries, or went right from school to work on the farms.

That was what it was like in the town of San Pedro. I loved working in the department store, because it was a small town, and you got to know and see everyone. The town itself was wonderful. People were very friendly. I didn't see my job as work—it was like a community job.

Everything changed for me on the day Pearl Harbor was bombed.

2.

Slide: That Sunday

TAMLYN: Haruko Hurt.

DIAN: I didn't even know where Pearl Harbor was. I was that naïve. But I soon found out. It was something that was just foreign to me. Something that country over there, Japan, did. It had nothing to do with me, as far as I'm concerned.

SHANNON: Mary Tsukamoto.

EMILY: I was about twenty-six, and we were in church. It was a December Sunday, so we were getting ready for our Christmas program. We were rehearsing and having Sunday school class, and I always played the piano for the adult Issei service. Of course, because there were so many Japanese, all of it was in Japanese. The minister was Japanese, and he preached in Japanese.

But after the service started, my husband ran in. He had been home that day and heard on the radio—

SHANNON: "The Japanese have bombed Pearl Harbor!"

EMILY: We just couldn't believe it. I remembered how stunned we were. And suddenly the whole world turned dark. We began to speak in whispers.

We immediately knew something terrible was going to happen. We prayed that it wouldn't, but we sensed things would be very difficult. The minister and all the leaders discussed matters, and we knew that we needed to be prepared for the worst.

SHANNON: Kay Uno.

DIAN: I was nine at the time of Pearl Harbor and I was in third grade. That Sunday, we were on our way home from church, and we had the radio on in our car.

Everybody was excited. We said "Oh, those Japs. What are they doing that for?"

When the war happened, my parents were really torn. Japan was their country. They were Japanese, and they couldn't have citizenship here. But, in a lot of ways, my parents were Americans. They flew the flag for every national holiday.

We lived six blocks from where I went to school, and I always walked. All the merchants and everyone knew me—

SHANNON: "Hi, How are you?"

DIAN: Monday, they turned their backs on me.

SHANNON: "There goes that little Jap!"

DIAN: I'm looking around. "Who's a Jap? Who's a Jap?"

Then it dawned on me, I'm the Jap.

After Pearl Harbor, the kids began to shun me. My friends. One person started it, and then pretty soon it went throughout the school.

My teacher and music teacher were both very supportive all through the time.

When I had to leave, one of them gave me a gift. A gold leaf pin. It was the first real piece of jewelry I ever had.

I still have it.

EMILY: President Franklin D. Roosevelt.

SHANNON: "Yesterday, December 7, 1941—A date which will live in infamy—the United States of America was suddenly and deliberately attacked by naval and air forces of the Empire of Japan."

TAMLYN: Yuri Kochiyama.

EMILY: On that very day, December 7, the FBI came and took my father.

He had just come home from the hospital the day before. For several days, we didn't know where they had taken him. Then we found out that he was taken to the federal prison at Terminal Island. Overnight, things changed for us.

The FBI took all men who lived near the Pacific waters, and who had anything to do with fishing. A month later, they took every fisherman from Terminal Island, sixteen and over, to detention centers in South Dakota, Montana and New Mexico.

The first group was thirteen hundred Isseis—my parents' generation. They took those who were leaders of the community, or Japanese schoolteachers, or were teaching martial arts, or who were Buddhist priests. Those categories that would make them very "Japanesy"—were picked up.

SHANNON: Mrs. Hama Yamaki.

DIAN: We had to consult a lawyer to get a permit to return home. Two weeks passed before we were able to return.

After we read newspaper articles about Nihonjin in Idaho being shot, we drove right home. We only stopped once at the restaurant to have coffee. Even though the rooms were dark, we could see the others staring at us. No one said anything to us, but we drank our coffees hurriedly and left.

As we were driving home during a snowstorm, our car stalled in the middle of a mountain road. We were very frightened. But a car drove right up and a Caucasian man offered to help us. Without a word about Pearl Harbor, he brought out his tools and worked on our motor. The car ignition started smoothly!

I wanted to clasp his hand in appreciation. But all I said was, "Thank you! Thank you!"

EMILY: Yoshiko Uchida.

TAMLYN: One evening, some friends and I were having a late snack in a restaurant in Berkeley. Suddenly, an angry Filipino man accosted us and vividly described what the Japanese soldiers were doing to his homeland. His fists were clenched and his face was contorted with rage. Fortunately, he had no weapon and left after venting his anger on us, but he had filled us with fear. It was the first time in my life I had been threatened with violence and it was a terrifying moment.

DIAN: President Roosevelt.

SHANNON: "The attack yesterday on the Hawaiian Islands has caused severe damage to American naval and military forces. Very many American lives have been lost."

TAMLYN: Masako Saito.

DIAN: I would be walking down to where I was working until the store closed. And people would come by and say—

SHANNON: "Jap."

DIAN: And then they'd split. I couldn't believe it. I mentioned it to my Chinese friends, and they said—

TAMLYN: "We'll lend you our 'I am Chinese' button."

DIAN: "Oh no," I said, "If they're going to hate me for being a Japanese, well, there's nothing more I can do—they're the ones who're wrong."

SHANNON: Amy Uno Iishi.

TAMLYN: That Sunday morning I was living as a domestic away from home, out in San Marino, and I had just served breakfast to the family when the news came on the radio that Japan had attacked Pearl Harbor. It's hard to describe the shock.

Even the people I worked for treated me and talked to me as though it was my own father who was piloting those planes out there at Pearl Harbor.

I remember they told me that I should go home. I said, "Why should I be suspected of anything? I've lived here in your home for many years now, nursed you when you were sick and fed you. And I never poisoned you once, and I'm not about to do it now."

But they said—

SHANNON: "You had better stay home until we can get the FBI to clear you."

TAMLYN: I felt like an ant. I wanted to shrivel up into nothing, and my mind was going a mile a minute, thinking, "What am I supposed to do? What am I supposed to say? All I know is I am an American, and yet now, at a time like this, people are going to say, 'You are a Jap,' and that turns the whole picture around."

I had never been called a "Jap" in my life. All these things were going through my mind.

By the time I got home, the FBI was at our house.

EMILY: President Roosevelt.

SHANNON: "I ask that the Congress declare that since the unprovoked attack by Japan on Sunday, December 7, a state of war has existed between the United States and the Japanese Empire."

DIAN: Mary Tsukamoto.

EMILY: Then of course, within a day or two, we heard that the FBI had taken Mr. Tanigawa and Mr. Tsuji. I suppose the FBI had them on their list, and it wasn't long before many of them were taken. We had no idea what they were going through. We should have been more aware.

One Issei, Mr. Iwasa, committed suicide.

DIAN: Amy Uno Iishi.

TAMLYN: The FBI were tearing out floorboards, taking bricks out of the fireplace and looking through our attic. Contraband, I guess. Looking for machine guns, munitions, maps, binoculars, cameras, swords, knives and what have you.

And my family, we just stood there. What could we say with military police standing out in front with guns pointing at the house? Telling us to stay right there in a particular room while they went through the whole house?

They didn't have a search warrant. They didn't have any reason to be coming in like this and tearing up our house.

And when the FBI left, they took my father with them.

DIAN: Mary Tsukamoto.

EMILY: Mrs. Tsuji's husband was also taken away by the FBI. But nobody thought about the family left behind needing food and money.

We finally arranged for the welfare office to provide food, and she cried because Japanese people are proud and they weren't willing to accept handouts. They had never been on welfare before, and she felt terrible.

But we told her this was different, because her husband was taken and because it's what you have to do. She had three children.

TAMLYN: Haruko Hurt.

DIAN: I did domestic work at the time. The employer, Mrs. Dunlevy, whom I was living with, said to me—

SHANNON: "Haruko—"

DIAN: She said, half smiling—

SHANNON: "I'm going to look under your bed to see if you have a radio transmitter hidden there."

DIAN: I kinda laughed. I thought she was joking.

I said, "By all means, look under there."

Can you imagine? I know she wasn't joking.

SHANNON: Mary Tsukamoto.

EMILY: We were supposed to turn in our cameras and our guns. Every day there was something else about other people being taken by the FBI.

Then gradually we just couldn't believe what people were saying. There was talk about *sending* us away, and we just couldn't believe that they would do such a thing.

DIAN: Amy Uno Iishi.

TAMLYN: There was also a very strict curfew law. We had to be in by five o'clock in the evening. We could not go out before a certain time in the morning.

We could travel only so many miles from our homes. If you worked a little further than that from your home, you had to give up your job.

SHANNON: Emi Somekawa.

DIAN: I think the thing that we felt the most was that the people who stopped in at our store thought maybe we should close it up. For our safety. But my husband said—

EMILY: "No, there's no need to do that. We're American citizens."

DIAN: When April came along, my husband started selling things in the store.

SHANNON: "*San Francisco Examiner*! Six a.m. Extra! Ouster of All Japs in California Near!"

TAMLYN: Mary Tsukamoto.

EMILY: It would be a situation where the whole community would be uprooted. But soon enough we were reading reports of other communities being evacuated from San Pedro and from Puget Sound.

After a while, we became aware that maybe things weren't going to just stop but would continue to get worse and worse.

SHANNON: Amy Uno Iishi.

TAMLYN: It was the most difficult thing, adjusting to having Dad away from home.

My mother and father had just celebrated their twenty-fifth anniversary. It was the first time they had ever been separated.

My mother was home with the children—but to have my father forcibly taken away from her, she was in a state of shock. Her blood pressure was really high, and it was a matter of trying to keep her composure.

She realized that she now had to be the head of the household, the backbone of the family.

It was very difficult when the young ones would say to my mother—

EMILY: "When is Daddy coming home? Where is he?"

TAMLYN: What kind of answers could she give? Could she tell the children truthfully that Daddy will be gone only a couple of weeks or a couple of months or a couple of years? She didn't even know.

The mere mention of my father would just break my mother up. It was just eating away at her.

Then the evacuation order came.

3.

Slide: Exodus

DIAN: President Roosevelt.

TAMLYN: Executive Order 9066.

SHANNON: "Now, therefore, by virtue of the authority vested in me as President of the United States, and Commander in Chief of the Army and Navy, I hereby authorize and direct the Secretary of War, and the Military Commanders . . . to prescribe military areas . . . [and to determine] the right of any person to enter, remain in, or leave."

DIAN: Amy Uno Iishi.

TAMLYN: That was really the biggest surprise of all. No one had an inkling as to where we were going to be sent and for how long.

DIAN: Mary Tsukamoto.

EMILY: I remember Mrs. Kuima, whose son was thirty-two years old and retarded. She took care of him. They had five other boys but she took care of this boy at home. The welfare office said—

SHANNON: "No, you can't take him. All families have to institutionalize a child like that."

EMILY: It was a very tragic thing for me to tell her, and I remember going out to the field—where she was hoeing strawberries—and I told her what they told us, that you can't take your son with you. And so she cried and I cried with her. A few days before they evacuated, they came to take him away to an institution. It was very hard for me to face that family. I felt as though I was the messenger that carried such tragic news for them. It was only about a month after we got to Fresno Assembly Center that they sent us a wire saying—

SHANNON: "He died."

EMILY: All these years she loved him and took care of him. He only knew Japanese and ate Japanese food. I was thinking about the family. They got over it quietly. They endured it. I just felt guilty, you know, just having been involved.

TAMLYN: Emi Somekawa.

DIAN: When we first realized that an evacuation would take place, it was a depressing feeling that's hard to explain.

I didn't know whether we'd come back to our home again, but it was a feeling that all these years we'd worked for nothing. That kind of a feeling, you know, that you're just losing everything.

EMILY: Yoshiko Uchida.

TAMLYN: As our packing progressed, our house grew increasingly barren and our garden took on a shabby look. My mother couldn't bear to leave her favorite plants to strangers and dug up her special roses, London Smoke carnations and yellow calla lilies to take to a friend for safekeeping.

One day, a neighbor rang our doorbell and asked for one of Papa's prized gladiolas that she fancied as she passed by.

It seemed like a heartless gesture, and I was indignant, just as I was when the people told me the evacuation was for our own protection.

15

But Mother simply handed the woman a shovel and told her to help herself.

She said—

EMILY: "Let her have it if it will make her happy."

DIAN: Eleanor Roosevelt.

SHANNON: "Approximately three months after Pearl Harbor, the Western Defense Command ordered all persons of Japanese ancestry excluded from the coastal area, including approximately half of Washington, Oregon and California, and the southern portion of Arizona. Later, the entire state of California was added to the zone from which Japanese were barred.

This separation is taking place now."

TAMLYN: Emi Somekawa.

DIAN: One thing that upset me, that was hard to take, was that we had this German family right next door, and they were as German as German could be, and they were free. They could do anything they wanted and nothing was bothering them. Why us? I felt like we were just being punished for nothing.

The day we left the house, this German lady came with a cake, and she said—

SHANNON: "If there was anything else we could do for you, call."

DIAN: So twice they came out to the assembly center. I think they were a bit displaced too. I don't think they could help but feel that way.

TAMLYN: Mary Tsukamoto

EMILY: I worried about trying to buy the right kind of things to get ready for a place I knew nothing about.

They said "camp." I thought "summer camp."

I thought we were going up into the mountains somewhere. I even bought boots thinking there might be snakes!

SHANNON: Amy Uno Iishi.

TAMLYN: We had to dispose of all our belongings. We stood by so helplessly when people whom we thought were our friends and neighbors, came by and said to my mother—

SHANNON: "I'll give you two dollars for your stove—"

EMILY: "A dollar and a half for your refrigerator—"

DIAN: "A dollar for your washing machine—"

SHANNON: "Fifty cents for each bed in the house, including the mattress and all linens."

TAMLYN: That really hurt because we knew—I was old enough to realize—it took my mother and father twenty-five years of hard work to put together a few things. And then to have this kind of thing happen.

We finally got rid of everything except—we had an old-fashioned upright piano that we were very fond of, and there was no way that my mother was going to let that piano go for two dollars. She just refused. She said she would take that piano out in the backyard and take an axe to it before she'd let anyone take it away for two dollars.

DIAN: Miyo Senzaki.

EMILY: I got married in March 1942. My husband used to come after me, and he found out that they were going to be evacuated. They already got their notice. That's when my husband said—

DIAN: "You either marry me or we just won't see each other."

EMILY: So I looked at him and said, "Marry you? You haven't even got a job."

We got married the day before the old Union Church was going to close. We got married so we could go to camp together.

TAMLYN: Monica Sone.

DIAN: On the day we evacuated, Dunks Oshima had offered to take us down to Eighth and Lane in a borrowed pickup truck. The menfolk loaded the truck with the last few boxes of household goods that Dunks was going to take down to the hotel for storage.

Puzzled, he held up a gallon of soy sauce—

TAMLYN: "Where does this go, to the hotel, too?"

DIAN: No one seemed to know where it had come from or where it was going, until Mother finally spoke up—

EMILY: "Er—it's going with me. I don't think we'd have shoyu where we're going—"

DIAN: My brother looked as if he were going to explode—

TAMLYN: "Mama, people will laugh at us. We're not going on a picnic—"

EMILY: "Nonsense. No one will ever notice this little thing. It isn't as if I were bringing liquor—"

DIAN: "Well, if Mama's going to take her shoyu, I'm taking my radio along. At least it'll keep me from talking to myself out there—"

TAMLYN: "That's enough! Two suitcases and a seabag a person, that's final! Now let's get going before we decide to take the house along with us."

DIAN: My mother personally saw to it that the can of shoyu remained in her baggage.

EMILY: Eleanor Gerard Sekerak.

SHANNON: I was teaching a criminology class at San Francisco City College when a field trip took us to observe a camp set up at

Tanforan by the Immigration and Naturalization Service after Pearl Harbor. This was my first contact with internment.

Later, in a graduate class on the Berkeley campus, the professor unexpectedly informed us that one of our colleagues would be giving his final oral presentation early. Hiro Katayama bade us—

DIAN: "Good-bye."

SHANNON: And left the classroom. His destination . . . Tanforan.

During hall duty, I had the occasion to admonish, almost daily, a youngster who always dashed by as though on roller skates. Once while reminding him not to run in the halls, I asked for his name—

TAMLYN: "Bill Oshima!"

SHANNON: After evacuation, the halls seemed very quiet.

EMILY: Nobu Miyoshi.

DIAN: We had chosen "voluntary evacuation."

One Sunday morning in February 1942, my sister Anne received a call from the War Relocation Authority office giving permission for us to leave Sacramento, California. The deadline for leaving was eight o'clock that evening!

The office had kept assuring us that we would have ample time for preparation, so we were shocked by this call.

We had not even collected boxes for packing our household goods. We and about twenty-five friends and neighbors went into high gear to dismantle our home. There were no consultations. Everyone did what they thought was necessary. And there was very little conversation or questions in the constant activity.

Suddenly, Esther Tani said—

TAMLYN: "This is against the Constitution. This is wrong."

DIAN: I was amazed to hear such a purely American expression. I heard no other Nisei openly call our government into question. I think most of us felt that we had no rights.

EMILY: Elaine Black Yoneda.

SHANNON: On the evening of Sunday, March 29th, the radio suddenly blurted out:

TAMLYN: "Attention, attention, all those of Japanese ancestry whose breadwinners are in the Manzanar Reception Center: You are hereby ordered to report to the Civil Control Station at 707 South Spring Street tomorrow from eight a.m. on for processing to leave for Manzanar by noon, April 2nd."

SHANNON: Had I heard correctly? What of the promise of "last ones out" and here it was only six days since my husband's departure? But soon the announcement was repeated.

I immediately called army headquarters but was told to call back after 7 p.m. for an answer to my question: "Does General DeWitt's Manzanar order include a three-year-old Eurasian child living with his Caucasian mother and grandparents?"

EMILY: "You do not have to go, Mrs. Yoneda, nor will you be allowed to go. But your son must go on the basis of the Geneva Accords. That is, the father's ancestry counts, and one-sixteenth or more Japanese blood is the criteria set."

SHANNON: After relating the conversation to my parents, I told them if my son had to go, I would go too, come hell or high water!

They agreed my decision was correct.

DIAN: Mary Tsukamoto.

EMILY: We never dreamed we would be separated—relatives and close friends, a community. We were just like brothers and sisters. These were our people. And we loved them. We wept with them at their funerals and laughed with them and rejoiced with them at their weddings.

And suddenly we found out that the community was going to split up.

We were just tied up in knots, trying to cope with all of this happening at once and so fast. I can't understand why they had to do this.

TAMLYN: Elaine Black Yoneda.

SHANNON: On Monday morning, my son Tommy and I took our places in the long line already formed outside the station. Suddenly an army officer and a priest came running to where we stood, telling us to—

DIAN: "Go right in. Don't wait in line."

SHANNON: I protested. But I was ushered in anyway.

There the captain refused to give me two application forms and the Maryknoll father kept saying—

EMILY: "We will have a Children's Village where our well-trained sisters will take care of your son. You needn't, nor will you be allowed to go. It will be *too hard* for you."

SHANNON: I turned to the officer said, "As sure as we are standing here, my husband will be in a khaki uniform like yours before the year is out! And I'll be there with our son to see him off!"

Then I turned to the priest, "Father, for all you know I may be an atheist, but I took an oath to love, honor and cherish, for better or worse, and that means something to me! I'll be with my child and my husband and never mind the 'too hard' bit!"

I demanded two forms and they were handed to me. I completed the applications and was given a typhus shot. I also informed them we would take the first train on April Fool's Day.

When we finally pulled into Manzanar, my husband Karl and I had a good, silent cry in each other's arms.

DIAN: Mary Tsukamoto.

EMILY: We had been a very happy family. When we left, we swept our house and left it clean, because that's the way Japanese feel like leaving a place.

I can just imagine everyone's emotions of grief and anger when they had to leave, when the military police came to tell them—

SHANNON: "Get ready right now. You've got two hours to get ready to catch this train."

DIAN: Aiko Horikoshi.

TAMLYN: I wouldn't describe myself as a resister but I kept defending my rights. I resisted the evacuation order during a long night prior to leaving for Pomona Assembly Center.

The night before evacuation, I climbed out of my bedroom window to meet my boyfriend, Tom, who was Caucasian. We drove around town for three hours.

I didn't want to be evacuated. I didn't want to leave, and I was rebelling with every fiber in my being.

But we were too young to elope. We talked about how we could get away from all this.

Finally at five o'clock in the morning I crawled back into my bedroom window and . . .

There was my father.

Waiting for me with open arms.

And he just held me real tight and said—

DIAN: "Thank you for coming home."

SHANNON: Mary Tsukamoto.

EMILY: There were tears everywhere. Nobody could take pets, and this was a sad thing for my daughter. Grandma couldn't leave her flowers. Grandpa looked at his grape vineyard. We urged him to get into the car and leave.

I remember that sad morning when we realized suddenly that we wouldn't be free. It was such a clear, beautiful day, and I remember as we were driving, our tears.

We saw the snow-clad Sierra Nevada mountains that we had loved to see so often, and I thought about God and about the prayer we always prayed.

DIAN: Florence Nakamura.

TAMLYN: Our family number was 19153.

In April 1942, on the day of departure, each member of my family had a cardboard tag with this number attached to his or her coat.

This tag was our identification.

SHANNON: Mary Tsukamoto.

EMILY: On the train, we were told not to look out the window. But people were peeking out. After a long time on the train, somebody said—

DIAN: "Oh there's some Japanese standing over there!"

EMILY: So we all took a peek, and we saw this dust, and rows and rows of barracks, and all these tan, brown Japanese people with their hair all—bleached. Dust had covered their hair. They were all standing in a huddle looking at us, looking at this train going by.

Then somebody on the train said—

TAMLYN: "Gee, that must be Japanese people in camp."

EMILY: We didn't realize who they were before. But I saw how terrible it looked: the dust, no trees—just barracks and a bunch of people standing against the fence, looking out. Some children were hanging onto the fence like animals, and that was my first sight of the assembly center.

I was so sad and discouraged looking at that. I knew, before long, we would be inside too.

SHANNON: Masako Saito.

DIAN: We did assemble, somewhere on Van Ness Avenue—my brother-in-law Frank came to pick us up. We then went on to the railroad station. We had to stay overnight in the old boxcar train we were on until they decided where to place us.

Finally, they took us to Santa Anita.

We lived in a horse stall.

4.

Slide: Somewhere in Between

TAMLYN: Mary Tsukamoto.

EMILY: When we arrived, we saw all these people, peeking out from behind the fence, wondering what group would be coming next, and, of course, looking for their friends too. Suddenly you realized that human beings were being put behind fences just like on the farm where we had horses and pigs in corrals.

It was hot, and everybody was perspiring. We were tired from the train trip, and here they were staring at us. It was humiliating to be stared at like that. And these were Nihonjin people staring us, Nihonjin people, our people.

We came dragging suitcases and luggage and all our clothing. We felt so self-conscious to be stared at, but of course I looked right back to see if I recognized anybody.

My father and mother and my cousins had gone a day or two ahead of us. I was looking for them, and they came looking for us.

Then we saw each other.

TAMLYN: Emi Somekawa.

DIAN: The Portland Assembly Center was terrible. It's just amazing how people can think of putting another group of human beings into a place like that. There was so much horse and cow manure around.

We were put into a cubicle that just had plywood walls and it was a horse stall with planks on the floor with about an inch of space between them.

In the corner, we saw this folding bed, an army camp cot, with mattress ticking, and we were supposed to go out there to fill it with straw so that we would have a mattress.

It's depressing we had to go into a place like that.

SHANNON: Mine Okubo.

TAMLYN: The room showed hurried whitewashing. Spider webs, horse hair, and hay had been whitewashed with the walls. Huge spikes and nails stuck out all over the wall. A two-inch layer of dust covered the floor. We opened the folded spring cots and sat on them in the semidarkness.

In the next stall, we heard someone crying.

EMILY: Eleanor Roosevelt.

SHANNON: "To many young people, this must have seemed strange treatment of American citizens. One cannot be surprised at the reaction that manifested itself not only in young Japanese Americans, but also in others who had known them well and had been educated with them, and who asked bitterly, 'What price American citizenship?' Nevertheless, most of them realize that this was a safety measure.

The army carried out its evacuation with remarkable skill and kindness.

The early situation in the centers was difficult. Many of them were not ready for occupation. The setting up of large communities meant an amount of organization which takes time.

But the Japanese, proved to be patient, adaptable and courageous."

TAMLYN: Haruko Niwa.

DIAN: I was kind of bitter at first. I trust the United States so deeply, its freedom and this Constitution. We are very proud about the United States, and I trusted this country so much.

But it all owes to wartime. I thought that no matter what, we have to obey military and government's order.

SHANNON: Mary Tsukamoto.

EMILY: We began to realize what it meant to stand in line—long hours standing to eat in the mess hall, standing in line for our bath, standing in line in front of the latrine. That was a shock, but I guess the Army's latrine is the same everywhere.

For us women and children, this was something which we couldn't . . . it was just a shock. I remember we got sick . . . we couldn't go . . . we didn't want to go. It was smelly, and it was dirty.

In the shower, the water was poured over you, and there were no partitions, and it was so cramped that we almost touched each other.

It was very humiliating.

TAMLYN: Chizu Iiyama.

DIAN: There was no privacy. And it was like that in camp—and we got over the feeling of embarrassment.

They had this huge shower room, half for the men, and the other for women.

Then they said some of the young men had made peep holes. I heard a lot of giggling that went on.

SHANNON: Monica Sone.

DIAN: The partition wall separating the rooms was only seven feet high with an opening of four feet to the top.

At night, Mrs. Funai next door could tell when my sister Sumi was still sitting up in bed in the dark, putting her hair up. Through the plank wall, Mrs. Funai would say—

EMILY: "Mah, Sumi-chan, are you curling your hair tonight again? Do you put it up every night?"

DIAN: And Sumi would glare at the wall.

SHANNON: Helen Murao.

TAMLYN: In the late thirties and forties in my neighborhood where I grew up with Caucasian kids, we were all just one big family. But as we approached our teen years, you know, sex started to become important, and boys and girls started to pair off. While

I was just great as a neighbor and a friend, all of a sudden, I wasn't right to be dated. So I had very strange feelings.

In camp, I discovered that among Japanese people I was really kind of an oddity, because I had lived among Caucasians. When the guys started coming around, I was thinking, "Boy, this is terrific I was getting offers for dates and stuff like that. This was just going to be great!"

It was this racial thing that I was just beginning to become aware of. I discovered that among the Nisei people, I was an equal. I could compete with the other girls for the boys' attention.

That summer I had this sorting out and coming to terms with my own self and my own life.

It was not an easy time.

DIAN: Yakuri.

EMILY:
Plate in hand,
I stand in line,
Losing my resolve
To hide my tears.

I see my mother
In the aged woman who comes,
And I yield to her
My place in line.

Four months have passed,
And at least I learn
To call this horse stall
My family's home.

SHANNON: Kiyo Sato.

DIAN: The assembly center was quickly built, temporary. Not a blade of grass, not one tree for the five thousand people living there behind barbed wire fences. And I wanted to see something growing—I would go around and see trees in the distance— oh—to be able to go out.

One day, I saw a whole bunch of people gathered around. I thought someone got sick or died—what do you do in a place like this if anyone got sick? So I went over to see what happened. You know what it was? A seed had sprouted. A seed had sprouted and everyone was there to look at it.

Everyday, no matter what time of the day I went, there was somebody there. And they built a little fence around it, so that it would be safe. I think it was morning glory.

It was amazing to me that all the Issei had packed seeds. My mother packed seeds, and they planted everywhere—between the barracks, etc. It was green everywhere—sometimes you couldn't see the barracks because the vines were growing. We were there for two and a half months.

SHANNON: Mary Tsukamoto.

EMILY: We had our July Fourth program. Because we couldn't think of anything to do, we decided to recite the Gettysburg Address as a verse choir. We had an artist draw a big picture of Abraham Lincoln with an American flag behind him.

Some people had tears in their eyes. Some people shook their heads and said it was so ridiculous to have that kind of thing recited in a camp.

I know it didn't make any sense but we wanted so much to believe that this was a government by the people and for the people and that there was freedom and justice.

SHANNON: Yoshiko Uchida.

TAMLYN: One of the elementary school teachers was the first to be married at Tanforan. She wanted to have the kind of wedding she would have had on the outside. She wore a beautiful white marquisette gown with a fingertip veil. We crowded into the church barrack that day, and the wedding was a moment of extraordinary joy and brightness. We showered the couple with rice as they left, and they climbed into a borrowed car decorated with "just married" signs and a string of tin cans. They took several noisy turns around the racetrack in the car. After a reception in one of the recreational centers, they began their married life in one of the horse stalls.

SHANNON: Haruko Niwa.

DIAN: I told Nobu and Aki, "From now on you kids have to be really strong and pray every minute, because whatever happens, you have to decide yourself.

"I cannot watch you constantly and we don't know from now on what kind of living we going to have. We don't know how we can continue as a family unit.

"We cannot protect you, so you have to stand up and protect yourself and decide what is wrong and what is right, because Mommy and Daddy can't follow all over, because we don't know what's going to be. We have to be closer than before."

That's what I told the two boys, you know.

SHANNON: Noriko Sawada Bridges.

EMILY: I recall one girl friend who decided she was one-hundred percent American. So when I would speak to her in Japanese, she wouldn't answer because she claimed she couldn't understand. She refused to eat rice because that was Japanese. She refused to use chopsticks because that was Japanese. She was viciously the other way. It's hard to survive in a camp like that, hanging on to those notions.

DIAN: Helen Murao.

TAMLYN: By Labor Day 1942, when we were to be moved inland to Idaho, I guess I was beginning to feel that I had no choice.

I had to quit being so angry and quit being so hateful. I had a job to do with my brothers, so I ran them like a drill sergeant.

People who met me in those years smile and laugh and talk about it now.

They said—

EMILY: "That Helen ran those boys like she was a drill sergeant."

TAMLYN: I wouldn't let them out after nine o'clock. I made them go to school. I made them study. I made them . . . you know. I had them help me scrub their clothes so that they would be clean.

Then somewhere during that time I came to feel, well, we're going to show these people. We're going to show the world. They are not going to do this to me. Nobody is going to make me feel this miserable. The United States government may have made me leave my home, but they're going to be sorry. You know what I mean.

I'm going to prevail. My will is going to prevail. My own life is going to prevail. I'm not going to kill myself.

I am going to prevail.

SHANNON: Yuri Kochiyama.

EMILY: I couldn't believe this was happening to us. America would never do a thing like this to us. This is the greatest country in the world.

So I thought this is only going to be for a short while. Maybe a few weeks or something, and they will let us go back.

At the beginning no one realized how long this would go on. I didn't feel the anger that much because I thought maybe this was the way we could show our love for our country.

SHANNON: Chizu Iiyama.

DIAN: When we were in a temporary detention center in Santa Anita, my mother cried and cried and said we were all going to get killed. But when she realized in a week or so that they weren't going to kill us—she perked up.

In fact, she took English in camp. She even took a class in American Constitution. And when the time came for her to become a citizen, she was one of the first people to.

TAMLYN: Mrs. Hatsumi Nishimoto.

EMILY: I do not recall any pleasant camp experiences—not even one.

What bothered me most was there was virtually no family dining. Young people ate with their friends. Men dined together. And women ate in their own groups.

Perhaps one positive thing about camp was that life was scheduled—without question. Everything occurred on time.

Life in camp could be described as happy, because we had time on our hands and could attend classes for free.

SHANNON: Yoshiko Uchida.

TAMLYN: I was an assistant at one of the three nursery schools at Tanforan.

Whenever the children played house, they always stood in line to eat at make-believe mess halls rather than cooking and setting tables as they would have done at home.

It was sad to see how the concept of home had changed for them.

SHANNON: Mary Tsukamoto.

EMILY: Soon we learned to cope and we managed to enjoy whatever we could and got busy. I taught English to Issei, which was a delightful experience. I also taught public speaking.

This was thrilling to me, because I found out that the Isseis really wanted to learn something that they did not have the opportunity to learn before.

One mother said—

DIAN: "I want to be able to write my son a letter. I'm always asking other people to write for me. When he's in the service and worried, I want him to know I'm all right. I want him to understand from my own letters that I care for him and that I'm okay."

EMILY: We used unfinished buildings for temporary classrooms, and we hastily tried to keep everybody busy. Soon, surprising things began to happen.

The Issei ladies were making crepe-paper flowers. They were taking classes from old Mrs. Nagao, who was a farmer's wife, brown and tanned and wrinkled. All I knew was that she was strawberry grower's wife, and I knew she could pick strawberries. Here she was—a teacher of the crepe-paper flower-making class.

Soon the whole camp was transformed.

Who but Nihonjins would leave a place like that in beauty? It was an inspiring sight. I felt proud that the Nihonjins who had coped through the heat of the summer, had faith enough to plant a garden.

Of course, it was probably torn down quickly because it was the Fresno Fairground.

DIAN: Eleanor Roosevelt.

SHANNON: "At first, the evacuation was placed on a voluntary basis; the people were free to go wherever they liked in the interior of the country.

But the evacuation moved very slowly, and those who did leave encountered a great deal of difficulty in finding new places to settle.

In order to avoid serious incidents, on March 29, 1942, the evacuation was placed on an orderly basis, and was carried out by the Army.

It was an entirely new undertaking for us.

And it had to be done."

EMILY: Wasco Fujiwara

TAMLYN: Fresno Assembly Center was just a temporary camp. We stayed there for three months.

We were then sent to a more permanent home in the interior, Tule Lake, because they had just finished that camp.

SHANNON: Monica Sone.

DIAN: When I got to the camp, I noticed a powerful beam of light sweeping across my window every few seconds. The light came from high towers placed around the camp where the guards with tommy guns kept a twenty-four-hour vigil. I remembered the wire fence encircling us.

What was I doing behind a fence like a criminal? If there were accusations made, why hadn't I been given a fair trial? Maybe I wasn't considered American anymore. Maybe my citizenship wasn't real. Then what was I?

Of one thing I was sure. The wire fence was real.

I no longer had the right to walk out of it.

Act Two

5.

Slide: Behind the Fence

TAMLYN: Katarine Krater.

SHANNON: After the bombing of Pearl Harbor, my husband had a grocery store down the main street, and all of a sudden these strange people began to come into the store—we thought we knew everybody in Owens Valley in those days—and these people were very uncouth, very unappealing.

We eventually found out that they were the people who had been brought in to build the barracks for Manzanar for the Japanese who were going to be interned there.

Well, I was very upset, and in those days I expressed myself, and I told these people that I thought this was unforgivable, and I didn't get a very good response. In fact, they were very unfriendly.

My husband told me I had better be quiet and not say anything about it. So, I didn't say very much about it.

EMILY: Haruko Niwa.

DIAN: My first morning in Manzanar, when I woke up and saw what Manzanar looked like, I just cried.

And then I saw the mountain, the high Sierra Mountain, just like my native country's mountain, I cried.

That's all. I couldn't think about anything.

TAMLYN: Katarine Krater.

SHANNON: The camp was enclosed in barbed wire and there was a tower at each of the four corners. It wasn't a relocation camp. It was a concentration camp, that's what it was. They were prisoners there. They couldn't leave and they couldn't move around at all. There were ten thousand at the time—it varied—But at one time they had a population of ten thousand which was more than the entire population of Inyo County.

There were people in Independence who were just frightened out of their wits. They thought the Japanese were going to break out of Manzanar and we'd all be slaughtered in our beds.

We know of at least two men who slept with guns under their beds all the time the Japanese were at Manzanar.

DIAN: Helen Murao.

TAMLYN: At Idaho's Minidoka, we were assigned our barracks.

At the same time, the camp was giving out bedding. The old and the infirm got beds with mattresses. The younger people got uncomfortable cots and pillow ticking that you had to fill with straw.

The guys in camps were teenagers. They were running down the block saying—

EMILY: "There's one over there!"

DIAN: "There's a good one over here!"

TAMLYN: They were pegging the families that were coming in that had—you know—good-looking girls. Finally, they came running up to me and asked where my parents were.

Since they did not know my parents were dead, I lied and said . . . "They weren't around."

They asked—

DIAN: "How many beds?"

TAMLYN: "Just one."

I managed to finagle a real bed with a real mattress from these guys using feminine wiles.

EMILY: Haruko Niwa.

DIAN: Aki was sitting on the front entrance step, he was crying with a drop of the tear like a marble. I know he missed the school in Westwood. He enjoyed so much the school activities that I know he missed that—all his friends in school and all that—and thinking about what is going to be his education and his future. Oh, he had the marble-size tear rolling down from his eyes, you know.

My other son, Nobu, was quiet sitting in the corner of the barracks. He was just sitting, just staring from the corner at nothing.

SHANNON: Noriko Sawada Bridges.

EMILY: When my mother was asleep, I would go to the library that was a block away and bring back books. She would accuse of me meeting boys at the library. She hated the library because I was being encouraged to be delinquent. She wouldn't let me go on dates. She just wouldn't allow anything.

It got to the point where I decided this wasn't worth living for. This was no life. Once I made that decision, I felt powerful and liberated. So then I took all my photographs and cut them up and burned them so she wouldn't have any evidence that I had ever existed.

Then I took a handful of her sleeping pills. But you know, they don't work all that fast. I was lying on the cot, and it was lunchtime and my father asked me if I wanted some lunch and I said sure. So he went to the mess hall and brought back my lunch and my mother's lunch and I ate it. That diluted the effects of the pills a lot.

Then my girlfriend came by and was being very chatty, and I said that I didn't feel much like chatting because I'm really committing suicide and I'm supposed to die any minute now. She ran for the doctor.

The doctor came and my mother told him that I was pregnant, which I wasn't. He was asking me the name of the boy and I was saying that I was not pregnant, and my mother was saying I was pregnant. Otherwise, no woman my age would be committing suicide. It was the haji, the shame of it all.

All of a sudden, it struck me as being really funny. I mean, here's this big moment in my life and I'm being accused of being pregnant and it's all like low comedy. So I began to laugh, and I laughed and I laughed. Of course, they're looking at me like I'm nuts and gone off my rocker totally.

The doctor made me drink some spirits of ammonia and then made my father sit at the foot of my bed. And every time I fell asleep, he poked me in the foot with a needle and that would wake me up. I was annoyed as all hell about the whole thing and swore I would never do it again.

Oh, my mother was also annoyed because the doctor was paying more attention to me than he was to her.

It was funny.

DIAN: Pauline Miller.

SHANNON: My daughter was just a little girl. I guess she was about four or five years old.

One time, we went for a dinner out at Manzanar, and they served all this beautiful food that they had raised. They raised their own vegetables and everything, and that's what they were showing.

And I couldn't get my daughter to take a bite, because she figured they were enemies, you know. She just had that in her mind. They were our enemies and you just didn't eat their food.

She just sat there.

TAMLYN: Toyo Suyemoto.

DIAN: Mother did not approve of her children "staying out" in the latrine building without parental supervision. Like other mothers in camp, she felt that discipline and respect for parental control were being ignored by the children.

One night, my two youngest brothers were not back from their showers though it was almost midnight.

Then Mother began putting on her cardigan sweater. I realized what she was about to do, and I told her she was not allowed to enter the men's shower area.

All she said was—

EMILY: "I will bring them back."

DIAN: And very quickly, she returned to our barracks with the two boys.

They pleaded—

TAMLYN: "Please don't ever do that again!"

DIAN: After that, she never had to remind them to be home on time.

EMILY: Helen Murao.

TAMLYN: I insisted that my two brothers and I eat together in the mess hall as a family unit. I insisted that we have grace before meals. And I insisted that they be in our room at eight o'clock at night. Not because I wanted to see them but because I thought that's we should do as a family unit—we should be together, spend our time together, and live as a family group—and I tried all the really childish ways to maintain us that way.

SHANNON: Anonymous.

EMILY: In our block, there was a woman whose husband began to beat her. Of course, everyone knew about it. How could you hide such a thing in those barracks? She was so ashamed that she wouldn't come out of her unit for days, even to eat.

Then one day—and I still don't know how she did it—she left camp, left her husband, and her two small children.

She must have suffered a lot to leave her children.

TAMLYN: Masako Saito.

DIAN: My mother was, well, it was hard on her, I guess—she's such an excitable woman—we tried to tell her how to do things, but she refused. When we were in camp, her main goal was to have her floor nice and clean.

But whatever it is—it was fate—as my mother would say. I know it was a feeling of sadness, being confined.

We felt it most when we used to go on Sundays to the grand-stand for our church services. And we would be singing our church hymns, and in the background we would see the trains wending its way, going around, and we thought, "Wouldn't it be nice to get out?" And that's how all of us felt.

I felt sad especially on a Sunday morning—in Sunday school.

SHANNON: Ada Endo.

TAMLYN: My sister and her husband and family are devoted Christians. I would never think of her doing anything out of line.

One night she came over and said—

EMILY: "You know, there is a lot of lumber down there and there is only one guard. Let's go down—and get some lumber."

TAMLYN: I looked at her, and I was sure surprised. I said, "Sure, why not?"

So we went down when the guard was not making his rounds or when he was on the other side.

We would go in and grab a piece of lumber, and we would wait awhile. And when the coast was clear, we would run back to the barracks. She held one end, and I held the other end.

I don't know how many pieces of lumber we brought back, but we divided it, and she took it to her barrack. I kept my half, and that is what we made shelves with.

We probably wouldn't ever do it again. We probably wouldn't even steal a penny, but we stole lumber that night.

DIAN: Anonymous.

EMILY: I remember one of my friends got engaged and married in camp. We gave her a shower.

What we gave her were carpenter nails because they were so precious. We went to the dump site and around the construction of new barracks, and sifted through the sand for them. I think I stole some from my dad's tool box. I wrapped them up in crepe paper so they resembled flowers and gave them to her.

She was very touched by it because she had to build furniture from scrap lumber for her new place.

SHANNON: Aiko Yoshinaga-Herzig

TAMLYN: I never had any sexual experience before going to camp. And so, making love on a straw mattress was noisy for me. Every time you moved a toe . . . you know.

SHANNON: Anonymous.

DIAN: We put up sheets to partition off our bed from the boys' beds. But we were always aware that they could hear everything, even a whisper. So my husband and I had no choice but to take "long" walks in the middle of the night . . .

TAMLYN: Noriko Sawada Bridges.

EMILY: I was trying to let my mother know what a crumb she was, and it wasn't working, and it would never work. When I realized that, I thought that I was sacrificing my life for nothing.

Things eased up a bit because when the doctor came back I told him why I made this suicide attempt, and so he told my mother that she should allow me to go to the library. And she should allow me to have dates.

So when a young man would ask me to go to a dance and I would say yes, and he would show up and he would say—

DIAN: "Hello, Mrs. Sawada."

EMILY: She wouldn't answer.

When we started walking off toward the mess hall where the dance was being held, not necessarily on our block, so maybe we would walk half a mile, my mother would follow us.

You know, walk a few paces behind and she would wait at the mess hall until the dance was over and then she would follow us home.

And that cured most guys of asking me the second time.

I was not the belle of the ball.

DIAN: Yoshiko Uchida.

TAMLYN: Sometimes as we walked, we could hear the MPs singing in their quarters and then they seemed something more than sentries who patrolled the barbed wire perimeters of our camp. We realized they were lonely boys far from home too.

Still, they were on the other side of the fence. Although at times they tried to talk to us, we never offered them our friendship.

EMILY: Mary Gillespie.

SHANNON: They built the camp and these men used to get very much provoked because we had to ration things—we were given just so much coffee, so much sugar—and they got everything, they were treated very good . . . they had all kinds of food and you know the Japs don't really live like that, they're used to fish and rice and their food.

The Japs had ham and bacon and all this stuff and it was said by some people who worked out at the camp that the garbage cans were just full because they weren't used to that kind of food.

They got the best of everything. They were treated very, very good. I'll say that for them.

EMILY: Teruyo Tamura Mitsuyoshi

DIAN: The food in the mess hall was terrible. They served a lot of stewed stuff—unidentified meat with rice—and Jello.

So whenever the food was unappetizing, we would return to the barracks for cocoa and spam.

To this day, I hate spam.

SHANNON: Aiko Horikoshi.

TAMLYN: I remember, in a department store in Powell, there were three Issei women who were looking at the material, and there were two local Caucasian ladies there, and me. We were the only ones in the store.

Those two ladies were talking about the three Japanese ladies, and they were calling them—

SHANNON: "Hicks."

TAMLYN: And I got all uptight about that. They didn't know what I was (I was half Japanese, half Caucasian).

I went over and said, "Don't you call us hicks. We are from Hollywood, California. You are such hicks you don't even have an escalator in the whole state of Wyoming."

I huffed and went away. They just stood there with their mouths open. They didn't even answer me.

EMILY: Mary Gillespie.

SHANNON: There were some real rough times at Manzanar because some of the internees tore down the American flag and they jumped all over civilian cars, but they moved them out to Tule Lake afterwards.

Well, all I can say is that when they were put into camp, they were royally treated—they fished and hunted. They were confined there but . . .

No, I never went to the camp. I had no desire to.

DIAN: Hisaye Yamamoto.

EMILY: Sears and Roebuck and Montgomery Ward catalogues would come in by the truckloads. And I'm sure they did millions of dollars worth of business.

SHANNON: Aiko Yoshinaga-Herzig

TAMLYN: We read those two catalogues from the two companies like bibles. I remember memorizing what page the chocolate candies were on in the Sears and Roebuck catalogue.

EMILY: Mine Okubo.

DIAN: When the cold days came in Tanforan, the War Relocation Authority distributed G.I. clothes to all those employed, both women and men. It was welcome if peculiar apparel—warm pea jackets and army uniforms. In sizes thirty-eight and forty-four! They were apparently left over from the First World War!

We also ordered our clothing allotment from the Sears, Roebuck summer catalogue. These clothes, with many substitutions, began to arrive.

Because of the catalog orders and the G.I. Clothes, everyone in camp was dressed alike.

EMILY: Eleanor Gerard Sekerak.

SHANNON: When my teaching contract did not arrive, I was informed by the dean that the district had decided to hire a man. This was long before the days one could rush into court claiming discrimination!

Then a telegram arrived and the wire read—

DIAN: "If you have not yet signed a contract, will you consider a position at Topaz, Utah? We are in desperate need of teachers."

SHANNON: I packed and caught a train for Utah, arriving there October 1st.

When I arrived at the staff women's dorm, a crew of young men delivered my trunk. One of the men shrieked upon seeing me and dropped the trunk on his toes. It was my hall-runner from Technical High—

TAMLYN: "Bill Oshima!"

SHANNON: He dashed away shouting—

TAMLYN: "Guess who's here? That strict teacher from Tech!"

SHANNON: By noon, the whole of Topaz knew that a Californian teacher had arrived.

Never was an ordinary teacher made to feel more welcome. People crowded around to ask questions, shake hands, bow and thank me for being there.

When questioners learned that I was from Oakland and from U.C., out the crowd emerged classmates from University High—and Hiro Katayama, who had told us "good-bye" only six months before.

EMILY: Helen Murao.

TAMLYN: I was still in high school, so I had to go to class.

My two brothers had to go too, and I lied a lot because I didn't want to go. I would stay at home, because the hot water in the mess hall and in the laundry rooms was available. I would scrub my brother's blue jeans and their clothes on a washboard and try to wring them out and also launder our sheets in the morning.

Then I would write a note saying, "Please excuse Helen for being absent, she was busy." And then I'd sign it, and the teacher would accept it.

I still managed to get good grades.

DIAN: Eleanor Gerard Sekerak.

SHANNON: I wondered how I could teach American government and democratic principles while we sat in classrooms behind barbed wire.

I never ceased to have a lump in my throat when the classes recited the Pledge of Allegiance, especially the phrase, "Liberty and justice for all."

On my first day, in our opening discussion, the students and I agreed that the whole evacuation process had been traumatic and could not last forever. And we could not permit academic achievement to be interrupted.

So they arrived for classes on time, with their homework completed. They worked diligently, took their exams and observed normal classroom standards.

We had one exception.

The day the first snow fell.

All the Californian Bay Area students and I rushed to the window to watch.

EMILY: Anna T. Kelley.

SHANNON: There were also teachers employed out there. Caucasians. They would come into Independence into Lone Pine. They met with a lot of hostility and were called "Jap Lovers." Some restaurants refused to serve them.

DIAN: Mary Tsukamoto.

EMILY: During the Christmas season, I renewed my letter writing with vigor and enthusiasm. I even wrote letters to President Franklin Roosevelt and his wife, Eleanor.

One day, the mailman delivered a letter to my barrack at 9-8-E. I wondered why a little parade of curious people accompanied him right up to my door. He handed me a letter, and his eyes were excited.

On the envelope were the gold letters that said "The White House." Who could possibly be sending a letter to 9-8-E in Jerome, Arkansas's internment camp from the White House?

I carefully opened the envelope—

SHANNON: "Dear Mrs. Tsukamoto,

Thank you so much for your letter. It was good of you to write to the President and me and your thoughtfulness is deeply appreciated. I am glad for you and wonder what your plans are for the future.

Very sincerely yours,

Eleanor Roosevelt."

EMILY: Eleanor Roosevelt wrote a letter to me!

TAMLYN: Mrs. Hama Yamaki.

DIAN: My son Bill was stationed in Minneapolis and could not secure a permit from the Army to enter Tule Lake. This was most distressing to me, because I had to wonder when we would meet again.

Shikata-ganai. It was the draft, he was a man, and he had to go.

In a letter, he expressed the thought—

TAMLYN: "It might be a long time before we see each other again."

DIAN: So I replied, "Do your best while on duty."

EMILY: Katarine Krater.

SHANNON: You know, of course, a good many of the Japanese girls are very beautiful, and this one girl was engaged to one of the boys who had enlisted from Manzanar. The girl was in camp and he was out. The girl was standing by the barbed wire fence saying good-bye to him, composed and undemonstrative, holding the barbed wire, and she didn't even realize that those barbs were cutting into her hands.

DIAN: Mrs. Tei Endow.

EMILY: My son Sho had originally served in Alaska. And then he was wounded while serving in the 442nd in Italy. Shrapnel missed his spinal column by a fraction of an inch.

When we first heard Sho had been injured, I received a very nice letter from the War Department that we were welcome to visit him.

I cannot help but think that perhaps we were treated more fairly during the war because we had a son serving in the Army.

Sho received the Purple Heart.

SHANNON: Mrs. Itsu Akiyama.

TAMLYN: My son, George, on leave before going overseas. Later, when I saw him off at the camp gate, I broke down crying. I did not know whether I would see him again. Even after I came home, all I could do was cry.

What troubled me most was that I did not really know how to pray for George's safety. In Japan, my parents had been Buddhist and prayed to a local shrine.

Here in America, I had no one to pray to. And I felt a desperate desire to pray.

DIAN: Eleanor Gerard Sekerak.

SHANNON: Just as we were settling down to a stable community, there was an uproar in the media outside the camps over Nisei registration for the draft.

As a consequence, "applications for leave clearance" were combined with registration of every man of military age into a single questionnaire.

The questions were worded for simple "yes" and "no" answers.

Question 27 concerned a person's willingness to serve in the armed forces. Question 28 asked for unqualified allegiance to the U.S. and the foreswearing of allegiance to Japan.

EMILY: Amy Uno Iishi.

TAMLYN: There were bad feelings among the Japanese people in the camps, because all the Niseis, the American citizens that were eighteen years and over, were made to sign a questionnaire, to state whether they would be faithful to this country or not. It was a loyalty questionnaire. Everyone called it "Question 27, Question 28."

It was worded something to the effect—

DIAN: "Will you be loyal to this country?"

TAMLYN: What is the justification of the government bringing questionnaires such as that into these barbed wire encampments where we were being "protected" when we didn't ask to be protected? When we didn't feel we needed to be protected?

They looked upon us as enemies of this country, and yet they dared to bring in this type of questionnaire asking us all to sign those questions saying—

DIAN: "Will you be faithful and loyal to this country?"

TAMLYN: How could we be anything but? They had us where they wanted us, under barbed wire, guard towers, searchlights and armed guards. So this was really a ridiculous thing!

It was really an insult to the integrity of the American people, to put forth these types of questions to the Japanese internees, and we *were* considered internees. And yet the boys still were forced to sign these questionnaires!

Many, many Japanese people said—

EMILY: "Don't sign it. By golly, they've got us here. If they want us to be loyal Americans, turn us loose, put us back where we were, send us home, and then draft our boys into the service. Then our boys would be justified to go and fight for this country and proved their loyalty to this country."

DIAN: Eleanor Gerard Sekerak.

SHANNON: All activities were suspended for a week while we interviewed the adult residents to complete the questionnaires

There were many meetings, many committees and much speechmaking.

EMILY: Amy Uno Iishi.

TAMLYN: My mother, brothers and sisters all agreed that the boys volunteer to go into service in spite of the fact that their father was interned in a so-called "hard-core enemy alien camp."

My mother—who had done nothing against this country except to raise ten children—was behind barbed wire. In spite of all of that, my mother felt—

DIAN: "If you boys go and serve this country and prove your loyalty, maybe they will turn Daddy loose, and at least give a chance for Dad to join Mother and the children and bring back the family unit."

TAMLYN: So the boys went to Camp Savage in Minnesota. They entered what you call Military Intelligence. They went as interpreters.

SHANNON: Florence Ohmura Dobashi

EMILY: Had I not wanted to leave camp, I might have answered "No" to both 27 and 28. But I chose to be practical and said "Yes."

It seemed foolhardy to make those sacrifices and feel like a lonely martyr, yet I was bothered by not answering honestly.

It was the only way out.

SHANNON: Chizuko Omori.

DIAN: When the questionnaires came out, my father rejected them, and asked for repatriation to Japan. Now that was very devastating for me personally.

I was like, thirteen years old. I think I protested very loudly, and when I would say "I'm not Japanese! I'm American!" And my mother would say to me—

TAMLYN: "Well, if you were an American, what are you doing here in this camp?"

DIAN: Well, I couldn't answer that, of course.

SHANNON: Miyo Senzaki.

EMILY: You learn from the time you're a child in school, from the first grade, to salute the flag. You believe in all the words that are said, you know.

And all of a sudden, you're in camp and you see the flag at half-mast, and you see the name of someone who volunteered for the army.

He's dead.

You think, can you salute that flag? Does it really stand for what it means? That was the time in my life when I didn't feel it stood for what it says.

I remember running over every day and see whose name would appear. We would see names of the kids we went to school with who died in the 442nd.

TAMLYN: Sato Hashizume.

DIAN: One family, the Nambas, created a shrine with a photograph of their uniformed son, his medals and a carefully folded American flag.

At lunch I stood by Mrs. Otaki. Her cheeks were tearstained, and her shoulders stooped with sorrow. I tried to speak, but could only muster up a nod.

SHANNON: Yoshiko Uchida.

TAMLYN: In Tanforan, my sister grew ill and spent many long days in bed, prompting a well-meaning Issei friend to bring her a small container of clear broth. She urged my sister—

EMILY: "Just take this, Keiko San, and you'll be strong and healthy in no time at all. I guarantee it will work."

TAMLYN: It wasn't until after Kay was up and around that the friend came again to see her.

EMILY: "It worked, didn't it? My broth?"

DIAN: "I guess it did—"

TAMLYN: My sister said.

Only then did the woman reveal she had made the brew with earthworms.

EMILY: "It's guaranteed to restore good health."

SHANNON: Emi Somekawa.

DIAN: There was a case at Tule Lake of a lady who was pregnant, and she had a very serious cardiac condition. All through her pregnancy she spent most of her time in bed, under medication. She didn't quite reach full term, but she went into labor.

The baby was in the neighborhood of about five and half pounds when it was born, and the mother fell into a coma at the time she delivered.

I was there at the time of her delivery. The doctor who was attending her said they didn't think that she would ever come out of it.

The mother wasn't able to nurse the baby or do anything for the baby, because she was constantly under an oxygen tent. This went on for about ten days and she never improved.

One day, her husband came and said—

EMILY: "I just can't stand watching her breathe. That very labored type of breathing, day after day. Will you please take her out of her misery?"

DIAN: I said, "Well, I will talk to the doctor and see what he says."

The doctor said—

TAMLYN: "We have nothing here to offer her, and if that's the wishes of the family, then I'll go along with it."

DIAN: The next day the husband came back again with his family. He had four children, and they were all still little. The first one might have been in grammar school, but not much older. They all came.

And the doctor told me—

TAMLYN: "Fix up a fourth of morphine."

DIAN: So I was there. There was a teaspoon with some water in it, and the father told each child—

EMILY: "Give your mother a sip of water."

DIAN: After the last child gave the sip of water, the father did the same thing, and then he was ready for the morphine.

Right away, the oxygen tent was removed and she just went to sleep.

That was it.

SHANNON: Aiko Horikoshi.

TAMLYN: I was a nurse aide at the hospital when I lived at Heart Mountain. We had a Caucasian chief nurse, Anna Van Dirk, who put a proclamation or a bulletin up ordering us to bow to her.

There was a lot of rumble especially among the doctors that they were ordered to bow to her. I was real irritated, and there was a lot of uneasiness in camp. The hospital staff decided to go on strike, and so I went on strike.

We used to call her Anna Van Jerk.

SHANNON: June Tsutsui.

DIAN: I still have the photograph of my firstborn son's grave. It always brings back painful memories.

I carried my baby full term. The delivery was intensified by the camp's inadequate medical care and by the doctor's late arrival.

I started hemorrhaging.

I believe that was aggravated by the hasty delivery on a hard flat table. I still think that a better-staffed hospital might have prevented it.

I endured such pain.

EMILY: Mabel Ota.

TAMLYN: I was in labor for twenty-eight hours, during which time no doctor came to check on me. When he finally came and examined me, he said they could not perform the operation because there was no anesthesiologist in camp.

They took me to the delivery room and gave me a local and I could see the knife he used to cut into me. Then he used those huge forceps and I kept watching that clock. He really had a hard time yanking her out, and I was conscious all the time. It was a horrible experience.

Then I remember looking at my baby and saying "Gee, I thought babies were bright red when they were born." And this one was very pale and they rushed her over to the incubator.

I didn't get to see my baby for three days. They said she was too weak to be moved. When I finally saw her, I noticed she had scabs on her head where the forceps had been used. There's one spot where hair has never grown.

I'm convinced my baby suffered permanent brain damage due to that procedure.

SHANNON: Miyo Senzaki.

EMILY: When I was pregnant with my second, that's when I flipped. I thought to myself, "Gosh, what am I doing getting pregnant?"

I told my husband, "This is crazy. You realize there's no future for us and what are we having kids for? We're behind barbed wire fence, the war could go on, what are we going to do? It's a crime to have children. We're not doing them any favors. I'm not going to have this child in camp."

Then, that night it bothered me so much, I wanted to get an abortion. I knew where a doctor lived, so I walked by his place.

I just couldn't go in. I thought, "Oh my god, I can't kill this child." But then I said, "If I have it, it's not fair. What am I doing?"

So I walked back. I figured the doctor is going to say no anyway. Then I cried and I told my husband, "I'm having this one in camp, but no more kids, unless you get me out of here."

DIAN: Yoshiko Uchida.

TAMLYN: One of the funerals I attended in camp was for the father of a friend of mine. She had returned from school in Colorado for the occasion, and it must have been devastating for her to see the bleakness of Topaz for the first time, knowing her father had spent his last days in such a place.

The funeral service was brief, and his coffin was decorated with cascades of crepe-paper flowers painstakingly made by some Issei women.

Many of those who died in Topaz were buried in the desert.

And it seemed ironic that—only then, they were *outside* the barbed wire fence.

6.

Slide: Outside the Fence

TAMLYN: Mine Okubo.

DIAN: Relocation programs were finally set up in the center to return residents to normal life. Students left camps to continue their education in colleges and universities willing to accept them. Seasonal workers flowed, to relieve the farm labor shortage.

Much red tape was involved, and "relocatees" were checked and double-checked. Jobs were checked by the War Relocation offices and even the place of destination was investigated before an evacuee left.

In January of 1944, I finally decided to leave. I plowed through the red tape, and through the madness of packing again.

I also had to attend forums on "How to Make Friends" and "How to Behave in the Outside World."

EMILY: Amy Uno Iishi.

TAMLYN: Before we left Heart Mountain permanently, my husband and I left to go to the small town out of Billings, Montana, to top sugar beets. This was when the government and the people on the outside realized that all the young people had fled the country and gone to the big cities to work in defense plants or had gone into the service. Who was there to harvest the crops?

They then realized they had a ready source in the camps. So they recruited us to go to these various farms.

The government made a big mistake in rounding us all up. It was costing them a lot more than they could afford to keep us behind barbed wire, so they were encouraging us to leave the camps.

So we asked permission from the WRA for a release, and they said—

SHANNON: "Yes."

TAMLYN: They gave us a one-way ticket to Chicago and twenty-five dollars.

DIAN: Mitsuye Endo, a twenty-two-year-old American citizen, once worked for the Sacramento Department of Motor Vehicles. In 1942, she was first sent to Tule Lake Center and later to Topaz.

In July, she challenged the Constitution by filing a petition for a writ of habeas corpus asking the courts to rule on whether she could be held indefinitely as a prisoner without being accused, tried or convicted of a crime.

EMILY: Mitsuye Endo.

TAMLYN: I never imagined it would go to the Supreme Court. In fact, I thought it might be thrown out of court because of all that bad sentiment toward us.

While all this was going on, it seemed like a dream. It just didn't seem it was happening to me.

DIAN: December 18th, 1944.

EMILY: United States Supreme Court Justice William O. Douglas.

SHANNON: "It is conceded by the Department of Justice and by the War Relocation Authority that Mitsuye Endo is a loyal and law-abiding citizen. They make no claim that she is detained on any charge or that she is even suspected of disloyalty.

Moreover, they do not contend that she may be held any longer in the Relocation Center.

Mitsuye Endo is entitled to an unconditional release."

EMILY: Justice Frank Murphy.

SHANNON: "I am of the view that detention in Relocation Centers of persons of Japanese ancestry regardless of loyalty is not only unauthorized, but is another example of the unconstitutional resort to racism inherent in the entire evacuation program."

TAMLYN: And that was our good-bye to the camp.

7.

Slide: A New Spring

DIAN: Mary Tsukamoto.

EMILY: I knew I would never live here again. The endless nightmare was behind me, and there was only hope for our future.

My last look at the barrack city brought me anguish mixed with exultation. I stood there for a moment taking one last look.

Here I was—a tired twenty-eight-year-old Nisei mother with her child, taking this big step onto the train and the gate.

Dad and my cousin were there to greet us at the station. Auntie, Uncle, Mother—they were all there, and it was wonderfully good to see them and hug them and, suddenly, I realized I was free.

I was in the real world, and I was free at last!

SHANNON: Helen Murao.

TAMLYN: I felt wonderful the day I left camp.

We took a bus to the railroad siding and then stopped someplace to transfer. And I went in and bought a Coke. A nickel Coke.

It wasn't the Coke, but what it represented—that I was free to buy it, that feeling was so intense. You get maudlin, sentimental about freedom. But if you've been deprived of it, it's very significant.

EMILY: Mrs. Hatsumi Nishimoto

DIAN: When we returned—in February or March 1945—we were distressed to see that our orchard had been neglected and our dwelling was filthy.

Our caretaker had been promised that our house would remain vacant, but another neighbor told us in confidence that the orchard foreman had lived in our home.

When I saw the condition of our orchards, I was quite downhearted. What was most cumbersome was the two of us had to do all the work. There were plenty of workers around, but we were unable to hire anyone. Our work was so exhausting that I lost six pounds in the first week!

It took us about three years to return our orchard to its normal condition.

EMILY: Amy Uno Iishi.

TAMLYN: Our only problem was we could not go back to our own house.

The house that we had lived in on Thirty-Eighth Street was not available to us when we came back. But we talked to the landlady, the Mexican family that owned the property. They wanted us to come back so badly. They were so happy to see us. They came and embraced my mother. Mrs. de la Puente never spoke any English.

When we were forced to leave our home there, the de la Puentes were very, very nice. They helped us. They asked if they could store some of our things for us. They promised us that, if we ever came back, the house was always ours to rent again. We lived in that house for eighteen years.

But at the time we came back, the government had frozen the business of housing and things. The people in the house had a lease on the house because they worked for the government, and the government would not allow the de la Puentes to throw them out. So until their lease had expired, they could not be made to move.

In the meantime, we lived out somewhere else. While there, my mother had a heart attack and died. The de la Puentes felt so badly because my mother never got a chance to come back and live in their house.

DIAN: Noriko Sawada Bridges.

EMILY: The Supreme Court decision was in 1944 and so the West Coast was opened and I came out to San Francisco.

As we were being oriented to the world outside, the relocation office would take groups of us who were going out and give us little lectures on how it was out there.

He would say—

SHANNON: "Don't congregate in groups of more than five.

Don't speak Japanese.

Don't be loud."

DIAN: Anonymous.

TAMLYN: We weren't to congregate among our kind. We shouldn't speak Japanese nor be conspicuous. We were not to talk about camp. In other words, we were not to be Japanese in any way.

But to the dominant society we were not only Japanese, we were "Japs." Certainly not American. So where the hell did that leave us?

DIAN: Noriko Sawada Bridges.

EMILY: When I got on this train the following year to Chicago, I went into the club car to get a drink. I was sitting there and some soldiers came in and they spoke to me in Japanese.

You know, all the signals went up and I was ready to fight or flee, but I looked through beyond them and they said—

SHANNON: "Oh, aren't you Japanese?"

EMILY: "No."

SHANNON: "Korean?"

EMILY: "No."

SHANNON: "What are you?"

EMILY: "I don't know. My mother was a lesbian."

I apologized to my mother at this point.

I felt like it was the only way I could get out of saying. "I am a Japanese American, I'm proud of it, and fuck you."

But I just couldn't do that.

DIAN: Fumi Kamada.

TAMLYN: Salt Lake City was nice—quiet—clean town. But—I remember one instance when my husband and I—Sunday— walking downtown and this young man in uniform approached us and asked for matches. He want to light the cigarette. So my husband reach in to give it to him.

Instead of taking the matches, he give my husband—you know—slapped him.

And then my husband tried to go back to him and I pulled him away because I don't want to get mauled, you know—get involved in a fight or anything. And he's wearing a uniform, and you're not suppose to hit a man in the uniform. Although my husband told him, "You know I was in the Army, TOO."

But he didn't care because us, you know, Japanese walking downtown, I guess he didn't like it.

He called him—

SHANNON: "You dirty . . . "

TAMLYN: Three word, you know.

EMILY: Emiko Omori.

DIAN: Immediately after leaving camp, I was busy trying to make ends meet that I had no time to think about what we'd been through.

I do remember being asked about the camps when I went to NYU in 1947, but always in the context of the Holocaust. All my friends were Jewish. You were made to feel apologetic, almost, about complaining of our "treatment."

But I do remember being annoyed during one of these discussions by a remark—

SHANNON: "Well, at least YOU weren't gassed or anything."

TAMLYN: Noriko Sawada Bridges.

EMILY: When the restrictive covenant was being taken off the deeds that ran with the land, I was getting signatures for a petition. I ran into this woman who said—

SHANNON: "Well, this measure, if it passes, means that if you want to live in the house next to mine and you have the money to buy it, you could move in?"

EMILY: "Yes."

SHANNON: "Weren't you in one of those camps?"

EMILY: "Yes."

SHANNON: "I don't want an ex-con living next to me."

TAMLYN: Haruko Niwa.

DIAN: It was August 15th, 1945.

I was riding a bus downtown coming home, and then all the
church bells rang, and whistles and firecrackers and all that,
and all the ladies in the seats in the bus kiss me and hug me.
We just kept crying.

The war was over!

It was so happy for all of us, and my husband hustle and
bustle for going back to West Los Angeles. Day and night he
was making a box and putting everything in.

We knew we were coming home.

8.

Slide: The Near Distance.

DIAN: Helen Murao.

TAMLYN: Camp wasn't a dreadful place. It wasn't a wretched place.
I did have some good times at camp. As I said, I met a lot of kids
and learned how to interact with my peer group, the Japanese.

But the overriding feeling that I had, without even being
conscious of it at the time, was the deprivation of freedom, and
that was a very traumatic thing.

You don't appreciate it until you don't have it. As I said, you
can flag-wave and you hear all these people who make it seem
so trite, but it isn't.

SHANNON: Chizuko Omori

DIAN: Well, you know what happened in our family. I mean, the fact
that our mother died at the age of thirty-four, a year out of the
camps, very suddenly of bleeding ulcers, the door on the whole
camp chapter of our lives was closed. And we didn't open it
again for years. It was like she was somehow connected with
that whole sorry incident and we were not gonna talk about it
anymore.

And we never did.

TAMLYN: Cara Lemon.

SHANNON: One of the reasons the internment is able to maintain its
obscurity is the absence of education and general knowledge
about it. The fact that I had absolutely no idea of the internment when I went to college is a testament to how little attention the subject has received.

Depictions of the Second World War in American public
schools still often present United States's efforts in the war as

sacrificial and heroic. The American role in the war is often portrayed as representative of democratic reason battling totalitarian regimes and ensuring justice for the future. Because of the United States's victory in the war, it is easier to remember it in that role. As a consequence, education about the Japanese American internment has received little attention.

The Japanese American internment is a reminder that we are not as far removed from racially motivated policy as we might pretend. Unfortunately, this important reminder has not reached many American citizens, especially younger generations.

The danger of not knowing about the Japanese American internment and its consequences is the inability to prevent the occurrence of a similar event.

TAMLYN: Yuri Kochiyama.

EMILY: I was one of these real American patriots then. Back then, I was all American. Growing up, my mother would say we're Japanese. But I'd say "No, I'm American."

At the time, I was ashamed of being Japanese. I think many Japanese Americans felt the same way. Pearl Harbor was a shameful act, and being Japanese Americans, even though we had nothing to do with it, we still somehow felt we were blamed for it. I hated Japan at that point.

So I saw myself at that part of my history as an "American," and not as "Japanese" or "Japanese American." That sort of changed while I was in the camp.

I hated the war, because it wasn't just between the governments. It went down to the people, and it nurtured hate.

The evacuation showed us that even though there is a constitution, constitutional rights could be taken away very easily.

TAMLYN: Mrs. Ethelyne Joseph.

SHANNON: Yes, at the time, I did, because of the war. I thought the Americans were doing a correct thing in incarcerating these people.

The camps were a necessity, because when you think of Pearl Harbor, naturally, if they would have made a return on Pearl Harbor, well, we would have been *done*. I think above everything else that it was a necessity. I'm sure we all felt the same way because we were at war. Naturally, we had a feeling of hatred toward them.

Since then, they have proven themselves, after having lost the war, and they're making their place in society, so I figure they're now equals.

But they had a lot of freedom in their little realm in Manzanar. They had their basketball courts and their tennis courts and their swimming pools. So they really didn't live as though they were in an internment camp. Other than the fact they were deprived of their autos and a few personal things. They didn't have it so bad.

And as far as their behavior and the conduct of the camp, and as far as Manzanar is concerned, there were beautiful relations.

In fact, internees still come back every year.

TAMLYN: Haruko Niwa.

DIAN: At first, when we have to evacuate, I was kind of hurt, you know. I was hurt, but I thought about it: it's wartime, so I thought, do the best we can whatever situations arise. We thought we do the best for the children.

I decided to stay here. I turned down my father's request to return to Japan, so I chose United States. I will obey the law of United States and everything. This is my country.

TAMLYN: Katarine Krater.

SHANNON: I think that the hysteria ran so high at the time, it went from President Roosevelt down. He was the one who signed the Executive Order, so the fault lies right on his doorstep, and right down the line.

I just can't believe this could ever happen again.

Are you familiar with General DeWitt, and his role in the affair? He heavily influenced the decision and, as a matter of fact, it was his plan, so to speak. It was his recommendation to the President.

And, of course, you read the telegram they sent to the President?

The Japanese American Citizens League sent this.

TAMLYN: "In this solemn hour we pledge our fullest cooperation to you, Mr. President and to our country. There can not be any question, there must be no doubt, we, in our hearts know we are Americans, loyal to America, we must prove this to all of you."

SHANNON: The telegram was sent on December 7, 1941.

Just *after* Pearl Harbor.

He ignored it.

DIAN: 1976.

TAMLYN: President Gerald Ford.

SHANNON: "February 19th is the anniversary of a sad day in American history.

51

It was on that date in 1942, in the midst of the response to hostilities that began on December 7, 1941, that Executive Order No. 9066 was issued . . . resulting in the uprooting of loyal Americans. Over one hundred thousand persons of Japanese ancestry were removed from their homes, detained in special camps and eventually relocated.

We now know what we should have known then . . . that evacuation was wrong."

EMILY: Helen Murao.

TAMLYN: My overriding feeling, and I've told my children, is don't let anybody else do something to you that you don't want to have happen to you. Don't let anybody control you. I have not wanted anybody to control me. My first reaction was "I'll show you." Well, I did show them.

So I guess I proved something, but I don't want anything to control my life. Hatred and bitterness can control you too, right? I think I resolved it.

But so, you know, we never forget.

DIAN: Mary Tsukamoto.

EMILY: I realized I needed to be angry not just for myself personally, but for what happened to our people. And also for our country because I really believe it wasn't just Japanese Americans that were betrayed, but America itself.

I'm saying this for the kids—the kids and their children and their friends and all the generations that are coming. For their sakes, we need to be angry enough to do something about it so that it will never happen again. I'm disappointed for America that it had to happen, and I want the record to be straight.

I know many Niseis who say, "That was all so long ago. Let's forget it and leave well enough alone." But I say, "We were the ones that went through it—the tears and the shame and the shock."

We need to leave our legacy to our children. And also our legacy to America, from our tears, what we learned.

TAMLYN: 1990.

EMILY: President George H.W. Bush.

SHANNON: "A monetary sum and words alone cannot restore lost years or erase painful memories . . . We can never fully right the wrongs of the past.

But we can take a clear stand for justice and recognize that serious injustices were done to Japanese Americans during World War II."

TAMLYN: Emi Somekawa.

DIAN: I hope that something like this will never happen to another group of people or to us ever again.

But sometimes I wonder.

(Pause.
Lights slowly fade to black.)

TAMLYN: Mary Tsukamoto.

EMILY: Yuri Kochiyama.

DIAN: Haruko Niwa.

SHANNON: Kiyo Sato.

TAMLYN: Monica Sone.

EMILY: Chizu Iiyama.

DIAN: Mine Okubo.

SHANNON: Elaine Black Yoneda.

TAMLYN *(Overlapping)*: Nobu Miyoshi—

EMILY *(Overlapping)*: Miyo Senzaki—

DIAN *(Overlapping)*: Emi Somekawa—

SHANNON *(Overlapping)*: Eleanor Gerard Sekerak—

TAMLYN *(Overlapping, softer)*: Amy Uno Iishi—

EMILY *(Overlapping, softer)*: Masako Saito—

DIAN *(Overlapping, softer)*: Yoshiko Uchida—

SHANNON *(Overlapping, softer)*: Ada Endo—

TAMLYN *(Overlapping, softer)*: Haruko Hurt—

EMILY *(Overlapping, softer)*: Noriko Sawada Bridges—

DIAN *(Overlapping, softer)*: Helen Murao—

SHANNON *(Overlapping, softer)*: Mabel Ota . . .

END OF PLAY

Bibliography

California State University, Fullerton Oral History Program, Japanese American Project; *Prisoners Without Trial* by Roger Daniels; *The Evacuation Diary of Hatsuye Egami* by Hatsuye Egami; *Japanese-American Internment Camps*, edited by Bryan J. Grapes; *Last Witnesses*, edited by Erica Harth; *Only What We Could Carry*, edited by Lawson Fusao Inada; *Starting Over: Japanese Americans After the War* from KCSM-TV; *Young Women's Everyday Resistance: Heart Mountain, WY* by Susan McKay; *Japanese American Women* by Mei T. Nakano; *Japanese American Internment During World War II* by Wendy Ng; National Japanese American Historical Society; *Citizen 13660* by Miné Okubo; Oral History Project of Japanese American Women's Exhibit; REgenerations Oral History Project; "A Teacher in Topaz" by Eleanor Gerard Sekerak; *Nisei Daughter* by Monica Sone; *Strangers from a Different Shore* by Ronald Takaki; *The Hood River Issei* by Linda Tamura; *We the People* by Mary Tsukamoto and Elizabeth Pinkerton; *And Justice for All* by John Tateishi; and *Desert Exile* by Yoshiko Uchida.

Chay Yew's plays include *Porcelain*, *A Language of Their Own*, *Red*, *A Beautiful Country*, *Wonderland*, *Vivien and the Shadows*, *A Distant Shore* and *Visible Cities*. His other work includes the adaptations *A Winter People* (based on Chekhov's *The Cherry Orchard*) and Lorca's *The House of Bernarda Alba* and the musical *Long Season*. His work has been produced at the Public Theater, Royal Court Theatre (London), Mark Taper Forum, Manhattan Theatre Club, Wilma Theater, Long Wharf Theatre, La Jolla Playhouse, Fattore K (Naples), Intiman Theatre, Studio Theatre, Portland Center Stage, East West Players, Cornerstone Theater Company, Perseverance Theatre, La Mama (Melbourne), TheatreWorks (Singapore), among others. He is also the recipient of the London Fringe Award for Best Playwright and Best Play, George and Elisabeth Marton Playwriting Award, GLAAD Media Award, Made in America Award and Robert Chesley Award. His plays are published by Grove/Atlantic, Inc. He is an alumnus of New Dramatists and is the Artistic Director of Victory Gardens Theatre in Chicago.

Last of the Suns

Alice Tuan

Author's Statement

Last of the Suns is the first play I ever wrote—

I remember the day I became a playwright. I was seventeen and living with my parents, sister Susan and grandparents in the San Fernando Valley. In my favorite state of sleeping late, I was awakened one morning by a continuous stream of high-piercing beeps from the kitchen. I find Yeh Yeh (Chinese for paternal grandfather) hunched over the microwave, pushing numbers, trying to warm his tea, but unable to find the start button. Years later, in a writing workshop at Los Angeles City College with poet Philomene Long, I scribed this short scene (my first ever), which was then read on LA lefty radio station KPFK, with my godfather Paul Chow performing Yeh Yeh with a singularly gruff and braying voice.

I consider myself an accidental playwright. What started as an exercise in the first amendment right of free expression—I wanted a more sophisticated U.S. existence as a gal of Chinese descent—became a writing laboratory to make sense of a cultural schizophrenia that was confusing and crazy-making. Raised in a household of Chinese values (from thriftiness to endurance) and schooled in U.S. suburban thought (from fun to freedom) I was never comfortable on one ground, when my foot was equally planted in another that contradicted it.

As a disaffected economics student at UCLA, I could make even less sense of "guns and butter" and its science of approximation when I was a citizen of a democracy that represented me with limited portrayals of minor character. And so I saved up enough money to live for six months without having to return to the dead-end secretary job in downtown LA that my economics degree yielded me. Through sheer will, I typed out a one-hundred-page draft of *General Yeh Yeh*—it read like a lame sitcom, because TV is what I fried on—and sent it to the Mark Taper Forum. There, the Mentor/Playwright Project and the Asian Theatre Workshop (as envisioned by Chay Yew) gave me a chance to learn a playwright's process and develop a theatrical voice. *General Yeh Yeh*—after 13 drafts and two productions—became *Last of the Suns*.

Now a playwright on purpose, I feel lucky to be a theatrical thinker as we pivot from the twentieth to the twenty-first century, from paper to ether. If the label "Asian-American" was sprouted from twentieth century U.S. multiculturalism, then the twenty-first century asks that the "Asian" values and sensibilities of the hyphenate be beefed up to match the American. In *Last of the Suns* I attempted to include "Chinese" in its language and character palate by having the parents speak broken English as their second language and speak fluid English as their native Chinese.

But I wonder if the time is ripening to perform this work as fully bilingual, where constant subtitling may allow the play to be accessible to both Chinese and U.S. audiences alike. Another thought is to elasticize the casting and not just faux-authenticate the Chinese family with any Asian countenance, but break open the ethnic specificity and give the play a diverse face where affinities live in character performance and not just surface representation.

A playwright can dream.

Production History

Last of the Suns received its world premiere in 1994 at Berkeley Repertory Theatre in California. It was directed by Phyllis S. K. Look. The set design was by Barbara Mesney. The costume design was by Lydia Tanji. The lighting design was by Kurt Landisman and the sound design was by J. A. Deane. The stage manager was Joseph Smelser. The cast was as follows:

YEH YEH	Sab Shimono
MONKEY KING / MAO CAP #1 / LT. GEN. KING	Michael Ordoña
EIGHT PIG / MAO CAP #2 / MAJOR GO	Kelvin Han Yee
TWILA / MAY LEE	Jacqueline Kim
FIRST WIFE / NI LEE	Jeanne Sakata
BUDDHA / HO PING	Alberto Isaac
SONNY	Sean San José Blackman

Last of the Suns was produced in 2003 by the Ma-Yi Theater Company in New York City (Ralph B. Peña, Artistic Director; Jorge Z. Ortoll, Executive Director). It was directed by Chay Yew. The set design was by Sarah Lambert. The costume design was by Rebecca Dowd. The lighting design was by James Vermeulen and the sound design was by Fabian Obispo. The production stage manager was Cynthia Curtis. The cast was as follows:

YEH YEH	Ching Valdes-Aran
MONKEY KING / MAO CAP #1 / LT. GEN. KING	Eric Steinberg
EIGHT PIG / MAO CAP #2 / MAJOR GO	Kati Kuroda
TWILA / MAY LEE	Tess Lina
FIRST WIFE / NI LEE	Mia Katigbak
HO PING	Ron Nakahara
SONNY	Pun Bandhu

Characters

YEH YEH / GENERAL SUN

MONKEY KING

EIGHT PIG

TWILA

MAY LEE (played by the same actor as Twila)

FIRST WIFE

NI LEE (played by the same actor as First Wife)

HO PING

SONNY

Setting

Los Angeles.
End of the Twentieth Century.

Note

The "Chinese" in this play uses the old-fashioned British romaniza-
tion Wade-Giles (since they are from Taiwan) instead of the modern
Pin Yin.

This play is dedicated to Shin and Ada Tuan,

and all parents who endure the treachery of their child's decision to pursue a life in the arts in the United States, and who ultimately support the endeavor, despite the unknowns.

Act One

The whole stage is an ice rink.

In darkness, we hear really loud, epicentric snoring. Lights up on General Sun, known to his family as YEH YEH, sitting in his throne. He is one hundred years old today. His eyeglasses are perched atop his head. He is awakened by his own snore. He registers that he is still in our world and immediately berates the sky.

YEH YEH:

    Let me die! Let me die! You!
    You are stubborn, stripping my eyes
    until all is the wool fog of Lu Shan.
    You will not let me sense the scenery,
    And leave me to memory.
    You let them tie plastic around my ears
    Pretending static is but my blurring brain,
    Or the echoes of a century's fears.
    You leave me hunched and ashamed
    Shriveled like dry anise plums
    and smelling like fermented eggs! *(sighs)*
    You've destroyed my scent
    As if all my prowess has been spent
    As if I'm not strapping anymore!
    Who can comfort me now, I implore?

Who can still feed my needs as a man?
No one! Nothing! You call this a life?
I command you this instant, to let me die!

(Silence.
Then Yeh Yeh throws a fit, stomping and pounding on his throne.)

ARRRGH AYYY AHHHHHH!

(His throne starts moving forward and we hear the voices of
MONKEY KING and EIGHT PIG.)

MONKEY KING: PUSH!

EIGHT PIG: Arg.

MONKEY KING: PUSH!

YEH YEH: HAH?!

MONKEY KING: PUSH!

EIGHT PIG: Arg.

MONKEY KING: PUSH!

YEH YEH: Who's there?

MONKEY KING: PUSH!

EIGHT PIG: Why are we . . .

MONKEY KING: PUSH!

EIGHT PIG: Why are we . . .

MONKEY KING: Shush!

EIGHT PIG: . . . pushing him . . .

MONKEY KING: Shush!

EIGHT PIG: . . . pushing him . . .

MONKEY KING: Shush!

EIGHT PIG: . . . pushing him back to the mortals?

MONKEY KING: Must I field any more your retortals?

EIGHT PIG: What?

MONKEY KING: Do I pinch up your snout 'til it snortals?

EIGHT PIG *(plugged nose)*: No.

MONKEY KING: So push just an itsy bit more—

EIGHT PIG: Tell . . . tell me why . . .

MONKEY KING: PUSH!

EIGHT PIG: Why?

MONKEY KING: PUSH!

YEH YEH: WHO'S THERE?
　　(The throne stops.)
　　Come out now!
　　(beat)

EIGHT PIG: You . . . you . . . promise you'll spare—
YEH YEH: I say NOW!

(*Monkey King and Eight Pig emerge from behind the throne and stand at attention.*
Yeh Yeh is looking for his glasses, trying to focus.)

YEH YEH: Who is it?
MONKEY KING: Who is it?
EIGHT PIG: Who is it?
YEH YEH: Who's there?
MONKEY KING: Who's there?
EIGHT PIG: Who's there?
YEH YEH: Dammit I can't find my glasses. Who is it?

(*He continues to search for spectacles. Monkey King and Eight Pig huddle.*)

MONKEY KING: We are his memories of *Journey to the West* . . .
YEH YEH: No talking behind my back.
EIGHT PIG: . . . Of China's fairy tales we are the most known and best.
YEH YEH: Help here a man of lack.
MONKEY KING: No light . . .
EIGHT PIG: . . . means fear.
YEH YEH: What say you?
EIGHT PIG: Severe.
YEH YEH: This isn't funny anymore.
MONKEY KING: It's pathetic . . . A BORE . . .
    outside so tough, inside so meek.
    We don't need anymore of these.
    (*Monkey King pulls out a scroll.*)
    Order here from our Monk Master Tang
    Words only spoken that should be sang
EIGHT PIG: Let's sing! Let's sing!
YEH YEH: Where are the damned things!
MONKEY KING: quote "Buddha cannot accept such a bloke
    of ego and attachment" unquote.
YEH YEH: Speak clearly!

(*Yeh Yeh finally finds his glasses atop his head and focuses.*)

MONKEY KING: I'm sure the western god would take him in
    but he'd end up in hell for his slanty-eyed sin . . .

YEH YEH: Lieutenant General King!

MONKEY KING: General Sun.

YEH YEH: Major Go!

EIGHT PIG: I'm no . . . (*monkey-nudged:*) Gen- Gen- General Sun.

YEH YEH: What took you so long?

EIGHT PIG: Our map seemed all wrong . . .

MONKEY KING: Our "journey to the far west" has taken . . .
    more than we . . . *imagined.*

EIGHT PIG (*in General's ear*): About time you awaken.

YEH YEH (*secretively*): . . . like a kite needs wind
    how do I say . . . I . . . I need May Lee . . .

EIGHT PIG: OO Wee!

MONKEY KING: Shush!

YEH YEH (*reverie*): Can you bring May Lee to me?
    I *need* her . . . one last time . . . do you understand?

EIGHT PIG: So why are we rhymers in his mind's land?

YEH YEH (*reverie*): I miss her lips . . .

MONKEY KING (*refers to scroll*): Says here we're his "unconscious" . . .
    his shadows

YEH YEH: Her curves, her hips . . .

MONKEY KING: We leap from the cracks of a brain that addles.

YEH YEH: Have May Lee prepared for me . . .
    Her little peach mouth . . . glossed and smoothed . . .

MONKEY KING: I'm sorry General, but you are the one who . . .

YEH YEH (*brusquely*): Stupid monkey can't you see?
    I'm rotten as a mandarin's orange peel
    under this vulgar California sun.
    Let's go. To that place. Where we become one.

MONKEY KING: Remember what Buddha said:

"Things seem to move, but are really at rest
And they seem to go away, but really sit . . ."

YEH YEH: Skip over the Buddhist texts.

MONKEY KING:

"Such things can only be understood by the spirit
And not in the dull, literal, humancentric folly of ordinary fact"

YEH YEH: I command you to relieve me of this tract!

MONKEY KING: You cannot be eaten as you are, so spiritually bland.

YEH YEH: Eaten? Ha!

MONKEY KING: So weak that you can barely withstand
  The small inconveniences of your existence.

YEH YEH: To die is to be eaten? Nonsense!

EIGHT PIG: Your mealy flavor so disenthralls
  The appetites of our lush undermass.

YEH YEH (*gathering pity*): The doctors have slashed my eyeballs.
  I cannot see without this framed glass
  weighing on my bridgeless nose.

EIGHT PIG: You chose not to hear and do ignore!

MONKEY KING: You're nothing but a century, propped for a pose.

YEH YEH: I cannot hear the quick-tongues of the young anymore.
  I only know the past . . . commanding five thousand troops in Szechuan for
  that luck bastard Chiang Kai-shek . . .
  beheading rows of reds, severing their spines,
  slicing the communist curves of their necks . . .
  assassinating mayors for their concubines.

MONKEY KING: The air here is benevolent and you, General Sun,
  stink it up with your small mundane histories.

YEH YEH: And there is no beauty in my life. No touch.

EIGHT PIG: You are not surrounded by beauty such?
  The stuffed chairs? The yarnish carpet?
  How many sheep shorn for such a sea of yarn?
  How many oranges pulped for that much
  color?

YEH YEH: I command you . . . EIGHT PIG . . . MONKEY KING . . .
  Enough of this . . . this . . . this playacting
  to your hideaway on Mount Flower and Fruit!
  Before banality finds me and chances pursuit
  We can be cohorts, as Chiang and I were,
  in the compounds of Lu Shan—
  where we lived so high atop that mountain,
  the fog below us like a snowy lawn . . .
  how could we not be gods?

MONKEY KING: Can't.

YEH YEH: What?

MONKEY KING: Have to consult your death agent.

YEH YEH: Who? Who is it?

MONKEY KING: The one who awakens you past this world of attachments.

YEH YEH: Who? Who is it? Who?

MONKEY KING: Ah, knowing how and who is inspired by enlightenment.

EIGHT PIG: And you have shoo'd her . . . (*covers mouth as if he's leaked and quickly exits*)

YEH YEH: Her. It is female!

MONKEY KING: The one you have failed.

YEH YEH: What?

MONKEY KING: You must woo . . .

YEH YEH: Who?

MONKEY KING: Woo!

YEH YEH: Who?

MONKEY KING: Woo this, this death . . . muse.

YEH YEH: How, when I cannot hear or see?

MONKEY KING: You are blind and deaf to both views.
What an epic void. Go, go drink your tea.

YEH YEH: I keep thinking. Thinking of what I've done . . .

(*TWILA stumbles in loaded, followed by Eight Pig. She collapses behind Yeh Yeh's throne, unknown to Yeh Yeh.*)

MONKEY KING: Time's a-ticking, General Sun!

YEH YEH: Who is it?

EIGHT PIG: She's awaiting.

YEH YEH: Tell me this instant.

EIGHT PIG: She's a-hating.

MONKEY KING: Where's she been?

EIGHT PIG: Tick . . . tick . . . tick . . . tick.

YEH YEH: It's May Lee!

MONKEY KING: Feel it!

YEH YEH: I'm sorry my May Lee, I'm sorry!

MONKEY KING: FEEL!

YEH YEH: I'm sorry . . . Come get me. I'm sorry!

MONKEY KING: Compassion, General Sun. Not these empty words!
Feel what you've done: Each stab. Each bind. Each murder.
Then you will know what a vile nausea you are to this world
and why it constantly convulses!

(*Monkey King skits away with distinctive laughter, followed by Eight Pig. Yeh Yeh retrieves his tea and walks towards the microwave during the next speech.*)

YEH YEH: This is absurd! Little mealy-mouthed icons telling me
to feel. Feeling is for the meek, who wait to be acted upon.

Nothing can get accomplished with feelings! You think Chiang Kai-shek bothered with feelings when surrounded by Japs AND commies? That he would buckle into his fear? NO! He thought about the treachery of Mao, skinning his country with this hairy, foreign Karl Marx beast. If I wanted feelings, I would have stayed in the village and remained a fisherman . . . felt the air waft through an empty gut. But my brain, the elders of the village saw my intelligence and cultivated it. I've passed all the texts, ascended in rank and commanded five thousand troops to . . . NEAR victory! I've spent a century thinking, thinking, and now I must bow my feeling down, kowtow to some death in the form of a woman? How many sorrys can one utter in a lifetime? Besides . . . what could one feel for a woman but pity for such useless inaction?

(Yeh Yeh attempts to warm his tea in the microwave, but cannot find the "START" button. The piercing beeps awaken Twila, his granddaughter, home after a five-year absence. She is punky, with spiky blond hair, blue contacts and combat boots. She rifles through her messenger bag, finds an empty pill bottle, then combs the bottom of her bag, getting a bit frantic.)

TWILA: Yeh Yeh!

(Beep beep beep . . .)

YEH YEH *(bent over, looking over his shoulder in an immense graveled voice)*: HAH?!
TWILA: Yeh Yeh! No! Not ninety-eight minutes. Too long!
YEH YEH: HAH?!
TWILA: Look, Yeh Yeh.
YEH YEH: HAH?!
TWILA: Look at the numbers.
YEH YEH: Is it broken?
TWILA *(holds Yeh Yeh's finger)*: ONE . . . ZERO . . . ZERO . . . START.

(Microwave starts.)

YEH YEH: Eyeh? Is it fixed?
TWILA: It's not broken, but to start . . . you need to press this button.
YEH YEH: This one?

TWILA: Yes . . . but not . . . again and again. Don't you see the light?

YEH YEH: HAH?! Say it again. Clearly. You know I can't hear.

TWILA: Yeah, Yeh Yeh. You only hear what you want.

(Monkey King's distinctive laughter.)

YEH YEH: What the hell are you talking about?

TWILA: BUTTON . . . ON . . . NO . . . PUSH.

YEH YEH: Okay, okay. Don't shout.

(She finally finds a pill at the bottom of the bag, blows dust off of it, pops it in her mouth. The microwave beeps. Yeh Yeh's tea is warmed.)

TWILA: Come, Yeh Yeh, your tea is ready.

YEH YEH: HAO!

TWILA: Come, let's sit and chat.

(She helps him to the table. They sit. He loudly sips.)

How . . . are . . . you, Yeh Yeh? How . . . are . . . you?

YEH YEH: How am I? Fine, fine. *(beat)* And . . . ah you?

TWILA: Getting by.

YEH YEH: Fine?

TWILA: Fine.

(Long uncomfortable pause as Twila, nauseous from pills and estrangement, tries to find words as Yeh Yeh continues to sip.)

TWILA: Happy . . . birthday, Yeh Yeh, happy . . . birthday!

YEH YEH: Birthday? Your birthday?

TWILA: No, you, Yeh Yeh, you. One hundred! One . . . zero . . . zero.

YEH YEH *(acknowledges with a smile that bucks his dentures)*: Sank you, sank you . . . hah . . . sank you.

(Twila assesses Yeh Yeh's comprehension.)

TWILA: Are you happy to see me?

YEH YEH: Happy! Happy birthday.

TWILA: Did you miss me, Yeh Yeh?

YEH YEH: Hah?

TWILA: Miss *me*. Twila *me*. Granddaughter me.

YEH YEH *(thumbs up)*: Ah . . . Twila . . . Good! Numbah one!

TWILA: Do you forgive me?

YEH YEH: Give me?

TWILA: For-give.

YEH YEH (*holds up four fingers*): Four?

TWILA: Just say, I . . . forgive you . . . Twila.

YEH YEH: You, Twila

TWILA: I . . . say, "I"

YEH YEH: "I"

TWILA: "For"

YEH YEH (*holds up fingers*): "Four"

TWILA: "Give you"

YEH YEH: "You"

TWILA: "Give you"

YEH YEH: "Gew"

TWILA: "Twila"

YEH YEH: "Twila"

TWILA: "I forgive you, Twila"

YEH YEH: "Four Gew, Twila"

TWILA: Close enough.

YEH YEH: You . . .

TWILA: One down. Two to go.

YEH YEH: You . . . skay-TING? Skay-TING?

(*Twila convulses.*)

YEH YEH: TWILA!

TWILA: Hah?!

YEH YEH: Have . . . you . . . taken break-fast?

TWILA: Hah?!

YEH YEH: Have you taken . . . lun-chee?

TWILA: No. Have you?

YEH YEH (*licking his chops*): Egg SANDWICH!

TWILA: Aha! (*she gestures*) One piece of bread or two?

(*He gestures "two."*)

TWILA: Dark bread or white bread?

YEH YEH: Egg?

TWILA: Dark or light?

YEH YEH: Egg! Egg Sand-wich!

TWILA: How many? One egg or two?

YEH YEH: How many? One. Just one. Cho-les-ter-ol.

TWILA (*New York waitress*): Oh, so ah tomato slices, prunes or cot-
tage cheese?

YEH YEH: Egg!

TWILA: Hashed, fried, mashed or baked?

YEH YEH (*demanding as a child chanting*): EGG SAND-WICH! EGG SAND-WICH!

TWILA (*falsetto subservience*): Of course, General Sun. Coming right up.

YEH YEH (*continued chant*): TWI-LA TWI-LA EGG SAND-WICH! . . . (*continued*)

TWILA (*concubinish*): Yes, General Sun, yes. Your command is my wish.

YEH YEH: Twila?

TWILA: Yo!

YEH YEH: What time is it?

TWILA (*whispers*): It's time TO die.

(*Pause.*)

YEH YEH: Two?

TWILA: Noon!

YEH YEH (*finger*): One?

TWILA: Close enough. Yes. It is one.

(*Twila looks closely at Yeh Yeh's face, feels the jowls of his cheeks, brushes his eyebrows with her finger.*)

TWILA: Yesterday. I was at the East River. With this bottle, you know, Yeh Yeh? I was gonna do it there. Put myself to sleep. The fog was thick. I mean . . . I know what's at the beginning, I see what's at the end . . . why should I forge into the middle? Whatever I do in life . . . ends up kinda pitiful . . . like you.

But then, right before my eyes . . . A mouthful of pills and right before my eyes, the fog clears. And the sky's canvas has a coupla blots of clouds . . . that become your face . . . YOUR face . . . and then thunder awakens me, like your hands applauding . . . you always clapped for me. I thought, Yeh Yeh is calling me. Yeh Yeh knows who I really am. The first one to skate with me. To-Pan-Ga. Let's go To-Pan-Ga. You held both my hands. My small hands. And the next thing you know, it was one hand. I could skate holding just one hand. And then it was one finger. You'd pull me along . . . I'd balance, just one finger . . . and after a month . . . no hands. You let go. I could on my own.

Yesterday.

Big puffy clouds were your cheeks and right above me . . . ragged streaks were these eyebrows . . . I spit all the pills out into the East River and rushed . . . and came here. Did you miss me, Yeh Yeh? Did you see my face in the sky? Do you even know I've been away for five years?

YEH YEH: Twila?

TWILA (*breakthrough?*): Yes, Yeh Yeh, yes?

YEH YEH: Is it one in the morning or one at night?

(*Disorienting light shines in Yeh Yeh's eyes. FIRST WIFE appears at the General's side. She is dressed in dark, rich Chinese apparel, circa 1920s China, with white hair swept back in a bun. She holds an onyx backscratcher.*)

TWILA: Gee, we have new neighbors, Yeh Yeh.
(*Yeh Yeh jumps at the sight of First Wife.*)
Something actually moved on this cul-de-sac.

FIRST WIFE: We found her in the well . . . again!

GENERAL SUN: First Wife!

FIRST WIFE: Pathetic stoned girl. Fell in the well again.

GENERAL SUN: May Lee is dead?

TWILA: When it is light, Yeh Yeh, is it day or night?

FIRST WIFE: Stop giving her the Szechuan junk.

GENERAL SUN (*squinting from the light*): She can't take the pain of her feet and complains and complains.

TWILA: Night or day, Yeh Yeh?

GENERAL SUN: She never shuts up and she's . . .

TWILA: Night or day, Yeh Yeh?

GENERAL SUN (*annoyed*): It is day. It is day.

TWILA (*salutes*): Very wise, General Sun. You will go far in your military career. I do believe it is . . . happy hour now.

(*She goes to search for a bottle of Scotch. The mindscape shifts. General Sun paces. It is Lu Shan, China, 1925. First Wife, played by the same actor as Ni Lee, stands at attention.*)

GENERAL SUN: Day, it is day . . .
Day is the worst time to move. All movement can be seen . . . so we must move swiftly . . . in fog. Fog is good! Fog is good! This thick woolly Lu Shan fog is best, for we can hide and move, hide AND move at the same time. Brilliant, General, brilliant. A perfect cloaking it is . . . like General George Washington. He crossed the river, in blind faith—he couldn't see, but he knew his enemy couldn't either. Cowards would wait 'til they

could see. But brave General George Washington . . . he rowed through the haze . . . clear about the other side. All was still and he moved invisibly . . . that's how we must be . . . invisible. And quiet. Invisible and quiet so the enemy won't know we are there. Did you hear that, May Lee? My little peach mouth, May Lee? I'm gonna need a little something of yours . . . May Lee!

(*Sound of May Lee laughing with Monkey King.*)

FIRST WIFE: She is drinking with that disloyal monkey of a lieutenant.
GENERAL SUN: Bring her to me.
FIRST WIFE: She's weakened you, General Husband.
GENERAL SUN: I need some amusement before we leave for Szechuan. Have her prepared for me right away (I like the glossy stuff).
FIRST WIFE: She is diseased.
GENERAL SUN: I'm having a little game of Lop with the other Generals. It's a good new batch of commie creeps to line up and lop. Last time it was ten, well, nine and a half . . . one didn't quite fall off his neck. But this time I'll do it. I will! Double Digit Lop.
FIRST WIFE: Sell her, I tell you, SELL HER!
GENERAL SUN: Let her drink, then drag her in. (*touches her*) You are a good wife. As I command.

(*General Sun exits gracefully, passes Eight Pig, who swigs from a bottle of Scotch. We hear May Lee's drunken voice.*)

MAY LEE: Giyuv . . . givutt you Beassst Frrreaks! Givit!

(*Monkey King rolls May Lee, played by the same actor as Twila, in on the kitchen table. She wears ratty Chinese opera garb, her hair a straight black falling length. She is vicious and flushed. Monkey King and Eight Pig play catch with the Scotch bottle, running in figure eights and then exiting. First Wife approaches, backscratcher raised.*)

MAY LEE: I'll have you minced and stuffed into bean sprouts, Pig! And don't think I can't clamp your head in this table, Monkey Freak, and eat your raw, pulsating brain . . . hah!
FIRST WIFE: Drunk again! When will you stop?
MAY LEE: Get off my back you monkey of a shriveled wench.

(*First Wife hits May Lee with the backscratcher. May Lee wavers.*)

MAY LEE: Again!

(*Hits.*)

MAY LEE: Again. Harder.

(*Many hits.*)

MAY LEE: Over here. You missed a spot.

FIRST WIFE: You thankless, worn harlot. You have duties. (*handing her the backscratcher*) Go tend to General Sun . . . . May Lee!

MAY LEE: That peeled rotten grape? He's a bowl of molded snot. (*hiccup*) You go suck on him for a while.

FIRST WIFE: You have been paid . . . silver drained from . . .

MAY LEE: DON'T tell me my price.

FIRST WIFE: We relieved your family of famine.

MAY LEE: Where're the other conks, ready to spread wet on his command? . . . and what a soft tiny command it is for such a loudmouth coward!

(*First Wife slaps her.*)

FIRST WIFE: You do not speak like that.

MAY LEE: But I do, Mother. Mother who sleeps with father who sleeps with me.

FIRST WIFE: I am not your mother. I am the First Wife of General Sun. YOU obey ME. I never wanted you in the consortium. That twist in your infant kick. Something was not right.

MAY LEE: The way you harangue . . .

FIRST WIFE: Where . . . are your . . . manners?

MAY LEE: Where are my feet?

(*She slams her feet on the table. They sport ice skates.*)

MAY LEE: Look at these: Prune pits for toes. Like a permanent blade in my arch. Where to balance? (*bitter*) There was no emperor when you purchased me for your husband. What about 1911? Dr. Sun Yat fucking Sen? Western puppet, huh! Democracy kicked in and he still had this done.
(*She slams her feet down.*)
How revolutionary to buck trend with a retrograde style, some ancient fashion for new power. Coward!

FIRST WIFE: Your parents agreed.

MAY LEE: My parents sold me. Such empty guts. How did they get so poor? *(toast)* Thanks, Mom. Thanks, Dad.

FIRST WIFE: Your parents couldn't melt fifteen thousand cocoons to spin these silk sleeves. Couldn't feed you tender rich flesh. Couldn't ornament your hair in glittering geometries, or pluck schools of ducks for softness to lay your stubborn head upon. Your belly sated, skin aglow, such a glut of beauty and all you do is wail.

MAY LEE *(piercing falsetto)*: My feet! My feet! My freak fucked feeeeeeeeeeeet . . .

FIRST WIFE: They cried their story . . .

MAY LEE: I am stuck to limp on stumps!

FIRST WIFE: They begged me . . .

MAY LEE: Oh stop it. Like this history is supposed to contain grief, posture some reason for enduring this mess. Pitiful people sell daughters to heroes of the highest degrees . . . Blanket. Basket. Pillow. Casket. This *(the booze!)* is so efficient.

FIRST WIFE: Drunk, babbling . . .

MAY LEE: Then kill me, kill me whole, not lollying in some halfway netherworld, some arrow for the ascending. If I can be bought, then I can be tossed. But don't keep breaking the arches. Kill me COMPLETE.

FIRST WIFE: Here we are but the silhouettes of General Sun's faulty memory . . .

MAY LEE *(piercing falsetto)*: My feet! My feet! My freak fucked feeeeeeeeeeet . . .

FIRST WIFE: He's blocked out the part where you were so inebriated from his fixes that you fell into the well . . . his memories are only of victories . . .

GENERAL SUN'S VOICE: Okay, gentlemen, line ten of those commie creeps up for me . . .

(Lt. Gen. King (Monkey King) and Major Go (Eight Pig) line up ten kneeling commie prisoners.)

FIRST WIFE: Go May Lee. Sober up and make him see you. Appeal to his heart and let us be done with this trapping head of his. We can be freed memories. We can end this hapless looping . . . I beg of you May Lee.

(May Lee wavers, faints, totally loaded. First Wife claps twice. Monkey King and Eight Pig roll May Lee away. First Wife follows. General Sun addresses the ten commie prisoners.)

GENERAL SUN: Well COMrades. Where is your fat red man to save you now? You were given the opportunity to change your minds. To stop believing in China's worst rat. The man who wants to wipe our great cultural slate clean, and fill it with the foreign babble of spineless idiots who glorify the low and dull.

Now, comrades. It seems the only righteous thing to do is to sever your head from your heart, and repurify your silhouettes. Silhouettes because you are not worthy enough to be made of flesh. You're in luck, comrades. Here now with one swift swing, I will relieve you of your red thoughts.

So stick those red necks out and let's Goooooooooooooooooooo . . .

(He makes one great swing, almost gets stuck at the tenth until it snaps.
A crowd cheers.
Ni Lee walks by.
The General pants heavily and falls asleep.
We continually hear his epicentric snore.
Monkey King and Eight Pig shake their heads.
The scene will slowly shift into a park, as we hear birds tweet and Monkey King and Eight Pig cast away from General Sun's victorious mind.)

EIGHT PIG: What happened?

MONKEY KING: He's wasted himself. No energy to think of us.

EIGHT PIG: So what now?

MONKEY KING: Well, we're back under in his *(refers to scroll)* "un-coon-shoos." Never needs us when he wins, only to console him when he loses, just like in his childhood days.

EIGHT PIG: Remember when we were his pals . . . when he was a loner because he came straight from the village to take the exams and all the other kids were from elite families and they were all laughing at his country-bumpkin jacket and the mending on his cloth shoes?

MONKEY KING: He read our hundred episodes of *Journey to the West* over and over again

EIGHT PIG: I think . . .

MONKEY KING: These mortals are perverse.

EIGHT PIG: Well, I think . . .

MONKEY KING: Looping nostalgia to get them through the present.

EIGHT PIG: Actually, I think . . .

MONKEY KING: Do you?

EIGHT PIG: I think . . .

MONKEY KING: Do you now?

EIGHT PIG: I think . . .

MONKEY KING: Get it Pig!

EIGHT PIG: The General fears death.

MONKEY KING: So?

EIGHT PIG: I thought he wasn't supposed to fear anything.
    (*Snooooooore.*)

MONKEY KING: Who told you that?

EIGHT PIG: Great men aren't scared. That's why they're great.

MONKEY KING: No, Pig. Great me ARE scared, yet continue never-
    theless.

EIGHT PIG: Continue nevertheless. That's stupid.

MONKEY KING: You're stupid.

EIGHT PIG: I'm not stupid.

MONKEY KING: You are.

EIGHT PIG: Just 'cuz I don't know every detail of your story?

MONKEY KING: Where was I born?

EIGHT PIG: From some stone egg on Mount Flower and Fruit.

MONKEY KING: What am I famous for?

EIGHT PIG: Why do we have to talk about you all the time?

MONKEY KING: What am I famous for, Eight Pig?

EIGHT PIG (*'tude*): Popping some immortal pills.

MONKEY KING: AND mastering the magical arts with the Taoist
    Immortal AND shape-shifting AND flying AND ridding the
    monkey kingdom of the monster AND my staff—

EIGHT PIG: You pass as one of them now . . . talking "oon coon shust"
    whatever.

MONKEY KING: Girth and size look to praise you . . . look at the big-
    mega-super-large-grand-gigantic-humongous-gargantuan-in-
    flated mentality of this western world . . .

EIGHT PIG: I'm hungry.

MONKEY KING: It will all POP!

EIGHT PIG: What's that?
    (*He spots a bag of pork rinds, runs to it.*)

MONKEY KING: We're here to awaken him, not dine.

EIGHT PIG: Live so long you end up eating yourself. Look! Look what they've done to our skins.

MONKEY KING (*grabs*): Abstain!

EIGHT PIG (*grabs back*): It's mine!

MONKEY KING (*grabs again*): What are your eight abstinences?

EIGHT PIG: Hey, you're mushing them. (*grabs back again*) That's where we came from. We're here now and . . . (*looks all around*) No abstinence in sight!

(*Eight Pig lustily crunches.*)

MONKEY KING: It is not food. It is amusement.

EIGHT PIG: Who could resist this crunch.

MONKEY KING: Perverse.

EIGHT PIG: My mouth is so loud.

MONKEY KING: One is to live out life reminded that one exists from the sound of a bite.

(*Invading light. NI LEE stands, as if addressing a press conference. From Hong Kong, she speaks English with a British accent.*)

NI LEE: Ice skating is the perfect combination of muscularity and grace.

MONKEY KING: Who is that?

NI LEE: You must be strong as a work horse, yet billow like a silk banner.

EIGHT PIG: Is it the Goddess of Mercy, bringing light?

NI LEE: You must duel as a prince, yet delight as a princess.

(*Big smile as cameras flash. Monkey King and Eight Pig twitch at flashes.*)

MONKEY KING: Let us move and hide.

EIGHT PIG: We are but thoughts flying around.

MONKEY KING: Just in case.

EIGHT PIG: The mortals cannot see us.

(*Invading light increases.*)

MONKEY KING: We are not as invisible as we think.

(*Monkey King and Eight Pig hide as Ni Lee takes a seat. Yeh Yeh's snores can still be heard, faintly.*)

NI LEE: Why do these thoughts come back now?
(*Monkey King and Eight Pig peer out.*)
Go away thoughts. Go away!

(*They hide. She composes herself, then sings a Chinese tune.*)

NI LEE: "Che lu tao, hsiang i tse ts'uan tsai yüeh yüeh li yao a yao

(*Monkey King and Eight Pig dance.*)

NI LEE: Gu niang yah, ni yeh tsai wo de shin huai li p'iao ah p'iao"
(*Ni Lee armors.*)
Don't try it . . . I have nothing in my purse.
MONKEY KING: Ah . . . we . . .
EIGHT PIG: She knows us!
MONKEY KING: SHHHH. (*to Ni Lee*) We are the . . . imperial . . .
EIGHT PIG: Gardeners . . .
MONKEY KING: Yes, yes . . . and you . . . you are here . . . to . . .
NI LEE: My car broke down. I'm just resting . . . headed *home.*
EIGHT PIG (*imitating her Hong Kong British accent*): *Home?*
MONKEY KING: Home, ah, yes.
NI LEE: Don't think I can't understand your peasant dialect. (*beat*)
Are you both from . . . Taiwan?
EIGHT PIG: Mount Flower and . . . (*monkey-nudge*)
MONKEY KING: Yes. And you?
NI LEE: I came here to study.
MONKEY KING: Ah, a scholar. A scholar of . . .
NI LEE: Mathematics
EIGHT PIG: Numbers. You are an accountant.
NI LEE: Yes. For the par-victorious General Sun. You've heard of him?
MONKEY KING: Why . . . YES!
EIGHT PIG: We're his "unt scon stoos."
NI LEE: His . . . ?
MONKEY KING: You are a worker of the General?
NI LEE: He's my father-in-law.
EIGHT PIG: Family of General Sun. Privilege.

(*They kowtow incessantly.*)

NI LEE: Oh stop it. It's America now. It doesn't matter.
MONKEY KING: Of course it matters of course . . . to us Chinese. And
you bear the General's heirs?

NI LEE (*beat*): I bear them.

EIGHT PIG: Warrior sons and (*licks chops*) delectable daughters.
  (*Monkey King severely elbows Eight Pig.*)

NI LEE: I have no daughter. (*pause*) Only a son.

MONKEY KING: A son is good. Better to carry the name.

EIGHT PIG: More useful.

NI LEE: Not here. Daughters do just as much. Some can make millions. Others can become champions. Here, anything is possible with hard work.

(*Ni Lee restrains tears, gets up to leave.*)

MONKEY KING: Kind daughter-in-law of General Sun . . . we don't
  mean to upset you.

NI LEE: Why did you say . . . daughter?

MONKEY KING: You said you had none.

NI LEE: I don't. (*suspicious*) How did you presume I did?

EIGHT PIG: I haven't taken lunch yet.

NI LEE (*circles them*): Are you some kind of communist spy? Seeking
  to take General Sun? To punish him for his past?

MONKEY KING: Why no . . . not us.

NI LEE: You know her? You know where she is?

MONKEY KING: No "she." There is no "she."

NI LEE: Surely you've heard of her. Twila Sun. World-famous ice
  skater?

EIGHT PIG: Who is she?

NI LEE: Our Asian American hope.

MONKEY KING AND EIGHT PIG (*confounded*): Asian American hope?

NI LEE: The whole world knows her. You must have heard of her . . .
  especially in Taiwan.

EIGHT PIG: Ah . . .

NI LEE: She's been missing for five years.

MONKEY KING: Well . . .

NI LEE: Whatever you are holding from me, gentlemen, whatever it
  is . . . if by chance you know of her . . . tell her . . . she is . . . a
  big success.

MONKEY KING AND EIGHT PIG: A big success?

NI LEE: Yes, tell her that she single-handedly killed . . . she broke . . .
  she lost . . . she lost the face of her mother . . . and only a shell
  . . . only a half shell of her mother is left.

(*Ni Lee continues her long march home.*)

Alice Tuan

EIGHT PIG: I am not understanding.

MONKEY KING: We must be careful.

EIGHT PIG: How can she know us?

MONKEY KING: Perhaps the mortals share thoughts. Not very original.

(A loud hip-hop bass beat startles Eight Pig and Monkey King. General Sun enters with his coat of metals and some sweatpants. The bass beat becomes General Sun's pounding on an upstanding coffin-like pantry.
We hear young Ho Ping's voice.)

GENERAL SUN: Ho Ping!

HO PING: Yes, sir.

GENERAL SUN: My youngest son.

HO PING: Yes, sir.

GENERAL SUN: How old are you today, Ho Ping?

HO PING: Eight, sir.

GENERAL SUN: You gonna grow up to be a brave general like your daddy, Ho Ping?

HO PING: Please, sir.

GENERAL SUN: Are you afraid to die?

HO PING: I cannot see in here, sir.

GENERAL SUN: You will get used to it. This is practice . . . to toughen you, my son. Are you afraid to die, Ho Ping?

HO PING: Please, Father.

GENERAL SUN: Answer me. Are you afraid to die?

HO PING: Can I come out, sir?

GENERAL SUN: Demons are watching you from walls, sharpening their teeth to devour you. Fear makes tender flesh and the longer you are shivering with that hole in your gut, the faster they will pluck you up and feast. Know this darkness. Know it.

(Kalump.
The booming hip-hop bass resumes.
General Sun gracefully walks to the table, in preparation for his egg sandwich. On his way over, he very unselfconsciously cuts a grand, epicentric fart. We have now completely shifted back to the Sun house in the present day.

SONNY, seventeen, enters. His hair is his mine and outrageously styled. He wears a walkman and holds a fistful of plastic packages—Radio Shack, Rite Aid, Paul Mitchell Salons, Sharper Image.)

SONNY:

    I'm proud to be American in every way
    Take a look at my hair I got lots to say
    Don't call me no sushi no chicken chow mein
    Taco Bell Big Macs take away the pain
    You like my style and my slick hard muscle
    Take a ride in my coupe feel its Lamborghini hustle
    Confucius that wimp talking mother Buddha fat
    Sturdy purdy quick chicks is what I'm smilin' at
    Flick-a my-a Bic-a and I'll burn you with ease
    I'm red white and blue, I only look Chinese

    (to Yeh Yeh) Hey dude. What's cookin'?
YEH YEH: Egg sandwich.
SONNY: Hah?
YEH YEH *(calls out)*: Egg sandwich!

    (Sonny turns off the beat, unplugs his ears.)

SONNY: Got the uniform on, huh?
    (Sonny rolls out an ancient hanger-in-the-antennae TV.)
    We gonna play soldier for your b-day, old man?
YEH YEH: Egg sandwich!

    (Twila appears with the sandwich.)

TWILA: All right, all right already.

    (Yeh Yeh loudly starts to devour the egg sandwich.)

SONNY: Whoa. Scary. Twila. Dude. Blond. Blue eyes. Wrong skin.
TWILA: Look at you, Sonny.
SONNY: Ladies and gentlemen!
TWILA: Look at you!
SONNY: Twila Sun—figure-skating LOSER of the world.
TWILA: Five years and you look like some action hero wannabe.
SONNY: Been workin' out. Benchin' two-fifty. What are you, out of
    some concentration camp? And eyes like tidy bowl.
TWILA: Someone piss in yours?
SONNY: There are rinks with your face grounded in like footprints
    at Grauman's Chinese. Couldn't hack the pressure? Couldn't
    get the gold? Now what's in your eyes? Pop 'em out Twila, pop
    'em out.

Alice Tuan

(He wrestles her, pokes his fingers in her eyes.)
Pop 'em out, whitey, pop 'em out.
(She breaks free.)

TWILA: Fuck you, Sonny. Steroid junky. Shrink your balls and turn your eyes yellow. What have you done lately?

SONNY: First-string Varsity left tackle.

TWILA: Countering the right testicle.

SONNY: You should know you've sucked so many.

YEH YEH: SON-NAY! Where . . . did . . . yo . . . come from?

SONNY: MALL! STORES! SHOPPING!

(Sonny pounds his fist into his hand.)

SONNY: You're dead to Mom you know . . . fossilized that moment you tore off from the rink. How . . . how . . . how could you rip her heart out like that?

TWILA: I'm not a machine! Had to stop the madness.

SONNY: Couldn't show her face in public. Would barely come out of her room. She just started going back to Chinese school, and you know how she was the queen of Chinese school, every Saturday morning . . . serving punch and cookies, ringing that little bell.

TWILA: So . . . so she's . . . she's okay now?

SONNY: I know about you and the hockey team.

TWILA: You don't know jack shit, Sonny

SONNY: Turning your hat tricks.

TWILA: They hid me.

SONNY: That's what crushed her.

TWILA: That I became invisible?

SONNY: I know about you, sister. You did the whole team. Night before your Olympic trials.

TWILA: I did not do the whole team.

SONNY: Then you did it for the whole team, right?

TWILA: You believe that shit in the press over your own blood?

SONNY: Look at me. *(kisses his bicep)* I'm a god. I'm the true champion in this household. There are colleges looking at me, looking to recruit me. I'm gonna make back the big bucks so Mom and Dad can at least get a new car.

TWILA: Whatever.

SONNY: They went into debt for you.

TWILA: Dreams cost.

SONNY: They're still paying off the red. Look at our bogus wallpaper, dingy dinette. We can't even get a new TV . . .

TWILA: TV is evil.

SONNY: Nothing gets replaced unless it falls off its last scotch-taped leg. Mom and Dad still wear clothes from 1981. (*beat*) All I know is it's not gonna be as simple as smoothing it over with a sorry. I don't know what's gonna get them through the sight of you.

TWILA: Sonny, I need you on my side . . . no, I need you to listen . . .

SONNY: Five years, Twila . . . not even a damned phone call! I had to bring them back from catatonia.

TWILA: Confucius said—

SONNY: Oh don't go Chinese on me.

TWILA: When parents are alive . . .

SONNY: That shit don't apply here.

TWILA: . . . a son, a SON should not go far abroad . . .

SONNY: Whatever.

TWILA: Or if he does, he should let them know where he goes.

SONNY: So?

TWILA: Doesn't say shit about daughters.

SONNY: Ah so. Confusion.

YEH YEH: WHERE'S BA-BA?

SONNY (*containing himself*): DAD? SHOPPING! God I'm sick of this namby-pamby three-year-old routine. Who cares where anyone is?

YEH YEH: WHERE'S MA-MA?

SONNY: Hairdresser's.

YEH YEH: HAH?

SONNY: HAIRDRESSER'S! God, where's the scotch tape?

YEH YEH: AH? WHERE DID SHE GO?

SONNY (*pointing to his head*): HAIRDRESSER'S HAIRDRESSER'S HAIRDRESSER'S.

YEH YEH: Your hair is shit!

SONNY: Bagging on my hair, old man?

(*He pulls out a piece of scotch tape.*)

YEH YEH: What did you say? Don't talk so fast.

(*Sonny tapes Yeh Yeh's mouth shut.*)

SONNY: There. Now ask.

(*Sonny switches on the TV, bang-bang-banging on it for reception.*)

TWILA: You fucking jerk, Sonny.

SONNY: What?

TWILA: This is your Grandfather! The man who commanded five thousand troops and killed communists. The man whose blood and seed you come from.

SONNY: I'm sorry. Is it Asian American history month again?

(Sonny turns his walkman on full blast. Yeh Yeh removes tape from his mouth, wadding it up into a small ball and throwing it at Sonny. Twila is numb.)

YEH YEH: Egg sandwich, good, Twila! Number one, Twila!

(BANG BANG BANG BANG BANG. Sonny tries to get reception.)

SONNY: Shitty piece of crap.

(BANG BANG BANG.)

TWILA: How can you even see through that debris?

SONNY: Takes an abstract mind.

TWILA: Knock knock on the plexiglass into Sonny's world.

SONNY *(chanting)*: Go, Twila, Go. Go, Twila, Go. Go, Twila, Go.

TWILA: What's in the bag?

SONNY: Go, Twila, Go. Go, Twila, Go

(She grabs it.)

SONNY: Unleash that.

TWILA: What is it?

(She looks in the bag.)

SONNY: Yeh Yeh's birthday present. Give it.

TWILA: You can't give this to Yeh Yeh.

SONNY: What am I violating now?

YEH YEH: WHAT TIME IS IT?

SONNY: See, it's perfect.

YEH YEH: Hah? WHAT TIME?

TWILA: It's one.

YEH YEH: Fucking twat, it's always one o'clock.

TWILA: Giving a clock in Chinese sounds the same as sending one to death.

SONNY: Whatever, Twila . . . I'm just being practical 'cuz the old man is fucking driving me insane okay? You're here after a long-ass time being absent . . . you haven't had to be entertaining the old man . . . answer all his inane questions. It gets kinda hard when the person you're trying to respect is fucking regressing back to a three-year-old, you know what I'm saying? Fucking "Hah? Hah? Hah? Hah?"

YEH YEH: Hah?

SONNY: So don't get all precious and knowing on me now 'cuz you just don't realize how hard it's been.

TWILA: Well it's been hard on me too, okay?

SONNY: I understand. I understand the pressure that was on you. I understand how Mom is a slave driver. I understand how dad is up to his ears in taking care of the old man but he can't stand to think of him in an old home with the tubes up his nose . . . I understand it all and I'd just appreciate it if you'd stop giving this unsolicited lame-ass Asian American advice. Just 'cuz I look it doesn't mean I have to inherit the pain and the injustice and the uh-uh-uh-uh stuttering and the victimness and oh how whitey has been unjust. I'm not into it. I like purity, looking at one culture at a time, okay? I know it's kinda shallow for you arty types, for you bi-people, for you hyphenates who want to maximize your beinghood, whatever. But dude this is my choice and in this country they still allow shit like that okay? Do you mind? Now please, move out of my line of vision. Please.

TWILA: I thought I could get into their head . . . you know the Chinese thing . . . but then, it's really split me apart, to think the Chinese believe that girls . . . that they are useless.

SONNY: They ain't the only ones.

TWILA: Sonny!

SONNY: What, it's true. That's why Ma was driving you so hard, away from that. You're blocking.

TWILA: Sonny, I need you to . . . I need you to help me back through. I'm . . . I'm dying . . . inside I'm . . . I'm . . . killing myself.

SONNY: Yeah, I feel your pain. But it's gonna take some time, Twila

(He signals her to move out of the way.)

TWILA: Yeah. Okay.

(She exits, holding her head as if a migraine has struck. Sonny watches TV. Yeh Yeh watches the pantry.)

YEH YEH *(whispering)*: Ho Ping, ah? This is death. Know it. Demons are watching you from walls, sharpening their teeth to devour you.

SONNY: Psssssst.

(Yeh Yeh sits still.)

YEH YEH *(still whispering)*: Ho Ping . . . are you afraid to die. Are you
Ho Ping? Afraid to die? . . . Fear makes tender flesh . . . longer
you are still and shivering with that hole in your gut, the faster
they will pluck you up and feast. Are you afraid to die?

SONNY: Psssst. Yeh Yeh.

(Yeh Yeh looks around.)

SONNY: Psssst.

YEH YEH: Hah?

SONNY: What's going inside of that hundred-year-old head? Who you
talking to in the pantry there, man?

(Sonny reaches into one of his bags and pulls out a Playboy *mag.)*

YEH YEH: Hah?

SONNY: C'mere, man.

YEH YEH: What's happened?

SONNY: Someone wants you to see them.

YEH YEH: You see Monkey?

SONNY: Dude, Yeh Yeh, spank some.

YEH YEH: Pig?

SONNY: You wanna torque some pork, man? This is totally, totally
universal, huh, old man? . . . Check out my latest wench.

(Yeh Yeh looks and looks and looks.)

YEH YEH: A white one.

SONNY: You want her, Yeh Yeh? You want her?

*(Sonny presses the centerfold against Yeh Yeh's face, then slowly
has the magazine go down on Yeh Yeh. Yeh Yeh laughs, claps.)*

SONNY: You like that, hohn, Yeh Yeh. How do you live life without
getting' any?

*(May Lee slowly moves out of the pantry, skates hanging around
her neck. She slyly approaches the General. Sonny is passionately*

*watching the Kings game on TV. The General is elated when May
Lee puts the blade of one of her skates up to his throat.)*

MAY LEE *(high like a willow)*: You ready?

GENERAL SUN *(sniffs)*: You stink of opium.

MAY LEE: I'mo mince you . . . and fry you up with some gar-lic. How's
that sound?

(The General throws May Lee to the ground.)

GENERAL SUN: How is one so lame to kill me?

MAY LEE: Fix me one more time please? Please? Please?

GENERAL SUN: This used up death-muse—

MAY LEE: Fix me.

GENERAL SUN: Let us get it over with. I'm ready.

MAY LEE: What? No Speech?

GENERAL SUN: One swift slice . . . right here . . . across this vein.

MAY LEE: Fix me first.

GENERAL SUN: Death cannot be this pathetic.

MAY LEE: Just fix me.

GENERAL SUN: They were soft and succulent. Your feet. Just the
length of my finger.

MAY LEE: Fix.

GENERAL SUN: I wanted to bite them off when I first saw you. One
day old. I wanted to preserve those tiny feet.

MAY LEE: We . . . had . . . the republic . . . a president. Queues cut.
Eunuchs restored. But I couldn't keep my . . .

SONNY: Yeah Kings! Kings Rule!

(May Lee sees the blue glow of the TV.)

MAY LEE: Blue . . . ray . . . *o* . . . *o* . . . *o* . . . *pyum?*

(She clicks into crave, crawls towards the TV with urgency.)

GENERAL SUN: It was more out of curiosity than taste. To have this
status symbol, upheld for hundreds of years.

(May Lee is in front of the TV. Bad reception. Sonny gets up.)

GENERAL SUN: But then your feet corroded into deformity that quite
frankly made me convulse. Not to mention the stench. Pus.
Decay. Uh . . .

(May Lee takes a hit off the TV. Sonny BANG BANG BANGS.)

SONNY: Gonna make me miss it.
MAY LEE: The cure . . . be-fore . . . disease . . . blue . . . rays . . .
I . . . crave
(She takes another hit. Sonny BANGS.)
Re-lief . . . sud-den . . . lids . . . like setting suns . . . I scream . . .
no . . . more

(She collapses. Sonny sits back down.)

SONNY: Go Kings!
GENERAL SUN: Go!
SONNY: Go KINGS!
GENERAL SUN: Go to your chambers. I have a new feather canopy
bed for you.
SONNY: Yeah!

(We hear the TV Commentator on the night of Twila's falling.)

TV ANNOUNCER: I don't know. I don't know . . . uh
I don't know what to say
I don't know. I don't know . . . uh
I don't know what to say
I don't know. I don't know . . . uh
I don't know what to say
I don't know . . .

(We hear the rustle of plastic bags.
Lights shift back to the Sun house in the present day.
Ho Ping, fifty-four, enters with plastic bags of groceries. He walks
a circle around General Sun. He stops in front of Sonny, dis-
gusted by his inaction.)

SONNY: Hi Pops.
HO PING: Whose junks is all this?
SONNY *(looking over his shoulder)*: It's not junk. It's Yeh Yeh's birth-
day present.
HO PING: Move it. Move all your junks.
SONNY: Wait, Kings are tied and commercial's almost here.
HO PING: MOVE! NOW!

(*Sonny slags over to his things, moves in slow motion. With impatience, Ho Ping slides Sonny's stuff off and puts his groceries on the table.*)

SONNY: Careful, Dad. There's breakable stuff in here.

HO PING (*knocking on Sonny's head*): And breakable stuffs in your head, too!

SONNY: Careful with the hair.

YEH YEH: Where did you come from?

HO PING: None of your business.

SONNY: Chill out, dude. You're bringing me down.

HO PING: Chill suh muh chill. I'm not no dude.

YEH YEH (*to Sonny*): Where did he come from?

HO PING (*to Sonny*): You didn't feed the dog last night.

SONNY: Well, I forgot, okay, old man? Just slipped.

HO PING: I working all day, come home, have to look at such mess and slob. Nothing moving.

SONNY: Don't worry, Dad. Cold War's over. Give you engineers your walking papers in no time.

HO PING: You tink some joke about my job? I be lay off, you no more fun. YOU work.

SONNY: Don't worry. Mom'll bring home the bacon.

HO PING: You tink you some kind emperor! I do everything and you can't remember small ting like feeding da dog!

TWILA: Ah, hi Dad. How's it goin'?

(*Long pause as Ho Ping adjusts his eyes on Twila.*)

HO PING: And what, you tink you da Empress Dowager? Go get da groceries.

TWILA: Nice to see you, Dad.

SONNY: Shit, I missed the goal. You made me miss the goal. Kings, fuck, Kings.

YEH YEH (*still trying*): Where did you come from? (*to Twila*) Where did he come from?

HO PING: Who are you? CIA spy? Don't ask so many questions.

TWILA: From YOU, Yeh Yeh. He came from you.

YEH YEH: Me? What about me?

HO PING (*to Sonny*): All you keep is ice head.

SONNY: I was pumping with Steve. We're up to two-fifty on the press.

HO PING: What about da poor family dog?

TWILA: All of us. All of us dogs.

(Twila exits to get groceries.)

SONNY: God, since when did the dog become such a force in the family?

HO PING: God, god, god. Anytime you not happy it's god, god, god. Get out of here! I don't want to seeing your slob.

(Sonny gets up, brawny.)

SONNY: Don't cross me, old man.

HO PING: Hey you watching da TV?

SONNY: You just told me to leave.

HO PING: I'm talking about if you don't watch, turn off it.

SONNY: Turn OFF it? You're fucking with me old man. Turn off it, shit. Speak right, wouldya? Speak right. Just remember, I'm benching two-five-o.

(Sonny exits.)

HO PING: Put you in street! Den you show me two-five-zero.

(Monkey King appears, well-tanned. Eight Pig is constantly crunching pork rinds—the noise of whose head?)

YEH YEH: Monkey King!

MONKEY KING: I have just returned from the furnace of the Imperial Palace where the Emperor ordered me burned. But I escaped with a mere tan. Don't I look fabulous?

YEH YEH: Never mind. My death-muse is defective.

MONKEY KING: Now why is that?

YEH YEH: Please, Monkey King, as your equal. Let me join you.

MONKEY KING: Impossible! I am to my hideaway on Mount Flower and Fruit where jasmine elixes and persimmon transfixes

YEH YEH: Take me from this bland suburb, where only bad memories haunt.

MONKEY KING: Bland? All these metal boxes, shiny and reflective.

(Monkey King presses a button on the microwave—beep—leaps away in pain.)

EIGHT PIG: O?

(Eight Pig keeps pressing buttons, to Monkey King's excruciating pain.)

MONKEY KING: Stop it, Pig!

EIGHT PIG: Just like in our story . . .

MONKEY KING: STOP!

EIGHT PIG: The Monk Master Tang always controlled the wild monkey with a cap that clamped down on his head . . . here, we can just push a button!

MONKEY KING: AHCH!

EIGHT PIG: Ha ha! Not so powerful after all, huh, Monkey King?

YEH YEH: Halt! I say HALT!

(Eight Pig does. Monkey King humbles Eight Pig.)

YEH YEH: It is fire by buttons. Needs magic to start. To my dull senses, it is broken. Please, take me away.

(Twila enters. Yeh Yeh sips tea loudly. Ho Ping puts groceries away.)

MONKEY KING: Who is she? So young with large feet . . . and hair of harvested wheat.

YEH YEH: My granddaughter.

MONKEY KING: YOUR progeny? You have twisted the spirits, dueled with nature and now the blight is apparent.

HO PING: I tought you never wanta see us again.

TWILA: Not many people live to be a hundred.

HO PING: Huh. You just come to see Yeh Yeh, no one else. Dere. Look. Satisfied? Now go.

TWILA: That's unfair, Dad. And untrue.

HO PING: Fair? You want fair? Fair is weather. Weather is fair. Dere. Take it. True? What is true?

YEH YEH *(to Eight Pig)*: What time is it?

TWILA: I missed you, Dad.

(Eight Pig gives Yeh Yeh the peace sign.)

HO PING: That is not true.

TWILA: It is. I did. I missed you.

HO PING: That is just word. Say it, it disappear. If you miss me, your action would tell me. You would write me a letter. You would call, so I don't worry. You would come back home work, to pay off . . .

TWILA: I couldn't Dad, I was lost I didn't know what to do to stop, to end it all . . . I'm not . . .

TWILA: . . . some excelling machine to brag to others about.	HO PING: . . . You come from good background not some BAG LADY, whatever you are.

TWILA: All of you are the ones with the bags.

HO PING: What, are you confused? You think you are man?

TWILA: Oh drag is equal opportunity.

HO PING: You look like sick. Maybe you do, the way you sleeping around.

TWILA: Gosh, Dad, I don't sleep around that much.

HO PING: As far as I'm concerned, you are a virgin!

TWILA: Hard to stay a virgin when you're showing it to the public. They looked at my crotch every time I kicked.

HO PING: You fall so many times! We watch on TV. It was first time that guy on TV didn't knowing what to say.

TWILA: Good! Silence is better than those babbling idiot heads.

HO PING: They cut away. Didn't want to showing such the American failure. People laughing at us. I can hearing it from the TV.

TWILA: I'm not the one to depend on for your victories.

HO PING: You broke us, Twila . . . Money. Spirit. Everything. You don't know.

TWILA: But I do know. That's why I'm here. I need to tell Mom . . . .

HO PING: There's nothing she wanting to hearing from you, believe me.

TWILA: Just to say sorry. I'm sorry Dad.

HO PING: Please, Twila. You didn't have to clean up after the quake . . . big and messy and I am too tired to live it again.

TWILA: Then maybe I was wrong. I was under the impression that family was blood, which means . . . which means whatever you do . . . or did . . . that . . . that family could see . . . smell past the stink . . . guide you through life no matter the mistakes. But . . . but this, this club . . . mindlessly following and following . . . SHIT! It's . . . family is a pack of lemmings that keep telling themselves "there is no cliff, there is no cliff," . . . it's a goddamned cult! And sometimes you gotta stop the brainwashing, make them open their eyes and look at the world as is, Dad, as is. Tradition is a warp of reality.

(*Monkey King whispers strategy in Yeh Yeh's ear. BEEP! Monkey King in pain. Yeh Yeh retrieves his tea, leaves the door open.*

Eight Pig watches Twila and Ho Ping's dialogue much like ping-pong.)

HO PING: The world is cruel, Twila.

TWILA: You don't gotta tell me that.

HO PING: And tradition, Twila, tradition is a pillow . . . a place to sleep with the cruelties more comfortably.

TWILA: Why didn't you just tell me that before? Huh, Dad? Just a clue like that . . .

HO PING: I am thinking of it now because I am too tired of it all.

TWILA: I'm at the end, Dad. This is my last try. I'm unable . . . to *love* without getting over it . . . that's why . . . that's why.

HO PING: Go back to where you coming from. Everything just starting to get better . . . maybe next year come you, please Twila . . . go away for your Dad because she just start now to have shine in her eyes.

YEH YEH: What time is it?

TWILA: Time to go, Yeh Yeh. What do you need, Yeh Yeh, what?

YEH YEH (*sighs*): I need nothing.

(Twila moves to leave, Yeh Yeh won't let her go. Monkey King counts down five-four-three-two and points at the microwave with open door.)

HO PING: How long dis door opened?

TWILA: Sonny used it last.

HO PING: SONNY!! SONNY!! COME HERE NOW!

YEH YEH: Who's there? Who's there?

(Sonny enters.)

SONNY: GAH what's wrong? All I hear is massacre down here.

HO PING: I have to scream and shout because nobody listening. You see da light on?

SONNY: Yeah.

HO PING: What does dat mean?

SONNY: Fucking quiz show hour. It means it's *open*. Did I get it right? Okay, okay I'll shut the door. Is that what you called me for? (*Sonny kicks the door shut. Eight Pig reacts. Ho Ping charges.*) Don't do it old man. I'm bigger. Can pop your head off with a twist.

HO PING: Watch so much TV. You tink it dat easy? Get out of here.

(*Eight Pig and Monkey King nod and encourage. Yeh Yeh takes General persona.*)

GENERAL SUN (*pointing at microwave*): Is it fixed?
SONNY: Dude, technically Yeh Yeh used it last.
HO PING: I am not no dude!
GENERAL SUN: Someone answer me! Is it fixed?
SONNY: We live in a democracy, and I have been falsely accused!

(*Sonny exits.*)

GENERAL SUN: IS IT FIXED?
TWILA: It's not broken.
GENERAL SUN: Then why didn't it work this morning?
HO PING: You do not touch dis oven. Understand?
TWILA: Not like he's playing with fire.
HO PING: Understand? I know you hear dis.
GENERAL SUN: What's all the screaming. Your banal tortures.
HO PING: You . . . DO . . . NOT . . . TOUCH . . . DIS!
GENERAL SUN: I touch what I like. Can you fix it?
HO PING: I do not want you to touch it, so don't touch it!
GENERAL SUN: I've touched it all and now you want me to stop. Is it broken?
HO PING: Just eat and sleep and go your own way!
GENERAL SUN: Is it broken?
TWILA: If it goes one hundred minutes, it'll kapow, kaboomy!
GENERAL SUN: That's my touch. Is it broken?
HO PING: YES! It's broken it's broken it's broken.
TWILA: True. What is true?
GENERAL SUN: Will you fix it, Ho Ping?

(*Ho Ping explodes. He gets his shiny red tool box and marches around with it.*)

HO PING: I WILL FIX IT! I WILL FIX IT! I WILL FIX IT . . . (*repeat like chant*)

(*Twila looks for her bag. Ho Ping culminates his tantrum by presenting his shiny red tool box.*)

HO PING: I will fix it.

(Pause.)

GENERAL SUN: When?

(Ho Ping slams the tool box in front of the microwave. Tools fly.)

HO PING: Now. I'll fix it now. Just don't ask anymore. Just don't ask.

GENERAL SUN: So temperamental, as a woman, and like her, you comply in the end.

MONKEY KING: Brilliant, General, Brilliant!

EIGHT PIG: You are the winner!

(Tableau of General and his victory. Monkey King and Eight Pig cheer.
Ni Lee enters as Twila exits.
Ni Lee tries to escape.
Twila blocks her path.)

TWILA: Talk to me, Mom. I'm not a ghost. I'm not a demon. I'm twenty-four years old now, Mom. *(struggle)* Even if I was world champion, my career *(struggle)* would be over by now. I wasn't cut . . . for ice . . . Mom, I'm here. I'm alive. I hate the world, too. I'm like you.

NI LEE: Don't touch me.

TWILA: I'm like you, Mom.

NI LEE: NO! You're not. You're not like me! Look at you. You disgust me.

TWILA: I'm like you inside. Inside I'm like . . .

NI LEE: Always, always against me. You're a loser. You haven't the flesh or mind for winning. You gave up . . . YOU GAVE UP! I should have known . . . I saw demons in the park . . . I should have known . . .

TWILA: Mom . . . Mother . . . Look at me . . .
(Ni Lee does not look at Twila.)
After all this . . . my losing and . . . and my hair? I'm much more. I'm a person. Please see . . . I'm your flesh and blood.

NI LEE: You are certainly not like me. YOU'RE NOTHING LIKE ME!

(Ni Lee storms off. Twila is numb.)

TWILA: Hi Mom. Hi Mom.

(Light fades.)

Act Two

The General is preparing to play mahjong. His cane is his sword.

GENERAL SUN: Is my enemy better than me? Huh? Better than me if he wins? Or just lucky, May Lee. Just lucky?

Come down and play, May Lee. Come down and play with me on my birthday . . . a nice civil battle of mahjong.

Try your hand, May Lee. A lucky hand, that's all it is. It takes no skill, no will, just luck in the end. Build the walls, stack them with the right sticks, the right winds the right words and WIN!

Yes, you, May Lee, you like the left. Because you could keep your feet and work like an equal. You really want to work? After a life of lounging and leisure? You think King Left was better? That Mao Tse-tung was better? Huh?

The bastard! All that talk of peasant and the blank slate. Bullshit! The beauty of the blank mind. Double bullshit! What does our good revolutionary friend do while the peasant is mindlessly chanting as if Mao is Buddha himself? Goes to Hangchou and Su-chou to capture the prettiest of concubines, oh excuse me, let's call them COMRADES. He himself fetishizes flesh and commands the rest to be neuter, to be blank.
(He picks up a few mahjong tiles.)

Why not just take each mahjong tile and erase its face . . . blank. How could we play?

All these cultures, Chinese culture, American culture, Chinese American, whatever: it's all just the faces of game pieces. Erase that face and there will be no game anymore. We'd use the tiles as debris, to throw at each other . . . yes, now that is civilized . . . back to rocks and beasts and weeds, oh my. I've spent *my whole life* to ensure the rituals of five thousand years of culture would continue for another fifty thousand years to leave with just rocks and beasts and weeds around!

(He makes a two-handed beheading gesture.)

Thwack! I kill your ideas, Mao. Thwack your Great Leap! Thawack your peasant collectives! Thwack your Hundred Flowers! Thwack your lies and bloated numbers. Thwack thwack thwack.

Then when all goes wrong, he turns, he appeals to the chaos of youth . . . turns his sons and daughters loose to destroy all that is old. To humiliate the old and glorify the new! How dare Mao . . . erase all of our precious culture. Keep the masses stupid while he fucks to his glory. Anything that came before . . . I CAME BEFORE! . . . gone. A blank slate. All my victories invisible, MY glories . . . we are of the same stock, yet I am on the losing side. I will not go down in the history books as the face-saver of my culture

(May Lee, balancing on ice skate, sings the last line of "Happy Birthday" to Generalissimo in piercing falsetto.

Ho Ping and Ni Lee are at the kitchen table. Ho Ping is taking apart two cabbage heads, which he will eventually mince into a bowl. They both speak in fluent American accents, as they communicate in their native language.
Cabbage SPLIT!)

HO PING: Never! Never will I comply.

NI LEE: Bring me some tea, Ho Ping

HO PING: Where? Where is it now?

NI LEE: I'm burned like this and all you care about is the car? I had to walk from DeSoto and Victory because . . . because . . .

HO PING: Was there smoke coming out?

NI LEE: I had to walk in this heat!

HO PING: It was the water.

NI LEE: A mechanical engineer! Ph.D.! The highest degree. You're supposed to know!

HO PING: Carburetor? . . . or . . .

NI LEE: All of a sudden, it just went clunk clunk clunk . . .

HO PING: The oil!

NI LEE: I could only wobble to the side.

HO PING: Was the engine hot?

NI LEE: All I know is red lights flashed.

HO PING: Which side? Which side red lights?

NI LEE: I don't know! (*beat*) The left side!

(*The General enters in full military drag, regal and confident.*)

GENERAL SUN: Come. Play mahjong.

HO PING: Can't you see I'm busy cooking?

GENERAL SUN: Where are King and Go?

HO PING: They come when they come.

GENERAL SUN: Ni Lee, come.

　　(*Ni Lee looks at Ho Ping.*)

HO PING: Go. Go play with yourself.

GENERAL SUN: May Lee! Come play!

(*He turns to exit.*)

HO PING: Crazy old man, still thinking about May Lee.

NI LEE: And now Twila!

HO PING: She just comes for Yeh Yeh's birthday dinner. Like the past. Never hear from her, then just shows up. No warning. Nothing.

NI LEE: I open the door. She is there. Ugly, UGLY as a demon . . . five years, FIVE YEARS and . . . unexpected, like some plague, she comes to our house . . . why is . . . WHY?

HO PING: She is still . . . our daughter.

GENERAL SUN'S VOICE: Come down, May Lee, come down and play.

NI LEE: I can never forgive her, Ho Ping. Losing my face in front of so many. Just like that. All, everybody, Canada, America, *CHINA*, the world watching and she can keep falling with that demon smile, like . . . like she loves to fall. And then just run, run away for so many years. Where? We think her dead. A black falling weight on my heart, and she dares come back like nothing happened, like a ghost and then say she's like me?

HO PING: The car . . . I must fix . . . where?

NI LEE: She could have made a mark on this world. The daughter could have been champion, world champion and I was helping her get there. She doesn't have the commitment on her own. She is lazy. Like you.

HO PING (*he shakes his knife at her*): She could have fought the world fine.

NI LEE: Don't shake your knife at me!

HO PING: Ni Lee, things happen in this world that have nothing whatsoever to do with you. There is more to life than accounts payable and received. Things do not solely turn around you.

NI LEE: Then how am I to be in this world? Anonymous? I want to make a difference.

HO PING: You have no control of day into night.

GENERAL SUN'S VOICE: I want you May Lee. Answer me.

> (*beat*)

NI LEE: What other daughter-in-law would let a lecherous old man live with her family?

HO PING: He is NOT a lecherous old man.

NI LEE: What about . . .

HO PING: You agreed. And you were praised for it, given his history. Perhaps the word was too steep.

NI LEE: You just don't know.

HO PING: You didn't tell me.

GENERAL SUN'S VOICE: Answer me, May Lee.

NI LEE: I did. You heard nothing.

HO PING: It was just a touch, you said. Just an old man. You said it like that. Not more.

NI LEE: It was not my home to tell any other way. The General's house. I live in the General's house. Always someone else's house, never my own.

HO PING: He mistook you for his first wife.

> (*Ni Lee storms out. Ho Ping following.*)

HO PING: He touched you by mistake.

> (*Monkey King and Eight Pig have joined the General and build walls with mahjong tiles at a card table.*)

MONKEY KING: Think she'll come down? . . . and play?

GENERAL SUN: Pitiful plaything. She battle wills with me?

EIGHT PIG: Doesn't know how to play anyway.

GENERAL SUN: We'll do the three-way. She'll always eat defeat.

MONKEY KING: That's not the point, General Sun.

GENERAL SUN: What is this bullshit about being my death-muse? She can't even walk, how is her task to be done?

EIGHT PIG: I'm starving. You got stuff stirring in the stews?

GENERAL SUN: Where are the cooks?

MONKEY KING: General, you have awakened to us. Now you must integrate, feel compassion for her, for the suffering of all human beings . . .

GENERAL SUN: What? Monkey? Is your heart a bleeding?

MONKEY KING: You must aim for the whole.

GENERAL SUN: I am aiming for her hole.

(He and Eight Pig snicker.)

MONKEY KING: Then let us go. You are not serious about Buddha.

GENERAL SUN:
Buddha is nothing but a word
All these cults around statues, absurd!

EIGHT PIG:
They couldn't even reincarnate me into the right womb.

MONKEY KING:
Pig, it's what you deserved.

EIGHT PIG:
I was so pissed I ate my mother and my little piggy brothers.

GENERAL SUN:
Lighten up, Monkey King, enjoy yourself.
This world, come to think of it, is bearably good.
Weren't you the one who relieved yourself
On Buddha's hood? What's happened to that
Monkey I loved so much? The one who can
Flip and change his own mass—

EIGHT PIG:
Yeah, relax, wouldya? Mr. Deny-Your-Past.

MONKEY KING:
Eight Pig, don't you want out of here?

(General discards a tile.)

EIGHT PIG:

I have a hand that will not only win, but *smear*.

GENERAL SUN:

Who draws?

EIGHT PIG (*draws*):

Hu! I win! Ha ha ha, I am the winner. Door clear,
double twins, same suit, no heads or tails and a jian pair.

GENERAL SUN:

Your door is not clear—you have east winds.
And, fucking cheater, it's only one twin!

EIGHT PIG:

Not so! You slid those there.

GENERAL SUN:

Get the cooks in here to slaughter this pig.

MONKEY KING:

A cheater's flesh is tough.

EIGHT PIG:

Things never change. You had my mother and sister and it's still
not enough.

GENERAL SUN:

I thought YOU had your mother and siblings that way—

MONKEY KING:

He IS you, General, there's barely a line—

GENERAL SUN:

Never mind, I'm hungry. I will slaughter this swine

(*Yeh Yeh swings his cane as a sword.*)

MONKEY KING:

Kill him and you are killing yourself.

EIGHT PIG:

That's right . . . we're your ah, ah "cunt on choose," What was it?

GENERAL SUN:

> You are my braised shank on a bed of tender fermented veg-
> etable . . .

EIGHT PIG:

> How you salivate, drool and spit!

MONKEY KING:

> His meat will spoil your meal!

GENERAL SUN:

> You are the morsels in my mooshu . . .

EIGHT PIG:

> Your eating me will change your fate!

GENERAL SUN:

> Mmm your feet stewed with garlic black beans.
> A feast that'll turn the reddest commie green . . .

MONKEY KING:

> General Sun, even this rancid sow is appetizing to you.
> Your longevity is a sham!

GENERAL SUN (*licking his lips*):

> In my egg sandwich, you are the ham.

EIGHT PIG:

> What about cholesterol?

GENERAL SUN:

> Get over here, you third-rate fairies,
> Your heads are going to roll

MONKEY KING AND EIGHT PIG:

> BUT OUR HEADS ARE YOUR HEAD.

GENERAL SUN:

> Kneel!

EIGHT PIG:

> What's gonna happen? What's gonna happen?

GENERAL SUN:

What is it about killing that makes me so horny? Kneel!

EIGHT PIG:

What's gonna happen?

MONKEY KING:

Someone gonna be oh-so-lonely again.

GENERAL SUN:

Stick your dead necks out and let's Goooooooooo!

(*Kalump. Kalump.*
Exhausted, the General falls to sleep in his throne, eventually backscoring with his epicentric snore.
Kitchen.)

HO PING: Sonny!! Sonny!!
NI LEE: Softly, Ho Ping. Softly.
HO PING: I told the punk to check the oil. He didn't do it. Or feed the dog. This isn't the first time. SONNY!

(*Sonny enters with video camera.*)

SONNY: Shit, crisis every minute. Nice hair, Mom.

(*Ho Ping returns to broken English, Ni Lee her Hong Kong British accent, as they now speak their second language.*)

HO PING: What I tell you last Monday?
SONNY: Feed the dog.
HO PING: Don't playing wise guy with me.
SONNY: What? That's what you said.
HO PING: What else I say?
NI LEE: That's enough Ho Ping. Just get the car to move again and I'll drive it until it explodes.
SONNY: The relic, Mom? Something happen?
NI LEE: Nothing happened. Nothing happened. Just go.
HO PING: No. What did I say to check?
SONNY: Oh, the oil!
HO PING: Now you talking.
SONNY: Oh man, I totally forgot. I'm totally sorry. Mom, I'm totally sorry.

NI LEE: Don't ever say sorry to me.

SONNY: You shoulda called.

HO PING: Do not tell your mother what should. Because you "totally forgot" your mother had to walk in heat while you make pumping in air-conditioned gym!

NI LEE (*sticks out feet*): Ho Ping, massage my feet.

HO PING (*to Sonny*): Go get da car. It's you responsibility to getting it and fix it!

SONNY: If you'd get the car Mom wants, she'd never break down.

HO PING: Come back here.

SONNY: A Lexus EP 800, hah Mom?

HO PING: DA car runs perfect when maintain proper.

SONNY: It's a hundred years old! Yeh Yeh fucking drove that car.

NI LEE: Nonsense.

SONNY: Now the engine's on its last and you blame it on me—

HO PING: I will not buy Japanese car. Not after what dey done to us.

SONNY: That was a hundred years ago!

NI LEE: And what did your father do to them? How many did he kill?

HO PING: Your histories are mixing up. He killed the reds not the Japs.

NI LEE: I heard he killed them all.

HO PING: You hear wrong.

NI LEE: And what of it. The Japanese. They can be slaughtered. You can kill them physically, but now look at the strong, enduring cars they have engineered and conquered the world with.

HO PING: Then who buy da American cars?

SONNY: American cars suck.

HO PING: Someone have to support da American car industry.

SONNY: Why us? I'm totally with you the whole way, Mom. I'd be stoked and proud to drive a Lexus. Not have to duck every time I pass by someone I know in that crappy Chrysler. No guts.

HO PING: Let me tell you one ting . . .

SONNY: Look at your face . . . Update, for Chrissakes.

(*Sonny starts shooting with the vid-cam. Ni Lee seems to awaken.*)

HO PING: A car take you from point A to point B. For one foreign car we can have two, three American car. We're not Kings. We're efficient. Nothing else in our life so flashy.

NI LEE: I don't want to hear it anymore!

HO PING: You want it car so bad. Be my guest. You make so much money, go ahead. Be my guest.

NI LEE: But I want you to go with me . . .

HO PING: Just like you want me to go to your family, smile and chat and joke. You want drag me to dat talk show, talk about myself like I'm famous or something. You don't need me going dere.

NI LEE: Can't you see it would make me happy?

HO PING: Happy? It make you happy but go against my principles. I'm already flexible, but I can't faking a smile.

NI LEE: If you could bend a tiny arch, it would spring such joy in me. I bend for you, letting Yeh Yeh stay here all our lives. Why can't you bend for me?

HO PING: That's not bending. Yeh Yeh take care of Sonny and Twila while you worked. We would have to paying a babysitter.

NI LEE: And your family? Where are they? They take one week out of their lives to talk and stroke and honor him. One week. And you, gallant Ho Ping, you explode day to day, shouting our lives away.

HO PING: It is my privilege to taking care of him.

NI LEE: Privilege. Huh! Pathetic. I'll go get the car! Nothing gets done around here unless I do it. I'm living with a bunch of cripples, loud-mouthed and spineless. And when I see cripples like you, you know what I want to do?

SONNY (*zooming in*): Rock and roll, MA!

NI LEE: I want to beat you, maim you . . . I want to beat and maim you so that your uselessness is more obvious to this already convulsing world!

(*She swings at the camera, the movements waking the General.*)

GENERAL SUN: First Wife. Have the servants finished slaughtering the swine?

(*Birds tweet in the park.*
Twila sits on the bench, speaks to a long black wig.)

TWILA: Loser.

You're a loser.

You don't deserve to live.

Never could jump high enough, kowtow low enough, double toe loop enough, triple axel salchow enough, spin fast enough, smile wide enough. What's wrong with you? You couldn't even be the first to quadruple! How dare you even exist, you loser!

How many times you'd wedged the blade into her face? To think that rink was her face, that is how you'd get out there, be willing to fall forty, fifty times a day . . . each chilled bruise a tattoo, a testament to her losing face. Get up to fall, AGAIN!, get up to fall, AGAIN!, get up and fall. And the one time, the one time I'd . . . I'd land, smack balanced on the blade, just gliding on God's popsicle tongue, no smile, no clap, just pursed lips and a frozen stare, I swear you were a ventriloquist . . . "again . . . again . . . again."

And that's all that will ever loop in my head if I don't clear this . . . this . . .

(Twila suddenly hears footsteps. Ducks behind the bench. Ni Lee approaches. Twila spies.)

NI LEE: I want a tree here, a tree is here. Litter some nests in the branches, all shit on cue. I want pansies around my feet, pansies are around my feet. Little rabbits with bent whiskers, they are there. I have the money, the power, the freedom, the will to build my own park. HOW?! . . . how have I produced such lame stock? Surrounded by the feeble and meek . . . what have I produced? WHAT HAVE I PRODUCED?
(Ni Lee weeps. Twila peeps out.)
Fools and Eunuchs!
(Twila hides.)
Fools and Eunuchs! I tried to breed Emperors and Emperors but only fools and eunuchs.

(Twila stands.)

NI LEE: A month ago, I had crawled out of my ice age, and accepted your disappearance. Five years it took me, but I did it. Now, of course, because fate is a fixed roulette wheel . . . of course you show up to humiliate me back into the tundra. What do you want from me? I am not American . . . I cannot wave happily to the chaotic. But you, Twila, you believe in a banner of stitched-together stripes and pasted-on stars, and that is so different a mind than a flag made of one whole cloth . . . I . . .
TWILA: May I sit with you, Mother?
NI LEE: What are you doing here?
TWILA: I heard nothing. May I sit with you, Mother?
NI LEE: There is nothing to say.
TWILA: I need a mother right now. May I sit with you, Mother?
NI LEE: You sit and I'll go.

TWILA: I . . . just, just *sit* with you, Mother. Sit.

(Ni Lee removes her handbag.)

TWILA: Thank you, Mom. Thank you.

NI LEE: Never ever, ever say "thank you" to me. It means nothing to me. In fact, it is vulgar. It insults me. Every time you say "thank you, Mom" to me, you might as well say "fuck you, Mom" to me. You might as well say "fuck you."

TWILA: Please, Mom.

NI LEE: Please is "fuck you, Mom."

TWILA: I'm sorry.

NI LEE: I'm sorry is "fuck you, Mom."

(Twila takes Ni Lee's hand and puts it to her cheek.)

TWILA: I love you, Mom.

NI LEE: I love you is worse than "fuck you." "I love you, Mom" is "I want to kill you, Mom."

TWILA: Then where? Where do I start? Your hand is frozen. How can I thaw it?

(Ni Lee takes back her hand. Twila rummages for the wig, dons it, then kneels down as a dog.)

TWILA: Go ahead, kick me. Kick me, if that's a start. Better than thank you please sorry I love you, better. Kick me, no words, just kick me. Kick the fuck out of me kick me.

(Twila takes Ni Lee's foot, helping her to kick.)

TWILA: Kick me for every fall, harder, kick me. Kick me for every rink you lost your face, kick me. Kick me down and I'll get back up. Kick me like you won't kiss me. Kick me kill me kick me. C'mon, Mom, kick me. KICK ME!

(Ni Lee breaks down. Twila gets up, puts her arms around Ni Lee, rocks her.)

Now, Mother. Start from the beginning. What is it? Tell me what came before me that froze your soul. Tell me your secret, Mom. Let us kick the shivering. Tell me, Mom. Tell me.

(Pause.)

I want to know about you, Mom. What were you thinking at ten? At twenty? Did you freak out at your period? *(Ni Lee cringes)* What was your first kiss like? I want to know. Don't you want to know about me? What I've done?

(Ni Lee breaks from the hug.)

NI LEE: I know what you've done.
TWILA: You know what I did. But after. Don't you want to know what happened after?
NI LEE: After you disappeared?
TWILA: After I defected.
NI LEE: There is no after. There is no after.
TWILA: Then before. Ask me something about the before.

(Long pause.)

NI LEE: What is the quadratic formula?
TWILA: What?!
NI LEE: What is the quadratic formula?
TWILA: You mean fetch?
NI LEE: You can't remember.
TWILA: What if I do? Will you know something about me?
NI LEE: Yes.
TWILA: It's not something personal about me. All the nerds of the world know the quadratic formula. That club.
NI LEE: I will know . . . that you know.
TWILA: What could it be but numbers? I know numbers.
NI LEE: You have no idea about numbers. One point zero. One point zero. One point zero. One point zero one point zero. How could one person fall so many times? In front of so many people!?
TWILA: I just wanted to kill myself in front of everyone. What could end it? What could be done so I'd never have to ever again?
NI LEE: What is the quadratic formula?

(Long pause.)

TWILA: I tell you the formula, you tell me a story? About you?
NI LEE: If it is correct.
TWILA: What? Why? . . . Arf arf arf arooooooooo. *(she pants)*

NI LEE: So many drugs.

TWILA: Not enough to break out of this pet trick.

NI LEE: That's why I never tell you.

TWILA: What? That you have a big frozen hole in the middle of your heart that you wanted me to melt with the sear of fame and fill with medals to hang on walls?

NI LEE: You think you're so smart because you can put so many words together so quickly.

TWILA: Think about it, Mom. Fifteen-thousand people you needed around you cheering when I landed square, smack in the middle of some fabricated wonderland. Applause, applause, and the possibility of warmth, the idea of a smile entered you.

(Pause.)

TWILA: Is that what you needed? A crowd around you? Reacting to me, to something I'd done to assure you, to assure you I was okay? And then perhaps, real?

(Ni Lee stands.)

NI LEE: Children don't tell parents what they should say.

TWILA: Then the parents have to share their life stories or their children will run screaming from the rink and find out about life from someone else.
(Ni Lee starts to leave.)
Mother, please, no, okay, not please, no pleasing. Just, just one. One story.

(Pause.)

NI LEE: You know why I never told you stories? My story? My story is precious . . . my story is secret. It's not something you discuss over a piece of toast or while the TV is blabbering. I don't waste stories on people who are not listening fully, listening full. You have to be here, completely with me, listening to my story.

TWILA: All ears.

NI LEE: See! This is a joke. This tells me you're not serious. You just listen as if I'm some kind of noise, some computer beeps, some car engine. You must record me like a camera. Silent, but everything.

(Silence.)

NI LEE: What story.

TWILA: Uhhhh.

NI LEE: What story?

TWILA: Coming here.

NI LEE: I walked.

TWILA: To America.

NI LEE: An airplane.

TWILA: That is data. That is not story.

NI LEE: Criticize me.

TWILA: Mom, Mom, no, what I mean is that story, that story is not . . . no, the story I really want is . . . you and Dad.

(Pause.)

NI LEE: He . . .

TWILA: Was he handsome?

NI LEE: He was . . .

TWILA: Was he funny?

NI LEE: He was . . .

TWILA: Just, how did you meet, I mean, where did you go on your first date? I mean, when did you know, Mom? When did you know?

NI LEE: He was chosen for me. Because he had the highest degree.

TWILA *(head down)*: Okay.

NI LEE: Sometimes, Twila, Know-it-all Twila, people want to spare you pain. I am your mother. I want good things for you, better than anything I ever had. The chance to move upward was lost on you. Your falling on the night that could have taken you to the Olympics and WORLD FAME! . . . better, bigger, greater than any Swedish prize for mathematics I could ever have . . . access like no other Chinese family could have.

TWILA: And that's all that will ever loop in my head if I don't clear this. I can't take back the past, can't take down the scores, or . . . or replace the defection. I am a loser in your shivering game, but you are my mother, and I will win you back.

NI LEE: It's too late, Twila.

(Ni Lee exits. Twila alone, looks up to the sky.
Trumpets sound and announce.
Monkey King and Eight Pig's heads pop up as MAO CAPS from the mahjong table, startling the General.)

MAO CAP I (Monkey King): LOP!

MAO CAP 2 (Eight Pig): LOP!

MAO CAP 1: LOP!

MAO CAP 2: LOP!

MAO CAP 1 AND 2: Loppity Lop

GENERAL SUN: HAH?!

MAO CAP 1: Remember me?

MAO CAP 2: You dismembered me.

MAO CAP 1: I was last in line.

MAO CAP 2: Had the hardest spine.

MAO CAP 1: Needed two whacks to rid me.

MAO CAP 2: WHACK.

MAO CAP 1: WHACK.

MAO CAP 2: WHACK.

MAO CAP 1: WHACK.

MAO CAP 1 AND 2: WHACKITY WHACK!

MAO CAP 2: You broke us.

GENERAL SUN: To stop your believing.

MAO CAP 1: You broke us for fun.

MAO CAP 2: Ha ha ha.

MAO CAP 1: Hee hee hee.

GENERAL SUN: Stop that communist nonsense.

MAO CAP 2: Hee hee hee.

MAO CAP 1: Ha ha ha.

MAO CAP 1 AND 2 (*suddenly serious*): You broke all of us.

GENERAL SUN: For your good.

MAO CAP 1 AND 2: OUR good?

GENERAL SUN: You worshipped Mao. Mao worshipped Marx. You all
    broke traditions. I was saving you.

MAO CAP 2: Oh please!

MAO CAP 1: I'm sorry!

MAO CAP 2: Oh thank you!

MAO CAP 1: She'll never come down and play.

GENERAL SUN: She must! I want her.

MAO CAP 2: You'll forever be alone.

MAO CAP 1: Just touching your own old self.

MAO CAP 1 AND 2: YUCK!

MAO CAP 1: Let us eat your medals.

MAO CAP 2: MMMMMMMMM.

GENERAL SUN: I earned these.

MAO CAP 1: Dry fry with soy.

GENERAL SUN: My accomplishments.

MAO CAP 1: Then forget it.

MAO CAP 2: Live as you are.

MAO CAP 1: Not quite alive.

MAO CAP 2: Not quite dead.

MAO CAP 1 AND 2: Treacherous, treacherous middle ground.

MAO CAP 1: Such a coward.

MAO CAP 2: COWARD.

MAO CAP 1: Such a coward.

MAO CAP 2: COWARD.

GENERAL SUN: I am not a coward.

MAO CAP 1: COW.

MAO CAP 2: COW.

MAO CAP 1: COW.

MAO CAP 2: COW.

MAO CAP 1 AND 2: COWARDY COW!

GENERAL SUN: I AM NOT A COWARD!

(The heads disappear.
The General prepares himself, fantasizing about May Lee.)

GENERAL SUN: Come, May Lee. Come to me. I am not a coward I am not a coward. Let me show you how I'm not a coward.

(The General rubs himself.)

No one wants hundred-year-old meat.
A century alive, no one wants to touch you in the end.
I need touch. I need touch. GIVE ME TOUCH!

(Twila walks in rather zombyish, still wearing the black wig. The general sees her as May Lee.)

GENERAL SUN: My precious!
(He walks over to her.)
My jewel. You've come down!

TWILA: I came to say goodbye, Yeh Yeh.

(Yeh Yeh pulls Twila close and puts his cheek to her chest.)

I missed you, May Lee. Thank you, thank you. I'm sorry. Please.

TWILA: You're the only one who sees light in me, Yeh Yeh.

GENERAL SUN: I'm sorry, I'm so sorry for what I've done.

(He kisses her.)

TWILA (*pushing him away*): I think you need to . . .

GENERAL SUN: You're always like that. You have feet and now you're like that.

TWILA: Where are . . .

(*She spots his pajama bottoms on his throne.*)

GENERAL SUN: It's this old meat, isn't it? It's not to your taste?

TWILA: C'mon, Yeh Yeh.

GENERAL SUN: Wait wait wait. We're just beginning.

TWILA: C'mon, Yeh Yeh.

GENERAL SUN: Your family was paid good money to do this—

TWILA: Hold still.

(*She starts to tie his pajama pants. He tries to push her head down to his crotch. She leaps back. Grabs his cane.*)

GENERAL SUN: You wouldn't hit an old man, would you?

(*She moves to exit. He blocks her.*)

TWILA: Yeh Yeh, I've helped you . . . when everyone else tried to silence you.

GENERAL SUN: Come, I want to give you money.

TWILA: I don't want your money.

GENERAL SUN: I want to give you everything.

TWILA: Skip the everything.

GENERAL SUN: You don't like to look at this shriveled body. It is still a body. A touching, feeling body. I am alive.

(*Yeh Yeh reaches for Twila's breasts.*)

TWILA: I am your . . .

YEH YEH: What of it . . . you must learn these things anyway. What better than . . . ?

TWILA: I already know.

YEH YEH: Another touch. I need fresh meat.

(*He chases her.*)

TWILA: NO . . . please . . . don't . . . NO.

YEH YEH: It's *purity*.

(*He pushes her on his throne and lands on her. She pushes him to the floor and lifts the cane.*)

AYYYYYYYYYY.

(*Twila drops the cane, rushes out.*)

AYYYYYYYYYY.

(*We hear breathing.*)

AYYYYYYYYYY.

(*Sonny rushes in.*)

SONNY: Yeh Yeh, dude. Oh shit. Are you all right? Who am I? Who am I? Oh Jeez. DAD! DAD!!

(*He listens for his heart.*)

SONNY: DAD! DAD!! COME QUICK! POPS! YEH YEH'S FALLEN! POPS! Yeh Yeh. You got to hold on. It's your birthday, man. I got you a present. You can't kick on your birthday. Hold on, okay, man . . . you're breathing. You're doing good, man.

(*Sonny helps Yeh Yeh back onto his throne.
Ho Ping enters.*)

HO PING: What are you screaming about? . . . Oh. What's happened?!
SONNY: I was walking downstairs and suddenly I hear this sound. So I come down here and he's on the ground. He's like fallen and he can't get up.
HO PING: Who am I? Who am I?
YEH YEH: Ay . . . chi tien le? (*What time is it?*)
SONNY: Hold it right there, be right back.
HO PING: Pu yao to chiang hua. (*Don't try and speak.*)
YEH YEH: Hah? Chi tien le? (*What time is it?*)
HO PING: Che mo tieh tao te? (*How did you fall?*)

(*Sonny rushes in with the vid-cam and his birthday present to Yeh Yeh and immediately starts shooting.*)

YEH YEH: I tien le? (*Is it one o'clock?*)
HO PING: Put that away, Sonny.

SONNY: What?

HO PING: This is a very serious moment.

SONNY: That's why I'm getting it. Happy birthday, Yeh Yeh

(*Hands the present in front of the camera, puts it in Yeh Yeh's lap.*)

HO PING: Put it down and come sit with us.

SONNY: Check it out. We have copies made, right? "As it happened, The Death of a Line—the New Oral/Visual History."

HO PING: Stop it. I don't want to be on da camera

SONNY: I'm thinking ahead, Pops. He's like famous in Taiwan, right? All his sergeants and lieutenants and stuff, and their families . . . WOW, say fifteen thousand at $29.95. We could clear three hundred grand! We could get out of debt and get Mom the car she wants.

HO PING: Nonsense!

SONNY: I could get into film school with shit like this. All right. You know what you gotta do, right Pops? Don't move. Stay there or you'll fuck up my zoom.

HO PING: Fuck, suh muh, fuck. You watch out. This is very important, serious moment.

SONNY: You can watch the end again and again and again.

HO PING: HOW! . . . (*gathers self*) How did you fall? How did you fall?

YEH YEH: Hah?

HO PING: Che mo shuai tao te? (*How did you slip?*)

SONNY: English, guys. This can't subtitle.

(*Clunking sounds of the camera are heard, as if something's caught.*)

HO PING: Che mo tieh hsia lai te? (*How did you fall?*)

SONNY: C'mon. You're breaking it with the Chinese. Not registering.

YEH YEH: Pu chih tao. (*I don't know.*)

SONNY: ENGLISH!

HO PING: Get out of here. We don want your direction!

YEH YEH: I . . . don't . . . know.

SONNY: He's my grandfather, you know, and this is how I choose to remember him.

HO PING: Shut up, Sonny, shut up.

SONNY: What? You're always beating on him. When did this moment get so precious?

HO PING (*to Yeh Yeh*): You were sitting . . . standing?
YEH YEH: Sitting . . . standing?
HO PING: Na li? . . . Che li? . . . Na li? (*Where? Here? There?*)
YEH YEH: Che li. Na li. (*Here. There.*)
SONNY: ENGLISH! ENGLISH! ENGLISH!

(*They watch his eight-second temper tantrum.*)

HO PING (*testing*): How many fingers?
YEH YEH: Fingers . . .
HO PING: Who am I? Who am I?
YEH YEH: I . . . You . . .

(*The camera conks out. Yeh Yeh has his last flicker.*)

SONNY: Shit. What's going on?
YEH YEH: Ho Ping . . .
HO PING: He knows me. He still knows me.
SONNY (*banging on the camera*): Shit, what's wrong. Where's the . . .
YEH YEH: Ho Ping? Tell me . . .
SONNY: Wait . . . don't do . . . don't say anything until I get a handle
    on this.
YEH YEH (*lifting head*): Ho Ping . . .
SONNY: Stop! Didn't you hear me? Nothing until I fix this.
HO PING: Yes, Father?
SONNY: Pops! Pops! Help me out. It's broken.
YEH YEH: Are you . . . Are you afraid to die?

(*Sonny shakes the camera.*)

HO PING: No, Father. I'm not afraid to die. I'm afraid to be like you.
    Live life overdue.
YEH YEH: Then be good to her . . . and she will kill you faster.

(*Yeh Yeh lays his head down. Sonny explodes, throws the camera
against the wall. Ho Ping jumps. Yeh Yeh doesn't.*)

SONNY: Yeh Yeh, man, no, not now, back, come back. Shit! I missed
    it. Seventeen years of bearing all that crap and I missed it. The
    end. I missed it! I missed it! I missed the moment. Missed it.
    Bullshit. Missed it.

(*Sonny goes on a rampage.*
Ho Ping takes his father's hands, examines them, puts them to his cheek, one last time. He caresses his father's head.
Sonny knocks over chairs and tables. He tosses Ho Ping's minced cabbage (from the top of the act) like confetti.
The TV gets bashed.)

Now they're broken. Really, really broken. Maybe you can improve, get some new shit going on here. Fix this, Pops.

(*He kicks over the microwave.*)

HO PING: Ni wang pa tan hsiao kuay. (*You sonuvabitch punk.*)
(*Starts slapping Sonny.*)
This is our home!

SONNY: I missed it, old man. Never can say goodbye. He'll never know I said it. You made me miss it with your ancient machinery. He didn't even open my present. I BOUGHT HIM A PRESEEEENT! . . . You gonna scotch tape this moment back together?
(*Sonny continues his steroid rage.*)
You skimp on everything . . . you're so goddamned cheap it makes me sick! Look at you. Wimpy father. You're an idiot. You coulda paid to get the old man out of your hair but NOOO you had to put us through these torture camps of HAH? WHAT? WHAT TIME . . . I'm sick of this shit!

HO PING: You want he die with strangers with da tupes up his nose in dat stinky dark place for one hundred dollars a day? It's inhuman!

SONNY: This is inhuman! It's the money, it's the money. Twila couldn't have broken us for this long! You've been blaming her for five years now. You have it, you just don't spend it. You're a fucking cheapskate! Don't be getting me angry like he used to. He was old but you're still middle-aged. Don't fuck with me!

(*Sonny grabs Ho Ping, shakes him then punches him in the stomach.*
Ho Ping goes down as Sonny bellows a coupla times and hulkily exits.
Ho Ping holds his stomach, rocking back and forth.
Sonny blasts far away.
    Silence.)

HO PING: I am . . . 54 years . . . next month.
How . . . many more . . . years . . . do I . . . have to . . . fix?

(Ho Ping convulses.
Ni Lee hurriedly enters, sees Ho Ping on the ground.)

NI LEE: What's? What's happened, Ho Ping? Who did . . . ? Those spies in the park.
HO PING: Worse.

(She kneels at his side.)

NI LEE: And did they find him?
HO PING: He's gone.
NI LEE: They took him?
HO PING: My father is dead.

(Ni Lee wavers between disbelief and a perverse sort of joy. She disguises this opening of heart.)

NI LEE: How!? . . . *(low)* How?
HO PING: He fell out of his chair. *(his stomach convulses)*
NI LEE: Did the spies beat you, too?
HO PING: There were no spies.
NI LEE: Demons?
HO PING: No demons.

(Ni Lee puts her hand atop Yeh Yeh's hands. Ho Ping releases his stomach.)

HO PING: This darkness that he made me brave when I was so young. I have waited for this . . . watched how ungallantly life was stripped from him, how it turned on him. I will never fight this darkness. I will not be like him.

(Yeh Yeh passes one last gas. A moment of green.
They look at each other, uncomfortable. Ni Lee immediately plugs her nose.)

HO PING: Ni Lee, NO! Don't plug it. *(whiff)* Smell it. Smell it now while you can. The stench of death.
NI LEE *(still plugging)*: What you kidding me, Ho Ping?

HO PING: It's awful . . . *(whiffs)* grotesque . . . *(whiffs)* It has a head and a tail and two small teeth. *(whiffs)* Smell it! Stop and smell it, Ni Lee . . . before it's gone! The last of General Sun.

(She releases her nose, makes a face. They both crack up.)

NI LEE: It's like a rotten century egg.
HO PING: Or just a plain rotten century.

(Ho Ping looks at Ni Lee, pulls her head close to kiss. She stops him.)

NI LEE: Do you . . . do you remember our . . . our first meeting?

(Ho Ping nods and pulls her close.)

Do you remember where?
HO PING: *(lips almost touching hers)* Yes.
NI LEE: Where?
HO PING: You know, why do you ask?
NI LEE: I want to know you know.
(Ho Ping pulls away.)
No, don't . . . *(she pulls him back)* . . . just tell me . . . here *(ear)*
HO PING *(whispers)*: Ice Capades.

(Ni Lee immediately beams a huge sunny smile.)

NI LEE: Yes . . . I do, too.

(They kiss deeply, the final kiss of a wedding vow. Monkey King and Eight Pig appear as the General's old cohorts.)

LT. GEN. KING *(Monkey King)*: Did he fall?
MAJOR GO *(Eight Pig)*: Was it an accident?
HO PING: We think in his sleep. Perhaps napping, he rolled and fell onto the ground.
NI LEE: We hope as gently as the autumn leaves.

(She looks Ho Ping in the eye. Questions start pouring into her mind as she looks around.)

LT. GEN. KING: You are a good son, Ho Ping. So patient and dutiful to take care of him into a century of life.

MAJOR GO: And you, Ni Lee, such a generous soul to allow him to stay in your house. I know my son's wife would never allow that.

NI LEE: We are dutiful people.

HO PING: We have completed our duties as Chinese.

LT. GEN. KING: You are one of the few who can still claim tradition.

MAJOR GO: Let us pay our respects to the lasting General Sun.

(Ho Ping points Ni Lee to bow.
They all take three bows: Lt. Gen. King and Major Go facing
General Sun, and Ho Ping and Ni Lee facing King and Go, to
show respect to the guests. Ni Lee exits to look for her son.
Ho Ping looks up to the sky as Monkey King and Eight Pig become
their selves.)

EIGHT PIG:
    So what's next?

MONKEY KING:
    It's not quite done

EIGHT PIG:
    The roast? I like it rare

MONKEY KING:
    Pig! The mission!

EIGHT PIG:
    But he's dead.

MONKEY KING:
    We'll see if compassion's still shunned.

EIGHT PIG:
    He's dead! He's done!

MONKEY KING:
    Not quite.

EIGHT PIG:
    Huh?

MONKEY KING:
    Pig, you'd never leave a bone unchewed.

EIGHT PIG:
True.

MONKEY KING:
A soup unstewed—

EIGHT PIG:
True.

MONKEY KING:
A crunch unruined—

EIGHT PIG:
O! The pork rinds!

MONKEY KING:
Never mind!

EIGHT PIG:
Souvenir.

MONKEY KING:
Leave them behind.

EIGHT PIG:
One last bag?

MONKEY KING:
My friend, no.

EIGHT PIG:
So we're almost free to go.

MONKEY KING:
Out of his mind. Yes. Almost.

(*The stage is an empty blue ice of netherspace.*
Yeh Yeh sits in his throne.
He waits to ascend.)

YEH YEH:
They ask me.
They ask me.

At the end, they ask me.
I lay packing my last thoughts, they are unutterable.
So I said nothing and "Who am I?" "Who am I"
Again and again as they chanted me away.

(A convulsing Twila staggers a figure eight, bumping into Monkey King and Eight Pig. She knocks into Yeh Yeh's throne, falls on him, continuing to convulse.)

YEH YEH: Twila? What are you doing here?
TWILA: Yeh-eh Yeh-eh Yeh-eh Yeh-eh

(He unclenches an empty bottle of pills from her hands as she falls off him to her hands and knees.)

YEH YEH *(with each "NO" he whacks her back)*: NO—Twila—NO—Twila—NO—Twila—NO.

(One last swift whack on her back and pills spill from her mouth, the sound of a breaking pearl necklace. She sits back, disoriented. Yeh Yeh holds her and rocks her.)

YEH YEH: Twila, Twila . . . why are you blanking yourself out?
TWILA: All I want is to be more invisible.
YEH YEH: Oh, Twila, Twila . . . think back to your happy times.
TWILA: None—
YEH YEH: Yes.
TWILA: No.
YEH YEH: What about that day, that first day—
TWILA: Last, I only remember the last.
YEH YEH: Only five years old, you wanted to go—
TWILA: I'm gone I'm gone.
YEH YEH: Skay-TING, skay-TING, you pull my hand and say, skay-TING, skay-TING . . . like a bell, that's how you'd say it, Twila . . . your music, your own music, say it, Twila, say it: skay-TING, skay-TING.
TWILA: skating, skating.
YEH YEH: TING . . . like a bell . . . TING TING TING.
TWILA: skay-ting skay-ting.
YEH YEH: Everyone else was swim-MING, swim-MING, no bell, no shine, but you, Twila, you, skay-TING.
TWILA: skay-TING.

YEH YEH: YES!

TWILA: skay-TING skay-TING.

YEH YEH: Then you'd say, "You, too, Yeh Yeh, you too . . . you too skay-TING, Yeh Yeh—"

TWILA: You, too.

YEH YEH: So we walk to the To-Pan-Ga ice, the To-Pan-Ga ice in Ca-no-ga Park . . . one hundred degrees, we march the long march to To-Pan-Ga ice. You had your little coins sealed up in an envelope. You saved, you saved to pay for the skates. You couldn't even lace them up: I had to tie them for you and you would pull me onto the ice. My cloth shoes all wet and you would hold so tight to me: two hands holding onto me, determined not to fall. All the big kids going by . . . you wanted to go fast like the big kids, but you wouldn't let go of me.

(Twila slowly comes back to life.)

YEH YEH: My old feet froze, feet were like popsicles. But you continued, continued skay-TING skay-TING, the TING of your song . . . you wanted your feet to go fast so you fell but got back up, fell, got back up, fell, got back up . . . I thought, this little girl fights like a boy . . . you have the Sun blood to fight.

Sometimes, Twila, sometimes you must go back to the first, the FIRST time, the beginner time when everything was new, and closer to true nature. Remember it . . . remember.

(Pause.)

TWILA *(back alive, yet distant)*: Why did you take your immoralness out on me? I was your ally.

YEH YEH: I mistook you.

(Twila slowly places her hand on Yeh Yeh's crotch.)

TWILA: I want to think, I want to think this . . . this is where my seed traveled from your sac. Your seed, through here, him and then me. I am touching this . . . bridge where you became me. I want to think this is some tube to my history . . .

YEH YEH: It is your belief . . . you must have belief.

(She removes her hand.)

TWILA: I don't care to . . .

YEH YEH: Your beliefs, Twila—

TWILA: . . . everyone else has so many

YEH YEH: You must.

TWILA: I know nothing,

YEH YEH: Then you are a blank slate to start anew! You are an original, Twila. Fill your head with firsts. With firsts.

TWILA: With firsts.

(He takes her hand.)

YEH YEH: Accept my touch as the last human stroke for old Yeh Yeh and nothing more than that.
    Forgive me, Twila.

(He kisses her hand and then pats it.)

YEH YEH: It's time, Twila. It is time. Go, go back. Skate yourself back into the world as if it was that first time, that first time, when it was pure. Go, Twila, go. Go. Go.
    Go. . . . . go . . . . go . . . .
    . . . . go . . . . go

(Yeh Yeh, Monkey King and Eight Pig slowly become Twila's mind silhouettes. She stands and prepares to take her first steps.)

TWILA: With firsts:
    Skay- *(she steps)* TING *(steps)*
    Skay- *(steps)* TING . . . . skay . . . .
    . . .TING

*(Twila gathers speed and joy as she skates around the light in a perfect infinite circle, skating herself back into the world.
Yeh Yeh strips to his natural being and moves to the next world.
Lights fade.)*

END OF PLAY

Alice Tuan is a playwright and teacher. She emerged in 2000 with recognition from the Richard E. Sherwood Award as well as the Colbert Award for Literary Excellence. *Ajax (por nobody)* premiered at New York's Flea Theater, played at Austin's Salvage Vanguard Theater and performed at the Melbourne Fringe Festival (2001). Besides being archived in the Billy Rose Theatre Collection at the New York Public Library for the Performing Arts, *Ajax (por nobody)* is also anthologized in *Play: A Journal of Plays* (2004) as well as *New Downtown Now* (2006).

Other plays include *Ikebana* (East West Players; Taper, Too), *Some Asians* (Perishable Theatre; UMass Amherst), *Manilova* (New Georges), *The Roaring Girle* (Foundry Theatre), *Iggy Woo* (Brown/Trinity Playwrights Repertory Theatre), a whole bunch of short plays for Atlanta's Dad's Garage, and the Virtual Hypertext Theater play *Coastline* (Serious Play! Theatre Ensemble; Edinburgh Festival Fringe). *BATCH: An American Bachelor/ette Party Spectacle*, her collaboration with Philadelphia's New Paradise Laboratories, was commissioned by the Actors Theatre of Louisville and premiered at the Humana Festival of New American Plays in 2007.

Ms. Tuan holds an MFA from Brown University in Creative Writing and has taught at the Los Angeles Theatre Center, East West Players and the Michener Center for Writers at the University of Texas at Austin. Performance works include a solo performance in *The Secret History of the Lower East Side* (En Garde Arts), *Sprawl* (with Rachel Hauck at the Actors' Gang) as well as the "conference performance" of *APACUNT* (Asian Pacific American Contemporary Unilateral Neo Theater) with Kristina Wong (Guthrie Theater; Theater for the New City).

Tuan has held one-year teaching posts in both Guangzhou and Shanghai, China. In December 2008, she gave a talk at the Beijing Foreign Studies University, entitled "The Contradiction of the Chinese American through the play *Last of the Suns*." She was invited to observe the Third European-Chinese Cultural Dialogue in

October 2010 in Shanghai. Continuing on the international front, she headed up an interdisciplinary, experimental performance/ design project with students at CalArts and Chung Ang University (of Seoul, South Korea), called *Lear/Layer* in January 2011.

She is currently the Head of Writing for Performance at CalArts.

$$x = \frac{-b \pm \sqrt{b^2 - 4ac}}{2a}$$

wAve

Sung Rno

Author's Statement

Chay Yew, who was running the Asian Theatre Workshop at the Mark Taper Forum, asked me to write a verse adaptation of Medea with a Korean American twist. I immediately accepted, with thoughts like "piece of cake" and "fun adaptation" swimming in my head. Several months later I realized that I fallen into a theatrical ambush of my own making—all my scenes seemed thin, I really started to dislike Medea and why did I keep hearing showtunes in my head? As I stared at the disjointed mess of pages slowly piling up on my  desk, I had the fear that I was becoming a Greek tragedy myself: playwright eaten alive by his own play. I was also fighting the pressures of writing a KOREAN AMERICAN VERSION OF MEDEA, you know, the one where Medea is a Korean war bride who falls for an American soldier from Kansas—*K Butterfly* meets *M*A*S*H*— which I was desperately trying to escape. Out of pure frustration, I started writing a sketch involving two characters named Chinky and Gooky, who vented all of my gathering bile—they were offensive, profane and ridiculous. With great embarrassment, I shared this scene with a few friends, and much to my surprise they fell on the floor laughing. I had inadvertently stumbled upon the raw nerve of this play. Chinky and Gooky became the satiric Greek Chorus, and with their blessing the adapted tragicomedy fell into place: Jason, a frustrated Korean American engineer, is tapped to play Mister Phnom Penh in the film musical version of *Miss Saigon*, while M loses her identity, one letter at a time, in the numbing plasticity that is Amurricah. And there *was* singing, over-the-top spoofs of showtunes. It was Mister Phnom Penh after all.

There was also wave/particle duality. Perhaps it was my physics background coming through, but I really just wanted to reflect the universal quality of Greek tragedy—it's not just someone breaking her heart, it's someone breaking the larger will of the gods. Wave/particle duality was a way of broaching Korean/American complexity in a more fundamental, universal way. If the very structure of matter is divided, then M would be even more so, because her very identity and passions have deepened this division. When working with the actors on the final rewrites of the play, we began to experience wave/particle duality at the theatrical level. Like Heisenberg meeting Beckett at a bar—a memorable moment was when we devoted one rehearsal to discussing the basics of quantum mechanics. Some actors expected a quiz. But this all helped the play pulse along in staccato rhythms, and then launch into the large, sweeping pull of a wave form. As we ramped up the tempo, Ron Domingo told me that he started feeling like a cartoon character, bringing my initial stage direction of "*Simpsons* meets anime" to real stage life. When the play finally found its true rhythm, oscillating wildly between dark and light, comedy and poetry, then we just tried to hang on and enjoy the ride.

Acknowledgments

Special thanks to Chay Yew, Daniel Dae Kim, Elaine Tse, Steve Park, Andrew Pang, Christine Simpson, Ralph Peña, Will Pomerantz, Chiori Miyagawa, Emily Morse, Todd London, Jorge Ortoll, Suzette Porte, Ken Leung, Ron Domingo, Michi Barall, Deborah S. Craig, Paul H. Juhn, Aaron Yoo, Patrick McNulty, Tom Moon, Rich Hahn, Mikey Suh, Mom and Dad and Helen for helping me find this play.

Production History

wAve was originally commissioned by the Mark Taper Forum's Asian Theatre Workshop and was developed at Imua! Theater Company, Ma-Yi Theater Company, Mark Taper Forum, Asian American Theater Company, Public Theater New Works Now!, Arena Stage, and Fluid Motion Theater Company.

The world premiere of *wAve* was produced in 2004 by Ma-Yi Theater Company in New York City (Ralph B. Peña, Artistic Director; Jorge Z. Ortoll, Executive Director). The director was Will Pomerantz. The set design was by Marsha Ginsberg. The costume design was by Carol Bailey. The lighting design was by Joel Moritz. The sound design was by Nick Borisjuk. The production stage manager was Christine D. Goutmann. The cast was as follows:

M	Michi Barall
JASON	Ron Domingo
MARILYN PART II	Deborah S. Craig
DR. YANG	Paul H. Juhn
WAVEMAKER	Patrick McNulty
JUNIOR	Aaron Yoo

wAve received its UK premiere in 2009 at the Yellow Earth Theatre in London (Phillipe Cherbonnier, Jonathan Man, Co-Artistic Directors). The production was directed by Jonathan Man. The set design was by Wai Yin Kwok. The lighting design was by Douglas Kuhrt. The sound design was by Cos Chapman. The production manager was Jim Leaver. The cast was as follows:

M	Louise Mai Newberry
JASON	Jonathan Chan-Pensley

MARILYN PART II   Tina Chiang
WAVEMAKER   Ashley Alymann
JUNIOR   Jay Oliver Yip

Characters

M, a fractured remnant of Medea, updated Korean American, bicoastal

JASON, her husband, like a cartoon, but Japanese anime meets *The Simpsons*

CHORUS, an assortment of comic characters including, but not limited to:

> LUCKY, a person of power and influence

> THE WAVEMAKER, a mysterious figure who really understands wave/particle duality

> JUNIOR, M and Jason's teenage son

> CHINKY and GOOKY, two Asian American TV personalities

> DR. YANG, a shrink

> MARILYN PART II, genetically reengineered from Marilyn Monroe's DNA

> DIRECTOR, a movie helmer

> ASSORTED JOURNALISTS, esteemed members of the media

Setting

That peculiar state of mind that happens where Korea and America meet, somewhere between *M*A*S*H* and Margaret Cho, between the 38th parallel, between two centuries, between McDonald's and Burger King. In other words, imagine that Los Angeles and New York have merged in space-time.

Time

Tomorrow.

Note

This is not a naturalistic play. It should be presented in the style of dream or nightmare or rock concert. It should have the logic of music, in the sense that transitions are not always explained, but simply occur. Music is important to this piece. Electric guitar with heavy distortion and feedback is suggested. Percussion could be used to further the effect of disorientation.

There should be as little as possible on stage. The use of visual projections to indicate physical settings is suggested.

Scene titles can be projected or announced before each scene.

. . . You are so far.
My loathing wrestles with the slow twilights.
But night comes and starts to sing to me.

—*Pablo Neruda, "Here I Love You,"*
translated by W.S. Merwin

Act One: Ripples

Prelude

A movie producer's office. Jason is sitting while Lucky is on the phone.

LUCKY (*on phone*): Fucking who said what? You can just sit there and tell me something like that? Look, don't mess with me here. I said I need a fleet of—what? Yes, it's essential to the vision. You think I'm just sitting around smoking my opium pipe, dreaming up expensive props to waste money on? Don't you get it? This is going to be an event, a happening, a zeitgeist-changing . . . movie is not even the right word, it trivializes it, demeans it. I mean, come on, a film version of *Miss Saigon*? *Mister Phnom Penh*. It doesn't get any better than this. They'll be nominating this for the Nobel Fucking Prize—years from now, people will remember where they were when this movie gets released, okay?

That's right, and we have an undiscovered talent. He's right here actually. Hey, I always trust my instincts about talent, and I have very strong instincts with this one.

This one's got everything: kick-ass martial arts—singing—romance—wind instruments—cooking sequences—helicopters—Marilyn Part II. But most of all, it's . . . multi-culti. This has the melting pot *and* the salad bowl, Charlie Chaplin *and* Charlie Chan, all wrapped up into one beautiful futo-maki of a movie, so dammit, when I say I want a fleet of helicopters, GET YOUR HEAD OUT OF YOUR FUCKING ASS AND GET ME A FLEET OF HELICOPTERS!

(*Slams down the phone. Turns to Jason.*)

Jason.

JASON: Yes?

LUCKY: Jason.

JASON: Hi.

LUCKY: Jason.

JASON: That's my name.

LUCKY: What do you do again?

JASON: Computers.

LUCKY: Computers?

JASON: I have a company called Argonaut Systems Services.

LUCKY: ASS?

JASON: Yes.

LUCKY: So you're an ass-man?

JASON: Excuse me?

LUCKY: I see a lot of your father in you, Jason.

JASON: You do? I didn't really know him all that much. He was always sending me away.

LUCKY: He had brains. Guts. Intuition. He did magical things with cabbage. He ate a lot of fish. Do you?

JASON: Do I what?

LUCKY: Eat a lot of fish?

JASON: No. Burgers.

LUCKY: Big Macs?

JASON: Whoppers.

LUCKY: I like that. I like your cojones. Just like your father. I liked his cojones too.

JASON: Oh?

LUCKY: He saved my life you know?

JASON: Yes, you told me.

LUCKY: Your life is going to change, my boy. In big ways. I'm serious. This is the biggest thing for your people since *M*A*S*H*. Did you read the script?

JASON: Yeah.

LUCKY: And?

JASON: I think I should read it again.

LUCKY: Oh?

JASON: I was thinking . . .

LUCKY: Yes?

JASON: I'm a little confused here. Why me? Don't get me wrong, I'm very excited about starring in this movie . . . *Mister Phomn Penh*. But I'm a computer guy. A techie. What do you see in me that makes you think—

LUCKY: That you could be a star?

JASON: Yes.

LUCKY: That's my job, Jason, to see things like that. Look, let me put it to you this way . . .

(*Singing softly:*)

> He's got the sun and the rain in his hands,
> He's got the moon and the stars in his hands,
> He's got the wind and the clouds in his hands,
> He's got the whole world in his hands.
>
> He's got everybody here in his hands,
> He's got everybody there in his hands,
> He's got everybody everywhere in his hands,
> He's got the whole world in his hands.

You understand now?

JASON: Ummmm . . . yeah, I guess.

LUCKY: Now, if you fuck this up, I'll kill you.

JASON: Right.

1. Blue

Lights up on Jason and M at home. They don't speak, but move as if they are ghosts. Jason takes off his work clothes, opens a can of beer, sits himself in front of the TV. M is busy in the kitchen preparing a pot of Asian noodles and soup. Both are in their own pools of light, with a minimum on stage.

The Wavemaker, an ethereal, strange, but powerful figure, hovers above them and speaks . . .

WAVEMAKER:
Ahhhhhh.
The silence. So it is.

Lips. Wet.
What do they taste?
Sea. Waves. Blue.
Myth. Blue.
Rolling. Lapping. Laughing.

Heart. Warm.
What does it feel?
A man. A woman.
A name. A letter.
Jason. M.

I'm what's known as a wavemaker.
I make the waves,
the vibrations in time and space
that slither and purr
kiss the back of your neck
make all the hairs on your history
stand on end.

Let me show you something.
Wave.

(Makes a wave motion with his hand. M freezes.)

Particle.

(Makes a particle motion. Jason freezes.)

See? It's all in how you look at it.

How do I know, you may ask?
How? 'Cuz I do.
Why? 'Cuz I am.
What? 'Cuz I be.

'Cuz I hear the laughter.
That's right.
I hear the H—2—OOOOOOOO-HO-HO-HO-HO . . .
The water is laughing in your face.
'Cuz the water knows that you're just fooling yourself,
'Cuz the water knows you're headed for a big
fall.

The H—2—OOOOOOOO-HO-HO-HO-HO knows
a good betrayal when it hears one.
Like a man goes to Korea to pursue his fortunes.
Comes back with a wife,
with the ch-ch-chi she stole from her family,
and the hungry desire for something more.
The very spirit, the ethos,
the essence, the soul of a family, a culture
that's what we're talking about here,
a woman stealing this chi from her family
for the man she loves, even to the point
of killing her own bro—
ahhhhhh, but I'm getting ahead of myself,
let's not Confucius the issue right now,
let's just listen.

Mmmmmmmm.
The silence. So it is.
Eyes. Open.
What do they see?
What do you see?

(*He looks to the audience expectantly, waits, then turns away.*
He makes a signal with his hand, and Jason and M start moving again. We hear the sounds of the basketball game that Jason is watching.)

M: I hope you're hungry. 'Cuz I cooked up something special. Real special. Better than anything you could buy. Better than McDonald's. Better than a value meal supersized.

JASON: Uh-huh.

M: Better than the Golden Arches. I only recently understood why have the Golden Arches. It's because of the M, right? Like my name.

JASON: YOU CALL THAT DEFENSE? WHAT THE HELL WAS THAT?

M: It's funny isn't it? That was the first meal we had when we finally made it here. I think I had a Big Mac. French fries. And a chocolate milkshake. When I think about what we had to go through just to make it here. That early morning. Fleeing Seoul. The waves . . . the boat. My brother's . . . eyes.

JASON (*Reacting to game*): ARE YOU KIDDING ME? THAT WAS NOT A FOUL! HOW CAN YOU CALL THAT A FOUL!

145

(He slaps the TV with his hand.)

M *(Aside)*: I feel my husband drifting. A woman can sense when it happens. It's like when you feel the current shift in the ocean, suddenly the water is pulling you out to sea.

(Jason takes a big swig of beer.)

JASON: Where's Jason Junior?

M: He's outside with his friends, doing heroin.

(Pause.)

I mean, he's at Kmart, buying a Glock semiautomatic.

(Pause.)

He's playing video games.

JASON: SHOOT! SHOOT THE DAMN BALL! YES! FROM WAY DOWNTOWN!

M: You know I'm getting worried about him.

JASON: WHAT? YOU SUCK! YOU ARE A FUCKING DISGRACE TO THE HUMAN RACE!

M: He seems withdrawn. I don't know what to say to him anymore.

JASON: What?

M: Do you love me?

JASON: Uh . . . honey, hold on a minute, it's the fourth quarter.

M: You don't listen to me these days.

JASON: BLOCK OUT! BLOCK OUUUUUUUUTTTT! GRAB THE REBOUND! GET—THAT—DAMN—BALL!

(M screams in anguish as she sees Jason pull out a semiautomatic pistol.)

M: NOOOOOOOOOOOOOOOOOOOOOOOO!

(Jason empties a few rounds into the TV.)

M: Jason!

JASON: Sorry.

M: That's four. Four in one year.

JASON: It's the Knicks. They do that to me.
  Mmmmm. Something smells good.

(He inhales deeply.)

I'm so glad I married a real-genuine-fresh-off-the-boat-cook-till-you-drop girl. Not some lame-ass-assimilated-college-educated-more-banana-than-Chiquita. They're too watered down, you know? They can't cook like this.

M: I was born with it I guess.

JASON: The way you can work with food. It's like magic. Come here. Let me kiss your magical hands. Your magical FOB hands.

M: You're more of an FOB than I am.

JASON: I ain't no FOB.

M *(playfully)*: F-O-B! F-O-B!

JASON *(angry)*: SHUT UP!

(Pause.)

M: I was just joking.

JASON: I have to go anyway.

M: Where are you going?

JASON: I have a meeting.

M: With who?

JASON: A producer.

M: A what?

JASON: It's complicated.

M: Our life is always complicated. I want things to be simple.

JASON: I get a call from this guy, says he's an old friend of my father's. Like they fought together in the Korean War. It turns out—he's in the movie business right now. He's a bigshot producer. I guess my father saved his life. Pulled him out of a foxhole . . . introduced him to kimchee. So, all these years he's really wanted to do something for my father. But it took him so long to climb the Hollywood ladder and now my father's gone. So he decided that at least he could do something for me. He wants me to be in this movie. To repay my father, he's making me the STAR.

M: He wants you to be the star?

JASON: That's what he said.

M: You're not an actor.

JASON: He says I have natural talent. I'm born to do this part.

M: What part?

JASON: It's a film version of *Miss Saigon*. It's called *Mister Phnom Penh*.

M: *Mister Phnom Penh?*

JASON: The co-star is Marilyn Part II.

(M starts to laugh.)

What's so funny.

M: Just the thought of you acting. I hope it's a comedy.

JASON: This is no joke, honey. Do you realize how . . . HUGE . . . this is? This has blockbuster written all over it. This will be like Citizen Kane for all the Asian people of the world, it'll be like Citizen . . . Kang.

M: What're you—what about us? Me? What we've built with our sweat. Our blood.

JASON: I don't want to be doing this my whole life. Making chips. Moving data. We're nothing but cyber-plumbers. But films, movies—that's getting at the deeper *thing* going on.

M: What deeper thing?

JASON: You know . . . Stories. Dreams. Myths. Not this dull, every-day reality where you're just trying to climb the food chain. You understand? You know how when you make noodles you sprinkle those scallions on the top? Well, I'm tired of being a scallion. I wanna be the broth, goddammit. I wanna be the soup. You know?

M: You want soup? Here's your soup.

(M slams a bowl of noodles in front of him.)

JASON: You're not pleased.

M: Oh, I'm overjoyed! I stay home all day while you make movie deals. What happens if you fall in love with your co-star?

JASON: Don't worry, that won't happen.

M: How do you know?

JASON: 'Cuz I know. After all we've been through? Come here.

(He kisses her.)

Now stop being silly.

(He starts eating.)

Mmmmmmm. You really outdid yourself this time.

(Slurping noodles noisily.)

You put something different in here, didn't you?

M: No.
JASON: Come on, tell me the truth.
M: Just the usual.
JASON: I can tell when you're hiding the truth.
M: Can you?
JASON: What's in the soup?
M: Just some special seasonings.
JASON: I knew it.

(Jason finishes with a large slurp.)

I gotta go. I love you.

(He kisses her with a flourish and exits.)

M: Love you too.

(M goes over to the pot of noodles and pulls out a black Converse tennis sneaker.)

Yeah. Seasonings.

(Throws shoe back in. She ponders this word . . .)

Hmmmm. Sea . . . son . . . ings.

Sea. Son.
Sea. Son.
Sea. See.

(She starts slicing vegetables. She speaks with the rhythm of her slicing.)

i see that day
clear that morning
jason and i woke
we ran
morning air
icy cold
we steal
our family ch-ch-chi
i take it
our family

spirit
essence
passed down for centuries
from generation to generation
i steal
i rob
i take

we run
hand in hand
the waiting boat

my father's angry
eyes
i feel
their heat
on my neck
i feel them

the night before
the night
i look into my brother's eyes
my brother's
i look
into
i look
his
his eyes
his eyes say
his eyes say everything

don't do this
they say
stay
they say
don't do
they say
stay
they say
don't
they say
stay

2. Screen/Dream

M and Junior, her son, sit in the living room. Junior stares at the television. M is reading a book.

JUNIOR: Mom?

M: Yes?

JUNIOR: This is a new TV. Did Dad break another one?

M: Yes.

JUNIOR: Isn't that, like, three TVs in one year?

M: Four.

JUNIOR: Was it the Knicks again?

M: I don't know.

JUNIOR: Did he shoot it or kick it?

M: He shot it.

JUNIOR: Probably the Knicks.

> (*Pause.*)

What're you reading?

M: Oh, nothing.

JUNIOR: Another one of your old diaries?

M: Maybe.

JUNIOR: Why do you keep reading those old things?

> (*She places the diary into her* Chinky and Gooky Guide to Cooking *book.*)

M: I'm actually reading this. *The Chinky and Gooky Guide to Cooking.*

JUNIOR: *Chinky and Gooky?* Why do you like that show so much?

M: I don't know, I just do.

JUNIOR: They're so fake though. (*Mimicking accent*) "Hi, I'm Chinky! I'm a Gooky!"

M: I think they're funny.

JUNIOR: They suck.

M: Don't say suck in front of your mother.

JUNIOR: They piss me off.

M: Don't say piss in front of your mother.

JUNIOR: I find their political views extremely disappointing.

M: That's better.

They make me laugh.

JUNIOR: I think I'm gonna go to McDonald's.

M: Okay.

JUNIOR: You want anything?

M: Uhmmm. Sure.

JUNIOR: What?

M: I don't know. Surprise me.

JUNIOR (*Turning to leave, stopping*): Mom?

M: Yeah?

JUNIOR: You don't want to come with me?

M: No. You know I'd rather stay here.

JUNIOR: I know you'd rather. But I think you should go outside.

M: No, really. It's fine.

JUNIOR: Mom, please?

M: No, thanks.

JUNIOR: You sure?

M: Yes.

JUNIOR: Mom?

M: Yes?

JUNIOR: You want yours supersized?

M: Whatever you're having.

(*Checking watch.*)

Don't take too long. My show is coming on.

JUNIOR: Yeah. Later, mom.

(*Junior exits. M puts her book down. As she flips on the TV, we crossfade to Scene 3.*)

3. The Chinky and Gooky Show

Bright TV music, like The Itchy and Scratchy Show *from* The Simpsons.

CHINKY: Hi, I'm Chinky.

GOOKY: And I'm Gooky.

CHINKY: And this is . . .

BOTH: *The Chinky and Gooky Show.*

CHINKY: Today we have Asian movie talk.

GOOKY: Yes, we talk all about movie.

CHINKY: That's why we say movie talk.

GOOKY: Okay.

CHINKY: Okay.

Today's first feature is an oldie but a goodie. Remember *Black Rain*, wiz ah Michael Douglas? American policeman go to Japan to track down Japanese Yakuza. You remember that scene when Michael Douglas say, "Hey, doesn't anybody fucking speak English around here."

GOOKY: Tha' not funny.

CHINKY: No. No funny.

GOOKY: That make me mad. Vely mad.

CHINKY: It make me so mad I can't see straight.

GOOKY: You can't see straight anyway, Chinky.

CHINKY: I can't?

GOOKY: No, you eyez is uh slanted. See like this.

(He makes Chinky eyes. They break up in laughter.)

CHINKY: Okay. Well, let's vote on *Black Rain*. I say, Solly Cholly.

GOOKY: I say, Mike Douglas, you need learn how to use chopsticks. Vely provincial of you.

CHINKY: He in that other funny movie, too, wasn't he?

GOOKY: *Basic Instinct*. Oh, yeah. I like that one. Sharon Stone. Mmmm. She dericious. I want to have her suki-yaki, you know what I say. I want her to steam my dumplings.

CHINKY: No, not that movie. *Falling Down*. I think that it. He like shoot at a Korean storeowner or something. Blow him away like it ain't no thang.

GOOKY: Oh yeah, but he wear those glasses like Chairman Mao. So, that a good thing. But I still give *Falling Down* a Moo Goo Gai PAN.

CHINKY: Me too. I say, Chicken Kung PAO even though he wear those Asian Style glasses.

Now, to our next movie. The biggest movie of all time.

GOOKY: *Star Trek II: Wrath of Khan*.

CHINKY: Idiot. *Titanic*!

GOOKY: Yah, *Titanic*. With that delicious water chestnut Kate Winslet. We like Kate because—

(Chinky sings two lines from the Titanic *song "My Heart Will Go On.")*

GOOKY: We like Kate because she work with Chinaman director Ang Lee in movies like *Eat Drink Man Woman*. I don't know she can

153

cook Chinese food like that. She could kick Iron Chef in ass, make any Asian man vely happy.

CHINKY: You stupid. She in *Sense and Sensibility*. With Emma Thompson.

GOOKY: You sure?

CHINKY: *Eat Drink Man Woman* all about Taiwanese father and three daughter. They not adopt Kate Winslet, okay?

GOOKY: That's true, Asian don't do that kind of thing.

CHINKY: But let's talk about movie. *Titanic*.

GOOKY: First of all, no yellow people in the movie. Not one single Asian.

CHINKY: So right away, we say—

BOTH: RACIST IMPERIALIST MOVIE!!!

GOOKY: In fact, there no people in that movie not white.

CHINKY: That's right. No people of color.

GOOKY: Mmmm.

CHINKY: And you know, on real *Titanic*—no Asians on *Titanic*. I mean, in real history too.

GOOKY: That's right, so we say—

BOTH: RACIST IMPERIALIST LUXURY LINER!!!

CHINKY: Why weren't any Asians allowed on *Titanic*? Because they considered dirty back then. We deserve to be on Big Boat too. We deserve to drown with all those white people too.

GOOKY: We must act now. We march with our fellow black and Hispanic and Native Americans. We march to Burbank and burn down some soundstages.

CHINKY: BURN PARAMOUNT BURN!

GOOKY: YES!

BOTH: BURN FOX BURN!

CHINKY: Then we re-release *Titanic*. We color in some of the victims on board.

GOOKY: We have them eat some shabu-shabu on board.

CHINKY: Some kimchee. And pad thai.

GOOKY: Some soul food. Some arroz con pollo.

CHINKY: Then we demand a cut of the profits.

GOOKY: Yes, we have Ang Lee redirect the movie.

CHINKY: YES!

GOOKY: POWER TO ANG LEE!

CHINKY: ANG LEE FOR PRESIDENT!

BOTH: WE LOVE ANG LEE!
ANG LEE! ANG LEE! ANG LEE!

(*Pause.*)

CHINKY: Okay . . . What next movie?

GOOKY: Another big movie, but with little people.

CHINKY: Ah yes. *Lord of Rings*. I love that movie. Make me sad.

GOOKY: Why so sad, Chinky?

CHINKY: Don't know. Maybe because Frodo so small. But feet so big.

GOOKY: Yes, but why no one call me to audition?

CHINKY: Gooky, you silly. You not right for part.

GOOKY: I can play hobbit. I can play elf. I speak elf language even. "Man kiluva lómi sangane, telume lungane, tollalinta ruste, vea qalume, mandu yáme."

CHINKY: What you just say?

GOOKY: I don't know.

CHINKY: Okay. Next week, we talk about an interesting remake— *Toro! Toro! Maki!*

GOOKY: Yes! All about courageous band of sushi chefs sent to internment camps during World War II, but we give away too much story. Until next week—

CHINKY: May your noodles be warm . . .

GOOKY: And your rice be sticky . . .

CHINKY: Goodlight!

GOOKY: Goodright!

BOTH: Ha-ha, just kidding.
Goodnight!

4. Dream/Scream

M in a pool of light—she is going through her diary and ripping pages out of it. Jason in a separate pool of neon light. M echoes words in bold.

JASON:

I want to live larger than I am.

I want to live in the minds of others.

I want to be their subconscious.

I want them to wake up and realize I've been dancing in their dreams.

I want to make love to them. All of them.

I want to see my name in two hundred–point type.

I want my mouth to be the size of the Grand Canyon.

I want my teeth to dwarf Mount Everest.

I want to say something seductive on an IMAX screen and have the audience gasp like they're being swallowed by King Kong.

I want to be a star. A nova.

I want to be a supernova that bursts into the night sky.

I want to explode in the air and leave remnants of my being in the interstellar calligraphy. So that centuries from now, some lonely astronomer on some lonely faraway planet will notice that there's light where there was none before.

And they will know. They will know that I did exist.

(Lights go out. Darkness.)

I did. I do. I SAID, I DO!!!

(Paparazzi flash bulbs go off.)

That's more like it.

JASON AND M:
I want. I want.

M:
I want.
I want to be dead.
I want to be the rain.
I want to be the concrete sidewalk.
I want to be a cigarette.

Please, someone smoke me.
Please, someone set me on fire.
Please?

(Lights shift back to M's living room, where a psychiatrist, Dr. Yang, has been sitting waiting for M to talk. There is a long silence. Dr. Yang keeps checking his watch, fidgeting, etc. M stares coolly ahead. Finally Dr. Yang exhales loudly and clears his throat.)

DR. YANG: Now, Mrs. Park—

M: Please, call me M.

DR. YANG: M . . . this is our fifth session, and I'm afraid that we haven't been making much progress.

M: You finally called me M. I would say that's progress.

DR. YANG: Yes, but I'm afraid we haven't made much headway with your phobia.

M: Maybe I don't want to.

DR. YANG: Your husband is paying good money for these sessions— I think you should at least make use of them.

M: I understand that I have certain fears. But I don't want drugs. I don't want therapy. I have a fear of social contact, but I want to keep it that way. I don't want to change.

DR. YANG: Why not?

M: I have my reasons.

DR. YANG: Would you please humor me and perhaps share one of these reasons?

M: No.

DR. YANG: Let's talk about your family.

M: What do you want to know?

DR. YANG: Tell me something about them.

M: Okay. My mother. Was a woman. Korean.
    And my father. Was a man. Korean. How's that?

DR. YANG: Mrs.—M . . . this is most frustrating.

M: Why?

DR. YANG: This kind of resistance to change. I usually see it with hardened criminals. Not . . .

M: Housewives?

DR. YANG: Yes.

M: Wasn't it Shakespeare who said that nothing is as it seems?

DR. YANG: Mmmmm.

M: What, you don't know?

DR. YANG: It sounds right.

M: What kind of a psychiatrist are you? If you don't know your Shakespeare, how can you understand the human psyche? Even growing up in Korea, I devoured Shakespeare.

DR. YANG: I don't see how this has anything—

M: Remember *Macbeth*? I used to love that play. The way a normal person could just turn into a murderer . . . given the right circumstances.
    "Here's the smell of the blood still: all the perfumes of Arabia will not sweeten this little hand."

DR. YANG: Nice.

M: What's your favorite Shakespeare play?

DR. YANG: My favorite Shakespeare . . . Oh, I don't know . . . Probably, *Romeo and Juliet*, I guess.

M: Ahhh. Of course.

(Long silence.)

DR. YANG: I'm not sure I understand where you're going with this.

M: Where am I going? I'm not going anywhere. But you are.

DR. YANG: I am?

M: Yes. Out.

DR. YANG: Out?

M: Out, out, damned Dr. Yang.

DR. YANG: But.

M: I'll see you next week.

5. Mister Phnom Penh, Take One

A movie soundstage. Sound of bombs, heavy artillery fire. Jason as Mister Phnom Penh and Marilyn Part II are on the top of the U.S. Embassy waiting for the helicopters.

MISTER PHNOM PENH: Marilyn. I can't get over how much we have in common. I mean, here we are separated by two totally different cultures, divided by war, and yet we're sitting here sharing a mai tai.

MARILYN: Oh, is that what this is. Where'd you get this anyway? We're in the middle of a war-torn battlefield.

MISTER PHNOM PENH: I bring a portable bar with me wherever I go.

MARILYN: Oh, Mister Penh.

MISTER PHNOM PENH: Please. Call me Phnom.

MARILYN: I've never met a man who shared my common interest.

MISTER PHNOM PENH: You mean long walks by the river while the napalm fumes mix majestically with the setting sun?

MARILYN: No, thumb wrestling.

MISTER PHNOM PENH: Thumb wrestling?

MARILYN: And you're so competitive. I like that in a man.

MISTER PHNOM PENH: I have strong fingers, from playing piano.

MARILYN: Can you keep a secret?

MISTER PHNOM PENH: Of course.

MARILYN: One day . . . when we get out of this godforsaken heathen-gook country—

MISTER PHNOM PENH: This is where I grew up.

MARILYN: Oops. When we get back to the States, I mean . . .

MISTER PHNOM PENH: Yes?

MARILYN: I want to turn pro.

MISTER PHNOM PENH: Pro?

DIRECTOR (*Offstage*): CUT! WHAT THE HELL IS WITH ALL THIS IMPROVISING? THUMB WRESTLING? THERE'S NOTHING ABOUT WRESTLING, THUMB OR NON, ANYWHERE IN THE SCRIPT. THIS IS A FAMILY PICTURE, MARILYN. CAN WE JUST STICK TO THE SCRIPT, PLEASE?

MARILYN PART II: I'm sorry, Steven, I was just trying out a new idea.

DIRECTOR: Marilyn, darling, we have done everything we can so that you don't have to think at all. We've got the teleprompter and the cue cards. We even made sure the character's name is your actual name. You don't have to worry about motivation, so please, don't think. Just do. Be. That's all we need.

JASON: Any notes for me?

DIRECTOR: Yes. You need to get inside.

JASON: Inside where?

DIRECTOR: Exactly.

JASON: I'm not sure I understand—

DIRECTOR: That's a wrap for today. See you all tomorrow morning.

(*Jason and Marilyn Part II hang out while the film crew goes home. She pulls out a cigarette, can't find a light. Jason offers her a light.*)

JASON: You were pretty good up there.

MARILYN PART II: Thanks. I'm not afraid of heights.

JASON: No?

MARILYN PART II: Yeah. You know, when me and Leo were going out. We used to like to sneak into tall buildings and go up on the roof and—you know.

JASON: What happened with Leo?

MARILYN PART II: Too wrapped up in himself. Also, believe it or not, I'm kind of a private person. I like doing things at home. People don't believe that, but I do.

JASON: Like what kind of things?

MARILYN PART II: Ikebana. Chinese herbal medicines. Jujitsu. Stuff like that.

JASON: You're related to Marilyn Monroe somehow, right?

MARILYN PART II: Yeah. Somehow.

Steven explained it to me once, but I don't quite get it. Somehow they preserved some of her DNA and they digitized it and I guess that's how I came to be.

JASON: So a part of you is digital?

MARILYN PART II: Part of me is pure media. Like if you take an X-ray of me, I really don't have bones. It's more like wires. But they say it's why I'm a born actress. It makes me more photogenic somehow. And I'm really good at interviews. That's what they say anyway.

JASON: I specialize in media.

MARILYN PART II: Really?

JASON: Computers. My wif—we . . . I build computer chips. We have the fastest chips out there. I could build a special chip just for you. Reinstate some of your organs.

MARILYN PART II: Wow. That would be cool.

JASON: Yeah. Wouldn't it?

(They hesitate, then kiss lightly.)

MARILYN PART II: That's weird. I felt that.

JASON: What do you mean?

MARILYN PART II: Usually when I kiss someone, I don't really feel anything. Like somehow my circuits don't get connected. But you—you've really got me wired.

JASON: Must be my electrical engineering background.

MARILYN PART II: Ooooooh, say that again.

JASON: I specialized in systems with a minor in biophysics.

MARILYN PART II *(Getting excited)*: What else did you study?

JASON: UNIX. JAVA. C . . . Plus . . . Plus.

MARILYN PART II: Where have you been all my life?

JASON: Home. Watching you.

MARILYN PART II: You said you specialize in chips. How many megahertz can you handle?

JASON: I deal in gigahertz these days. And one day we'll achieve the Holy Grail of computing . . .

MARILYN PART II: You mean?

JASON: Yes. A terraflop chip.

MARILYN PART II: Really? How?

JASON: I have . . . the ch-ch-chi.

MARILYN PART II: The secret essence to our spirit. You have that?

JASON: Yes.

MARILYN PART II: Ohhhh . . . you're that Jason. Jason and the Astronauts.

JASON: Argonauts. My company is called Argonaut Systems Services.

MARILYN PART II: ASS?

JASON: Yeah.

MARILYN PART II: I'm very into mythology. I think it's because I've been raised on pure pop culture. Something inside me thirsts for more . . . history.

JASON: I was raised in a Confucian home.

MARILYN PART II: STOP! You're overheating my circuits. Whew.

(Pause.)

Wait a minute, aren't you married?

JASON: Uhhh. Yes. And No. Kind of.

MARILYN PART II: I don't take marriages all that seriously anyway. My mother was married, what, how many times?

JASON: I lose count.

MARILYN PART II: Exactly.

6. Value Meal

M at home. She opens the front door, stares at the world outside. She takes a step outside and starts to have a panic attack.

M *(Having attack)*:
>Don't
>Don't be afraid
>Don't be afraid of the dark

>I come here
>I came here
>I come here
>I came here

Come a speeding, come a screeching, bump . . . bump, airplane smell like plastic stale wet sock crammed into mouth and now

the cabin is rocking and a can of coca cola is spilling onto my lap and I feel sick to my toes and I feel I have to go to the bathroom and I go and the room is too cramped and I don't understand where to put the paper and the toilet flushes and all the air is sucked out of the little room

and I can't
and I can't breathe
for a moment

and I can't
and I can't breathe for a year

(She shuts the door, calms down as she comes back inside. She opens a page from her diary.)

only yesterday i was a little girl only yesterday i was a young woman falling in love with this strange man only yesterday i was a young bride only yesterday we landed in a strange airport it was like we had just woken from a dream the smog was clogging my nose i was scared i knew this would never be home to me i knew that the bright colors and neon and plastic would never welcome me completely but i had no choice i had divorced myself from my family my home my country that first night i ordered a big mac stared out at the street the endless noise and motion i was thinking of *the wizard of oz* one of my favorite movies how in the end oz was just a man behind a curtain i wanted to find the man behind this curtain maybe it was ronald mcdonald maybe he was the key behind everything or if he wasn't it was someone but who but who no one seemed to know i was sad that night sad as i ate my french fries because i was so alone alone with this man i really didn't know alone with a child on the way i looked back on myself my former life i couldn't see the shape of it anymore i couldn't tell what was real and what wasn't it was as if all of it had been written in sand and the water had washed it away.

7. Koreansomething

Jason, M and Jason Junior sit eating in silence.

JASON: This is good. Really good. Pork?

M: No.

JASON: Chicken?

M: No.

JASON: Whatever it is, it's really, really good.

M: It's Converse.

JASON: What's that?

M: A new kind of meat.

JASON: Yeah? Like Spam?

M: Something like that. Tomorrow's Puma.

JASON: Whatever it is, I like it.

(*Pause.*)

M: How's the movie?

JASON: Going well. Lotta work. I had no idea about the hours they put in. I mean, I have a lot more respect for movie stars now. You think all they do is do drugs and screw around, and maybe they do, but they do work hard. They deserve all the perks they get.

M: You get in really late every night.

JASON: I gotta, honey. I'm the new kid on the block. How's school, Junior?

JUNIOR: Okay.

JASON: You picking up any sports or anything?

JUNIOR: Math team.

JASON: Math team? Ugh. Was that your teacher's idea?

JUNIOR: No.

JASON: Anything else?

JUNIOR: I'm thinking of joining the gun club.

JASON: The gun club?

M: Can you believe that?

JASON: You mean, you learn about guns and the history and all that stuff?

JUNIOR: No, they give you a Glock 9 and you go out to the range and practice.

M: I think it's horrible, we should write a letter to the school board.

JASON: Now, honey, we live in different times now. Who came up with this idea anyway?

JUNIOR: Charlton Heston visited our school and said if more school kids were armed, there would be less violence and stuff. So they started this club. Can I go? I'm done.

JASON: Sure.

(Junior starts to exit.)

Junior.
JUNIOR: Yeah?
JASON: Give me a hug.

(After a moment, they embrace.)

JUNIOR: Is this your sweet good-byes?
JASON: What does that mean?
JUNIOR: Nothing.
JASON: Now don't go bringing an uzi home, alright?
JUNIOR: Yeah. Haha. Funny.

(Junior shuffles out.)

JASON: He still loves me doesn't he?
M: Uh-huh.
JASON: He doesn't show it, but I can tell.
M: So.
JASON: So.
M: Do you have anything to tell me?
JASON: Me? No. What?

(Pause.)

I could tell you about the movie.
M: I don't want to hear about the movie.
JASON: How was your session with Dr. Yang?
M: Fine.
JASON: Did you say anything?
M: No, not really.
JASON: Look, you have to work with me, here. The other shrink didn't work out, so I got you this one, a Korean one.
M: I told you I don't want any shrink.
JASON: Well, I want you to get over this . . . this . . .
M: What? Problem? There's no problem, okay, I can't help it if I feel overwhelming guilt all the time. Or that I can't talk to other people about it. I don't want to talk to other people about it. I'd like to talk to you about it, but you never want to.
JASON: We've talked about it. Over and over. I don't see the point of dwelling in the past. You did what you had to do. I did what I had to do. No, it wasn't pretty. But look at the alternatives.

M: I've been seeing him.

JASON: Who?

M: You know damn well who!

JASON: Where?

M: Around the house.

JASON: Yeah, what does he say?

M: He doesn't. He just stares at me. You can see how that can be disturbing.

JASON: I need to go.

M: Go ahead. Run. Like you usually do.

JASON: Stop blaming me. I didn't kill your brother. If anything, your father is the one to blame. He was so against me that we had to do something extreme to be together.

M: Don't drag my father into this!

JASON: You're protecting him? After he's disowned you? After we basically have to live in the witness protection program to get away from him?

M: Don't you realize what I've done for you? I have nothing anymore. Everyone, everything died for me the day we left Seoul.

JASON: We're not in Seoul anymore. We're here. This is our home. We have to make things work here. We can't turn back the clock.

M: It's easy for you to forget. You can always move on to the next thing. The next hobby.

JASON: This movie is more than a—

M: You smell different at night. You smell like perfume.

8. Mister Phnom Penh, Take Two

A movie soundstage. Sound of helicopters continues. The scene in which the U.S. Embassy falls is being filmed. There is considerable wind and noise on stage.

MISTER PHNOM PENH: Wait, Marilyn—come back!

> (*Marilyn Part II is hanging from a ladder that is connected to the helicopter.*)

MARILYN: I'm sorry Mister Penh.

MISTER PHNOM PENH: Please, call me Phnom.

MARILYN: Phnom. I can't stay here with you.

MISTER PHNOM PENH: But, but . . .

MARILYN: What?

MISTER PHNOM PENH: What about our love for each other?

MARILYN: What?

MISTER PHNOM PENH: Our love for each other!

MARILYN: I CAN'T HEAR YOU!

MISTER PHNOM PENH: OUR FUCKING LOVE FOR EACH OTHER!

MARILYN: Oh, that. Maybe I can best express it in a song.

(To the tune of "Memories":)

It's tooooooo baaaaaaaaaaaad
We aren't both Ameriiiiiiican

It's kinda saaaaaaaaaaaad
That I have to gooooooooo

But I'm not
Meant for rice fields and bombs

Watch out Phnom
Here one comes

(She ducks. There is a deafening explosion.)

Saigon iiiiis falliiiiiiiiing
Saigon iiiiis in flames
But soon this will come to pass
'Cuz I'm good at saving my ass

MISTER PHNOM PENH: NO! I won't let you leave!

(He pulls out a pistol.)

MARILYN: No, don't kill yourself! Please, PHNOM!

MISTER PHNOM PENH: You fool! I want to kill you!

(He takes a wild shot at her, but misses.)

MARILYN: I'm sorry it had to end this way. Let me say good-bye in song again.

(To the tune of "Happy Birthday":)

Sayonaraaaaaaa to you
Sayonaraaaaaaaa to you
Sayonaraaaaaaaa to you . . .

MISTER PHNOM PENH: NOOOOOOOOOOOO!
DIRECTOR: CUT!

(Lights and wind die down.)

ALRIGHT, WHO FUCKED UP THE LIGHTS? I SAID
I WANTED HONEY-TONED SKIN. YOU THINK THAT'S
HONEY-TONED SKIN? THAT'S SHIT-TONED SKIN! WE
ALREADY HAVE ENOUGH TROUBLE WITH THE ACTING,
NOT YOU MARILYN, THE LAST THING WE NEED IS
BAD LIGHTING. THEIR SKIN SHOULD BE SO GOLDEN
SWEET THAT YOU WANNA STICK YOUR TONGUE OUT
AND LICK IT. HONEY-TONED. GET IT? SOMEONE GET
ME AN OMELETTE, I'M STARVING.

9. Dissonance

*M alone, washing her face in front of a basin. Chorus echoes words
indicated in bold.*

M:

I miss my family—
I miss
I miss my country—
I miss my

Beyond hate right now
Beyond citizenship
Skin
Hair
Eyes

Beyond waiting for him to come home
Beyond smelling another woman on him
Beyond love
Beyond beyond

167

I used to have a name
I used to be
    MikyungMinsunMinjungMinaMiriamMadelineMedea
Something like that
But then I came here
And I lost things
Innocence. Hope. LETTERS.
Vowels. Consonants. Gone.
I was left with one letter.
"M."
Just M.

You can describe a wave
But you can't be the wave

In the end the wave
rides its troughs and crests

and is gone

I burned bridges
For him
I burned
For
I
him
For
him
I
him
I
him
I
burned
burn
burrr
brrrr . . .

(We transition into a flashback. We are in Korea, several years ago.
    Two pools of light: one with M, one with her brother. Both of
them face out to the audience. It is night. M's brother is in bed.
    M stands watching her brother sleep. He opens his eyes.)

BROTHER: What're you doing?

M: I don't know.

BROTHER: What time is it?

M: Uhmmm . . . late.

BROTHER: Something wrong?

M: No.

Yes.

Maybe.

BROTHER: You're stealing our family ch— . . . You are, aren't you?

M: I have to.

BROTHER: I have to stop you.

M: I know.

That's why I'm here.

Sorry.

BROTHER: For what?

(He stares into her eyes.)

Oh.

(Pause.)

You don't have to.

M: I know. But I do.

BROTHER: For him?

M: For me.

(M pulls out a knife. She makes a swift upward slash. Her brother's shirt becomes drenched in blood. M bows her head. Lights out on M. Her brother slowly gets up—)

BROTHER: In the morning, our father discovered my body. Our father was so overcome—with grief, rage, shock—he had a stroke, was dead within a week. Our mother retreated from the world. She became a ghost. Our family withered away that day.

It was my sister's plan. She knew that killing me would distract them, make them stop chasing.

But she had to be sure. Or maybe he did. So they cut my body up. Chopped it into pieces. Dumped them. Into the Han River. They knew that my father would take the time. He would look. He would try to recover every piece. Of me. They knew.

When I looked into my sister's eyes that night. I saw water . . . waves . . . surf. She had already left. She was already looking ahead. I could see that she was doing it all out of love. She had no control. She was being pulled out by the tide, and she knew . . . she knew it would all end badly.

They escaped in a boat. They made it to Japan, then hopped on a plane. To that other country.

(He slowly slumps back into bed.)

Act Two: Convergence

1. Node

A TV announcer.

ANNOUNCER: In entertainment, Marilyn Part II has a new love in her life. The twentysomething bombshell has been seen around town with newcomer . . . uh, what's his name again . . . that Asian Guy, anyway, it's her co-star in the upcoming blockbuster *Mister Phnom Penh*. Marilyn, who is this new man in your life?

MARILYN PART II: He's incredibly talented. In fact, he's PHE-Nom-enal!

ANNOUNCER: Here we see the hot new couple at a karaoke club together.

(Jason sings two lines from the song "Desperado" by the Eagles.)

Marilyn was coy about the couple's future plans.

MARILYN PART II: Well, okay, it was supposed to be a secret, 'cuz there's like his wife and stuff, but yes—we are engaged to be engaged. Do you like my ring? It's infused with the ch-ch-chi. Oops. Can you edit that out?

(Crossfade to M watching TV. She stares at the screen for a long time, then pulls out a pistol and empties several rounds into the TV. It explodes.)

M: Guess it runs in the family.

2. Particles

M is emboldened to venture down the street to a bus stop.

M:

I'm tired of being invisible
I'm tired of just being me
Me is just me
I want to be her
I want to be him
Then they'll talk
Then they'll say "look at her/him"
Isn't that her/him?

What
　　　　What am I
　　　　　　What am I about to
　　　　　　　　　　　　　　do
　　　　　　to about I am what
　　　　　I am what
What
What
What

(She's interrupted by the Wavemaker, who is posing as a homeless guy sleeping near the bus stop bench. He startles M and makes her very uneasy.)

WAVEMAKER: Whine, whine, whine.
M: What?
WAVEMAKER: You heard me.
M: I wasn't talking to you.
WAVEMAKER: You were talking weren't you?
M: To myself.
WAVEMAKER: Your words violated my airspace. So I can respond can't I?
M: But I don't want any response.
WAVEMAKER: You think you're a real big shot, don't you? If you have so many problems with this country, go back to where you came from.

M: Why don't you?

WAVEMAKER: Because I'm from here.

M: No one's from here. There's no here to speak of, for one thing.

WAVEMAKER: I'm one hundred percent American. My father's father's father's father's father's father's father's—How many was that?

M: I don't know.

WAVEMAKER: Doesn't matter. Should be like seventeen. Fathers born here. We were here before the Indians, before the Eskimos, before Time itself. So I don't have to go anywhere. This is where I come from. So you just go back.

M: Before Time?

WAVEMAKER: Yeah. I'm part Glacier, see? I was part of the molten lava that spewed forth when the tectonic plates were grinding against each other. I'm part tectonic, baby, I was born from the friction of those plates, those geophysical thighs rubbing, heating things up, firing up the rocks and soil with their lava lust. Until all America broke loose, understand, until dreams were spewing forth in pressurized steam, forced through the cracks and crevices of stalactite. That's where I'm from.

M: Okay. But I'm here now. I'm a citizen.

WAVEMAKER: I don't care. You complain. You whine. Get out. If you can't stand the heat, get the hell out of the cineplex. A famous American said that. Like Andy Warhol, some politician like that.

M: What are you doing here anyway?

WAVEMAKER: I lost my job.

M: Oh yeah?

WAVEMAKER: Used to be a professor.

M: What did you teach?

WAVEMAKER: Wave/particle duality. The scientists talk about light and quantum theory and all that shit. But I'm talking about people. You and me. Take love for instance. That's a particular kind of wave. You can see the shape of that. Or say I'm eating a Big Mac. Now that's another type of wave. So all of us have like millions of waves going on, all at once, resonating, going up, down, crossing each other out, creating weird peaks and resonances.

M: And the particles?

WAVEMAKER: Every once in awhile all those waves kind of happen to be resonating with the same frequency, and they all build up together, and they become this huge pulse, this huge packet of energy.

M: It's an interesting theory.

WAVEMAKER: It ain't no theory. It's the truth.

M: How do you know?

WAVEMAKER: How? 'Cuz I do.

Why? 'Cuz I am.

What? 'Cuz I be.

'Cuz I'm a wavemaker.

M: Okaaaay.

WAVEMAKER: 'Cuz I hear the water laughing. The H—2—
OOOOOOOOOO-HO-HO-HO-HO.

M: Yeah. I know all about that.

WAVEMAKER: You've heard it too?

M (*Remembering*): One morning. I was in a boat. It was far away
from here.

(*Wavemaker circles M, examining her.*)

WAVEMAKER: Oh, yeah. Mmmmmmm. Yup. That's what I thought.
You got both things going on right now.

M: What things?

WAVEMAKER: You got waves . . .

(*He makes the wave motion with his hand.*)

and you got particles.

(*He makes a fist.*)

You got it all goin' on, I'd be careful if I were you.

M: Careful?

WAVEMAKER: You got turbulence all in your face. After turbulence
comes violence. After violence comes tragedy.

M: Why are you saying this, why?

WAVEMAKER: Just saying what I see.

M: THIS IS WHY I NEVER LEAVE THE HOUSE! WHERE THE
HELL DO PEOPLE LIKE YOU COME FROM?

WAVEMAKER: Shit, people like you is why I stay out here.

3. Uncertainty Principles

*Junior is playing videogames. M goes to him and sits next to him. They
both stare at the screen. Silence. Suddenly Junior stops.*

JUNIOR: Mom?

M: Yeah?

JUNIOR: Why are you all wet?

M: I went outside.

JUNIOR: You did?

M: Yes.

JUNIOR: How was it?

M: I met a wavemaker.

JUNIOR: A who?

M: It was just to the bus stop, but it was progress. I guess.

(*Pause.*)

JUNIOR: You wanna play?

M: Uhhh . . . sure.

(*They play together for awhile.*)

JUNIOR: You're better than Dad.

M: Yeah?

JUNIOR: Dad sucks at this game.

M: Yeah, Dad sucks.

JUNIOR: Mom—

M: What?

JUNIOR: Nothing.

(*Pause.*)

You're gripping the controller too tight.

M: I am?

JUNIOR: See, you have to let it flow.

M: Yes.

Flow.

Yes.

(*She relaxes.*)

Oh. This is fun.

JUNIOR: Hey, you cleared a level. Now go pick up the extra weapons. The uzi. The grenade launcher. The titanium knife. Cool. You're good, Mom.

(*M becomes engrossed in the game.*
Junior is thinking.)

Mom?

M (*Distracted*): Mmmm?

JUNIOR: Can I ask you a question?

M: Sure . . .

JUNIOR: How come you and Dad never talk about the past?

M: The past?

JUNIOR: Yeah. Like, you know, our history.

M (*Blasting away*): WHY . . . WON'T . . . HE . . . DIE? YES! Next
   victim.

JUNIOR: Sometimes it feels like our family is an island. Like Korea.

M: Korea is a peninsula, honey.

JUNIOR: Oh yeah.

M: Sandwiched between China and Japan. So we were always getting invaded.

JUNIOR: Mmmm. Is that why it's always a war at home?

4. Electrons

M and Jason are in the middle of a fight.

M: I despise your petty desires, your dick stuck between countries.
   Your silly grasp towards a deeper identity. "Who Am I?" you
   ask in that whining voice. WHO THE FUCK CARES? Nobody.
   I renounce you as I would one of the Japanese soldiers taking
   my father to one of the work camps. Taking my mother to be a
   comfort woman. Face it. You're no more American than a bowl
   of kimchee stew, hot and fermented, opening your nostrils to
   the pigmented pigskin of your fucked up identity crisis.

JASON: Do what I do. I reoriental myself. I see life in a different way.
   I see beyond the bad memories clogging your pores. I hire a web
   designer and airbrush history into oblivion.

M: You've fallen for the Silicon Valley Girl. Blonde thing with Intel
   breasts, ass by Microsoft, legs by Pixar. Mmmm.

JASON: It's not a personal thing. I explained this to you. (*Aside*)
   I hope she hasn't been reading my blog.

M: I guess I'm just too old school. I'm analog. You're digital. I'm
   Chinese characters. Pre–Steve Jobs. I'm pre-Gutenberg. Pre–
   pen and ink. I think in pictograms.

JASON: I Googled myself the other day. I got chills.

M: You're an ass, you know that? Have you given any thought to our . . . your . . . my son?

JASON: When he's grown up a little, I think he'll understand. I know this is hard, for all of us. But I'm doing this for him in a way.

M: How do you figure that?

JASON: I'm trying to make it a better world for him to grow up in. I'm trying to open doors for him. It's just a movie, but it will have a ripple effect: tearing down barriers, shattering myths. There will be more opportunities for our people—the delivery boys, the sweatshop workers, the accountants—for the generations that come after us, so that we can truly fulfill the dream of this country, the dream that has drawn millions of immigrants to these shores. In the words of Emma Lazarus, "Give me your tired, your poor, your huddled masses, yearning to see their name in lights."

M: I miss the ocean. You remember when we used to go there on the weekends? We would take long walks on the beach.

JASON: We ran into the water.

M: It was night. Dark.

JASON: You dared me to dive in. And I did.

M: No, you didn't.

JASON: I did.

M: You didn't. You were afraid of dealing with things. Even then.

JASON: Look, I didn't plan this.

M: Is that supposed to make me feel better?

JASON: I never stopped loving you. I still love you.

M: I thought she was making wedding plans.

JASON: That was just the media blowing everything out of proportion.

M: So now it's the media's fault?

JASON: You know they distort everything.

M: Chinky and Gooky don't.

JASON: They don't?

M: Well, they do, but underneath, they don't.

JASON: See, that's the difference between us. I'm trying to take our people to the next level and you're talking about Chinky and Gooky.

M: Our people? So now you're Moses?

JASON: I see that you don't understand.

M: I'm trying. Make me understand.

JASON: You know how it can be really sunny outside, when all of a sudden you're caught in a flash thunderstorm. Then just as fast it came, the storm leaves. So now it's sunny again, but it's still wet and the whole world feels out of balance, like everything is standing on its head.

M: What the hell are you talking about?

JASON: It's like I've fallen into a dream. And I'm not sure I want to wake up.

M: I don't dream anymore, because I can't even fall asleep. Don't you see? My nightmare is always happening, replaying before my eyes like a horror film that I can't stop.

JASON: My heart is still yours.

M: I don't want your heart. That's just an outlying province, a coastal city. No. I want the whole country. I'm not interested in a colony. Or being colonized. I want democracy. Or at least monarchy.

JASON: Sometimes anarchy is more natural.

M: Riots.

JASON: Passion.

M: Chaos.

JASON: Freedom.

M: Violence.

(*Pause.*)

JASON: Remember, no one else knows what we went through to get to this point, this very moment in space and time. No one ever will. So no matter what happens, know this: I love you.

M:

I . . .
I love . . .
Yes. Still.

I had gotten you a present. For your new career. I was going to throw it away. But you should have it.

JASON: You sure?

M: I know how you have a lot of gun scenes in the movie. You are "Mister Phnom Penh" after all. So I got you this—

(*She produces a beautiful handgun.*)

It's handmade.

JASON: Wow. Hugo Boss. Thank you.

(Pause.)

I'm overwhelmed.

M: This is specially made for stage and film work. I hear that Chow Yun-Fat has one. And Robert De Niro.

JASON *(Holding the gun)*: It has great balance. It's so light. I feel like I'm holding a Stradivarius.

M: Try to make it sing.

JASON: I will. I'll make you proud. I promise.

M *(Aside)*:

I
I feel
I feel so
I feel so cold.

(She exits.

Jason is in love with his new gun. He plays with different ways of holding it. He tries different ways of holstering the gun—in his pants, from the back, from his socks, etc. He imitates Travis Bickle from Taxi Driver . . . *)*

JASON *(As Bickle)*: You talking to me? You talking to me?

(He pulls his gun out—it clatters to the floor. He tries once again.)

You talking to me?

(Crossfade to the sound of videogame gunfire and Jason Junior playing a violent videogame.)

JUNIOR: What're you doing, Dad?

JASON: Uhhh, nothing.

JUNIOR: Why are you acting like Travis Bickle?

JASON: I don't know what you're talking about.

(Pause.)

What game is this?

JUNIOR: *K.S. 6.*

JASON: K.S.?

JUNIOR: Kill Spree.

JASON: Lovely. Who got you this game again?

JUNIOR: You did. For Christmas.

JASON: Right. What was I thinking?

JUNIOR: Yeah, Dad, what were you thinking?

JASON: What's the difference between *K.S. 6* and *K.S. 5*?

JUNIOR: When you shoot someone in *K.S. 5* they get blown to bits but it's kind of mechanical. But in *K.S. 6* they make these facial expressions.

JASON: Uh-huh.

JUNIOR: It, like, makes you feel bad.

JASON: And that's fun?

JUNIOR: Sure. What's the point of hurting someone without seeing them show it.

JASON: I can't argue with you there.

    Son, we need to talk.

    Look. I don't know if you heard, but your mother and I are . . . you know, when you get older, you'll understand, I mean . . . what I'm trying to say is . . .

JUNIOR: Dad . . . I know. Don't worry. I'm a big boy.

JASON: Alright. Whew. I'm glad we had this talk.

JUNIOR (*Rolling his eyes*): Yeah, me too.

(*Pause.*)

    So is she good?

JASON: What?

(*Pause.*)

JUNIOR: Mom.

JASON: She's a tough woman, son. She's . . . we're all gonna get through this fine.

JUNIOR: Yeah.

JASON: Can I play . . .

(*Junior ignores him.*)

    Son . . . ?

JUNIOR: Lemme finish.

JASON: Come on, let your . . .

JUNIOR: Hold on.

JASON: LET YOUR FATHER PLAY!

(Beat.)

JUNIOR: Here.

(Hands Jason the controller. He plays.)

JASON: Everything alright with school?

JUNIOR: Yeah.

JASON: What's your favorite subject these days?

JUNIOR: I don't know.

JASON: We haven't gone fishing in awhile, have we?

JUNIOR: Dad, we've never gone fishing.

JASON: Yes, we have.

JUNIOR: No. We bought all the equipment, but you had a business meeting and we had to cancel.

JASON: Well, we'll definitely go soon.

JUNIOR: Sure.

JASON: Son. Believe it or not, I understand how you feel. I do. I know you're angry. Not just at me, but the whole world. Okay, maybe you're angry at me most. I've been angry too. When I was your age. And even now. In fact, I may be more angry now. But it's an anger that's deep in my bones. You know how your mother marinates the beef for hours and hours, until the sauce gets deep inside the meat? That's how it is with me. The anger has seeped into everything I do. I live it, breathe it. The same anger you feel is why I'm doing what I'm doing.

JUNIOR: What *are* you doing?

JASON: What am I doing?

JUNIOR: Yeah.

JASON: I'm trying to move forward, son. I'm trying to move all of us forward. Not sideways. Not backwards. Forward.

JUNIOR: Uh-huh. Can I see your gun?

JASON: Sure.

(He hands him the gun. Junior looks it over, checks the chamber. For a moment, he points the gun at his father.)

JUNIOR: You had the safety off. Now you're all set.

(He hands the gun back.)

JASON: Thank you.

(*Beat.*)

How am I doing?

JUNIOR: Alright.

JASON: Just alright?

JUNIOR: Mom's a lot better than you.

JASON: She is?

JUNIOR: Yeah, Mom could kick your . . . she's better.

JASON (*Seeing the reaction in the game*): Whoa! I see what you mean. This makes me feel terrible.

JUNIOR: Yeah. Isn't it fun?

(*Jason hands controller back to Junior.*)

5. Chinky and Gooky Redux

Another episode of The Chinky and Gooky Show.

CHINKY: It's us again.

GOOKY: I'm Chinky.

CHINKY: No, I'm Chinky.

GOOKY: That's right. I'm Gooky.

CHINKY: AND THIS IS . . .

BOTH: *The Chinky and Gooky Show!*

CHINKY: So, today we talk about things important from ancient time, but still have big meaning today. Myth.

GOOKY: Yes. We look at identity and value of young women today. Very hard to be young woman these days.

CHINKY: Young woman?

GOOKY: That's right, you say we talk about Miss. Young woman.

CHINKY: No, no, myth. Not miss.

GOOKY: That's what I said.

CHINKY: Aiyayai—it's like you eating with just one chopstick sometime, you know?

GOOKY: So I make mistake. Nobody perfect.

CHINKY: Ang Lee is.

GOOKY: True.

CHINKY: Let's look at myth number one.

GOOKY: Meeees Numba One!

CHINKY: Da flute.

GOOKY: Yes. Every time we see yellow face on TV or movie, what happen?

CHINKY: We hear some flute music come out nowhere. Like I think, where the fuck that flute player come from?

GOOKY: He hiding in the closet?

CHINKY: Even on CNN the other day, they do story about China, and this flute music come from nowhere. So let's get this straight. Most Asians don't play flute. For instance, I don't play flute. Gooky?

GOOKY: Yes?

CHINKY: Do you play flute?

GOOKY: I play clarinet.

CHINKY: Okay. But no flute, right?

GOOKY: I ain't no pie piper.

CHINKY: Alright. Let's look at another myth now. Math wizard.

GOOKY: Yes. You know you in math class in junior high school okay, like every time there's a test, why is the person sitting next to you asking for your answers? I'm not born to be good at math.

CHINKY: Gooky, what's two plus two?

GOOKY: FIVE!

CHINKY: What's derivative of sine wave?

GOOKY: FUCK YOU!

CHINKY: What's A squared plus B squared?

GOOKY: Fool! That's Pythagorean theorem—oops, I mean, A SQUARED MY ASS!

CHINKY: Okay, well, maybe Gooky's good at math.

GOOKY: Hey, we forgot another meeeth. The model minority myth.

CHINKY: Ahhh, an oldie but a goodie!

GOOKY: Okay, we know there are a lot of stereotypes out there: blacks are all homeboy!

CHINKY: Latinos—good lovers . . .

GOOKY: But Asians—good SATs.

CHINKY: Now, some Asians get mad about this.

GOOKY: They say, hey, stop putting me in accounting department.

CHINKY: The problem is, Gangbanga—bad, but cool, stereotype. Latin Lover—bad, but cool, stereotype. Model minority—not same thing. We need your help. We need to work at glassroots level. We need more of you Asians to create bad, but cool, stereotype.

GOOKY: We need more Asian crack dealers.

CHINKY: More lazy Asian.

GOOKY: More evil Asian.

CHINKY: It's not like you not out there. Gooky, your mother, for instance—

GOOKY: Don't go there, Chinky.

(Beat.)

CHINKY: Okay, we have CNN do big special on bad Asians.

GOOKY: We hire Jethro Tull play flute music soundtrack.

CHINKY: Then we achieve ultimate achievement in American society—

GOOKY: Big house?

CHINKY: No.

GOOKY: Big dick?

CHINKY: No! BIGGEST VICTIM STATUS—

(M walks into the studio and sits down next to Chinky and Gooky.)

M: Hi!

(Pause.)

GOOKY: Okay—it look like we take commercial break—we be light back, okay?

CHINKY: Don't touch that dial, or we come to you house and rearrange all the furniture, screw up your feng shui.

(Pause.)

How you get in here?

M: I've been watching you guys every morning. I'm sick of watching. I want to play a more active role. I want to be a part of Chinky and Gooky.

GOOKY: Excuse me?

CHINKY: You want to be us?

GOOKY: She clazhee.

CHINKY: Too much bird nest in her soup.

M: I even came up with my own name: "Slanty." *(Singing)* "It's the *Chinky, Gooky, and Slanty Show!*" What do you think?

GOOKY: Let me say this nice way: NO!

CHINKY: Also, Slanty a little, how shall I say, OFFENSIVE?

M: Offensive?

GOOKY: Yaaaah, I agree, not PC. Not Mac either.

M: Chinky and Gooky are okay, but Slanty's not?

CHINKY: It's subtle difference. Like difference in Szechuan or Hunan, McDonald's or Burger King. But people who know, they know.

GOOKY: Anyway, doesn't sound right. "Chinky and Gooky." That sound good. Balanced. Like Yin . . . Yang, moo shoo . . . pork, Lennon . . . McCartney. But "Chinky and Gooky and Slanty" . . .

CHINKY: Unbalanced.

GOOKY: Bad chi. No good for my Tae-Bo.

M: It doesn't make sense. Can I talk to one of your producers? Can't I at least audition?

GOOKY *(Dropping accent)*: Look, lady, we're trying to be nice, but we don't have time for this now—it's sweeps season—I'm in the middle of changing antidepressants—so would you please get the hell off our set!

(Pause.)

M: Hey . . . what happened to your accent?

GOOKY *(Resuming accent)*: Excuse me?

(He starts coughing.)

CHINKY: He have flu, you know, there are arrergies in this studio too—

M: He lost his accent!

GOOKY: SECULITY! CAN I HAVE SECULITY PREASE!

(Gooky and Chinky try to get security, but then M's meltdown makes them stop and watch.)

M: You guys are fucking frauds! Oh my God . . . I trusted you . . . You two were the last ones . . . but even you . . . now I'm realizing. Now it's all making sense. Evolution is a cruel joke, and the punch line makes you laugh so hard it hurts. I don't blame you. I forgive you in fact. Oh my . . . oh my . . .

OH SAY CAN YOU SEE the waves of rolling Viagra/Nothing comes between me and my MTV/JerryRegisEllenDaveConan O-O-OOOOOOOOOOOOOOprah/two all beef patties special BY THE DAWN'S EARLY Whopper SUPERSIZE ME BABY! DAAAA Big King Big Mac Big One Big Momma Big Daddy Notorious B.I.G. Big Killer Big Opening Big Movie Big Star Big Dick Big Tits Big Big Big Big Biggity DAAAA BIG BANG EXPLODING FUCKING UNIVERSE CREATION OF ALL TIME AND SPACE ATOMS SQUEEZING INTO ELECTRONS INTO QUARKS FLAVORS CHARMS—OH MOMMMMMMMMMA—OH MY FUCKING HEAD!

(M collapses. Chinky and Gooky aren't sure what to do.)

GOOKY: You okay?

M: What happened?

CHINKY: You said all this stuff. Then you passed out.

M: Right. I think I feel better now.

GOOKY: You want us call ambulance?

M: No. I think I'll be okay. Thank you. Really.

(She stumbles out.)

GOOKY *(Accentless)*: That was weird.

CHINKY *(Accentless)*: Yeah.

GOOKY: You think that's a sign?

CHINKY: Of what?

GOOKY: To move on.

CHINKY: No.

GOOKY: I'm serious. Maybe we've been fooling ourselves. I keep thinking, I'm just doing this till something better comes along. But maybe nothing will. Maybe this is it. My fiancée told me she loved me the other day, and you know what I said? "I rove you too." You see? I don't want to be Gooky my whole life. I don't know what I'm doing anymore.

CHINKY: You shouldn't have dropped your accent in front of her. That was totally unprofessional.

GOOKY: At least I have an accent to drop.

CHINKY: Hey, I went to Juilliard. I studied with George Takei for four fucking years.

GOOKY: Maybe you should have studied harder.

(A buzzer sounds. They're back on camera. Both resume accents.)

CHINKY: And we're back.

GOOKY: We sorry about that little interruption few minute ago. We so popular, we have many admirer.

CHINKY: Yes, sometime they admire us too much. Then they become stalker.

GOOKY: Yes . . . next week we have vely special guest. It's secret, but I give you hint.

CHINKY: Once I love someone too much. His name was Bob. I become stalker too.

GOOKY: Tiger hiding. Dragon crouching. Ehhhh?

CHINKY: I do nothing too bad. Just ring his bell and set his car on fire. That's all.

GOOKY: Uhhh, Chinky?

CHINKY: We have new book in bookstores next week! *Chinky and Gooky Guide to Tofu.*

GOOKY: Most people think tofu only for eating.

CHINKY: We show you other use for tofu. Like when you putting new tile in bathroom. Good for caulking.

GOOKY: Or you have headache or tired eyes? Tofu mask.

CHINKY: Just nineteen ninety-five. So cheap even Gooky can afford it.

GOOKY: Ha-ha, funny. We say good-bye for now.

BOTH: Bye bye!

6. Tangent Wave

M is being detained by The Chinky and Gooky Show *security guards. Dr. Yang shows up to take M back home.*

DR. YANG: Hello, M.

M: Hello, Dr. Yang.

DR. YANG: Your husband couldn't come.

M: He's busy.

DR. YANG: Should I take you home?

M: They're not pressing charges?

DR. YANG: No. Someone talked to them.

M: Who?

DR. YANG: I don't know the details, but someone spoke on your behalf and they're letting you go.

M: Hmmm. I hope it wasn't Jason.

DR. YANG: I have no idea who it was.

M: I'd almost rather stay if it was him.

DR. YANG: Please, M.

M: Are you proud of me at least?

DR. YANG: Proud?

M: Yes. I had a breakthrough. I made it out of my house, even past the bus stop. I actually rode the bus. I was on television even. Just for a few seconds.

DR. YANG: This isn't quite what I had in mind.

M: Well, it felt good to me. I had a meltd . . . a discussion with Chinky and Gooky. It helped. It cleared my head. So I want to thank you.

DR. YANG: But I've done nothing but come to your house and sit in silence for hours on end.

M: Silence is highly undervalued these days.

DR. YANG: Shall I take you home?

M: Please.

DR. YANG: I do notice a slight change in you, I must admit.

M: I think I'm free, Dr. Yang.

DR. YANG: Free?

M: Yes, I've been in a muddle all these years. The past was swallowing me whole. I doubted everything. My life, my family, my . . . self. But the past is washing out of me. I only have the now. This very moment. I don't have to be paralyzed. I can fight back. I can do something.

DR. YANG: And what is that?

M: I'm not sure yet. But something . . . something.

DR. YANG: I don't want you to do something rash.

M: Life is all about doing something rash. Without it, we're just puddles, waiting for something exciting to happen.

DR. YANG: I'm not sure I agree.

M: You're satisfied with being a puddle, Dr. Yang?

DR. YANG: I don't consider myself to be a puddle.

M: You're more like a pond. A little one. Calm. Maybe a few fish swimming around in it. A little bit of scum and algae floating around. But very very still.

DR. YANG: You obviously have a high opinion of me.

M: Don't you want to be the ocean instead? Don't you want towering waves crashing onto the shore? The wind in your face, the salt and foam?

DR. YANG: I can't swim.

M: I can teach you.

DR. YANG: I have a better idea. Let me take you home.

M: But that's just it, don't you see. I'm already home. All this time I've been afraid to leave. But I already left. So when I go outside I'm not really leaving, I'm arriving. Instead of saying good-bye, I should say hello.

DR. YANG: Hello?

M: Good-bye.

7. Mister Phnom Penh, Take Three

Movie soundstage. The same scene in which the U.S. Embassy falls, as before.

Jason pulls out a pistol.

MARILYN: No, don't kill yourself! Please, Phnom!

MISTER PHNOM PENH: This is for you, dumbass.

MARILYN: I have faith in you, Phnom. I know that your Confucian values would never allow you to kill an innocent woman like myself.

MISTER PHNOM PENH: Good-bye, Marilyn. If I can't have you, no one can.

MARILYN: Wait! Remember how it was when we first met?

(To the tune of "Maria":)

The most beautiful sound in the world
I ever heard
Phnom
Say it loud, and it's like lemongrass boiling
Say it soft, and it's like bulgogi broiling
Phnom, Phnom, Phnom,
Phn-e-no-mh . . .

(Jason blasts her with his gun.
Marilyn screams, falls off the helicopter and bursts into flames.)

MISTER PHNOM PENH *(To the tune of "Oh, What a Beautiful Morning")*:

I've got an imperialist feeeeeeling
I've got a Kissinger viiiiiiibe
I've got an Asian domino theoorrrrrryy
Everything's going my waaaaay—aaaay!

DIRECTOR *(Offstage, talking through a megaphone)*: CUT!

(Sound and movie lights cut out. Jason goes to where Marilyn had fallen and looks for her body. All he finds is a CD-ROM disc. This is what Marilyn has been reduced to.)

JASON: What the hell?

DIRECTOR *(Offstage)*: Jason, where's Marilyn?

JASON: I don't know.

DIRECTOR: What do you mean you don't know?

JASON: She fell. But there's no body. There's only this.

DIRECTOR: What the hell is that?

JASON: It's a disc.

DIRECTOR: What kind of disc?

JASON: I think it's a CD-ROM.

DIRECTOR: Don't fuck with me, Jason.

JASON: I'm not fucking with you! Look!

DIRECTOR: Let me see your gun. (*Jason hands the Director his gun*)
Your gun is very unique.

JASON: Yes, it's Hugo Boss.

DIRECTOR: Not only that, it has an electromagnetic distortion device built into it.

JASON: It was a gift from my wife.

DIRECTOR: I didn't know you were married.

JASON: Yeah, well . . . you know.

DIRECTOR: Intense magnetic fields probably overwhelmed her fragile internal wiring. You turned her media into mush.

JASON: Shit.

DIRECTOR: Yes, "shit" is a good way of putting it. And "fuck." And "game over" because this picture is shit-canned, done, finished. Dammit. I knew I shouldn't have listened to my wife: "Do the Asian musical, it will be cultural." Cultural, my ass. THAT'S A WRAP EVERYBODY! Jason, thank you very fucking much. You might want to get a lawyer. And a bodyguard. Your ass is in deep poo-poo.

(*Lights begin shutting off. The soundstage gets cleared. Jason is left all alone with the electronic remains of Marilyn Part II.*
Long pause.
The final light shuts off, leaving Jason silhouetted in darkness.)

8. Static

CNN news flash.

ANCHOR: Mac Camerintosh here on the CNN National News Desk with some late-breaking news. Marilyn Part II has been shot, apparently the victim of a freak accident on the set of her latest blockbuster, *Mister Phnom Penh.* We now join our White House correspondent. Angela, what is the mood in the White House?

REPORTER: There is much sadness here . . . a twinge of melancholia . . . and a smidge of wistfulness. I'm detecting a hint of rosemary too, perhaps because Nigella Lawson is visiting today.

ANCHOR: Is that flute music I hear in the background?

REPORTER: Why, yes, Mac, there happens to be a flute quartet playing at the White House this afternoon. It is rumored that Congress will issue a ban on selling firearms to all actors of Asian descent. The Pentagon has announced that a new national security color code of Fuchsia will be introduced as a way to pay tribute to the tragic passing of this young talented starlet. Fuchsia will most likely be placed between Yellow and Orange, although there is some concern that this will further confuse an already confused American public. Defense Secretary Donald Rumsfeld had this to say about today's development: "We are looking for the answers. It's the old glass box at the gas station, where you're using those little things trying to pick up the prize, and you can't find it. All these arms are going down in there, but you keep dropping it and picking it up again and moving it. Some of you are probably too young to remember those glass boxes, but they used to have them at all the gas stations when I was a kid." The White House was unavailable for further comment.

(Pause.)

Uhh, Mac?

ANCHOR: I'm sorry, Angela, I was listening to the flute music. Really beautiful stuff. Reminds me of my time in Korea, and the lovely time I had there . . . MyungHee, MyungHee, where did we go wrong . . . sorry, we'll talk about this next time. Mac Camerintosh, CNN.

9. Feedback

M has been dropped off by Dr. Yang. She slowly enters her house. It is as if she sees her surroundings in a different light.

M:

the sun rises and the world awakes
my son rises
I hear my son
I hear the sun

it's whispering
words that fall round me
like liquid heat

that crash round my feet
disappear
like a wave washes over you
it's there for a moment
you can see it
it's coming towards you
and then
it's gone

my son
I look at him
I look
he looks just like
him
jason
my
former
my

a feeling washes over me
a feeling wash
es
ZZZ

I see
   I see my
       I see my brother's face
          I remember
             his eyes
             terrible
             eyes his
          remember I
       face brother's my see I
   my see I
see I
see
see

(*The wail of an electric guitar. A fluorescent light is flickering on and off.*

The bedroom door to M and Jason's son's room is open. Light streams from the room. She approaches it, but becomes too scared.

Now it's like a reprise of M murdering her brother . . . two pools of light: One with M, one with Junior. Both of them face out to the audience. It is night. Junior is in bed. He wakes up and notices M.)

JUNIOR: What're you doing?
M: I don't know.
JUNIOR: What time is it?
M: Uhmmm . . . late.
JUNIOR: Something wrong?
M: No.
        Yes.
        Maybe.
JUNIOR: You're leaving us, aren't you?
M: I have to.
        That's why I'm here.
        Sorry.
JUNIOR: For what?

(He stares into her eyes.)

Oh.

(Pause.)

You don't have to.
M: I know. But I do.
JUNIOR: For who?
M: Me. You. Us.

(M takes a knife out and gets ready to kill her son; the Wavemaker steps in behind her.)

When I looked into my brother's eyes that night. I saw land . . . trees . . . green. He had already left. He was already letting me go.
JUNIOR: Mom?
M: Shhhh . . .
JUNIOR: You don't have to, you know.
M: I know . . . but . . .

(She readies herself.)

I know . . . but . . .

(She raises the knife.)

I do.

(Blackout.)

10. Cyberia

M is sitting in her dining room with her long overcoat on. She has a small bag packed. Jason enters. Long silence.

JASON: Hey.

M: Hi.

JASON: You must be proud.

M: Why?

JASON: Your gift. Your gun. It did the trick.

M: You were leaving me. What else could I do?

JASON: Well, you could have killed me.

M: True.

JASON: But you didn't.

M: It would have been too easy. Boring. Lacking in imagination.

JASON: I've changed, M.

M: I wanted to hurt you. Truly hurt you. I thought of different ways
     to do it. Having you shoot her. But that wasn't enough.
     I'm leaving, Jason.

JASON: No, no, wait. You don't understand. I learned from this.

M: What did you learn?

JASON: That without you, I'm nothing. We need—I need for all of us
     to be together. I've learned that the hard way. I had no control
     over the situation. It was like a dream. Movies really are myths,
     but it's all smoke and mirrors. That's exactly what I'm—I want
     to make amends, that's for sure. I want to be a good husband
     again. A good father again. And I think we can. I believe that.
     Even with everything that's happened between us.
     Where's Junior?

M: I don't know.

JASON: If you did something to our son, I swear I'll—

M: Don't threaten me.

JASON: Did you do something?

M: I don't owe you an explanation.

JASON: What did you do?

M: I did what I had to do. Just like I always have. That's all you need to know.

JASON: Tell me.

(*He stops, listening.*)

What's that noise?

(*Suddenly, the deafening roar of helicopters. Their house is flooded by the piercing glow of search lights.*)

What the hell is this?

M: I made arrangements.

JASON: With who?

M: A Wavemaker.

JASON: A Wave who?

M: There are waves. And there are particles. And sometimes you can't be both. You have to choose.

JASON: What the hell are you talking about?

M: It's quantum mechanics. Go look it up.

(*Two figures burst through the door, the Wavemakers' agents. It turns out that they're Chinky and Gooky. They speak without accents.*)

CHINKY: A wave is not a particle.

GOOKY: A particle is not a wave.

CHINKY: You are not me.

GOOKY: I am not you.

JASON: Do I know you?

CHINKY: Shut up.

JASON: M. Hey. (*To Chinky and Gooky*) Can you get the hell out of my house? (*To M*) Can't we just talk?

M: I thought you were tired of talking.

JASON: No, no, no, I mean, yes, I was. But that was then. Right now, everything's different. Right now I want to talk.

(*Pause.*)

M: Okay, let's talk.

(*Pause.*)

Well?

JASON: I'm thinking.

(*Wavemaker enters.*)

Who are you?
WAVEMAKER: You know.
JASON: No, I . . . excuse me, I'm trying to talk to my wife.
WAVEMAKER: But you aren't.
JASON: Who the fuck do you think you are?
WAVEMAKER: You know who I am.
JASON: No. I do not.
WAVEMAKER (*With Chinky and Gooky*): I know you do.
How do I know, you may ask?
How? 'Cuz I do.
Why? 'Cuz I am.
What? 'Cuz I be.

(*M starts to exit.*)

M: Junior!

(*Junior runs in.*)

JUNIOR: Dad. Hey.
JASON: Son. Come here.
M: Come to your mother.
JASON: Your father still loves you.

(*Junior hesitates for a moment, but then goes to M.*)

Wait, Junior, come back here. M, can't we just talk and work
things out. Come on, I fucked up. I know that. I'm a man. Men
fuck up. It's in our genes.
M: You and I don't harmonize. We should have similar peaks and
valleys, but instead we're canceling each other out, creating distortion and white noise. I want convergence. I want oneness,
not duality.
JASON: Where are you going to find that?
M: I don't know. But at least I know where I can start.

(*M and Junior start to exit with Chinky and Gooky.*)

JASON: No, wait! Come back here. Hey, what about our love for each other?

M (*Leaving*): What?

JASON: Our love for each other!

M: I can't hear you.

JASON: OUR FUCKING LOVE FOR EACH OTHER!

(*She and Junior are gone. Jason is alone with the Wavemaker. Wavemaker makes a signal and all the lights black out.*)

Now what?

WAVEMAKER: I pulled the plug.

JASON: What plug?

WAVEMAKER: You know. The juice. The fireworks. The show. I took down the show.

JASON: Why?

WAVEMAKER: Trust me, it's what you need.

JASON: So I'm supposed to sit here in darkness for the rest of my life?

WAVEMAKER: Maybe you've been sitting in darkness your whole life and didn't even know it. Ever thought of that?

JASON: That's deep.

WAVEMAKER: There's a difference between light and enlightenment.

(*He produces a candle and lights it for Jason.*)

Edison, though he invented incandescence, was not necessarily incandescent. A blind man can see clearly, while a man with an electron microscope can be blind as a bat. Men travel to Nepal to speak with a prophet when all along the truth has been sitting on their dining room table.

JASON: I get the vague sense that you're insulting me.

WAVEMAKER:
> Not insulting . . . consulting.
> Not demeaning . . . delighting.
> Not depressing . . . impressing.
> How do I know? 'Cuz I do.
> Why?

JASON: 'Cuz you are. You be. I get it.

WAVEMAKER: Do you?

I know you hear the laughter,
but do you really hear it?
The tragedy in those hydrogen bonds.
The sadness floating in that oxygen.
The hyena laugh of the
H—2—OOOOOOOO-NO-NO-NO-NO . . .
That siren water song was meant for you
a beautiful melancholy wail
she's been warning you
all this time
about the hot-blooded surf
avenging tides
jealous storms
and the waves lap against the shores
of your memory in a chorus of
loss
loss
loss . . .

JASON: So how long is this going to last?

(Pause.)

How long?

(Pause.)

Hey. Wavemaker?

(The Wavemaker has left. Jason sits down, stares at the candle.
He notices The Chinky and Gooky Guide to Cooking book that
M had been reading. He opens it and one of M's old diary entries,
which she had been using as a bookmark, falls out.
He opens the old, wrinkled paper and starts to read.
As he does so, we see the ocean in the background.)

(Reading:)

And so we skimmed the water
that morning. grim. up. down.
a wave

brought us up high,
for a moment we soared

above the water,
we saw the land break through
we saw her shores,
and as we hung
suspended,

*(M and Junior enter the ocean space. At some point Junior retreats
and it is M alone watching the waves.)*

we saw a glimpse
of a human figure
her stark outline against the sky
she was waving
a white cloth

JASON AND M:
she was beckoning

M:
welcoming
us

and for that one
brief
fleeting moment
we felt
so together,
so complete,
so in love.

(M remains silhouetted by the ocean.
Jason finishes reading.
We see his face by candle light. After a moment of reflection,
he blows the candle out, as we fade to black.)

END OF PLAY

Sung Rno's plays include *Behind the Masq*, *Weather*, *Cleveland Raining*, *Gravity Falls From Trees*, *Drizzle and Other Stories*, *New World*, *Yi Sang Counts to Thirteen* and *The Trajectory of a Heart, Fractured*. His work has been produced and developed by Pan Asian Repertory, East West Players, Thick Description, Asian American Theater Company, Northwest Asian American Theatre, San Diego Asian American Repertory Theater, Dance Theater Workshop, Immigrants' Theatre Project, Seoul International Theatre Festival, New York International Fringe Festival, Sanctuary Playwrights Theatre, Second Generation, Changgo Theater (Seoul), Yellow Earth Theatre (London), Silk Road Theatre Project, Public Theater, Mark Taper Forum, Arena Stage, Foundry Theatre, Mabou Mines/Suite, and Ma-Yi Theater Company. As an NEA/TCG Resident Playwright with Ma-Yi Theater Company, Sung founded the Ma-Yi Writer's Lab. Other honors include the New Dramatists Whitfield Cook Prize, a New York Fringe Festival Best Overall Production Award, two Van Lier Fellowships (with New Dramatists and New York Theatre Workshop) and first prize in the Seattle Multicultural Playwrights' Festival.

His plays and poetry are anthologized in *Savage Stage*; *Manifesto Series V.1*, edited by Erik Ehn; *But Still, Like Air, I'll Rise*; *Premonitions*; *Echoes Upon Echoes* and *The Nuyorasian Anthology*. His screenplay for *Crumple* (directed by C.S. Lee, featuring Paul H. Juhn) won the first annual 64-hour Film Shootout at the Asian American Film Festival. Current projects include *Happy*, commissioned by Second Stage and the Time Warner Commissioning Program; *Galois*, commissioned by Ensemble Studio Theatre and the Sloan Foundation; *Infinitude*, commissioned by Ma-Yi Theater Company and *Free Verse*, a screenplay.

Sung holds a BA in physics from Harvard, and an MFA in creative writing from Brown. He is an alumnus of New Dramatists.

Swoony Planet

(Play One of The Suitcase Trilogy)

Han Ong

Author's Statement

Swoony Planet is as romantic as its title suggests.
I was twenty-four when
I wrote the play and I guess
twenty-four is the time of
romance. What sustains
your days and nights then
is the thought, the hope of
greatness ahead. Soaring
opera. Grand ambition.
This is what the play's protagonist Artie is possessed by. He is
convinced of his potential artistry and his big future—feelings which
transfer to the protagonists of two successive plays with which
Swoony Planet forms *The Suitcase Trilogy* to Farouk/Freddie,
Kirtana's lost son who, in the second play, *Autodidacts,* finds a footing
in America, and to the young wunderkind Albert in the last play
Virgin. Three young men of color who are the bearers of hope for a
galaxy of their family and friends.

I was twenty-four when I wrote *Swoony Planet.* Living in Los
Angeles and working at the Mark Taper Forum. Was I poor? Yes.
I wasn't making that much money but then again my overhead was
low, and besides—as I like to tell young artists today—L.A. is the
place to be when you're poor (is this still true?); so yes, there wasn't
much money but I didn't feel the pinch.

What I felt was the nag of ambition. *I have to write.* This
was not torturous but in fact its opposite: a pleasurable thrum of
dissatisfaction, like a second heartbeat.

I loved the movies but I loved words more and since the movies
were not a place for words, not really, I wrote plays. By the time
I started *Swoony Planet,* I had written two other plays. *I have to
write.* It was part of my self-education: learning by doing. Though

the word "education" gives this episode in my life the feeling of a trudge. Far from it. It was fun. I had yet to read the short stories of Chekhov or Tanizaki's *The Makioka Sisters*—greatness ahead. But did I feel I was missing out? Nope. I didn't know the extent of what I didn't know: the ignorance of youth, out of which greatness might arise, as an accident, as a gift, as a moment of grace, quickly given and just as quickly confiscated.

The writing of *Swoony Planet* was fun. Smooth. I was gaining in confidence, two plays behind me, each illustrating the parameters of my abilities. *Swoony Planet* would be—at least in my head—an even further pushing out of said abilities. It would be grand in style, tone and ambition—though at the time of its writing, I had no idea there would be Plays Two and Three to form a trilogy. A critic of a San Francisco production of my second play said, among other disparaging things, that my writing was "too arty." Hence, Artie in *Swoony Planet*. Nothing fazed me. And I knew I was right to keep on writing, disparagement or not. Twenty-four being the age of total certitude. The romance of repudiating authority, of learning on the job and of gathering strength as you went along: all that infused the writing of *Swoony Planet*.

Leoncillo—I don't know where I got the name from. Later, somebody would tell me it means "lion cub" and that would make a kind of counterintuitive sense given the character whom it refers to. But Leoncillo was a character that has always been strangely within my wheelhouse: the embittered old man. In *Swoony Planet*, I was just discovering this. So capturing the character's bile was part of the thrill of writing the play. And really, being twenty-four and without formal education, there would be a lot more disparaging critics ahead for me: so bring on the vinegar, let us swim in its life-giving properties.

The writing of *Swoony Planet* was easy (I didn't have long periods where I stopped to figure out what happened next) and *alive*—both the characters and myself at the writing desk (in my off hours at the Taper, on their Jetsons-y computer) felt so alive. Reading it these many years later, I feel that aliveness, that palpable twenty-four-year old heartbeat. Writing it was like trying to make velvet: making something luxurious in its word-drunkenness, lyrical, and really, I have to admit, a little too much. But that was the ambition—a *little too much* dictated by a young central character who was a tad precious and whose growing up would entail meeting a long-lost father who would dispense a necessary slap of cold water: the possibility of a big future for someone like you in this country, says Leoncillo to Artie, is a mirage. Agree or disagree with them, after so much romance and swooning in the play, Leoncillo's lines arrive like a tonic.

Today I live in New York city—the perpetual capital of twenty-four-year-olds everywhere but also, paradoxically, and more and more, the world capital of Money. I have lived here for seventeen years. Since *Swoony Planet*, I've had many other lives: I've written novels. I've taught playwriting. It's been a long time since I thought of *Swoony Planet*, since I reminded myself of all that went into its writing. But in playwriting class I teach something that I call "aliveness" inasmuch as aliveness can be "taught."

"Aliveness" is a word I use for its wide embrace of many virtues, though principally it's about trying to write characters who are always *people* unpredictable, willful, seeking—and not simply functionaries for your ideas. It's hard and not everybody succeeds in the first go. The goal—inasmuch as this is possible—is the erasure of the writer's *self*.

It would seem that the writing of *Swoony Planet* was a repudiation of this: what else was I doing but celebrating *self*, being twenty-four and writing a character that was in the same time of life? So maybe there is another way to write a play that I'd long forgotten about. And the lesson might go something like this: *When you wake up, you are forty-three. You remain forty-three as you brush your teeth, have breakfast, check your email. But when you switch to a clean document that is the beginning of your next play, you are no longer forty-three. Suddenly, you are twenty-four. Write the first line.*

Production History

Swoony Planet was commissioned and given an initial workshop by the Mark Taper Forum, Center Theatre Group, Los Angeles, CA.

The New York workshop of *Swoony Planet* was produced in April 1997 by Ma-Yi Theater Company in New York City (Ralph B. Peña, Artistic Director; Jorge Z. Ortoll, Executive Producer). The director and set designer was Loy Arcenas. The lighting design was by Blake Burba. The sound design was by Fabian Obispo. The production stage manager was C. Renee Alexander and the assistant director was Andrew Sachs. The cast was as follows:

ARTIE	Kaipo Schwab
JESSICA	Mia Katigbak
KIRTANA	Natsuko Ohama
KUMAR	Harvey Perr
MARTIN	David Teschendorf
LEONCILLO	Thomas Ikeda
BUGLE BOY	Forrest McClendon

Swoony Planet received a staged reading in 2006 produced by Ma-Yi Theater Company (Ralph B. Peña, Artistic Director; Jorge Z. Ortoll, Executive Director) in association with Pregones Theater. It was directed by Ron Daniels. The stage manager was Karen Hergesheimer. The cast was as follows:

ARTIE	Kenneth Lee
JESSICA	Sophia Skiles
KIRTANA	Gita Reddy
KUMAR	Harvey Perr
MARTIN	David Bishins

LEONCILLO	Mel Duane Gionson
BUGLE BOY	Yusef Miller
GUARD, MAGICIAN, ATTENDANT	Triney Sandoval

Characters

ARTIE, early twenties, Asian

JESSICA, early forties, Asian

KIRTANA, mid-thirties, Asian

KUMAR, twenties, Asian

MARTIN, forties, White

LEONCILLO, an old man, Asian

BUGLE BOY, young, Black

ATTENDANT, played by the same actor as Martin

GUARD, played by the same actor as Leoncillo

MAGICIAN, played by the same actor as Kumar

Setting

No set at all.
Any environ that parallels abandoned factories, shelled-out churches.

This play is dedicated to Jessica Hagedorn, Eduardo Machado and Irene Fornes.

1.

AIRPORT. Bench. Smoke all around. Clouds. A Guard enters. (An actor who will later play Leoncillo.) Addresses the smoke.

GUARD:
Excuse me

(Obscured by the smoke is Kirtana, an Indian (Asian) woman, mid 30s. She becomes visible in increments, as the smoke slowly dissipates.)

KIRTANA:
Please go away

GUARD:
There is no smoking here

KIRTANA:
I'm not smoking

GUARD:
What's all this then

KIRTANA:

A woman preceded me to this spot
Why don't you go ask her

GUARD:

Four hours ago
Someone was here four hours ago
Since then
You've remained stuck here Alone
For four hours

KIRTANA:

I'm collecting myself

GUARD:

For four hours?
What's left that still needs
collecting after four
hours? I'll help you
catch it

KIRTANA:

This is a public place
It says public
An arrow points here saying, Public
Besides I don't see a crowd
Why should I be cleared out

GUARD:

You're a security risk

KIRTANA:

You're a cow
You beat your wife
Clear her out of the bathroom
each night after work don't you
so you can rush in there
can't wait to rush in there
to scrub clean the soil
that sticks to your skin
underneath that uniform

GUARD:
This is my job

KIRTANA:
HOW
You lousy cow
HOW am I a security risk

GUARD:
I look at you—

KIRTANA:
Your eyeballs wheel
everywhere for a wife substitute
I get the picture

GUARD:
And you are a woman—

KIRTANA:
Hooray
You are per*cep*tive

GUARD:
—who's alone
so that's strike one
in this type of environment
where interstate smuggling
is on the rise

KIRTANA:
Go away
Please go away

GUARD:
Am I breaking you down
Because—
           Good
Because the sooner you get out of here
the safer you'll
         we'll all be

KIRTANA:
Please
Just a few more hours

GUARD:
Where are you from?
India?

KIRTANA:
(*A return to pissed:*)
YOU should talk

GUARD:
I was born here

KIRTANA:
Well hip hip hooray
I'm from
Iowa, I came from Iowa if you wanna know

GUARD:
And before that India right

KIRTANA:
Before that I have no memory

GUARD:
You're a traitor then is that what you are

KIRTANA:
Immigrant
How could you possibly claim to have been
born here you don't even speak
the language

GUARD:
Traitor that's what we call people like you
I speak English
For you, English says see under: Traitor

KIRTANA:
Move off
If I'm a traitor what does that make your parents

GUARD:
They were born here

KIRTANA:
Well believe me
you are DESCENDED from Traitors

GUARD:
If I were your husband—

KIRTANA:
Well you're not
I'm a woman who's alone
but not defenseless
I have claws and teeth—

GUARD:
You ARE from India
Well if I were your husband
I'd come pretty quick
to collect you
before the jungle reclaims your
manner

KIRTANA:
Are you DEAF
I'm husbandless
I don't need one
And if this is your way of applying
for the post, well then
FUCK OFF BUDDY

(*Lights dim on them. Guard leaves. Kirtana remains.*)

2.

Simultaneous: From stage left enters Martin. White. 40s. From stage right enters Artie. Filipino American. Early 20s. Martin in white undershirt and white boxers. Artie in yellow undershirt and yellow boxers. Each has in both hands a shirt and pants, white. They stand on opposite sides, facing forward, flanking Kirtana. Tight light on each.

Each line they speak is punctuated by an arm being fitted into a sleeve, leg into pant, buttons being buttoned, etc.—gestural, like dance.

MARTIN:
When you were young

ARTIE:
When I was younger

MARTIN:
I used to look at you

ARTIE:
You keep looking at me still

MARTIN:
And I would open my mouth

ARTIE:
You'd open your mouth
Martin I know all this

MARTIN:
Before you go just listen to me
My mouth would open

ARTIE:
Into an O

MARTIN:
It would curve up

ARTIE:
Then down
A little cave
Your words like bats flying out
each one blind

MARTIN:
Not the words
But their destination
Which was you

It would curve up
Then down
And I'd say looking right at you

ARTIE:
What would you say Martin

MARTIN:
I'd say Daddy
I'd peek at you through bars of a crib

ARTIE:
I was never in any crib Martin

MARTIN:
And I'd say, Call me Daddy
And one day

ARTIE:
And one day

MARTIN:
You did

ARTIE:
All of a day

MARTIN:
All of a *year*

ARTIE:
And you said

MARTIN:
An entire year hearing
your mouth curve up then down
your voice a junior
saying exactly what I said
saying Daddy

ARTIE:
And you said

MARTIN:
And I said
all full of joy

ARTIE AND MARTIN:
Now we're alike

(At this line, Artie and Martin have finished dressing and do indeed
look alike. White pants, white long-sleeved shirt. Except Martin has a
leather belt around his waist, which doesn't fit him anymore.)

MARTIN:
Alike enough to be father and son

(Struggles with belt. Won't fit. Gives up.)

Jesus Christ

(Removes belt. Lifts it in one hand towards Artie.)

ARTIE:
I don't want it

MARTIN:
The body fucks up
sneaks up on you
and then one day looking right in the mirror
from crib to middle age in just one glance
That's what a father is for
Take it

ARTIE:
I don't want your belt

MARTIN:
To tell about the tyranny of the body
That's what a father is for
To give a well-notched belt
each puncture letting a little air out
until

ARTIE:
The belt's not my style Martin

MARTIN:
Until you float up a little less each year
To make you earthbound
That's what a father is for

ARTIE:
Martin
The belt may be the right belt
The story behind it may be the right story
(*Beat*)
But you're not the right Father
Somebody else's but not mine
(*Beat*)
I'm sorry

(*Lights fade on Martin. Back up on Kirtana at the airport bench. Artie walks to Kirtana.*)

3.

ARTIE:
Taken?

KIRTANA:
You wanna sit?

ARTIE:
I'd like that yes

KIRTANA:
Sit

(*Artie sits.*)

This is Illinois

ARTIE:
Are you talking to me

KIRTANA:
Do you live here

ARTIE:
Not for long

KIRTANA:
It's not a big place is it

ARTIE:
Big enough to have an airport

KIRTANA:
But not too big

ARTIE:
Actually quite sleepy

KIRTANA:
Restful

(Beat.)

ARTIE:
Sleepy

KIRTANA:
I've been too awake
So this sounds completely
to me
Some sleep
is more than I've had in the last three days
The plane took three days

ARTIE:
Really? Where did you get on?

KIRTANA:
They keep telling me three hours
but I'll swear to you
it's been three days with no sleep
Iowa We started surrounded by corn fields all yellow and green and
by the time the plane tipped this way all we could see looking down
was miles and miles of black

ARTIE:
What was black

KIRTANA:
Razed grass I think
and structures going up
and it seemed to bode great speed
something far ahead I can't catch up with
like my son

(Sees Guard approach.)

Listen
There's a man coming this way
who's been hitting on me all night
I wanna stay a bit longer
Don't let him clear me out OK
Pretend you're my son

ARTIE:
What

KIRTANA:
Call me Mom
Say you've come to meet me
and take me home
He won't bother you

GUARD:
This is a final warning

KIRTANA:
(To Artie:)
That's the man

GUARD:
Who is this

KIRTANA:
He's my son
(To Artie:)
That's who's been assaulting me

GUARD:
Wait a minute now

ARTIE:
Leave my Mom alone

GUARD:
This is your Mom?

ARTIE:
    Didn't you hear what I said
                    I said, Leave my Mom alone

GUARD:
A woman alone in an airport is a recipe for trouble

KIRTANA:
How

GUARD:
I told you, interstate smuggling

KIRTANA:
I'm not afraid of guns

GUARD:
Easy enough to say

KIRTANA:
I know what it's like to be in the middle with guns pointed
from both sides
I've been living that way for months

GUARD:
It's never the same—

ARTIE:
—you don't seem to understand
this is not an invitation to debate
Leave my Mom alone—

GUARD:
—A real gun is something else
So's real blood
particularly when it spills onto the whiteness
of airport floors
Never more sobering and redder than then

ARTIE:
I really don't see what good all this talk of blood's doing

GUARD:
It's my job
to keep it off the floor

ARTIE:
Well my Mom's blood isn't on the floor is it?

GUARD:
Take her home

KIRTANA:
He'll take me home
(To Artie:)
Let's go home Farouk

GUARD:
(To Artie:)
That's your name?
What kind of crackpot name's that*

ARTIE:
I'm calling the cops

GUARD:
I *am* the cops

KIRTANA:
(In response to *:)
It's a king's name

GUARD:
(To Kirtana:)
A son with a king's name and
Unafraid of guns:
Get down from the clouds where you live lady
(To Artie:)
Take her home
Lock her up

KIRTANA:
(To Artie:)
Take me home Farouk
Don't ever let me go
(Whispers the following in Artie's ear:)
Say it back to me
Come on
Say it and he'll leave us

ARTIE:
(Not quite sure of all that's transpiring.)
I'll take you home Mom
and lock you up

KIRTANA:
And you'll never go

ARTIE:
And I'll never go

KIRTANA:
Give us a kiss

(He kisses her. Slowly.)

GUARD:
(To Kirtana:)
I wish I had a mother like you

ARTIE:
(To Guard:)
You can fuck off now

GUARD:
(To Kirtana:)
That's not a mother's kiss You don't fool me

(Exits.)

KIRTANA:
Do you have a mother?

ARTIE:
I have a mother yes

KIRTANA:
She's lucky having a son like you

ARTIE:
I'm better in the abstract

(Lights dim as an airplane flying overhead is heard.)

4.

Lights return. Same place. Empty. Enter Jessica. Filipina American.
Early 40s. Cigarette in hand.

JESSICA:
I'm looking for my son
(Looks around)
Anyone?
(No one)
The thing about hands is
Hands knead
and in the absence of a son (who's
the right kind of dough)
they grope elsewhere
Cigarettes for instance

(Guard enters.)

GUARD:
There's no smoking here
Are you coming or going

JESSICA:
Neither

GUARD:
Listen it's three a.m.
and you're not the first crazy lady
I've had to help so if
you've got no business—

JESSICA:
I'm looking for my son

GUARD:
This is an airport
not an orphanage
And there's no smoking here

JESSICA:
He's flying out

GUARD:
There you go
He's gone
Will you put out that cigarette

JESSICA:
A hand needs a cigarette
I don't do it for the smoke

GUARD:
I don't care ma'am

JESSICA:
(*Throws cigarette on floor, grinds it with undue emphasis with her feet.*)
I'm sorry
I'm not myself

(*Lights fade.*)

5.

In the darkness, a song. Sung live by all performers, who are offstage.

Song:
>Half the world
>is packing a suitcase
>The other half's
>tossing in bed
>
>The first half dies
>with no proof or trace
>no memory of dinner talk
>any remnant of grace
>no azure stroll
>never a leisurely pace
>instead a bolt a run
>perpetual lunging for Place
>
>Half the world
>is packed tight in Samsonite
>The other half's
>clobbered by sleep
>
>This half lives
>underwater not flying by air
>that avenue of dreamtime
>the long-uncut hair
>of the past stretching yards
>and years back to where
>we once had an estate
>>once had a guard dog
>>once had a sun
>>>>>constant in heat
>This half may be rooted here
>but all the while
>it breathes
>the air of
>another year
>another currency
>another God
>miles away

Half the world
is doing is making
is acting the act
The other half
is watching is waiting
and forever holds back

(Lights fade up. All seven characters emerge into a lineup, an inverted triangle whose final point is Artie, closest to the audience. The song is sung once more, this time accompanied by the percussion of the singers stomping on the ground, or beating out a rhythm on their chests, or clapping. It should end with a series of claps or stomps or beats, speeding urgently, then a sudden stop. Everyone deserts the stage, but Artie.)

6.

Lights fade tight on Artie to suggest nighttime.

ARTIE:
It's a motel room in Arizona
                              That much I know
Some numbers splay across a wooden door
Fixing me to:
                    this room
                    this specific shoebox in the world
                    This is where I am
                    not lost at all
That much I know
(Beat)
That I am here
(Beat)
Here is Arizona
And I've come so far
                              so fast
(Beat)

And I'm still packing my suitcase
And tossing in bed
Packing my suitcase
And tossing in bed
Packing my suitcase

And tossing at sea: those twin feats one must learn
to master without a father's precedent
without benefit of example
in the great
American magic act

(Beat)
Here goes
Watch this trick
Now you see me

(Lights out.)

ARTIE'S VOICE:
Now you don't

7.

*Lights. AGENCY. Two chairs, facing each other. On right, Kirtana.
On left, notebook in hand, pen too, Jessica.*

KIRTANA:
You do see

JESSICA:
There are freeway systems in this country
is what I'm saying
And they complicate things beyond comprehension

KIRTANA:
He ran away as teenagers do
Nobody beat him

JESSICA:
No one's saying you did

KIRTANA:
Fifteen

JESSICA:
Nobody's going to blame you

KIRTANA:
Seduced by the promise of neon and
a constant buffet of hamburgers.

JESSICA:
It's foolish to think that
the finger will be pointed at
you here
There are other agencies
the church for example
in which blame is placed
        blame is always placed
on the parent
           the source of all wrongdoing
It's something we don't abide by
in this agency
We counsel

KIRTANA:
And track right?

JESSICA:
We *help* track
to the best of our abilities

KIRTANA:
I've come very far
    come carried by good word of mouth
                so many mouths talking about this
place you don't know

JESSICA:
And they say what? Good things?

KIRTANA:
A magic act, they say

JESSICA:
The success
when it's come
has come against great odds

KIRTANA:
But not—
            Not insurmountable
People leave tracks
have fingerprints

JESSICA:
People do leave tracks—

KIRTANA:
Some larger than others yes
And a boy like Farouk
            like no other

JESSICA:
But you take a look out any window in any city
and you'd be hard-pressed
to second-guess destinations
I mean
I've been here years
                        half a lifetime
and I'm *still* not used to it
this ludicrous tic-tac-toe of cars
Wheels are like—

KIRTANA:
Feet He's left footprints

JESSICA:
A little yes
But he *escaped*

KIRTANA:
Not escaped. Left

JESSICA:
OK Left
And wheels are the perfect conduit for that
Invented for just that purpose
And yes there are license plates to be written down
Sightings

But those things when they happen are the *exception*
And wheels
The thing about wheels is that
they're better than brooms
Footprints may have been laid down
But wheels sweep them so clean you'd hardly know
anyone had been there
They guarantee
Often they guarantee exits so speedy—

KIRTANA:
You're not painting a good—

JESSICA:
No not good
Practical
We don't operate on false hope

(Beat.)

KIRTANA:
But where else can I go
If you fail me who else

JESSICA:
There are detective agencies—

KIRTANA:
They cost

JESSICA:
I know
But sometimes they're better equipped
for—
Complications come
in the form of
in many forms
some we're not equipped to handle

KIRTANA:
Such as

JESSICA:
In the instance of abductions

KIRTANA:
He'll escape
I know he will

JESSICA:
This has happened to him before?

KIRTANA:
Back in India
His father's parents
vindictive
people
They took him away from me
And he came back
Ran halfway across the country
(And it's not—
        there are hills and haters of children—
                           not
a simple matter of running track)
He came back to me
(Beat)
And now he's gone

(Beat.)

JESSICA:
We'll find him

KIRTANA:
I know you will
It's our particular fate
Jar the symmetry
Fifteen
and
He'd look at television: Mom we jar the symmetry

JESSICA:
You have a local address?

KIRTANA:
I'm staying at a motel
The Six of Hearts

JESSICA:
Why don't you go back to Iowa
It could be—

KIRTANA:
Weeks, months
Have you heard of the Bob and
Cowboys' Grill?

JESSICA:
Yes

KIRTANA:
I waitress there
You can put that down
on the form
When no one's looking I sneak some
Indian spices into
whatever's brewing
One day it was beef stew
And the manager

JESSICA:
Bruce

KIRTANA:
You know him?

JESSICA:
The entire female population
has been warned to stay miles away
He hasn't—

KIRTANA:
No, no
He's been very kind
Very kind and very stupid Thicklike

JESSICA:
And nothing else

KIRTANA:
He kept bragging about
the beef stew, calling it
Great American Food
saying how you will never go bankrupt
selling American people
American food (and sure
enough, that batch of beef
stew sold out quicker than
any other before it) but little did he know
those spices
scumming around the top
were mine
(Beat)
How about you
You're from somewhere else too

JESSICA:
Manila
I grew up there
This agency is founded entirely by immigrants

KIRTANA:
Manila is
the Philippines?

JESSICA:
PI

KIRTANA:
What's that

JESSICA:
Philippine Islands

KIRTANA:
is Marcos?

JESSICA:
Was
Not that I keep up
I don't anymore

KIRTANA:
You have no family back there

JESSICA:
They're all dead

KIRTANA:
I have relatives in India

JESSICA:
Do they know about your son

KIRTANA:
(*Shakes no*)
They're the same as dead
More my husband's family than mine actually

JESSICA:
And you're not married now

KIRTANA:
I never divorced him
just left
Escaped, to use your word
A suitcase in one hand, a knife in the other,
my boy on my back, we cameled our way
out of there
(*Beat*)
Are you married

JESSICA:
Twelve years

KIRTANA:
Is he Filipino too

JESSICA:
(*Shakes no*)
American
I meant
I promised I'd stop doing this

KIRTANA:
What

JESSICA:
Substituting that word for white
My husband is white
It's something my mother did too
even after years of living here
Mom *you're* American now, I said
but she never quite took to it

KIRTANA:
You shouldn't beat your head over
just a word

JESSICA:
Yes but—

KIRTANA:
There are more important things
(*Beat*)
Such as a son
(*Beat*)
Farouk

8.

*Martin and Jessica. PATIO. Sounds of crickets. Night. Shadows of
leaves play.*

JESSICA:
He crept in

MARTIN:
Crept in how
We invited him

JESSICA:
Just snuck up on me

MARTIN:
What piece of news was he gabbing on about
You shouldn't have screamed

JESSICA:
Look at you Martin
Always the diplomat
He asked what had happened over the weekend

MARTIN:
The robbery

JESSICA:
The break-in, he kept screaming, tell me
And I said—

MARTIN:
—furniture stolen—

JESSICA:
—gave him an itemized listing—

MARTIN:
—So why'd you scream

JESSICA:
—no suspects, I said
and he kept saying, Any person you know who might
have access to the house, and then and there
I should have known to
stop the conversation dead
but instead I said Carol

MARTIN:
That's why you screamed

JESSICA:
I said, Carol our housekeeper
and then he asked if we'd put Carol
through some police check

MARTIN:
He wouldn't say something like that
He's got this one-of-a-kind brain
that processes (it's what
we use him for)
numbers and diagrams
Where others see crisscrossing
lines of no conceivable use
he sees their application
how to translate them into freeways

JESSICA:
The same thing had happened to his
family and they'd done a checkup
on their housekeeper and wouldn't you
know she'd been siphoning loot for
years, at which point that
wife of his
little bird in Chanel yellow
and white teeth
began to crack jokes

MARTIN:
What jokes

JESSICA:
How can they expect it'll go over well
with me these jokes—Do they think
I'm some sort of
us-not-them kinda gal expecting me to throw
my head back and laugh
The one thing
about you Americans—

MARTIN:
We Americans: not that refrain again

JESSICA:
—you have beautiful teeth but you
reveal them in the aftermath of an ugly joke
Yes we invited him
but we certainly

gave no indication he
had podium rights

MARTIN:
You go to work
and see these people
for whom you've developed—

JESSICA:
I go to work. Yes.
I bring no one home
And if I did
Not one of them would
think, Carol

MARTIN:
—and relative to that kind
of partisanship,
between needy and
sponsor
which is
this cult of
suffering you've built up—

JESSICA:
A family, Martin

MARTIN:
—is nobody can compete
You think
because we're doing
well and belong to this
set—

JESSICA:
The smart set

MARTIN:
—we become automatically guilty—

JESSICA:
Since when*

MARTIN:
—as if we were
causing them
misfortune
(*In response to* *:)
Since you mentioned it
two nights ago

JESSICA:
You talk
because you're missing a son

MARTIN:
He's a friend—

JESSICA:
I don't want him back

MARTIN:
—and he's a—

JESSICA:
I said

MARTIN:
And I'm telling you what
          What do you expect me to tell you

JESSICA:
I'd rather be robbed
than entertain people like that

MARTIN:
I'd much rather do anything but be robbed again
How much more violated do you
want to get Their grubby
hands through our drawers
MY clothes
picking and choosing as if
I were dead
You want a family?
What do you have

One broken lock
And a son out the door.
And now you
don't want friends

JESSICA:
The right kind of friends

MARTIN:
What do you end up with?
An even emptier house

9.

*HILL. Bugle Boy. He sings a song, in dim spotlight. Behind him, a
field of stars.*

Song: "Outskirts of Town"

BUGLE BOY:
    Wind blows through
    making tin cans rattle
    Losers pass through
    making each woman tattle
    Why don't you
    and I take shelter
    away from the townsfolk
    with their radio and rumor
    run out to the tracks
    gleaming their poor man's humor
    Darling can you
    and I try marriage
    and be mindful of us only
    as we weave and we wear the exile's gown
    Sweetheart let's you
    and I cast our luck
    with hearts that are lonely
    who bear and who grieve on the outskirts of town.

(Lights fade on him. He remains there. A silhouette against stars.)

10.

Tight lights on faces: Artie standing. Jessica seated. A phone conversation. Phone receivers may or may not be used. They are both on one half of the stage, as the other half is still occupied by Bugle Boy.

JESSICA:
You said you'd call earlier

ARTIE:
I'm calling now

JESSICA:
What's that music Where are you

ARTIE:
Arizona

JESSICA:
What kind of bar

ARTIE:
Mom I'm a fag

JESSICA:
Don't get snippy with me

ARTIE:
Just stating a fact

JESSICA:
You want a fact exchange
This is mine: He ran out on us

ARTIE:
I'm still gonna see him

JESSICA:
He ran out on you

ARTIE:
I know you don't want me to

JESSICA:
It's not that I don't

ARTIE:
Where you work
You have
Access to information

JESSICA:
Access?
This is a man who hasn't called
hasn't written for sixteen years!

(No response.)

What's this going to accomplish?

(Lights up on Bugle Boy. Artie is in both scenes.)

BUGLE BOY:
(Points up.)
What's that
Three points that end
No eight
Eight points that tip into
a blade

ARTIE:
(To Jessica:)
What's that star
composed of eight points
which come to a blade

JESSICA:
I don't know

ARTIE:
Aurora Borealis?

BUGLE BOY:
That's not it

JESSICA:
Head in the stars
That's where you are

ARTIE:
Mom
I gotta go

JESSICA:
He's beautiful in the distance

ARTIE:
Who

JESSICA:
Your Dad
(He doesn't even deserve the name
Martin's been talking about you)

BUGLE BOY:
The bear
It's the bear

ARTIE:
(*To Bugle Boy:*)
Ursa Major
(*To Jessica:*)
He's not my Dad

JESSICA:
No your Dad shines so much
brighter because he vanished
before you could find him out
for the fraud that he is
That's what I've been
telling Martin:
Abandon him and *then*
he'll start thinking highly of you

BUGLE BOY:
That doesn't sound right

ARTIE:
I gotta go

JESSICA:
Will you call me

ARTIE:
When

JESSICA:
As soon as you get to California

ARTIE:
I can't promise anything

(Lights fade on Jessica.)

BUGLE BOY:
Will you come with me

ARTIE:
Where

BUGLE BOY:
(Points)
See that rainbow down there
Carnival's in town
Only time anyone would
be caught dead there

ARTIE:
What do I call you

BUGLE BOY:
I told you

ARTIE:
But it's—

BUGLE BOY:
Bugle Boy

ARTIE:
A strange name

BUGLE BOY:
My father gave it to me

ARTIE:
Thinking what

BUGLE BOY:
Is there supposed to be a story behind everything

ARTIE:
Fathers and sons

BUGLE BOY:
What do you do

ARTIE:
Mainly I listen

BUGLE BOY:
You get paid to listen

ARTIE:
Then I sift
Then I write down
What do *you* do

BUGLE BOY:
Certainly not a writer
What do you write
        You write about your people

ARTIE:
Who's that

BUGLE BOY:
Privilege

ARTIE:
I'm not

BUGLE BOY:
You don't work

ARTIE:
I'm not rich

BUGLE BOY:
What kind of muscles does that give you Writing
Not calves

ARTIE:
You're checking out the wrong part

BUGLE BOY:
What should I be looking at

ARTIE:
(Lifts hands.)
Veins

BUGLE BOY:
I like a body to read in the dark
I like to run my hands through skin
and run into
a scar Scars And say This body is not
a stranger to work
                or discomfort
What I don't like is smoothness
                and ease
Because it's a world I don't
think I'll ever know
And besides those things
make you flabby
And that's one thing I
don't intend to be

ARTIE:
I've earned veins in the right places
And *you*

BUGLE BOY:
Veins in my name That's one

ARTIE:
Tell me the story

BUGLE BOY:
I didn't know till my Dad
screamed at me one night:
I called you Bugle Boy direct from
the Bible expecting you to be
                                    some sort of angel
                                    some herald
of Good News from now on but all your grown-up life
                                                    ever since you
                                                    were thirteen

all you kept trumpeting was a rap sheet

ARTIE:
What kind of rap sheet

BUGLE BOY:
Petty thievery

ARTIE:
Cars?

BUGLE BOY:
It's a country dependent on freeways
Cars don't sound petty to me do they to you
(*Beat*)
I've killed a couple of dogs in my time
Mailman's prerogative
(*Beat*)
So you wanna come with me

ARTIE:
Where

BUGLE BOY:
Carnival
A magician who gives late shows

ARTIE:
And after that

BUGLE BOY:
My place

ARTIE:
Where's that

BUGLE BOY:
On the outskirts of town

11.

Blue light isolates Kirtana, standing center.

KIRTANA:
At the University of Bombay where I went
before giving up
thought to be by my husband's
side, a professor told me
You are where history is
going to be made
How absurd thinking yourself
important enough to stencil into books

But I think now
(It's all I do now is think)
Meera Kherjee, the star debater
of the University of Bombay, not
only smart but glamorous, so ripe
for history-making, is
today behind a fat
tyrant she married, a permanent
lock on her lips. From debate to
complicity: no limit to the
perverseness of God's game
plan. And me.
Here in America. History. My footprints so lonely.
So at night to console myself I say,
                    But you're making history
          I say,
                    repeating after the professor,
                              Despite ourselves
                              We are history

We lie in bed and toss
Our days are bad and our clothes a mess
still we're history
(*Beat*)
I say that at night and yet I know inside this heart
I would give up History in a minute in exchange for some
Company
my son back at my side

12.

CARNIVAL: red, yellow, green lights. Magician enters. Stops center.
Artie and Bugle Boy enter, crouch flanking facing Magician.

MAGICIAN:
(*Facing audience; takes off top hat.*)
In this hat
ladies and gentleman
my first trick
a rabbit out of my hat
(*Beat*)
Did I hear a snicker
For what is this
snicker ladies and gentleman

(*Cocks ear.*)

Lack of originality? Did I hear
someone say, LACK OF ORIGINALITY?
Well let me defend myself: Magic need
not be original The only demand
on Magic is that it be
MAGICAL
I used to be a bus conductor
would you have guessed
all day long I strode the same
narrow corridor which cuts
through the bus's middle yelling
                              All Aboard
punching tickets and yelling

Come one come
All aboard the Homebound Express
(what a beautiful word,
homebound)

I varied
I *tried to* vary
these little choruses everyday
Some days I'd shout
(*Singsong:*)

Hey there ho there
we're all going home
after a hard day's work
Clap hands

(*He claps.*)

Clap hands

(*He claps.*)

Day in day out running after
ORIGINALITY that's what
I'd do
And did you think I'd get some show of thanks for this? Nooooo
And now you ask me for
ORIGINALITY? After history
has proven to me its
uselessness has proven it
unappreciated? Puh-leeze

A rabbit out of a hat
That's what you're getting so
Shut Up or Get Out

(*Waves fingers, incanting.*)

Yabba dabba doo
Yabba dabba dee
A rabbit a rabbit

(*Reaches into top hat, pulls out a rose.*)

What the

(Keeps pulling out rose after rose after rose; into top hat:)

Where the fuck are you

(Rose after rose after rose; to audience:)

OK
You asked for originality
You got it
No rabbit just flowers
Are you satisfied
ARE YOU SATISFIED!

DESPITE MYSELF I'M ORIGINAL!

(Lights fade on Magician, who exits, and rise on Artie. He rises, wobbles. Bugle Boy goes to him.)

BUGLE BOY:
Steady

ARTIE:
The earth just tilted

BUGLE BOY:
You felt the earth tilt

ARTIE:
More people with luggage*
got off the plane and we
tilted some more

*(At * Martin enters. With him is a small-scale architectural model of a strip mall, which he rests on the floor in the exact spot where the Magician was earlier.)*

BUGLE BOY:
You're just swooning

ARTIE:
(Ironic:)
'Cause I'm in love with you?

BUGLE BOY:
'Cause you're in love with me
but you don't know it yet

(They exit.)

13.

Jessica enters.

MARTIN:
You walk around believing you
have a target glued to
your forehead and
think people will
come and bash you in
Ghosts ringing our
doorbell at night now
he's not coming back
It's in his blood

JESSICA:
I am not afraid of change

MARTIN:
I've been watching you—

JESSICA:
You keep watching me

MARTIN:
How you rearrange the furniture
preparing for what is it

JESSICA:
I've let him go

MARTIN:
And this latest
it's *change* too—

JESSICA:
Change flows two ways: forward and
back Which is this, you
haven't even bothered
asking yourself
I never thought
It'd get this complicated

MARTIN:
Well it is

JESSICA:
It doesn't have to be

MARTIN:
Bullshit

JESSICA:
The wrong friends, the right friends

MARTIN:
What you do is civics, not economics

JESSICA:
What I do feeds more
than what you do ever will

MARTIN:
It's progress
Where do you stand
With the future or with the past

JESSICA:
A wheat field into a mall?
We drive by there every day
A daily reminder

MARTIN:
You want the geography to be
impervious to progress just so
we can have a scenic drive

JESSICA:
Who are the financiers

MARTIN:
What've you got against
the Japanese

JESSICA:
I'm a professional sympathizer I have
more than enough sympathy to spare

MARTIN:
But not for them

JESSICA:
Money

MARTIN:
The root of all evil

JESSICA:
Doors open when they land
while for my people—

MARTIN:
How proprietary

JESSICA:
They would love to be thought of
as mine—

MARTIN:
Do you teach them to be afraid
like you Your heart skipping
a beat every time we drive
onto a freeway

JESSICA:
—they live here
while the Japanese
leave and don't have to sustain

                I do
                I'm the one who has to sustain

MARTIN:
A mall
is not a nuclear plant

JESSICA:
It attracts listless—

MARTIN:
We give them jobs

JESSICA:
—aimless youth

MARTIN:
Because you're depressed you want
everything around you to spin in
the same circle No change
possible until you're good and ready

(They stand silent.)

14.

Artie and Bugle Boy bring a bench in. Set it so that it covers the architectural miniature from view. Train station. Jessica and Martin remain. Artie, with backpack, and Bugle Boy, stand side by side, in front of the bench. Sound of a train. They look left.

BUGLE BOY AND MARTIN:
I guess that's it

ARTIE:
Here it comes
You have my address*

JESSICA:
I guess so

(Jessica and Martin exit. Each on opposite sides.

*Bugle Boy pats breast jacket pocket. In response to *:)*

ARTIE:
Will you call

BUGLE BOY:
You're not the kind who should be given
a head start You'll bolt and then
you'll outrun me

(Beat)
I'll call

ARTIE:
Do that

BUGLE BOY:
On the road

ARTIE:
Handing out telegrams in shorts
to show off calf muscles

BUGLE BOY:
Hitchhike your way
to California using veins as bait

ARTIE:
Can't get too far on that

BUGLE BOY:
Why not

ARTIE:
Veins aren't too popular around here

BUGLE BOY:
Do I get a kiss

ARTIE:
Sure

(Bugle Boy looks, sees no one, kisses.)

You look then you kiss

BUGLE BOY:
You take what you can

ARTIE:
And then you run?

(*The space between them widens. Mainly it's Bugle Boy who moves, walking off. They wave and mouth the following lines, all drowned out by the boom and hiss of a train pulling in.*)

Bye

BUGLE BOY:
Take care

ARTIE:
I'll see you

BUGLE BOY:
Promises promises

(*If there is to be a break, it should occur here.*)

15.

RESTAURANT. *Spill, offstage, red-blue off-on neon. Table. Two benches, similar to train station bench, flank it. Kirtana, in waitress uniform. Jessica seated.*

JESSICA:
Kirtana regarding Farouk

KIRTANA:
This is strictly social

JESSICA:
This is social

KIRTANA:
Unless of course you've news for me

JESSICA:
No I'm afraid that's what I was announcing

KIRTANA:
As soon as you get news I'm sure you'll tell me

JESSICA:
Of course

KIRTANA:
But till then we'll be social
We can be social can't we

JESSICA:
Of course

KIRTANA:
I'll be back with the food and then
you should tell me all about
your life How exemplary it's been

JESSICA:
Far from it

KIRTANA:
No don't say that Of course exemplary If
not you then who

(*She exits, to return with two plates. Sets before Jessica and herself. Sits.*)

JESSICA:
This your concoction

KIRTANA:
Beef I pollute all the stews now
Bruce has no idea why he's doing so well
Just pockets the money and pats
me on my bottom

JESSICA:
You should sue

KIRTANA:
No

JESSICA:
You *could*

KIRTANA:
And then what

JESSICA:
And if you don't, what

KIRTANA:
More waiting
Case after case tied up in the courts like
a long ball of yarn unwinding
To knit what
            what kind of fabric

JESSICA:
Someone steps on your rights
you have recourse to that

KIRTANA:
It's called unemployment

JESSICA:
You certainly
don't believe
this is all you have to look
forward to

KIRTANA:
What marketable skills do I
possess to begin with

JESSICA:
Nothing that training can't remedy

KIRTANA:
Night classes

JESSICA:
(Detecting something askew in Kirtana's voice.)
Yes?

KIRTANA:
I've tried them

JESSICA:
And what's wrong with night classes

(Beat.)

KIRTANA:
Full of backward geeks consigned
there by pathological social
ineptitude and failure Impossible to
miss the scent of failure in all
those rooms Don't think I haven't
forced myself to try Night
after night just sitting
hoping to extract some hope from all this

JESSICA:
And there is

KIRTANA:
This is not what I came for
In just a few nights watching
a roomful of elderly students each
pouched heavy with dismay you
begin to understand this country
It only has time for winners And
What winners need more than
anything else is a batch
of geeks to make *them* look
winners in comparison
a batch to clean up after
parties and victory
celebrations So the skills those schools
teach, the skills they would
profit from teaching
are service industry ones
of smiling and serving soup

JESSICA:
But I don't understand
How is what you're afraid of different
from what you're doing right now

KIRTANA:
I went to the University
of Bombay I want you to know that

JESSICA:
No one's taking that away from you

KIRTANA:
I'm telling you now I come
from a family of proud women
each one bearing pride in a
different manner, but all
equally proud nonetheless
I have pride in my accomplishments
(*Beat*)
Eat your stew
(*Beat*)
I'm sorry

JESSICA:
This is wonderful

KIRTANA:
I wanted to thank you

JESSICA:
For

KIRTANA:
Introducing me to that group

JESSICA:
Are they good people*

KIRTANA:
(*Simultaneous with *:*)
Who'd have thought in the
middle of Illinois these
Indians

JESSICA:
I'm glad you liked them

KIRTANA:
I walked through this door
the room all of a sudden
parting in equal rhythm*
to take me in all full
of smiles asking after me
The kind of confidence I can only
associate with having been
born here not boat-tipsy in any
way not like me who's constantly afraid

JESSICA:
(*Simultaneous with* *:)
I've heard so much about them
but just haven't had the time
to check up

KIRTANA:
A group of
people so tip-top they
could've been issuing from
a TV set
Except

JESSICA:
Except what

KIRTANA:
Well not except really but
There's this guy

JESSICA:
Really

KIRTANA:
Oh don't smile like that I feel silly enough

JESSICA:
An Indian guy

KIRTANA:
He wears this ten-gallon hat
and walks into rooms as if preceded
there by a ticker-tape parade
An Indian John Wayne

JESSICA:
And

KIRTANA:
He's bullish

JESSICA:
He's asked you out

KIRTANA:
We've gone out

(*Kumar, unseen, enters.*)

JESSICA:
On a date Was this a first date

KUMAR:
Speak of the devil

KIRTANA:
What are you doing here
Walking so stealthy I couldn't
even hear

KUMAR:
I thought we had a date

KIRTANA:
I don't think so

KUMAR:
So you've forgotten

KIRTANA:
Maybe it's *you* who's confused

KUMAR:
This was to be our
(Looks at Jessica) second date

KIRTANA:
We weren't talking about you Kumar

KUMAR:
I'm Kumar

JESSICA:
Nice to meet you

KUMAR:
(Kisses Jessica on the hand.)
Very nice to meet you
Kirtana speaks highly of you

KIRTANA:
Spoken Just that one time
Don't make it
sound like routine

KUMAR:
Not yet

KIRTANA:
Tell Kumar we weren't talking about him Jessica

JESSICA:
I'm afraid we really weren't

KUMAR:
My ears were buzzing

KIRTANA:
Ear infection A sign of old age

KUMAR:
(To Jessica:)
She's wonderful isn't she
Always a line for everything

KIRTANA:
I've had to

KUMAR:
There she goes again

JESSICA:
So what is it you do if you
don't mind my asking

KUMAR:
I'm into several ventures—

KIRTANA:
Speculation That's
how you described it Your lips
biting into that word as if
tasting fruit

KUMAR:
—real estate being one of them

KIRTANA:
It's the perfect word
to characterize his
approach to life—Speculation—Isn't
that right Kumar

KUMAR:
My approach to life?

KIRTANA:
How you pursue things
romantic and otherwise
mere speculation You convince yourself
of something long enough you begin
to believe it

KUMAR:
Such as

KIRTANA:
(To Jessica:)
Thicklike
Kumar I don't think we planned
something for tonight

KUMAR:
I'm sorry then my mistake
so Should I come back

KIRTANA:
Call first

KUMAR:
No you're not the kind who
should be given any warning
because you'll bolt and
then you'll outrun me

KIRTANA:
Believe me if anyone's bolting
it's not me If you have to know
I'm practically glued here

KUMAR:
So what is it keeps you
glued Certainly not a husband

KIRTANA:
(Acknowledging Jessica:)
Friends

KUMAR:
I have those The problem with
them is they can only carry so far

KIRTANA:
Maybe you have the wrong kind

KUMAR:
I know who to surround
myself with One gift of mine

JESSICA:
Maybe you should introduce me to some
of *your* friends

KUMAR:
But despite their friendship they
never seem to be good
for lonely nights spent
by yourself in big houses
lightning licking the surfaces
of windows making you feel
like a seven-year-old

KIRTANA:
Sounds like an advertisement
for a mother to me
(To Jessica:)
Doesn't it

KUMAR:
What's wrong with wanting a mother
Perfectly natural tendency

KIRTANA:
My hands are full

KUMAR:
I don't see any rattles trailing
behind you

KIRTANA:
It's the other way around

KUMAR:
I don't understand

KIRTANA:
You're not meant to
Call next time Kumar

KUMAR:
All right I promise

KIRTANA:
You always do but your
promises have a way of never working out

KUMAR:
Not the ones that matter

(Beat.)

JESSICA:
Such as

KIRTANA:
Jessica

JESSICA:
No this is a friend of mine
I'd like to know what intentions
you have Because you seem to have
strong ones and I'd like
to know As a friend

KUMAR:
Honorable ones

KIRTANA:
Honorable

KUMAR:
You sound skeptical

KIRTANA:
I haven't heard that word
in such a long time

KUMAR:
No It's not a popular word

JESSICA:
An Old World word

KUMAR:
That's where I'm from

KIRTANA:
But not entirely
Something not quite Old
World about you Kumar what
is that

KUMAR:
Is that the part you like

KIRTANA:
I don't know

KUMAR:
But it's the part you don't
mind Because I know you *do*
mind from the way you
speak, curling your
lips the way you do Not that
I understand why Because I'm fit
if not fitter than most

KIRTANA:
It's the part that won't
let me write you off
completely

KUMAR:
An amalgam

KIRTANA:
Is that what they call it
these days

KUMAR:
(To Kirtana:)
Just like you're one
(Beat)
I should leave now but before I
do can I say one other thing
A defense of what you called
my speculative
life which is not true at all

I don't believe in poverty
not for myself it's true
but I don't
I'm not hazy and unforthright either
which is what I understand
speculative to mean
Like I said
I know who to surround myself with—

KIRTANA:
Kumar I'm sure Jessica isn't
interested in all this

JESSICA:
No I am

KUMAR:
Are you sure

JESSICA:
Go on Please

KUMAR:
You're quite sure?

JESSICA:
I don't understand why
you should be so surprised

KUMAR:
A history of indifference
from women which as I remarked
is beyond my understanding

JESSICA:
You were married before

KUMAR:
No never
A lifelong bachelor

KIRTANA:
And you want me as a habit-breaker

(Beat.)

KUMAR:
Not when you put it like that no

KIRTANA:
And how should I put it Kumar

KUMAR:
I don't know Nicely maybe

JESSICA:
Go on You were saying something

KUMAR:
As an example of my—

KIRTANA:
Unspeculativeness

KUMAR:
—honorable
(Beat)
habits
What I've been doing
lately I've been trying to convince
these Vietnamese fisherman in
Texas whom the natives
are accusing of encroaching on
their territory, and with
these people who have no conception
of the importance
    the immense need for public representation
(because it's the public who'll vote
on whether or not their fishing
rights are extended) it's
key with these people to
talk, to
illustrate
by improvising ballpoint maps or using
cartoon representations
how this country works

and how if they are ignorant of how
it works they cannot therefore
demand
through legitimate means
what it is that is their due It's a very
jealous age we're living in They have no idea
and must be told
have to be educated
and that's what I do One example
of what I do

JESSICA:
That sounds wonderful

KUMAR:
But it's an uphill struggle
With these people
you can't be who I am

KIRTANA:
Which is what

KUMAR:
A dark-skinned
man Can't knock on
their doors and expect ears
to listen attentively,
beg for your
presence You have to
keep coming back and each day
they make damn sure you know
your presence is some form of
encroachment
Who better to cast their
lot with I'm in the
same boat But
Skin always in the way
(*Beat*)
Thank you for hearing me out
(*To Jessica:*)
It was nice meeting you

JESSICA:
Nice meeting you I
hope we'll see each other again

KUMAR:
Kirtana

KIRTANA:
Kumar

(*He exits.*)

JESSICA:
Is he who we were talking about

KIRTANA:
(*Nods.*)
He took me out

JESSICA:
Was this a date

KIRTANA:
Not a date really Well
OK a date He's buying a house

JESSICA:
Here?

KIRTANA:
This is where he wants to
settle Originally he's
from Kentucky but
he's buying a house
he wants to buy a house in Illinois
So he took me prospecting

JESSICA:
And

KIRTANA:
You're smiling You keep smiling

Han Ong

JESSICA:
Isn't this good news

KIRTANA:
You've seen him

JESSICA:
It's not good news

KIRTANA:
He took me out to this wheat field
His hands were dancing wildly the whole time
                conjuring things from the air and
                saying, Here I'm gonna build a recreation
                        room and
                here the study and
                here the bedroom
and he held my hand
I mean I've only known him a few days but
he was holding my hand

JESSICA:
And you didn't want him to

KIRTANA:
It's not that I don't
want him to It's just
I didn't feel

JESSICA:
Give it time

KIRTANA:
It's not about time
He took me to this wheat field and his hands were dancing
                        and the wheat was dancing
                        (a whole field of wheat
                        you should've seen how
                        beautiful it was Just
                        swaying
                        back and forth and I would
                        love to live there don't get
                        me wrong) but

ATTENDANT:
Under no circumstances are you to
frighten
scare
drop any bombs
He's very excitable

ARTIE:
I don't want to scare him

ATTENDANT:
And his name's Leoncillo
That's what everyone calls him

ARTIE:
He goes by his last name

ATTENDANT:
His bingo name

ARTIE:
What's he look like

ATTENDANT:
You'll see
And under no circumstances are you to say
we helped you find him or anything else

ARTIE:
What's he look like
So I won't drop my jaw

ATTENDANT:
This is an old person's home
What do you think he looks like
Why'd you come

ARTIE:
Excuse me

ATTENDANT:
He's not a nice man

ARTIE:
I don't know him

ATTENDANT:
If he gets nasty
(*Points*) press that button by that column

ARTIE:
Why's he here
a home for Jews

ATTENDANT:
Why should you be surprised

ARTIE:
Like I said, I don't know him
(*Beat*)
If you hadn't seen your father in
years wouldn't you—

ATTENDANT:
If only that were so
Instead *I've* had to labor
under that sonofabitch's shadow
Sixteen years
that little weasel has had
me to marshmallow around
Can you imagine that SIXTEEN
YEARS doing little errands
scooping up after him
Boy oh boy was I glad when
he finally croaked Except where I
used to wake up with this
intense feeling of aliveness every
morning plugging me up in every
part—this wish for him to just
shrivel up into the ground—now I
wake up empty and I don't know
if that's such a good thing
(*Beat*)
Go back home
I'm sure you have a nice
family waiting for you

ARTIE:
You're not my father are you
Bring him in

(Attendant exits. Pause. Artie sits. Rests backpack on bench. Attendant wheels Leoncillo in to table. Artie gets up.)

LEONCILLO:
Who is this boy

ATTENDANT:
It's your son

LEONCILLO:
(To Artie:)
Who are you

ARTIE:
I'm Artie

LEONCILLO:
Who

ARTIE:
Arturo

LEONCILLO:
(To Attendant:)
Get me out of here motherfucker

ATTENDANT:
He just wants to have a talk with you
Not that that's possible if history's
to judge

LEONCILLO:
(To Artie:)
I DIDN'T DO ANYTHING
YOU GOT THAT

ATTENDANT:
Well in that case you'll have nothing to fear

LEONCILLO:
(To Attendant:)
How much is he paying you

ATTENDANT:
It's not the money
Just payback for years
of having to put up
with your crap

LEONCILLO:
How much is he shelling out
I'll triple it

ARTIE:
I just want to talk

LEONCILLO:
Who are you Who is this boy

ARTIE:
I'm your son

LEONCILLO:
Which one
I have hundreds

ARTIE:
Jessica's son
What do you mean you have hundreds

LEONCILLO:
I was a handsome motherfucker
Of course I had hundreds
(To Attendant, who's starting to exit:)
Where are you going

ATTENDANT:
I'll be within distance

LEONCILLO:
Ear to keyhole

ATTENDANT:
It's a slow news day

LEONCILLO:
Come back

(*Attendant gone.*)

ARTIE:
I brought you something

LEONCILLO:
Listen You *could* be my son

ARTIE:
I am

LEONCILLO:
—but what could I give you Now
Look at me
I used to be handsome and now
look at me

ARTIE:
I just want to talk

LEONCILLO:
What'd you bring me

ARTIE:
(*Reaches into backpack; takes out box, which he gives to Leoncillo.*)
Here

LEONCILLO:
(*Puts it to ear, shaking it.*)
What's in here Candy?

ARTIE:
Some chocolates

LEONCILLO:
CHOCOLATES?! Don't you know I have
a weak heart

ARTIE:
(*Unfazed; reaches hand out.*)
I'll take it back

LEONCILLO:
NO
I love chocolates

ARTIE:
I can take it back

LEONCILLO:
I said, I love chocolates

ARTIE:
I won't be responsible for your death

LEONCILLO:
Might as well go with a smile on my lips

ARTIE:
Do you want to know anything about me

LEONCILLO:
Like what

ARTIE:
Like who I am

LEONCILLO:
You're my son

ARTIE:
Would you like some ID You don't have to take it on faith

LEONCILLO:
You look like me when I was young
God I hate you
You're a handsome motherfucker too aren't you

ARTIE:
(*Hands Leoncillo his ID.*)
That's me

LEONCILLO:
What is this

ARTIE:
My driver's license

LEONCILLO:
You drive?
What is this? Illinois

ARTIE:
That's where we live

LEONCILLO:
You're Jessica's kid?

ARTIE:
Did you love her

LEONCILLO:
Illinois She stuck it out huh
God I hate the Midwest
    I loathe the Midwest
Rednecks
How's she doing
          she been lynched and tarred

ARTIE:
No

LEONCILLO:
How's she doing

ARTIE:
She's happy
She converted Left Catholicism Just like you

LEONCILLO:
I meant financially
is she happy

ARTIE:
Very
Why'd you convert

LEONCILLO:
Judaism suits me

ARTIE:
How

LEONCILLO:
HOW?

ARTIE:
I'm curious

LEONCILLO:
In the Midwest CURIOUS boys stare at you
and say, You're our first
Asian

ARTIE:
Why Judaism

(*Beat.*)

LEONCILLO:
They know what it's like to be under Foot
(*Beat*)
It's founded by people who've had firsthand experience
of an exodus and
don't resent the modern-day version
At least I don't think they do

(*Pause.*)

ARTIE:
Did you love her

LEONCILLO:
Did she love me

ARTIE:
I don't know I'm not her I can't answer
Did you

LEONCILLO:
I've planted so many little
flags in so many different
places Didn't have time
for love

ARTIE:
Is that what I am A little banner

LEONCILLO:
Like I said, You look like me

ARTIE:
I'm not flapping for you
Do you see me flapping for you

LEONCILLO:
What's all this then if not
one big flap You're the
flag I'm the sun

ARTIE:
Can I have my ID back

LEONCILLO:
(Takes one more look at it.)
I take it back You're not so handsome

ARTIE:
I don't care

LEONCILLO:
(Hands ID back.)
You got a girlfriend

ARTIE:
I'm married

LEONCILLO:
Got any kids

ARTIE:
Four

LEONCILLO:
You're fuckin' with me

ARTIE:
How would you know

LEONCILLO:
They got any ID

ARTIE:
I killed them all

LEONCILLO:
You killed them

ARTIE:
Better than abandonment

LEONCILLO:
You don't even remember me How could you feel abandoned
Listen Arturo

ARTIE:
Artie

LEONCILLO:
Artie
Do you want to get to know me *Now* get to know me?

ARTIE:
Don't be ridiculous

LEONCILLO:
Did you want to help hold my hand through sunsets

ARTIE:
No

LEONCILLO:
Did you want to spoon-feed me liquefied food

ARTIE:
I came to see you
I came to see California

LEONCILLO:
I traveled
Mainly I wanted out of the Midwest
Jessica wouldn't
My feet itched And hers were golf shoes
                              spiked into the ground

ARTIE:
What are you explaining

LEONCILLO:
I traveled so much
Too much now I realize
but that's the price you pay
logged so many lonely nights in exchange for—
                                        in exchange for what?
                                        I don't
even remember
                So as not to let this country catch up
lonely nights equal in number to yours
or maybe more
                probably more because I was older
                                        when loneliness and
                                        foreignness feel
                                        more
acute
All I have to show
All I have to show
                is a trunkload of bus and
                                train chits and
                                plane tickets all
punched telling: This man has gotten away from hooks
fists
and nooses
I still have it
that trunkload of tickets
Hoping one day for someone to show up
so I could give it away
It's yours Just say the word

ARTIE:
What would I do with it

LEONCILLO:
Burn it Make a fire
     or Build a church
the only two choices left in this country
Do you want it

ARTIE:
No
(*Beat*)
What are you trying to explain

LEONCILLO:
Why I left You were going to ask me why I left

ARTIE:
No she told me

LEONCILLO:
Exactly like that?

ARTIE:
But without the tickets

LEONCILLO:
But you still want to know some other things

ARTIE:
I'm not good at this
So I've written
(*Takes out notebook from backpack*)
down some questions

LEONCILLO:
What's that

ARTIE:
It's just a notebook

LEONCILLO:
Your notebook

ARTIE:
Yes

LEONCILLO:
She asked you to take notes

ARTIE:
It's mine

LEONCILLO:
Not hers?

ARTIE:
She has nothing to do with me

LEONCILLO:
What do I get
If I pass this test

ARTIE:
It's not a test

LEONCILLO:
Everything's a test

ARTIE:
The real test you failed years ago
This is just some post-failure survey

LEONCILLO:
I need some incentive
For twenty-five years California was one
Big Incentive Blue sky
        White light
        Invisible Life
What incentive you got to give me

ARTIE:
Sorry

LEONCILLO:
I need an incentive

ARTIE:
If you don't answer these questions
I take the candy back

LEONCILLO:
The candy's mine

ARTIE:
No I gave it too early
thinking you'd cooperate

LEONCILLO:
The candy stays with me

ARTIE:
I'm younger
    stronger
I'm not in a wheelchair
If I want that candy back how much money you willing to bet
I won't get it

LEONCILLO:
Is that a threat

ARTIE:
I could push you
The wheels would do the rest

LEONCILLO:
That's an incentive

ARTIE:
(Looks at notebook.)
First question
Did you think of me

(Long pause.)

Did you think of me

(Beat.)

LEONCILLO:
I like watching TV

ARTIE:
What kind of answer's that

LEONCILLO:
No I didn't think of you
    I watched TV
    Plenty of TV to watch No time for memory
Next question

ARTIE:
Question number two
Did you think of me

LEONCILLO:
That's the same question

ARTIE:
No It's question number two
I've crossed out question number one and
I'm looking at question number two

LEONCILLO:
What's the differnece

ARTIE:
The difference is that there's a number two in front of this one
Question number two Did you think of me

LEONCILLO:
I have no regrets
Next question

ARTIE:
Question number three
If my name weren't Artie what name would you give me

(*Beat.*)

LEONCILLO:
Junior
I've always wanted a Junior

(*Pause.*)

Is that it

ARTIE:
Question number four
Would you recommend I go back to the Philippines

LEONCILLO:
Why

ARTIE:
Don't answer a question with a question
Question four Should I return to the Philippines

LEONCILLO:
There's nothing there for you

ARTIE:
Have you been back recently

LEONCILLO:
You see footage on the news don't you

ARTIE:
It's Western eyes It could easily be pejorative

LEONCILLO:
Trust me
If there's any good I can do
It's to let you know that there is nothing back there for
you or for me
A book closed when we left You got that?
A book closed You can return and go through the same words
as I have but the story won't change Not even for you It's
the same sad poverty story

ARTIE:
Is that why we left?

LEONCILLO:
You should thank me

ARTIE:
You should answer me

LEONCILLO:
If you'd known you would thank me
Why do you want to go back

ARTIE:
Maybe this isn't my country
(*Beat*)
Why did we come here?

LEONCILLO:
Word of mouth
(*Beat*)
People look at you funny?

ARTIE:
No

LEONCILLO:
They call you names?

ARTIE:
(*Irritated.*)
Like what

(*No response.*)

Not that I've heard no

LEONCILLO:
They don't give you things you feel you deserve

ARTIE:
But I can't say their reasons are—
I just don't feel—I can't put my finger on it

LEONCILLO:
The Midwest is like that
makes you fingerless
nothing to point with to say, This is my own piece of land

ARTIE:
Is that why you left

LEONCILLO:
I've answered that
How many more questions

ARTIE:
(Looks at notebook.)
Question number six

LEONCILLO:
What happened to Question five

ARTIE:
You answered it

LEONCILLO:
You didn't ask

ARTIE:
I didn't have to

LEONCILLO:
You think you're so smart

ARTIE:
Question number six
I'm six Pretend I'm six
You have an entire day to spend with me
Where would you take me

LEONCILLO:
Where would I take you?

ARTIE:
Where would you take me

LEONCILLO:
Where you wanna go

ARTIE:
Your choice not mine

(Long pause.)

LEONCILLO:
You're six

ARTIE:
And I've never been out in my life

LEONCILLO:
Stuck in the Midwest

ARTIE:
Well maybe once or twice But that's it

LEONCILLO:
Stuck and six

ARTIE:
I'm still six yes

LEONCILLO:
And being six you need a lesson
                         some kind of lesson

ARTIE:
But fun at the same time

LEONCILLO:
I thought this was my choice

ARTIE:
Sorry

(Beat.)

LEONCILLO:
I would take you to the zoo
I would take you to two cages side by side to learn a
fundamental lesson of this country: On one side a white dove
                              on the other a crow
You know what a crow is

ARTIE:
I know what a crow is

LEONCILLO:

On one side a dove
on the other a crow

        Both motiveless and acting
          as instinct decrees
And outside these two cages are people
called Americans
And for the dove they applaud
And for the crow they cringe
That's why I would take you to the zoo

ARTIE:

I don't understand You're telling me this isn't my country
and yet you're also saying

          Don't go back to the Philippines

LEONCILLO:

I'm not telling you this isn't your country
I'm telling you:

        Know your cage

ARTIE:

Know my cage

LEONCILLO:

Know your cage

ARTIE:

To do what

LEONCILLO:

Know your cage well
memorize its dimensions
        its distinguishing traits
so that when you go to bed
in the instant before you pitch into black
that's what you see the clearest and
you'll know

        if you run or
        if you kill or
        if you—What do you do

(*Pause.*)

LEONCILLO:
What is it you do

ARTIE:
I want to write

LEONCILLO:
if you run or
            if you kill or
            if you write
If and *When* you remember your cage
you'll know *why* you run and
            why you kill and
            why you write.

(*Beat.*)

ARTIE:
Have you ever killed anyone

LEONCILLO:
Out of a countryful of sons
how come it was you who
showed up

ARTIE:
You don't have to answer

LEONCILLO:
There's a young Indian boy
here
changing sheets
Doesn't say a word I told him what
I've just told you
Thought
Of anyone here he'd still
have skin thin enough to
soak things up
Asked him what his name was
and he said Billy
One day I thought
(just a passing fancy) I'd

adopt him Give him my name
He looked so nameless
(*Beat*)
But now that you're here

ARTIE:
I don't want anything of yours

(*Beat.*)

LEONCILLO:
yes I've killed someone

ARTIE:
I guess that's it

LEONCILLO:
I get to keep my chocolate

ARTIE:
(*Nods; rising.*)
One more thing
It's a request: can I take your picture

(*Takes out an instamatic from backpack; hoists backpack on.*)

LEONCILLO:
You gotta stand far back
Not a close-up

ARTIE:
That's fine

(*Backs off.*)

This far?

LEONCILLO:
Farther

(*Backs off some more.*)

ARTIE:
How's this

LEONCILLO:
Some more I'm vain I'm a vain man
It's true I don't mind saying it

(Artie keeps backing off until he disappears.

Leoncillo begins to tear at his box.)

Chocolate Give me my chocolate

(Tears open box:

Brings out rose after rose after rose after rose.

Sixteen in all.)

What the hell—

(Pricks himself.)

Ouch
OUCH
SOMEONE
I'M BLEEDING

(Artie reappears.

Leoncillo hides his hands.)

ARTIE:
Wait
I want to know

LEONCILLO:
You want to know what

ARTIE:
I remember the carpet

LEONCILLO:
Carpet

ARTIE:
Green
Like grass chewed off
by horses
I want to know what it
is you remembered about

LEONCILLO:
The plane

ARTIE:
When we landed
When we first
What you felt
I want to know
everything

17.

Lights cross fade dim white to Attendant, standing upstage center.

ATTENDANT:
Listen Billy
fold the sheets
Look at my hands
and do accordingly
fold
the south end
layer on top of the west
a pie crust
kneaded into place

Now Billy
don't be afraid
of blue skin
how
cold
like some midnight bloom
and the veins

Don't be afraid of veins
because they're
finally at peace
If anything you should be
afraid when they're still
boiling like kettles
And remember to always
close their eyes
because the eyes
are the repository for
hardships little
crime-scene witnesses who
cannot help but look
agitated no matter how peaceful
the life led always some crime
lurking behind there somewhere the eyes refuse to
give in to Death They always lodge
the final protest And when
the relatives come
as they do the day after
obituaries are telephoned
always tell them when they
ask How did he die,
always tell them, Peacefully
Because that word will
carry them through
(Just a simple word but
you can't imagine how
long it'll carry them through
their lives)

It's a good trade to learn Billy
Don't be ashamed
When I leave here
besides a handful
there'll be you

Do as I do Billy
It'll be just like
in the old days fathers
passing trades to sons

Look it's done
The south end over the west
and then tie the knot
It'll never pooch
never loosen
Always remember that

18.

White light fades to blue.

BUGLE BOY:
It's not often you meet
someone like you
who's young
and confused
and wanting to do something
anything
so I tell myself
What are you afraid of
Bugle Boy
Open up
Open
and meet your match
Love
Love doesn't have to make
you flabby
I'm going
I'm getting there
I have your address

19.

KIRTANA:
Farouk?
Your body's so small Farouk
I hope you have clothes beyond
those holed jeans you prefer
or I hope you're
in a warmer climate

Surfing Farouk
Surf back home to me

20.

JESSICA:
Artie?

(Martin appears.)

MARTIN:
I'm here

JESSICA:
I was—

MARTIN:
I heard you call me

JESSICA:
I was

MARTIN:
Here I am

JESSICA:
That's all I wanted to know

MARTIN:
Everything's all right
Let me take care of you
Why don't you just let
me take care of you

JESSICA:
Go to sleep

(Martin walks out of the light. The blue light holds for a beat on Jessica, then it widens.)

21.

Jessica goes and positions two chairs, as in scene seven, at the AGENCY. She sits in one. Bugle Boy enters and stands by the other.

JESSICA:
He looks more skeletal each year

BUGLE BOY:
He takes pride in that

JESSICA:
Looking thin?

BUGLE BOY:
Looking poor

JESSICA:
Look at his closet: nothing if
not the opposite But he goes
around wearing holed
articles instead That's what your
generation likes

BUGLE BOY:
I don't know what that word means

JESSICA:
They want to project
indifference but one arrived
at by very meticulous means Holes
in exactly the right places

BUGLE BOY:
The holes I
have I've worked hard to get rid of

JESSICA:
You should talk some sense into him

BUGLE BOY:
That's not what I'm here for

JESSICA:
You mentioned you were friends

BUGLE BOY:
I'm sick and tired of having to educate
people Of constantly being
expected to do that

JESSICA:
I'm sorry

BUGLE BOY:
And no, not friends I thought
we'd be friends to begin with,
but I don't think it's possible

JESSICA:
Was it something I said

BUGLE BOY:
I saw your
house Not inside But out Looking
at how the entire thing cuts against
the sky

JESSICA:
An empty house

BUGLE BOY:
He said he wasn't from privilege But the way he
held himself told a different story

JESSICA:
You see where I work
This is it
Does this look like privilege to you

(No response.)

Does it

BUGLE BOY:
Charity work to quiet guilt

JESSICA:
This is who I am
Not the house

BUGLE BOY:
Your neighbors wouldn't help me
They peeked out from windows and
I expected sirens to
screech their way to where I was

JESSICA:
Until recently they did the same to me

BUGLE BOY:
What do they have to protect looking at me like that?
Sign of privilege to me

JESSICA:
Why do you keep coming back to that
What's it to you

BUGLE BOY:
It's not for me

JESSICA:
It's not for me either

BUGLE BOY:
I'll believe it once I see it
Thanks for your time

JESSICA:
What do I tell Artie

(*Kirtana enters.*)

KIRTANA:
You lied to me

JESSICA:
Kirtana

KIRTANA:
I took in what you said
just staring at that wallpaper
all day long thinking about your
news—

JESSICA:
What news

KIRTANA:
—before realizing, It's not true
What you were trying to relay—

JESSICA:
What NEWS Kirtana

KIRTANA:
—when you were trying to relay—
You said possibilities

JESSICA:
Our leads?

KIRTANA:
Stop using that word Nothing further from the truth
All dead ends, I'm telling you

BUGLE BOY:
I'm going

JESSICA:
No no please stay

KIRTANA:
(To Bugle Boy:)
Don't trust them
They claim omnipotence here
but they lie
    They leak and
                sputter all the while claiming to be Magic

BUGLE BOY:
(To Jessica:)
Tell Artie—
(Beat)
I don't know

JESSICA:
That you came?

BUGLE BOY:
Good luck with his veins

JESSICA:
What's that mean

KIRTANA:
It's not him Jessica

JESSICA:
(To Bugle Boy:)
What's that mean

BUGLE BOY:
He'll know

(Bugle Boy exits.)

JESSICA:
Kirtana

KIRTANA:
It's not my boy

JESSICA:
We have received reports of sightings

KIRTANA:
Another Indian boy

JESSICA:
This one's clearly a runaway

KIRTANA:
Another Indian runaway

JESSICA:
(*Impatient.*)
Suddenly they've become legion is that it
Early on you said rare

KIRTANA:
But not singular

JESSICA:
You want a photograph taken would that
constitute concrete proof to you

KIRTANA:
Do you have a photograph

JESSICA:
It could be arranged

KIRTANA:
You'll be wasting your time

JESSICA:
Why are you purposely striking down
a possibility

KIRTANA:
This is the *only* possibility you
can offer?

JESSICA:
Not the only one—

KIRTANA:
What others

JESSICA:
—but it's the only one that's
turned into something definite
A track

KIRTANA:
Look elsewhere

JESSICA:
On what recommendation Yours?
We have sightings, witnesses
What do you have

KIRTANA:
A mother knows

JESSICA:
Are you afraid of being
reunited is that it

KIRTANA:
Don't waste your time on Seattle

JESSICA:
It's a *substantial* lead

KIRTANA:
(*Disbelief:*)
Male prostitution?

JESSICA:
It's a possibility
which doesn't mean Yes
            It means Could

KIRTANA:
My son's not a homosexual

JESSICA:
Kirtana listen to me
You're not hearing what I'm saying

KIRTANA:
No you said
      you clearly said in the last meeting, Mixed up
with male prostitution

JESSICA:
If I did that was an unfortunate
choice of words
All I said
All I *remember* saying was, He's been spotted
in an area in Seattle that's populated primarily
by runaways

KIRTANA:
And you said, Male prostitutes

JESSICA:
And in these areas—

KIRTANA:
Male prostitutes

JESSICA:
—male prostitutes and drug dealers
To keep alive yes

KIRTANA:
And that's supposed to make
me feel better

JESSICA:
We don't paint—

KIRTANA:
Not paint no You
scratch away

JESSICA:
You asked us to find him
and we *did Maybe*
Just a name A spotting
somewhere by witnesses who'd
seen a tacked-up Wanted sheet
with his photograph

KIRTANA:
The fact remains—

JESSICA:
You asked us to find him not render
him like some storybook We track
the *physical* body

KIRTANA:
The fact remains that Farouk is neither
homosexual nor a drug addict

JESSICA:
(*Impatient:*)
How would you know

KIRTANA:
Why are you talking like this

JESSICA:
Why are *you*

KIRTANA:
I see pictures at night

JESSICA:
We all do Kirtana

KIRTANA:
Pictures of him floating in some river

JESSICA:
Don't be SILLY

KIRTANA:
A mother knows these things

JESSICA:
You're saying to me what
                    That you'd much rather see him
dead in some river than
alive

KIRTANA:
Not if he's in Seattle doing
what you claim Not that kind
of life he might as well be dead

JESSICA:
That's absurd You're a
sensible woman Always
you've struck me as being
this sensible person

KIRTANA:
I've never told you
my history

JESSICA:
History of what

KIRTANA:
Premonitions that have come
true one by one I don't
know whose joke it was to
gift me with this But I
never asked for it
(Beat)
I'm telling you, My
boy's in some river

JESSICA:
Who put him there

KIRTANA:
Murderers everywhere

JESSICA:
You sit alone watching
the patterns of the wallpaper
all night after work
refusing to socialize—

KIRTANA:
With whom
Who do I know besides you
and how do I know you won't
start resenting me
like this dog constantly hanging around

JESSICA:
Kumar

KIRTANA:
That's not what he wants
To socialize

JESSICA:
And pretty soon you can't
tell the pattern of the
wallpaper apart from your life
You see murderers burning into
focus along the corners of the room

KIRTANA:
I have to marshal facts at night now

JESSICA:
But isn't that what I'm giving you

KIRTANA:
Giving me what

JESSICA:
Facts

KIRTANA:
Facts

JESSICA:
The solace of facts

KIRTANA:
But not yours Your set
of facts don't provide
solace at all

JESSICA:
He can be brought back
Rehabilitated

KIRTANA:
That's not what we came here for

(Sits.)

JESSICA:
Do you want some tea

(Kirtana shakes No.)

Go back and take the day off Get some sleep

KIRTANA:
I quit

JESSICA:
What do you mean you quit How
Have you got any money saved up

(Kirtana shakes No.)

What are you going to do

KIRTANA:
There's always Kumar

JESSICA:
He'll loan you money?

KIRTANA:
I'll live with him

JESSICA:
Since when

KIRTANA:
It got so I wouldn't even
leave the restaurant after work
Just spend the night on the floors

JESSICA:
Does Kumar know you want to
live with him

KIRTANA:
Believe me he'll be ecstatic

JESSICA:
Oh I don't doubt that
But does he know why

KIRTANA:
A clean start No son I have
no son Jessica He doesn't need
to know a thing No better qualification
for a new wife than to be without history
Besides he doesn't want
someone to talk
                    tell their story
He wants someone to listen
to *his*, ears always
buzzing after what he has to say

JESSICA:
Do you love Kumar

KIRTANA:
You want to know what I've learned

JESSICA:
What

KIRTANA:
One can't do without diversions Not
here Not have emotions
so unalloyed like—

JESSICA:
One makes do*

KIRTANA:
—like me
(*In response to* *:)
Have you

JESSICA:
I've made do yes

KIRTANA:
But not entirely You have
this house Beautiful and large

JESSICA:
Somewhere along the line
I can't even account for
it I lucked out

KIRTANA:
Some lottery that I can enter
as well?

JESSICA:
You already have
(Beat)
Do you love Kumar

KIRTANA:
Does that matter

JESSICA:
I thought it did to you

(From Kirtana's bag, she takes out a cow noisemaker.)

KIRTANA:
This makes me laugh

(Dips it; it moos.)

JESSICA:
Do you love Kumar

KIRTANA:
It's this country's main
business isn't it

JESSICA:
Toys?

(Stretches her hand out as a gesture of asking for the toy.)

KIRTANA:
(Hands toy to Jessica.)
The manufacture of diversions Always
something else besides the wound

But never a cure,
just its diversion

JESSICA:
It's good to laugh
(*Beat*)
Do you love Kumar

KIRTANA:
You keep asking that

JESSICA:
Because what you said
about swooning
        why you've held out
stayed with me

KIRTANA:
(*A sudden burst of adrenaline; escalating quickly into mania:*)
Believe me
I'm SWOONING all right
I will not change
Do you hear that
This country changes you but
NOT ME It changes you for
the worse but not ME
Not my son either
He's not turning homosexual
Only because it's a new country
If there's anyone who'll change it's
this country
This country and not me
If the food's not to your liking, you change it
                        COOK IT YOURSELF
Right Isn't that right
If the wallpaper's not to your liking, rip it out
"You have recourse to that": aren't those
your words? If this country lies
to you

(*Snatches toy from Jessica and begins to stomp on it.*)

If this country lies to you, fuck it
Then fuck it
(*Beat; more calmly now*)
I will not be moved
I will not be moved
I will not be moved

(*Lights fade on everything but the crushed moo-toy, at center.*)

22.

Dim lights upstage center in preparation for the next scene. Stage right: Kirtana, smoking a cigarette. Stage left: Leoncillo, sitting in a wheelchair. Lights remain on the moo-toy as well. Beside Kirtana, a phone. Throughout the scene, she plays unconsciously with her hair. Throughout the scene, Leoncillo coughs.

LEONCILLO'S VOICE:
You want to know what

ARTIE'S VOICE:
I remember the carpet

LEONCILLO'S VOICE:
Carpet

ARTIE'S VOICE:
Green
Like grass chewed off
by horses
I want to know what it
is you remembered about

LEONCILLO'S VOICE:
The plane

ARTIE'S VOICE:
When we landed
When we first
What you felt

LEONCILLO'S VOICE:
And you're writing this down

ARTIE'S VOICE:
In my notebook

LEONCILLO'S VOICE:
I remember cows
seeing them through the porthole

ARTIE'S VOICE:
Window

LEONCILLO'S VOICE:
I'd never seen cows
I was so excited
What can I say
We're allowed moments of
stupidity But I was so excited
This pulsing Black against white
Never seen these balloon things
Certainly not in the Philippines
Carabaos, they had
You know what that is

(Silence, during which we presume Artie shakes no.)

LEONCILLO'S VOICE:
A Filipino water buffalo
It appears on the flipside of the five
centavo piece in the currency

ARTIE'S VOICE:
Of the Philippines

LEONCILLO'S VOICE:
In the currency* of the Philippines

(*At this word, Kirtana's phone starts to ring. She looks at it, impassive. Lets it ring once, twice, thrice, four times, five. It dies. All the while the voiceover continues.)

The five-cent piece

ARTIE'S VOICE:
And it's called a what

LEONCILLO'S VOICE:
Carabao

ARTIE'S VOICE:
Could you spell that please

LEONCILLO'S VOICE:
You want me to spell that

ARTIE'S VOICE:
Could you please

LEONCILLO'S VOICE:
You want me to SPELL that

ARTIE'S VOICE:
(More authoritative:)
Yes I want you to spell it

LEONCILLO'S VOICE:
You want me to spell carabao

ARTIE'S VOICE:
Is there anything wrong

LEONCILLO'S VOICE:
You don't know how to spell carabao

ARTIE'S VOICE:
Would I ask you if I did

LEONCILLO'S VOICE:
You want to hear it spelled

ARTIE'S VOICE:
Forget it

LEONCILLO'S VOICE:
Maybe you should go back

ARTIE'S VOICE:
Just because I don't know how to spell carabao

LEONCILLO'S VOICE:
It's C-A-R-A-B-A

(*Before he can say O, an amplified moo-toy sound, or a real cow moo-ing is heard. As soon as it starts, the lights quickly die on Kirtana and Leoncillo. The moo-toy sound fades soon after.*)

23.

The Attendant, upstage center, visible in the dimness because of his white male nurse's uniform, and who has been there all throughout, smoking, is now better seen.

ATTENDANT:
(*Sings:*)
> The first half dies
> with no proof or trace
> no memory of dinner talk
> any remnant of grace
> no azure stroll
> never a leisurely pace
> instead a bolt a run
> perpetual longing for Place.

(*Speaks:*)
Don't be afraid Billy
of blue skin
and veins
Everything must end

(*He picks up a phone, dials. Rings. Jessica revealed. She picks up.*)

JESSICA:
Hello

ATTENDANT:
Hello?
May I speak to
Artie Leoncillo please

JESSICA:
Who is this

ATTENDANT:
Who am I speaking to

JESSICA:
I'm his mother
Who is this

ATTENDANT:
Oh

JESSICA:
He's not here

ATTENDANT:
Ma'am

JESSICA:
Has something happened to him

ATTENDANT:
No ma'am
I was calling
to let Mr. Leoncillo know
His father

JESSICA:
Yes

ATTENDANT:
His father has

JESSICA:
Oh my God

ATTENDANT:
You have my condolences
Are you his wife mam

JESSICA:
No
How
How did he

ATTENDANT:
In his sleep mam

JESSICA:
So it was

ATTENDANT:
It was very peaceful

JESSICA:
Thank you

ATTENDANT:
He was at peace

JESSICA:
Thank you

(*Jessica remains. Light fades.*)

END OF PLAY

Han Ong is the author of more than three dozen plays, including *The L.A. Plays*, *The Chang Fragments*, *Middle Finger*, *Watcher* and the plays that comprise *The Suitcase Trilogy*: *Swoony Planet*, *Autodidacts* and *Virgin*. He has also been a performance artist appearing in works such as *Symposium in Manila*, *Corner Store Geography*, *Play of Father and Junior* and (with Jessica Hagedorn) *Airport Music*. These works have been produced at American Repertory Theater, Magic Theatre, Berkeley Repertory Theatre, the Public Theater, Ma-Yi Theater Company and the Almeida Theatre in London. He is a novelist as well, and has published two novels: *Fixer Chao*, a *Los Angeles Times* Best Book of the Year and cited by the *New York Times* as a new immigrant classic, and *The Disinherited*, nominated for a Lambda Literary Award.

Ong is the youngest playwright to be awarded a MacArthur Fellowship, and has also been the recipient of fellowships from the Guggenheim Foundation and the National Endowment for the Arts. He was most recently awarded a Berlin Prize from the American Academy in Berlin. He has been a guest lecturer at Columbia University, Long Island University and the New School, and has taught playwriting at New York's 92nd Street Y for the last five years.

Durango

Julia Cho

Author's Statement

I wrote *Durango* know-
ing it would be the final
play in a group of three
plays all set in the desert
(the previous two were
The Architecture of Loss
and *BFE*). At the time,
I thought of the three plays
as a trilogy, but "trilogy"
makes it sound more gran-
diose than it was. I was just a neophyte playwright, trying to make
sense of what being Asian in America is. I found the desert—a place
of extremes and harsh beauty—lent itself well to exploration and
metaphor. And so I set different variations of the Asian-American
family in the desert not just once but several times, each broken in
its own way and trying to make itself whole.

But the desert isn't really the focus of *Durango*, the road is.
Boo-Seng and his sons are on a journey, and like almost all travelers,
they go a very long way just to come back to where they began. But
that seems to me the nature of trips, especially family road trips. The
point is never the destination: we pile into cars and hit the road out
of the hope we will become closer, tighter . . . better.

The reality, of course, is often quite the opposite: we fight, we
argue, we complain. Yet the family road trip tradition continues
unabated, as popular now as it was when I was a child. Call it our
American optimism. We long to be the best version of ourselves and
persist in the belief that somewhere, out there on the open road,
we'll find it.

Acknowledgments

Durango would never have been birthed without the administrations of many people: Center Theatre Group, which commissioned it; Wendy Goldberg, Artistic Director of the National Playwrights Conference, where the play was developed; and Chay Yew and Gordon Edelstein, who saw the play in its earliest stages and believed in it. Portions of the play were written during a residency at the MacDowell Colony.

Production History

Durango was commissioned by Center Theatre Group in Los Angeles, California. It was written with support from the MacDowell Colony and the Juilliard School and subsequently developed at the Eugene O'Neill Theater Center National Playwrights Conference, the Ojai Playwrights Conference and the Public Theater's New Work Now! series.

   Durango premiered in 2006 at the Public Theater in New York (Oskar Eustis, Artistic Director; Mara Manus, Executive Director) in association with the Long Wharf Theatre (Gordon Edelstein, Aristic Director; Joan Channick, Managing Director). It was directed by Chay Yew. Set design was by Dan Ostling. Costume design was by Linda Cho. Lighting design was by Paul Whitaker. Sound design and additional music was by Fabian Obispo. The production stage manager was Buzz Cohen. The stage manager was Christina Lowe. The cast was as follows:

BOO-SENG LEE	James Saito
ISAAC LEE	James Yaegashi
JIMMY LEE	Jon Norman Schneider
THE RED ANGEL / BOB	Jay Sullivan
JERRY / NED	Ross Bickell

Durango received its Midwest premiere in 2008 at the Silk Road Theatre Project in Chicago (Jamil Khoury, Founding Artistic Director; Malik Gillani, Founding Executive Director). It was directed by Carlos Murillo. The set design was by Marianna Csaszar. The costume design was by Carol J. Blanchard. The lighting design was by Rebecca A. Barrett. The sound designer and composer was Robert Steel. The stage manager was Jen Poulin. The cast was as follows:

BOO-SENG LEE	Joseph Anthony Foronda
ISAAC LEE	Dawen Wang
JIMMY LEE	Erik Kaiko
THE RED ANGEL / BOB	Austin Campion
JERRY / NED	Walter Brody

Characters

BOO-SENG LEE, a fifty-six-year-old Korean man

ISAAC LEE, twenty-one, Boo-Seng's son, awkward

JIMMY LEE, thirteen, Boo-Seng's other son, well-developed for his age

THE RED ANGEL, a beautiful, blonde, young sun god

BOB, late twenties to early thirties, Boo-Seng's co-worker, played by the actor who plays the Red Angel

JERRY, late fifties, a security guard

NED, fifties or sixties, a retiree, played by the actor who plays Jerry

Setting

The Southwest.

Time

The near present.

Note

A smarter playwright than I invented the use of a forward slash (/)
to denote where a character begins an interruption or an overlap.

Em dashes (—) do not indicate overlap. They indicate when one
word or line is immediately followed by the next. Please make sure
the word before the dash is actually spoken.

Ellipses (. . .) do not indicate overlap, but they are not exactly a
pause or break. They indicate a word or thought is sustained through
to the next word—left hanging, so to speak.

Words in brackets are thought and meant but not actually spoken.

For James Joong-Suk Cho.

1.

Lights up on Isaac with a guitar. He sings.

ISSAC:

Main Street isn't busy much anymore;
the girl diver's become a lonely sight.
She's a neon girl all dressed up with nowhere to go
and soon she'll be diving
in the dark.

Who thought this would be some kind of big destination?
Who stays in all these dusty motels?
The girl dives into a sign that says, "Vacancy."
You see her dive and then you just drive on.

Oh whoh oh
whoh oh
Oh whoh oh
whoh oh

Doesn't she ever, doesn't she ever get lonely?
And doesn't she ever, doesn't she ever get bored?

Doesn't she ever get sick of what she's doing?
I think she wants to hit the road.

Oh whoh oh
whoh oh
Oh whoh oh
whoh oh

Main Street isn't busy much anymore;
the girl diver remains a lonely sight.
She's a neon girl all dressed up with nowhere to go
and she's diving
in the dark.

2.

An office. Boo-Seng is sitting behind the desk. Jerry, a security guard, sits in a chair.
    Boo-Seng's desk is clean except for a framed photo.

BOO-SENG: How old are you, Jerry?

JERRY: Letsee now . . . fifty . . . fifty-eight.

BOO-SENG: You can retire soon.

JERRY: Yeah, if I last that long.

BOO-SENG: Full benefits.

JERRY: That's the idea.

BOO-SENG: And then what?

JERRY: Oh, I don't know . . . maybe travel. Play golf. See my grand-kids more. Usual stuff, I guess.

BOO-SENG: Back where I come from, you know, lot of my old friends, they are quite successful now.

JERRY: Is that so?

BOO-SENG: One is the owner of his own company, big company. Another is very high in the government, you know, close to president. Another is president of university.

JERRY: Must be quite a reunion when you guys get together.

BOO-SENG: No, I haven't seen them in long time.

JERRY: Why not?

BOO-SENG: I haven't gone back in over twenty years.

JERRY: Not even once?

BOO-SENG: Here is my home.

JERRY: Sure.

(Jerry reaches for the framed photo.)

These your boys?

BOO-SENG: Yes.

JERRY: Good-looking kids.

BOO-SENG: This one, Jimmy, he's a swim champion. No one can beat him in backstroke.

JERRY: He looks like a winner.

BOO-SENG: He is. He'll get scholarship for swimming I'm sure. Which is good. Hard to get into college without some kind of, you know, special thing.

JERRY: Yeah, grades aren't enough anymore. Getting so competitive.

BOO-SENG: And my other son, Isaac, he's going to be doctor. He just came back from his interview at the University of Hawaii. That's in Honolulu. Very good med school. Very hard to get in.

JERRY: Tell me about it. My Lisa applied everywhere and only got in one place—and that was by the skin of her teeth.

BOO-SENG: Your daughter? Is in med school?

JERRY: Doctor now. One more year of residency. Pediatrics.

(Jerry hands the photo to Boo-Seng who puts it into a box behind the desk. Boo-Seng sets the box on the desk.)

You ready?

BOO-SENG: Jerry?

Sometime, in the morning. I don't know my face. Inside, I still feel the same, same as when I was young . . .

JERRY: . . . exactly the same . . .

BOO-SENG: . . . but then I have this old face.

(Pause.)

JERRY: Would you like a moment, Mr. Lee?

(Boo-Seng nods.)

BOO-SENG: Thanks, Jerry.

JERRY: Don't mention it.

(Pause. They sit there.)

BOO-SENG: Jerry. Maybe a moment . . . alone?

JERRY: Well, if it were up to me, of course, but—

BOO-SENG: What am I going to do?

JERRY: Oh, I know you wouldn't *do* anything, it's just . . . you know the rules.

BOO-SENG *(Softly)*: I don't want everyone see you walk me out like I'm a criminal.

JERRY: It won't be like that.

(Boo-Seng cleans out his last drawer. There are letters and a brochure. The brochure is old and folded up. He unfolds it and looks at it.

Maybe, very briefly and very faintly, there is the sound of a breeze, of wind moving through leaves.)

Mr. Lee?

I have to be at another office by four.

Let's go.

(Boo-Seng puts the brochure in his pocket. He picks up the box and stands.)

BOO-SENG: Yes.

Let's go.

3.

The kitchen. Isaac is playing the guitar.
Jimmy is stirring something in a pot.

JIMMY: I thought Dad told you to get rid of that.

ISAAC: Screw Dad. You gonna tell him I still have it?

JIMMY: Nah, I don't care if you play.

So what was it like?

ISAAC: Warm.

JIMMY: Duh, warm. Arizona's warm. I mean, what else?

ISAAC: It's a totally different kinda warm. Arizona's putrid warm. Arizona's like the armpit of the United States warm. And Honolulu . . . Honolulu's like the promised land. I mean, they've got soy sauce at the fucking McDonald's, right by the ketchup. You can get kimchi at the corner store, that's what I'm talking about.

JIMMY: No.

ISAAC: Yes! And everyone goes around in swimsuits, I shit you not. Grocery shopping, filling up their gas—in swimsuits, man, girls and guys. And they're all beautiful. Tan. Slender. You've never seen such beautiful people. I didn't see a single pimple on anyone the whole time I was there.

JIMMY: What'd you do after your interview?

ISAAC: I don't know. Just hung out.

JIMMY: Didja talk to any girls?

ISAAC: Yeah . . . but no one really interesting. I mean, they *look* good, but. *(He shrugs)*

JIMMY: I can't wait to visit.

ISAAC: You know how hard it is to get into med school, Jimmy?

JIMMY: It's hard.

ISAAC: Shit yeah, it's hard. And for someone who isn't exactly a four-oh, organic chemistry major who also runs a homeless shelter on the side, one might even say it's impossible.

JIMMY: But you got to the interview, that's a good sign, right? Right?

ISAAC: Check this out. Listen to this chord. *(He plays a chord)* Isn't that a cool, fucking chord? I just found it.

JIMMY: You know, we had an assembly today and the marching band from your old high school came and played. And the sax player, he played the theme from that old show they show on TV sometimes, *The Benny Hill Show.* It was pretty funny.

ISAAC: Uh huh. *(He looks at his fingers)*

JIMMY: It made me think. Made me think of quitting swimming.

ISAAC *(Not listening)*: Sure. *(Listening)* What?

JIMMY: I could do something else, right?

ISAAC: Like what?

JIMMY: I could learn to play the sax.

ISAAC: Jesus, why not just pick up the clari-fucking-net?

JIMMY: I kinda want to be in band.

ISAAC: Oh, you're killing me. You are NOT going to be a band geek, Jimmy, okay? Over my dead body.

JIMMY: I think band would be more fun than swimming. It's like when you swim, you swim alone. But when you're in band . . . you're in a *band*.

ISAAC: Do you *want* to get picked on? Is that it?

JIMMY: Look, it's not like when you went to school. I don't let myself get picked on.

ISAAC: You think I *let* myself get picked on?

JIMMY: Joining math club, what did you expect?

(The sound of the front door opening.)

ISAAC: Shit.

(He hides his guitar and starts setting the table. Boo-Seng enters.)

JIMMY: Hey, Dad.
ISAAC: What's up.

(Boo-Seng walks right through the room without acknowledging either Jimmy or Isaac. He leaves.
    Jimmy and Isaac just look at each other.)

JIMMY: Is he okay?
ISAAC: Is he ever?
JIMMY *(Calling offstage)*: Dad? Dinner's ready.

(Jimmy puts rice on the plates and then puts beef stew on the rice. Isaac starts eating. Jimmy sits down.
    Boo-Seng enters and sits at the table.)

JIMMY: How was your day, Dad?

(Boo-Seng closes his eyes, as if deep in thought. He breathes heavily. Jimmy looks at Isaac, who just shrugs. They eat in silence. Boo-Seng finally opens his eyes. He clears his throat.)

BOO-SENG: Tell me what you think.

(Pause.)

JIMMY: 'Bout what, Dad?
BOO-SENG: I think it is time for family trip.

(Isaac looks alarmed. Jimmy looks eager.)

JIMMY: Really?   ISAAC: What?

ISAAC: Dad, I just got back from a trip. I'm tired.
BOO-SENG: What tired? You sit on plane, that's all.
ISAAC: But I've got classes, you've got work—
BOO-SENG: I have some time off . . . I always thought you need to see more of where we living.

ISAAC: What's to see? It's all the same, it's all dirt and rocks.

BOO-SENG: Jimmy need to see.

JIMMY: Cool. When can we go, Dad?

BOO-SENG: This weekend.

ISAAC: I have to study. You know, for my bio test on Monday and orgo and—

BOO-SENG: Just a short trip. Drive up north maybe. Take a look around, drive back. Different up there. Not desert. Tree.

ISAAC: Yeah, but Jimmy's probably got a swim meet, right, Jimmy?

JIMMY: No, we don't have a meet until—ow! (*Isaac has kicked Jimmy under the table*) Coach said we could have the weekend off to— quit it, Isaac.

ISAAC: But you need to rest, right, Jimmy?

BOO-SENG: He can rest in car.

JIMMY: Yeah. So where we going, Dad? Where d'you want to go?

BOO-SENG: Durango.

ISAAC: What the hell's that?

BOO-SENG: You don't know Durango? Everyone know Durango.

(*He takes out the brochure and looks at it.*)

BOO-SENG: There is train . . . very famous train. Silver train. It leave from Durango and go up into the mountain.

JIMMY: Durango.

ISAAC: Never heard of it.

BOO-SENG: It's famous.

ISAAC: Well, never heard of it.

JIMMY: Is it a long trip?

BOO-SENG: No. Just a few hours.

JIMMY: We could do that, Dad, if you want to.

BOO-SENG: I wanted to for long time. Now is last chance, maybe.

(*He puts the brochure away.*)

JIMMY: Yeah. Soon Isaac'll be in Hawaii.

ISAAC: Yeah.

JIMMY: Then let's do it. C'mon, we can do it, right?

ISAAC: I don't feel up for it . . . I'll stay here and watch the house, someone's gotta watch the house, right?

JIMMY: You can't just not go. It's a family trip.

ISAAC: Well, I don't want to go, okay? I just got back from one trip, I'm not / about to go on

JIMMY: But we've never done this, we've never all gone on a trip.
ISAAC: Yeah, we have.
JIMMY: *I* haven't.
BOO-SENG: We leave tomorrow morning.
ISAAC: Does anyone hear a word I'm saying? No.
JIMMY: You're going.
ISAAC: *You* go, go with Dad. Have fun.
JIMMY *(To Boo-Seng)*: Dad. You gonna just let him punk out on us?

(Boo-Seng sets down his fork and frowns.)

What is it? What's wrong?
BOO-SENG: Somehow . . . doesn't taste right.
JIMMY: Did I make it wrong?
BOO-SENG: No . . .
ISAAC: Maybe he's just sick of Dinty Moore Beef Stew. Are you,
Dad? Are you sick of Dinty Moore Beef Stew?

(Boo-Seng gets up.)

BOO-SENG: I'm going lie down.
Jimmy. I will wake you at six.

(Boo-Seng leaves.)

JIMMY: C'mon, Isaac. Please.
ISAAC: Gee . . . let me think about it no.

*(Isaac scrapes the food off Boo-Seng's plate onto his own plate
and starts eating.*
Jimmy looks at him in disgust.)

(Mouth full:) What? Did you want some too?
JIMMY: Such a jerk.

(Jimmy leaves.)

ISAAC *(Calling)*: You're not exactly a ray of sunshine either.

(Isaac stops eating.
He gets his guitar from where he hid it.
He holds it but doesn't play.)

4.

Jimmy's room.
  Jimmy is sitting at his desk, drawing in a sketchbook.
  Isaac knocks at the door.

ISAAC: C'n I come in?
JIMMY: No.

  (Isaac comes in anyway.)

JIMMY: I said no.
ISAAC: What're you drawing? C'n I see?
JIMMY: Go away.

  (Isaac flops down on Jimmy's bed.)

ISAAC: Your bed is so much more comfortable than mine. I don't get
    that. How come you get the better bed? Oh, wait, I know, it's
    because:
      (Imitating their father:) An athlete needs his sleep.

  (It's a joke they usually share, but Jimmy keeps ignoring him.)

Yeah . . . I should take up a sport.
    Hey, Jimmy, can you think of a non-strenuous sport?
    Jimmy.
    Hey.
JIMMY: Go to your own room.
ISAAC: Why do you want to go on this road trip, huh? It'll be dead
    boring. Cooped up in a small car with Dad and me. I mean,
    Jesus, is that your idea of a good time?
JIMMY: That's not the point. The point is he asked. He asked to spend
    time with us. He never asks that.
ISAAC: What're you talking about? He goes to every single one of
    your swim meets.
JIMMY: Yeah, and you know what he does? He comes, sits in the last
    row of the bleachers and he times me. And then he writes down
    all the times in this little book and after I swim, he comes and
    finds me, and tells me down to the last tenth of a second how
    far off I am from my personal record or the city record or what-
    ever. Sometimes I'll be like getting ready for my next event, like
    at the starting blocks right before the relay or something, and

he'll just come barreling up and I can't make him shut up, he'll just stand there, rattling off all these times at me while I'm putting on my goggles. It's like he's there to check up on me, not to support me. And definitely not to spend time with me.

And the one time he offers to spend time with us—all of us together—you act like he's just asked you to chop off a limb.

ISAAC: I get carsick.

JIMMY: Shut up, you love to drive.

ISAAC: Jimmy.

JIMMY: Just get out.

ISAAC: Jimmmmy.

You know what I remember? After all those trips? What I remember is how we drove hours and hours to get to the Grand Canyon. And it wasn't even where we were headed. We were just going up to Flagstaff but Dad had to go see the Grand Canyon—no, he had to pretend he was going to see it really *for us*, for me and Mom. Course me and Mom just want to go home; we're hungry, we're tired, but does Dad care? No.

So we drive and we drive and we finally get there. But it's taken us so long that now it's sunset. Five minutes after we park, the sun's gone down and I can't even see my hand in front of my face let alone the Grand fucking Canyon.

I mean, shit. The Painted Desert. The Petrified Forest. Yellowstone. Yosemite. Bryce Canyon. Zion Canyon. Monument Valley. I am so fucking *sick* of national monuments. All those hours and hours on the road with Dad screaming his head off about how "we are going to have a good time OR ELSE" and Mom not saying a word—*a word*. I get sick just thinking about it.

JIMMY: But that was a long time ago.

ISAAC: So? You think this shit changes? It doesn't change.

JIMMY: It's not fair. It's not fair that you got to go see all these places and then by the time I get big enough no one wants to go anywhere anymore.

ISAAC: Why do you think it's going to be so great?

JIMMY: I'm not expecting it to be great. I just want to go. It doesn't have to be this great adventure. But you, me and Dad, we never do anything all together. Let's just go, Isaac. Please. Let's just go.

(*Pause.*

Jimmy turns back to his drawing.)

You *are* selfish.

ISAAC: Who says?
   Dad?
   Or you?
JIMMY: Me.

(Beat.)

ISAAC: All right . . . You want to go so bad . . . show me what you're
   drawing.
JIMMY: What? No. Why?
ISAAC: 'Cause I'm curious. You're always drawing. See your light on
   late at night. All secretive.
JIMMY: Forget it.
ISAAC: Hey, I thought you wanted to go . . .
JIMMY: Even if I did show you, you'd just welsh on the deal.
ISAAC: Welsh? What kind of word is welsh?
JIMMY: You going to renege on this deal?
ISAAC: Ooh, renege. What is that, an SAT word? Fine. I won't *renege.*
   I promise.

(Jimmy gives Isaac the sketchbook.)

JIMMY: Just this page. Don't flip around.

(Isaac looks at the sketchbook.)

ISAAC: Superheroes? You're drawing superheroes?
JIMMY: It's my comic, shut up.
ISAAC: Nah, it's good. Really.
JIMMY: Yeah, right. Just give it back.

(Jimmy grabs it from him.)

   That's enough.
ISAAC: Didn't know you could draw like that.
JIMMY: Deal's a deal, right? *Right?*
ISAAC: Yeah. What the hell. I'll go.
JIMMY: You'll see—it'll be fun.
ISAAC: Uh huh.
JIMMY: It'll be like, like, the three of us together. And maybe Dad will
   finally be, you know. Happy. With us.
ISAAC: Night, Jimmy. Get some rest.
   You're going to need it.

(Isaac salutes and leaves.)

JIMMY: What's that supposed to mean?
  (Calling:) What's that supposed to mean?

(He turns back to his desk.
  He starts drawing again.
  The Red Angel appears. He is a beautiful, blonde, young man.)

JIMMY: He grew up in a small, dusty town. He was just an average kid.
  Or so he thought.
RED ANGEL: Did I know I was different? Somehow, somewhere? Was there, underneath it all, some kind of recognition?
JIMMY: The morning of his thirteenth birthday, two little bumps appeared beneath his shoulder blades.
RED ANGEL: They terrified me. I hid them with sweaters, I never took off my backpack. But no matter what I did, they grew larger and larger.
JIMMY: And then: tragedy! His house was on fire! He made it out but his parents were trapped! They waved frantically from the second floor window—who could save them?
RED ANGEL: And then I understood—
JIMMY: who he was—
RED ANGEL: what I was—
JIMMY: the bumps on his shoulders:
RED ANGEL: They were wings.

(The Red Angel unfurls his wings.
  Jimmy lifts up his drawing into the air, as he makes a sound of flying.)

5.

The family car.
  Isaac slouches in the front seat. Boo-Seng sits behind the wheel, alert. Jimmy's bouncing around the back.

BOO-SENG: Air conditioner off?
JIMMY: Check.
BOO-SENG: Back door locked?
JIMMY: Yup.

BOO-SENG: Side door?

ISAAC: Why do we have to leave so early?

BOO-SENG: Have to get early start. I don't like to drive when it's too hot.

Uh . . . (*He's lost his place*) . . . back door . . . Jimmy, what was I—?

JIMMY: Side door. And check.

BOO-SENG: Window locked?

ISAAC: . . . Oh, for Christ's sake . . .

BOO-SENG (*Sharp*): Isaac, this is important.

JIMMY: Windows are locked. Check.

BOO-SENG: Okay.

Okay.

Let's go.

(*He starts the engine. The car gets underway.*
Boo-Seng smiles. He's glad to be on the road.)

JIMMY (*Sing-songy*): Road trip, road trip. We're going on the road—

ISAAC: Shut up, Jimmy.

BOO-SENG: So quiet outside.

ISAAC: That's because it's six friggin' a.m. in the morning.

BOO-SENG: Clear weather. Good sign. What is word for that? Good sign?

JIMMY: Lucky?

BOO-SENG: No . . . *Aus*-pi-shss.

JIMMY (*Correcting him*): Aus*pi*cious.

BOO-SENG: Aus-*pi-shuss*.

JIMMY: Auspicious.

ISAAC: Someone wake me up when we're there.

(*Isaac settles in and closes his eyes.*)

BOO-SENG: Isaac. You know. I wanted to say. That was very big job you did. Go to Hawaii and come back by yourself.

ISAAC: It's no big deal.

BOO-SENG: So what did my friend say when you saw him?

ISAAC: What friend?

BOO-SENG: My friend, I told you, I gave you his number.

ISAAC: Oh, I didn't see him.

BOO-SENG: What?

ISAAC: I got busy. Plane was a little late . . . and then I had to get ready for the interview . . .

347

BOO-SENG: But I told him you would call him. I told him. Isaac. This is serious.

ISAAC: Well, I'm sorry.

BOO-SENG: He is a busy man, Isaac. He did you great favor.

ISAAC: I know. You don't have to remind me, okay?

BOO-SENG: He is my oldest friend; he was *waiting* for you.

ISAAC: Well, you didn't tell me that.

BOO-SENG: He was *expecting* you.

ISAAC: Then why did you make it sound like I should *maybe* just call him up? That's what you said: *Maybe* you can call him *if* you have time.

BOO-SENG: That means call him.

ISAAC: Then why didn't you say so? Say: *You Have To Call Him.* Don't make it sound like it's an option if it's not.

BOO-SENG: Are you so stupid, you can't understand what I mean?

ISAAC: It's not my fault you don't just say what you mean, I'm not some friggin' / mind-reader

BOO-SENG: The most basic thing, and you can't even / do what is right

ISAAC: Look, I filled out fifteen med school applications for you. I got on an airplane for ten hours for you. So don't tell me I don't / do anything for

BOO-SENG: For me? FOR ME? Is THAT what you think it's for?

ISAAC: Of course it is, so that you can tell your friends that your son is a doctor so that you'll look good, right?

BOO-SENG: I DON'T CARE ABOUT LOOK GOOD. You don't have any talent to be anything else, *that's* the point. Selfish *Ba-boh. Ee Na-pu-nom Seh-ki.* My friend, you know how long we know each other? Since we are twelve years old. I remember how poor we were. We were always hungry. And in the winter, our hands were cold—

ISAAC (*Muttering, underneath*): Yeah, yeah, yeah . . .

BOO-SENG: —no gloves—

ISAAC: Just one holey mitten that you had to, like, share among all seven of your brothers and sisters . . .

BOO-SENG: You have no idea what is like to be cold. To be hungry. A hundred degree below freezing—

ISAAC: That's impossible.

BOO-SENG: YES IS POSSIBLE. A hundred degree below, up in the mountains. That's why Americans had such hard time, because not used to how cold it get and hungry, you never know how hungry,

ISAAC (*Talking under his father*): Once a month, if we were lucky, we got a little bit of bone with a little flap of marrow hanging from it and my brother, he was the favorite, so he always got the bone to gnaw on

BOO-SENG: there was never enough to eat. If my friend or I got some money, we would buy a little food and then we would eat it together, share—

BOO-SENG (*He cuts Isaac off wherever he is*): **He is my best friend.** He did so much for you and you, / you—

ISAAC: FINE, DAD, I'm a horrible person, okay? Your friend was kind enough to pull strings to get your loser of a son an interview and how do I repay him? By not calling him up and falling over myself thanking him. I'm useless, I'm an idiot. I'm hopelessly spoiled. You're absolutely right. I should've never been born—you and Mom should've ABORTED ME WHEN YOU HAD THE CHANCE.

(*A silent fury fills the car.*
   Jimmy sits quietly in the backseat.
   A long silence.)

JIMMY (*Tentatively*): So.
   When will we get there?
   Dad?
   Dad, when d'you think we'll get there?
   I'll look in the map. Where exactly is Durango? Near Flagstaff
or . . .
BOO-SENG: Colorado.

(*An enormous pause fills the car.*)

ISAAC: What?
BOO-SENG: What.
ISAAC: What did you say?
BOO-SENG: I said Colorado.
ISAAC: Durango's in Colorado?
BOO-SENG (*An affirmative grunt*): So?
ISAAC: You said a few hours. That's what *you said*. I asked, how far and you said—
BOO-SENG: The train is a few hours. Just up and down the mountain. Once you get there.

ISAAC: Are you KIDDING me?

BOO-SENG: DON'T SHOUT.

ISAAC: Are you telling us this stupid train is in COLORADO?

BOO-SENG: SO?

ISAAC: YOU DIDN'T TELL US THAT.

BOO-SENG: I SAID DON'T YELL. **Durango is in Colorado, everyone know that.**

ISAAC: WE didn't. We didn't know that we were embarking on a trip that actually crossed STATE LINES.

BOO-SENG: LINE. State LINE. Arizona, Colorado. THASSIT.

JIMMY: It's not so bad, Isaac, just don't—

ISAAC: SHUT UP, JIMMY. Stop the car.

JIMMY: We're already on the way—

ISAAC: I'll hitch a ride home—

BOO-SENG: Let him go, fine! Feel sorry for whoever pick him up!

JIMMY: NO. Dad, don't pull over.

C'mon, Isaac. This is supposed to be a family trip.

ISAAC: Family? Family?? I've been kidnapped.

BOO-SENG: WHO KIDNAP? **I am your father.**

JIMMY: Just calm down, everyone, okay? Dad? Isaac? It's fine. We'll go, we'll see the train or whatever, we'll come back. No big deal. Okay? Okay.

ISAAC: Colorado. Colorado!

(A long silence.)

JIMMY: I always wanted to go to Colorado.

ISAAC: Shut it, Jimmy. Just. Shut it.

6.

Jimmy and Isaac look out the window of the car. They are unbelievably bored.

BOO-SENG: Now, if we compare with United States, Korea is very small country. But Korea has very long history. Unfortunately, only a little bit of the history is written down. Only two thousand year out of maybe five thousand. But there are many thing to be proud of. Pottery. Korean pottery: very good. And Kumgangsan, which is very beautiful mountain, in fact the most beautiful

mountain in the world. But unfortunately, it is in North Korea,
so we cannot go see it. There are many trees in—
JIMMY: Right there, Dad—pull in.
BOO-SENG: Uh?
ISAAC: There. *There.* Don't miss it, you're missing it—
BOO-SENG: I see it, I see it.

(Boo-Seng turns in.
    He stops the car.)

Okay.

(Boo-Seng stops the car and Isaac and Jimmy jump out of the car
like animals that have been let out.
    Calling after them:)

That is the first Korea lesson. We continue after lunch.

(Boo-Seng sits in the car.)

Aus-*pi*-shus.
Aus-pi-*shus.*

(Lights up on Bob.)

BOB: Hey, Boo. You got a minute?
    Step into my office. Let's have a talk.

(Bob's office.
    They sit down.)

You know I like you, Boo. Always have. You've been a good team
member.
BOO-SENG: My reports are always good, right, Bob?
BOB: They're very accurate, it's true. That's why I try to watch out for
you. Because I know that among the team, there's the tendency
to, sometimes, to exclude you—
BOO-SENG: Somehow people are not comfortable around me. I don't
know why.
BOB: Now, I wouldn't say that. But I wanted to speak with you about
your progress reports.

BOO-SENG: My reports are good, you said that.

BOB: No, I'm not talking about the reports you make. I'm talking about the reports on you. Job performance, Boo. Some members of the team are . . . how can I put it . . . concerned about you.

BOO-SENG: Concerned? Why?

BOB: Yes. It seems . . . well, there are some areas where you're a bit . . . less effective . . . team building . . . communication skills . . .

BOO-SENG: Maybe I get too focus on my project, on my work, but that's not a problem.

BOB: Well, Boo, it kinda is. When you don't attend team exercises, staff meetings—

BOO-SENG: Two meetings, I didn't go because no one *told* me—

BOB: There are memos, Boo, it's not anyone's job to—look. You've been a good worker, that's not the issue. But you know we lost that big contract, and they're looking to dissolve two of the ten units at this location and one of them, one of them, is yours. Now, we're trying to relocate people, but it's just not possible in every situation, I mean, in every case. We simply don't have that many openings, Boo. I'm sorry.

BOO-SENG: I'm sorry?

BOB: It's not my decision, I mean, if I had my way—

BOO-SENG: You are telling me what? Say it clearly.

BOB: I am saying it clearly, Boo. Clear as I can. I'm sorry, I'll slow down. It's not just you we have to lay off, fifteen percent / of the workforce

BOO-SENG: But but but I have this watch, you gave me this watch, see? There was a cake. Twenty years of service. See?

BOB: That's right and that's for you to keep and I'd be happy to be a reference / for you to anyone

BOO-SENG: To who? Who's going to hire me, Bob? I'm fifty-six.

BOB: I know, I know—

BOO-SENG: In four years, I can retire with full benefits, Bob—Bob.

BOB: You'll get a good severance package, Melissa in HR will / take care of

BOO-SENG: Who's going to pay my health insurance?

BOB: Severance comes with five months paid insurance, after which I'm sure / there are some great values

BOO-SENG: You gave me this watch. You want it? Take it. Take it.

(He starts to take it off.)

BOB: No, no, Boo, it's yours. C'mon. I don't want it. You've earned it. Just think of it as early retirement. Travel. Huh? When was the last time you went somewhere? Or take up golf. There's a golf course on every block. Just keep it in perspective, okay? It's not the end of the world. Now, I've got a meeting . . .

BOO-SENG: **Don't walk away from me, Bob.**

BOB: What, you threatening me, Boo?

BOO-SENG: No, no, of course I'm not—

BOB: 'Cause I'll call security, I will.

BOO-SENG: I'm fifty-six, Bob.

BOB: My hands are tied, Boo. My hands are tied.

(The office is gone.

Boo-Seng looks at his watch. He takes it off and then he hurls it from him as far as he can.

On his naked wrist is the pale outline of where the watch used to be.)

7.

On the patio of a fast food place. Isaac and Jimmy sit at a table, eating.

JIMMY: He'll be bigger than Batman, bigger than Spider-Man. The superhero of the future.

ISAAC: Hate to break it to you, but Stan Lee? Not Asian.

JIMMY: I *know* that.

ISAAC: I'm just saying . . .

JIMMY: Look, it's not an issue. My superhero's going to be normal. He's not going to be, you know, like us.

ISAAC: Well, excuse me.

JIMMY: I just don't want to be limited.

ISAAC: Look in a mirror, Jimmy. What do you think you are? All right. What're his powers?

JIMMY: I haven't figured it all out yet. But he's basically invulnerable.

ISAAC: So nothing can hurt him?

JIMMY: He's sort of like Superman except without kryptonite.

ISAAC: Well, that won't work.

JIMMY: What do you mean?

ISAAC: Superheroes are *defined* by their flaws.

JIMMY: I don't want my superhero to have any flaws. That's the point. He always wins.

ISAAC: That's boring.

JIMMY: Is not. Shut up.

ISAAC: Think about it: Charles Xavier—stuck in a wheelchair; Nightcrawler—looks like a freak. It's like that. You have to have some kind of irony because that's how life is. It might be super-cool you can read minds or whatever, but it's got to come at some great cost.

JIMMY: But why? Why does it have to cost you something? Why can't you just have the cool powers?

ISAAC: Because then it's not real.

JIMMY: So?

ISAAC: Okay, who's your favorite.

JIMMY: Who do you think? Wolverine.

ISAAC: And why do you like Wolverine?

JIMMY: Cause he kicks ass.

ISAAC: Wrong. You know what makes Wolverine so compelling? All the other X-Men, their powers tend to be big and dramatic. But Wolverine's power is simple: he's got a healing factor, that's it. Everyone else, their powers *prevent* them from getting hurt. But with Wolverine, it's the opposite. Wolverine was *made* to get hurt. He was *made* to suffer. That's what his gift *is*. And because he suffers, because he feels pain, we see in him the truest expression of what we, as humans, experience. *That's* why he's the greatest X-Man. Not because he's the most powerful but because he's the most human.

So this comic, the Red Angel? He's all powerful, fine. But what makes him human? What is it about him that when we look at him we see ourselves?

(Pause.)

JIMMY: Wow. I didn't know you liked Wolverine so much.

ISAAC: I don't. I like Magneto.

JIMMY: What? He's like pure evil.

ISAAC: Yeah, but you know what makes him human? Two words: the Holocaust. He's the best fuckin' villain ever, and you know why? Because you sense that maybe, just maybe, he coulda been a hero. Maybe, if the world hadn't fucked him over so much, he mighta been someone—done something—good.

(He throws his crumpled up food wrappers at the trash basket. He misses.)

He still over there?

(*Jimmy looks past Isaac at Boo-Seng who is doing old-fashioned stretching exercises, e.g., rotating from side to side, rotating his arms, etc.*)

JIMMY: Yeah.
ISAAC: What's he doing?
JIMMY: I have no idea.

(*Isaac turns around and looks.*)

ISAAC: Oh God. Come on.

(*They get up. Jimmy looks at his palm.*)

JIMMY: I wish I were a mutant.

(*Isaac looks at their father.*)

ISAAC: I think we kinda already are.

(*They walk towards Boo-Seng.*)

Dad. Dad!
　What're you doing?

BOO-SENG: Stretching. Good for back.
ISAAC: Someone's going to see you.
JIMMY: Are you hungry, Dad? We brought you some food—
BOO-SENG: No. Not hungry.

(*Isaac and Jimmy get in the car.*)

JIMMY: C'mon, Dad. Let's get a move on.

(*Isaac leans on the horn.*)

ISAAC: Let's go!

(*Lights go briefly up on Jerry.*)

JERRY: Mr. Lee?
Let's go.
BOO-SENG: Yes. Let's go.

(*Boo-Seng gets into the car.*
They drive away. Boo-Seng waves good-bye to Jerry, who waves back.
Jimmy looks back.)

JIMMY: Who you waving to Dad?
BOO-SENG: Jerry.

(*Jimmy and Isaac look back but don't see anyone.*
They look at each other and Isaac just shrugs.
They drive on.)

8.

Time has passed. The car. Jimmy sits in the front. Isaac is in the back.

BOO-SENG: So after the king invented his own alphabet, then we had Hangul. Very smart man. But still, you know, we use Chinese character for some thing. For instance, in the—
JIMMY: Dad—where's your watch?
BOO-SENG: What?
JIMMY: Your watch.
BOO-SENG: I lost it.
JIMMY: What? Where?
BOO-SENG: It fell off.
JIMMY: You loved that watch.
BOO-SENG: No.
JIMMY: You hardly never took it off.
BOO-SENG: I only like because it was free.
JIMMY: Listen, Dad, maybe you should eat something? We brought you some food.
BOO-SENG: I feel fine.
JIMMY: You're probably hungry.
BOO-SENG: No . . . I feel good. Clean.
JIMMY: Well, how about just some fries for now. Isaac, hand me the fries.
ISAAC: Oh . . . were you saving those?

JIMMY: Isaac! Those were for Dad!
ISAAC: Well, no one said—

(The car hits something with a loud thud as Boo-Seng swerves.)

JIMMY: Dad!
ISAAC: What the hell was that?

(Boo-Seng pulls over to the side of the road.)

JIMMY: Something ran out, I saw it.

(All three get out of the car.
They look down at the bloody body of an animal.)

ISAAC: Oh, God . . .
JIMMY: It's a dog.
ISAAC: No shit, Sherlock.
JIMMY: Where'd it come from?
ISAAC: I don't know.
JIMMY: It's gotta belong to someone.
ISAAC: It's still breathing.

(Boo-Seng goes to the trunk of the car and walks back to the front holding a hammer.)

JIMMY: It's in pain, Isaac.
    Isaac, do something. Isaac!
ISAAC: What do you want me to do?
JIMMY: I don't know, help it.
ISAAC: Do I look like a friggin' vet?
JIMMY: We can't just let it suffer.
ISAAC: I *know* that, will you just—

(Boo-Seng quickly swings the hammer down onto the dog's head. It lands with a sickening sound. Isaac and Jimmy both jump.)

Jesus.

(Silence.
Boo-Seng throws the bloody hammer away. He gets into the car.)

BOO-SENG: Let's go.

(Jimmy and Isaac get in the car. Jimmy in front, Isaac in back. No one says a word.)

9.

Night. The Palms Motel.
A room with two double beds. Isaac is fiddling with the AC. Jimmy comes in from the bathroom.

JIMMY: I just stunk up the bathroom, royally.
ISAAC: Thank you for sharing.
JIMMY: Why's it so hot?
ISAAC: AC's on. Be patient.

(Jimmy gets into a bed.)

What do you think you're doing?
JIMMY: Going to bed.
ISAAC: So share with Dad. That bed's mine.
JIMMY: That's not fair.
ISAAC: All right, but touch me while I sleep and you're a dead man.

(Jimmy settles in.)

JIMMY: He still out there?

(Isaac looks out the window.)

ISSAC: Yeah.
JIMMY: What's he doing?
ISAAC: I don't know. He's just standing by the pool. Like staring at the water.
JIMMY: He hasn't said anything for the last few hours.
ISAAC: Gee, how unlike him.
JIMMY: But it's not like usual. It's not like he's angry, he's just . . . I don't know.
ISAAC: Ugh. Fucking motel smell. I feel like I'm six years old again.
JIMMY: I kinda like it. Smells clean.
ISAAC: Trust me, it ain't that clean.
      I don't get it. Shouldn't we be there by now?

JIMMY: Well . . . maybe we were kind of going the wrong way for a little bit.

ISAAC: What?

JIMMY: I was looking at the map in the car and I don't think Dad knew where exactly he was going. He took this long route that kind of dead-ended. I think he tried it thinking it was a shortcut, but it doesn't connect back up to the interstate. It looks like it does but I think that's just the crease of the map.

ISAAC: So he was doubling back?

JIMMY: . . . Yeah.

ISAAC: Oh God.

Why didn't you say anything?

JIMMY: I didn't know. Not till it was too late. And you were asleep so . . .

Anyway, we're almost there. I bet we'll get there by noon.

ISAAC: No, we won't. We'll be in the desert forever. Like Moses. We'll fucking die here.

(Isaac doesn't move. He's splayed out on the bed, like he's been shot.)

JIMMY: Well, I'm going to sleep.

(He turns off the light.)

Good night, Isaac.
    Good night, Isaac.
        Good night—

ISAAC: Good night.

(Outside, Boo-Seng stands by the pool. It emits a green glow. The water and light cast shapes and patterns on Boo-Seng's face.

He kneels down. He washes his hands, rubbing them hard. There's blood on his shirt from the dog. He tries to wash that too.

Tears seem to seep from his eyes. He washes his face and the water from the pool mingles with his tears. He stares into the water. He is exhausted and spent.

Ned enters.)

NED: There something in there?

BOO-SENG: Wha?

(Boo-Seng stands.)

NED: In the pool?

BOO-SENG: Oh. No. Just the light in the water . . .

NED: Kind of hypnotizing, isn't it?

You staying here?

BOO-SENG: Yes. With my boys.

NED: I'm here with the wife. Grand Canyon. You?

BOO-SENG: Durango.

NED: Durango!

BOO-SENG: You know it?

NED: Of course I do! Durango! It's famous!

BOO-SENG: It is!

NED: Everyone knows Durango!

BOO-SENG: Exactly!

So you been to Durango?

NED: No. Would like to. You know, someday.

BOO-SENG: Are you retired?

NED: Yup. Look it, don't I? It's the hat. Kids gave it to me. I hate it.

BOO-SENG: How do you like it? Retirement?

NED: Oh, it's great. Plenty of time. Freedom. Get to travel, do whatever I want.

(Pause.)

I'm bored out of my fucking mind.

BOO-SENG: I am too.

I am bored out of my fucking mind.

NED: Since you retired?

BOO-SENG: Since . . . always.

NED *(With perfect understanding)*: Yeah . . . Yeah.

May I offer you a beer?

BOO-SENG *(He is about to say no)*: Yes.

NED: Wait right here.

(Ned leaves. He returns with a beer.
He and Boo-Seng sit on lounge chairs.)

Ned Harmon.

BOO-SENG: Boo-Seng Lee.

NED: What is that?

BOO-SENG: Korean.

(Ned leans in.)

NED: Ahn-nyung-ha-seh-yo.

(Boo-Seng looks at him, confused.)

Means hello!

(Boo-Seng smiles and nods.)

BOO-SENG: Yes. Hello.

NED: Don't you speak your own language? *(He laughs)*
     So. Boo-Seng. How long you been retired?

BOO-SENG: Oh, I'm not . . . I was laid off.

NED: Holy shit. After how many years of service?

BOO-SENG: Twenty.

NED: Twenty! Those bastards!
     I was a teacher—high school—so thank God I didn't have to deal with that kind of shit. Used to be that a company would take care of its own. But not anymore. Everything's disposable now. People most of all.
     So bottoms up, my friend. Bottoms up.

(They drink.)

BOO-SENG: Being teacher is very important job.

NED: I like to think so. I mean, yeah, it could be a pain in the ass, but at the end of the day, you got to watch these kids grow and change. And sometimes kids would come back, kids I'd taught years before who now had kids of their own. And that always felt good. To be remembered. How about you? Did you like what you did?

BOO-SENG: . . . Funny, you know? You look back at your life . . . at all the things you chose . . . and . . . you don't know how you got here.

NED: So true.

BOO-SENG: I did not like my work. But I did it. Every little thing have to be put into computer. Make a report and another report and another. All day long, every day, day after day . . . I did. And if I didn't get laid off, I would still be there, doing. And I would feel . . . lucky. Lucky to have some place to go every day. But why? Why did I want so little? Where did I learn to want so little for myself?

NED: Well . . . what is it you want now?

BOO-SENG: I . . . I want . . .

NED: Go on . . . just say it. What?

(The enormity of all the things Boo-Seng wants silences him.)

BOO-SENG: I don't know.
Not anymore.
Too late. All of it. Too late.

(He is utterly lost.)

NED: Hey . . . it's okay . . .

(Ned puts his hand on Boo-Seng's leg.
Boo-Seng jumps to his feet, almost knocking the beer out of
Ned's hand.)

Whoa, whoa—

BOO-SENG: I'm sorry, I—I—it's late—

NED: No, no, no, I shouldn't't've—

BOO-SENG: I am very tired, too much time in car—

NED: No prob, my wife's probably wondering where I am anyway.
It was nice talking to you. Have fun in Durango. And good
luck to you.

BOO-SENG: Thank you. For beer.

NED: Don't mention it.
Well. Take it easy.
Hey, how do you say, "Take it easy"?

BOO-SENG: I don't think there is expression for that.

(Ned leaves.
The motel room.)

JIMMY *(Whispering)*: Isaac?
(Louder:) Isaac?
(Louder:) Isaac!
Are you awake?

ISAAC: I am *now*.

JIMMY: I can't sleep.
C'n I ask you something?

ISAAC: C'n I stop you?

JIMMY: What was it like? To be part of a family?

ISAAC: You are part of a family.

JIMMY: But a whole one.

ISAAC: Shit, I don't know. Why're you thinking about this now?

JIMMY: I think about it a lot. Don't you?

(*Pause. Isaac does.*)

She was a good cook, right?

ISAAC: Yeah.

JIMMY: What was her best dish?

ISAAC: Wasn't like that. Everything she made tasted good. She could pull food out of the fridge like a magician pulls a rabbit out of a hat, make stuff out of nothing.

And she always smelled good, like really good. Not like perfume. Just the way she was. The smell of her skin.

JIMMY: Do you think she'd like me? How I've turned out?

ISAAC: Yeah, Jimmy. I think she'd like you a lot. I was the one who was too much trouble.

JIMMY: You were?

ISAAC: Oh yeah.

JIMMY: Why?

ISAAC: I dunno. I always pushed her, tried to see how far I could get. She was always having to whale on me. Keep me in line. Don't know why I'm that way but I am. Not like you.

JIMMY: What do you mean?

ISAAC: You're a good kid, that's all. You try to make people happy. Try to make things easier.

JIMMY: I don't mean to.

ISAAC: No, it's a good thing. People *like* you; you get along. That's important.

JIMMY: You wanna see something?

(*Jimmy goes over to his sketchbook. He slides out a plastic sheath—a cut down version of the kind that usually holds comics. Inside the plastic is a photo and a white piece of poster board.*

Jimmy carefully takes the photo out and shows it to Isaac.)

ISAAC: Where'd you get this?

JIMMY: It was in a photo album in dad's closet. I found it when I was looking for Dad's old trench coat for my Halloween costume last year. You remember? How I went as a detective?

ISAAC: Yeah.

JIMMY: It was up on a shelf. This one's from Christmas. It's you and
Dad and Mom and me.

She looks happy, huh?

ISAAC: You keep it with you?

JIMMY: Yeah.

Was it a good Christmas?

ISAAC: No. I don't think it was.

JIMMY: Why not?

ISAAC: They fought.

They fought a lot.

*(Isaac hands the photo back to Jimmy. Jimmy carefully takes it
from Isaac and slips it back into the bag. And then he carefully
slips it back into his sketchbook.)*

Doin' much sketching on this trip?

JIMMY: Nah. You know why I draw?

ISAAC: 'Cause you're bored?

JIMMY: No. It's like, like lotta times . . . lotta times I *need* it. I need
to draw. I think it started when I was really little. I was copying
some panel of Cyclops, you know, after Jean Grey dies. And
she's going to come back, you know, be reborn as Phoenix,
except he doesn't know that yet. And I'm drawing him and then
I see these, like, dark spots on the paper? And I can't figure out
what they are. And then I realize they're tears. I'm drawing his
face, but it's *my* face . . . I mean, it's the same. My face is all . . . like
in the same expression as the picture. Isn't that weird? That I feel
what I draw? That it's the only time that I really feel anything?

ISAAC: Did you think . . . Mom was Phoenix?

JIMMY: I'm not a moron, Isaac. People aren't superheroes. People are
just people. And they don't come back.

(A moment.)

ISAAC: Hey, you want to hear about this movie I saw once?

JIMMY: What movie?

ISAAC: It's called *Motel Hell*.

JIMMY: Shut up, Isaac—

ISAAC: These people are staying at this motel that's got, like, a diner
attached? And this diner is known for its amazing steaks, like
the most tender, juicy steaks in the world. And this is all based
on a true story.

JIMMY: Stop it.

ISAAC: Listen, it's not scary. Thing is, people start *disappearing* from the motel. And it turns out—

JIMMY: Shut the hell up, I mean it / la la la la la la la I can't hear you la la la la la

ISAAC: It turns out that the cook—the cook is like killing them in their sleep and then dismembering the bodies and putting them in the freezer and—

(The sound of a splash outside.)

What the hell was that?

(Isaac springs out of the bed.)

JIMMY: What? What's going on?

(Isaac opens the door.)

Jimmy, stay here.
    Where're you going? Isaac!

(Isaac rushes out.
    Jimmy sits up, a little freaked out.
    He opens his sketchbook.)

The Red Angel haunts the city at night. He hides in the shadows and no one ever sees him pass by.

(The Red Angel appears.)

RED ANGEL: He wears a mask so no one can see his face.

JIMMY: His eyes are cruel. The Red Angel is compassionate towards two things and two things only: children . . .

RED ANGEL: And animals.

JIMMY: In his spare time, he plays the sax.

(Suddenly, a yellow water polo ball bounces across the stage.
    Jimmy and the Red Angel look after it.)

RED ANGEL: Aren't you going to get that?

(Neither moves.
The door opens.
The Red Angel disappears.
Isaac reenters with his arms slung around his father, helping him in. Boo-Seng is soaked.)

JIMMY: Dad! Are you okay?
ISAAC: Get some towels.

(Jimmy runs to the bathroom and reenters with an armload of towels.)

Here, take off your clothes. We'll hang 'em up to dry.
BOO-SENG: Turn off the light.
ISAAC: You're getting all modest now?
BOO-SENG: I'm your father. Turn off the light.

(Isaac turns off the light.
Boo-Seng takes off his shirt and pants. Isaac throws his clothes over the chair and Jimmy helps towel Boo-Seng dry.)

JIMMY: What happened?
BOO-SENG: I . . . lost my balance.
ISAAC: You could've drowned, Dad.
      Give me your clothes. You done?
      Come on. Get in bed.
BOO-SENG: Cold . . .
ISAAC: Just get under the blanket.

(Boo-Seng gets in bed.
Jimmy gets in his.)

JIMMY *(Whispering)*: He okay?
ISAAC: Yeah.
JIMMY: He didn't eat today.
ISAAC: He didn't?

(Boo-Seng shifts in the bed.
They continue to talk in lowered tones.)

JIMMY: No—the food we got him is still in the bag in the car.
      Isaac. He is okay, right?

ISAAC: Yeah, Jimmy. Just—go to sleep.

(Isaac pulls Jimmy's blanket up and tucks him in.
Suddenly, the neon sign of the motel switches on. It consists of
three parts, aligned vertically.
The top section is a girl piking in mid-air.
The middle section is the girl straight in the air, diving towards
the water.
The bottom section is the girl entering the water with a splash.
A soft glow beats on the room as each part of the sign lights up
in succession. The girl dives again and again. Isaac sits there with
that rhythm of light on him.
  1-2-3.
  1-2-3.
  1-2-3.)

10.

Isaac remembers his Mother.

ISAAC *(As his mother)*: Isaac-ya, why you still awake? *(She sighs)* I know.
Sometime sleep not come. My father was like that. I am like
that. Maybe you are like that too, mm?

He was banker, you know. Very smart, kind of genius. He
could look at whole row of number—big number—and add all
up in his head, no paper, no pen, nothing. We were so wealthy
we had a telephone, very first one in whole town. Our phone
number was six. But it was little useless you know, because
there was no one to call.

I was plainest of five girls. When I was born, my father was
quite discourage. So when you were born, I sent him photo and
you know, he write me back right away saying: *This one going to*
be big man, important man.

I was so proud to have son. Should not matter, but everyone
like first one to be boy. And second one, boy or girl is okay.
So this baby *(She touches her stomach)*, boy I am happy, girl
I am happy. Okay, maybe little happier if girl, but that's secret,
okay?

Isaac-ya. You want another secret?

(She whispers:) You are always my first baby. My very first
one. And you are most special, because you are first baby I ever,

ever love. And no matter how much I love new baby, I never, ever love in exact same way I love you. Okay? Okay. Happy? Happy. Good. Now go to sleep. Give me kiss. *(She is kissed)* Such good son. When you want to be. But I know my father was right. Big man. Great man. Everything is inside you. It just take time.

11.

Morning. The motel room. Boo-Seng is gone. Isaac heaves the blinds up so that the sun pours in, waking Jimmy.

JIMMY: Turn it off.

(He turns over and pulls the blanket over his head.)

ISAAC: Rise and shine.
JIMMY: Where's Dad?
ISAAC: Waiting for us. Get up.

(He snatches all the blankets off Jimmy's bed.)

JIMMY: Isaac.
ISAAC: Up! Here.

(He tosses him a toothbrush.)

JIMMY: Where'd you find a toothbrush?
ISAAC: Front desk. Toothpaste is on the sink.

(Jimmy stumbles out of bed and into the bathroom.)

Gotta get a move on. I want to be there by lunch. Sooner we get there, sooner we get home.

(Jimmy opens the door. He's brushing his teeth.)

JIMMY: You were talking in your sleep.
ISAAC: I was?
JIMMY: You said—here, I wrote it down.

(He opens his notebook.)

I think it says—it was dark—"The sun is mittens. Hold the dime."

ISAAC: What does that mean?

JIMMY: You said it.

(*Jimmy goes back into the bathroom. The door opens and Boo-Seng enters with two cups of coffee.*)

BOO-SENG: Ready?

ISAAC: Yeah, almost.

(*Boo-Seng hands a cup to Isaac.*)

Thanks.

You sleep okay?

(*Boo-Seng nods.*

Boo-Seng seems a little embarrassed about the previous night and Isaac doesn't pursue it. Instead, they drink their coffee.

Jimmy comes out of the bathroom.)

JIMMY: Where'd you get that?

BOO-SENG: Lobby. It's free.

(*Boo-Seng and Isaac are clearly savoring the coffee.*)

JIMMY: Can I have some?

ISAAC: Since when do you like coffee?

JIMMY: What, I can't drink coffee?

BOO-SENG: I'll go check out.

JIMMY: I'll come with.

(*Boo-Seng and Jimmy leave.*

Isaac sees Jimmy's sketchbook. He hesitates and then opens it. He finds the photo and looks at it. A page catches his eye. He stares at it hard.

He flips around and stares at some other pages. He puts the photo in the sketchbook back and sets it back where he found it. Jimmy appears at the door.)

Hey.

ISAAC: Hey. No coffee?

JIMMY: They were out. What're you doing?
ISAAC: Nothing.

(*Jimmy grabs his notebook and goes to the door.*)

JIMMY: You coming? Dad's waiting for us in the car.
ISAAC: Yeah. Let's go.

12.

The car. Isaac is driving. Jimmy is in the passenger side, reading the map. Boo-Seng is asleep in the backseat.

ISAAC: Lots of interesting stuff in this area, you know that, Jimmy?
    Ruins, that big ol' hole in the ground where that comet hit . . . all
    sorts of stuff. Ghost towns too. You want to stop and see some
    of it?
JIMMY: I thought you were sick of tourist sights.
ISAAC: Yeah, but some of it . . . like Four Corners, you know, stand-
    ing in four states at once. It's kind of cool.
JIMMY: I just want to get there.
ISAAC: Sure, no prob.

    (*Isaac looks back to make sure Boo-Seng is still asleep. Boo-Seng
    is quietly snoring away.*
        Isaac pulls over to a rest area.)

JIMMY: What are you doing?
ISAAC: Let's get out of the car. Stretch our legs a little.
JIMMY: Dad, you want to—
ISAAC: Just let him sleep. He looks like he needs it.

    (*They get out of the car and walk several yards away.*)

    So Jimmy: can I ask you something?
JIMMY: Okay . . .
ISAAC: How's school?
JIMMY: That's your question?
ISAAC: One of 'em.
JIMMY: It's fine.
ISAAC: Kids make fun of you?
JIMMY: No.

ISAAC: How about girls, any cute girls?

JIMMY: Isaac, why we are we talking about this?

ISAAC: Well, it's like . . . I thought we should have a talk. Man to man. You know, Dad never taught me how to shave. It's a simple thing, right? The kind of thing a man should teach his son. But he never showed me. So for years, I shaved the wrong way. I shaved against the grain. Which you're not supposed to do. I mean, I guess some guys do it because it's a closer shave or whatever, but most guys, you get ingrown hairs and cuts if you shave against. You're supposed to shave *with*. But see, I didn't know this. So I'm talking years of bad shaves. Bleeding. Pimples. And when I finally figured it out, I was so mad because, he could have just told me, you know?

So see, Jimmy, there are things, like, man things that men pass on to each other. And you're getting to be about that age when you and I should talk about, talk about . . . well, I should tell you about . . .

JIMMY: You want to show me how to shave?

ISAAC: Sex, Jimmy. Maybe we should talk about sex.

JIMMY: Yeah, like you know anything about sex.

ISAAC: I know more than you. Anyway, this isn't about me. I wanted to ask you, Jimmy, and you can be honest, okay? Are you . . . (*He lowers his voice and says something very, very quietly in Jimmy's ear*)

JIMMY: What?? NO.

ISAAC: C'mon, Jimmy, it's me, you can tell—

JIMMY: Why would you even ask that? Why would you even *think* that? *You're* the one who's never even had a real girlfriend, I mean, what's *that* about—

ISAAC: Yeah, well *I* don't draw figures of naked men, do I?

JIMMY: What?

ISAAC: Jimmy, I'm sorry, I wanted to look at that photo of Mom again and your sketchbook was sitting there and I didn't—

JIMMY: YOU JERK.

ISAAC: The fact is, I saw them, Jimmy. I saw them.

JIMMY: Those were figure studies, asshole.

ISAAC: Well, I didn't see any figure studies of female superheroes. And last I checked, superheroes actually wore costumes, they didn't go around naked. With enormous erections.

(*Silence.*)

So are you?

JIMMY: No.

ISAAC: 'Cause you know, I—

JIMMY: I'm not. I'm not a . . . I like girls. I want a girlfriend. Heather Spiro, she's got a crush on me. Her friends all say so.

ISAAC: Well, I'm sure she's very cute.

JIMMY: There're a coupla guys like that in my class and you can tell, everyone can tell. Way they talk. Way they walk. I'm not like that.

ISAAC: Well . . . good. 'Cause you know, it's not that I've got anything personal against gays, I mean, I like Erasure, you know—

JIMMY: Don't be such a hypocrite, you totally hate fags and you know it.

ISAAC: That's not true—

JIMMY: Anything you don't like it, you say it's "gay"—

ISAAC: It's an expression.

JIMMY: Don't lie.

ISAAC: Jimmy, I don't have anything against homosexuals, okay? But our family is built on a very simple equation. And that equation is that you are the golden boy—the savior—and I am the fuck-up. Do you realize, I mean, I don't even know if there is a Korean word for "homosexual." I don't know if Dad has even the slightest idea what that is. So I'm just saying, it's a good thing you're not . . . [gay]. If you were, I'd still love you, we'd still be brothers, all that stuff. But life—our life, yours, mine and Dad's—would be a hell of a lot harder. Because that man's got his hopes built on you. You're his golden boy, his favorite—

JIMMY: Oh, come on.

ISAAC: You are! You are. You know you are.

JIMMY: But that's not fair—I never asked for that. How come I have to be the hope of the family? You're the one who's going to be a doctor, who's going to med school—

ISAAC: Yeah, well . . . I'm not sure about that . . .

JIMMY: Are you kidding? Dad's oldest friend practically runs the program—

ISAAC: Well, you're the swim champion who's going to get a full ride anywhere you want to go.

JIMMY: No, I'm not.

ISAAC: You've got coaches drooling all over you—

JIMMY: I quit the team.

ISAAC: What?

JIMMY: I quit the team.

ISAAC: You quit the team?

JIMMY: Yes, because I hate it. I've always hated it.

ISAAC: What are you talking about? You love the water. You're like a fucking fish. You win every meet you go to.

JIMMY: Doesn't mean I like it.

ISAAC: You can be that good at something and not like it?

JIMMY: Yeah.

In fact, you can hate it.

ISAAC (*Pause*): Well.

I didn't go to my interview.

JIMMY: What?

ISAAC: I didn't go.

JIMMY: Bullshit. Dad took you to the airport, picked you up.

ISAAC: No, I went to Hawaii. I just didn't go to the interview.

JIMMY: Isaac.

ISAAC: I made it to Honolulu. Got to the hotel . . . I even steamed my suit, you know, ran the shower and let my suit hang. Like they say to do. And I walked out of the lobby with every intention of getting into a cab and going to the University of Hawaii. I gave myself plenty of time to spare. But I never made it.

You know what I did instead?

I went to some outdoor mall. There was like this little café and I sat at this tiny plastic table with an umbrella over it. I felt like I was in a tropical drink. There was some kind of bad open mic going on. I sat there until the sun went down. And then I went back to the hotel room and watched porn till dawn.

Dad's going to kill me.

The porn cost a lot.

(*Jimmy looks at him, speechless.*
Finally:)

JIMMY: Well.

Was it any good?

ISAAC: No. As a matter of fact, it sucked.

JIMMY: What was it?

ISAAC: I think it was, um, *Edward Penishands*.

(*Jimmy starts to smile.*)

You think this is funny?

(*Jimmy starts laughing.*)

Well, I'm glad you think this is so funny. Dad's going to kill me and you think it's funny.

(Isaac starts to smile too. They both start to laugh, really laugh, the contagious kind that escalates the more they try to stop.
The laughter finally subsides.
They are quiet.)

JIMMY: Maybe it's good. I mean, you don't have to be a doctor. You could do other stuff.

ISAAC: Yeah, 'cause there's so much stuff I'm good at.

JIMMY: You could be a musician.

ISAAC: I don't want to be a musician, Jimmy.

JIMMY: Why not?

ISAAC: Because it's something I just do for me. And besides I suck at it, the way I suck at most things.

JIMMY: That's not true—

ISAAC: I'm not like you, I'm not good at everything I touch, which, I mean, do you have any idea how *annoying* that is?

JIMMY: You just don't try—

ISAAC: What are you talking about? You think you were the only one to try swimming? You think they didn't throw me into a pool and hope that I'd be the next Mark fucking Spitz? What a joke that was. I was hopeless in the water. But one day, you just kinda stumbled into the water when no one was looking and that was that. I mean, no one even had to teach you how to swim, you just *knew*. Sometimes I think the only thing that kept me from smothering you in the crib was how fucking cute you were, all innocent and shit, like you were brand shiny new and maybe I could help keep you that way. I mean, you're even good at things you hate. Who does that?

JIMMY: I don't hate swimming. I mean, I don't *like* it, but. That's not why I quit.

ISAAC: That's not why you quit.

JIMMY: No. I quit because. It's stupid.

ISAAC: If it made you quit, it's not stupid.

JIMMY: No, it didn't, I mean, nothing *made* me quit.

(Beat.)

Sometimes we end practice early. Coach lets us go.

ISAAC: Uh huh.

JIMMY: So I was waiting for Dad to come pick me up. And me and Charlie, we're throwing around one of the water polo balls. 'Cause we're so bored. But Charlie, he's such a dumbnut, he throws the ball too far. It goes way above my head, right into the shed.

Shed's where they keep everything, you know, lanes, the big clock that times us, the kickboards, everything.

So I go in there to get the ball and it's real dark, right? There's no light in the shed, so I can barely see where I'm going and I hear this sound, and I think it's me knocking into something except then I realize I haven't really moved, that this sound isn't me, that I mean, I didn't make it.

Someone else is in there. And it's this guy. This senior.

He's in there changing. He's by this small, high window, I guess 'cause it's the only place where he can see what he's doing. But thing is, he's standing in the only place where I can see him too. And I guess it's no big deal, I mean, I see other guys all the time in the, you know, the locker room or whatever.

But this guy . . . he is. Different.

(The Red Angel appears. We see him as Jimmy must have seen him: golden in the light, sculpted, like a David come to life.)

ISAAC: Different how?

(Jimmy can barely breathe.)

JIMMY: Different . . . perfect. He's perfect.

(The Red Angel picks up the ball.)

RED ANGEL: Here.
    You looking for this?
    Hey.
    Kid?
    You okay?
    Take the ball. Take it.
JIMMY: I couldn't move.
ISAAC: Why?
JIMMY: I don't know.
RED ANGEL: What's wrong with you? Take the ball.
JIMMY: I turned and ran.

ISAAC: Why? Did he do something?

JIMMY: No.

But he called me a, a—

RED ANGEL: Hey—you

JIMMY: —little faggot	RED ANGEL: —little faggot

RED ANGEL: **Take the goddamn ball.**

(He hurls the ball at Jimmy. He is gone.)

ISAAC: Why'd he call you that?

JIMMY: Because he saw my, he saw my.

I couldn't help it and he saw my.

So I ran.

ISAAC: You got a?

JIMMY: Yeah. That happens, right? I mean just 'cause one guy makes me—that's happened to you, right?

(Isaac tries to nod his head "yes" but it turns into a shake "no." He doesn't know what to say.)

I don't want to be a faggot, Isaac.

I don't think I'm a faggot.

I'm *not* a faggot.

I am not.

(A beat.)

ISAAC: Then.

I guess you're not.

(Silence.
Jimmy holds out his pinkie.)

JIMMY: Don't tell Dad. Please.

(Isaac squeezes Jimmy's pinkie with his own.)

ISAAC: Tell him what.

13.

Jimmy imagines his mother.

JIMMY (*As his mother*): Dear Jimmy,

You have to understand that sometime not all my words are good. English is hard language, you know?

I am dying. Maybe in Korean I could come up with more better, more beautiful way to say, but in any language, it is same sad. But maybe it is good you never see me old or sick. Not have to clean my poo or wash me. I am like Marilyn Monroe, always young and pretty.

You know in Korean I am very funny. I always used to make everyone—even your father—laugh. But somehow in American I have lost all my humor.

But to matter at hands. I have a few thing to tell you. Help Isaac and Dad. They are both exact same: stubborn. You are third way. Very gentle, like my mother. So you can help them. You have big heart, Jimmy. I can tell. So you can love them and love *for* them when sometime they cannot.

Other thing: be good. Dad has lot of pain. Story too long for here. But he has lot of sadness. Kind of disappoint. Having good children maybe help heal him. I was not such good wife, maybe. That is another long story. Be kind to your father. He may seem hard but inside he is more easy to break than you think.

Last thing: this is my recipe for my special kal-bi. Some day, you marry nice girl and you can make this together, eat and be happy.

Because most of all, be happy. This is the thing I wish for you.

Love, Mom

14.

The car.
   Isaac is driving.
   Jimmy is in the backseat and Boo-Seng is in the passenger side. They're both asleep.
   Isaac sings quietly.

ISAAC:

I don't have the greatest voice
I don't have the sharpest mind

All I have is a few worn tools
and a lot of my own time

(Isaac hears music.)

I don't have the brightest face
I wasn't born with the cleverest hands
All I have is a few good chords
and the lack of any plan
Making a lot with just a little
Making what you can with what you got
Days pass and the hours run out
whether you made something or not

(The music begins to taper off, or maybe it's already gone.)

So if you don't mind, I would rather be singing
Even if my voice slips off the key
I know I was not made to sing
but I hope singing will make me.

15.

Boo-Seng wakes up.

BOO-SENG: Where are we?
ISAAC: Hey. Sleep okay?
BOO-SENG: Where are we?
ISAAC: Colorado somewhere. We'll be in Durango soon.

(Boo-Seng rubs his eyes.)

BOO-SENG: Thank you. For driving.
ISAAC: No problem.

(Pause.)

BOO-SENG: Isaac . . . I know you didn't want to come. But you'll like
Durango. I know you will. It is very beautiful place.
ISAAC: Sure.

(Pause.)

BOO-SENG: When we get home, I want you to call my friend.

ISAAC: What friend? The one in Hawaii? Why?

BOO-SENG: To apologize.

(Slight pause.)

ISAAC: Fine.

BOO-SENG: You know, he never had kids. I always send him picture of you and Jimmy, he kind of watch you grow up. And he was so looking forward to—

ISAAC: Yeah, I get it, I'll call him.

So how come he never had kids?

BOO-SENG: Never marry. Surgeon is very busy you know.

ISAAC: Well, if you guys were such good friends, how come we never met him?

BOO-SENG: Mom and him not get along so well.

ISAAC: Why?

BOO-SENG: She didn't like we spend so much time together. But he was my oldest friend. He was . . . like Gregory Peck, you know? That's what he look like. Very smart. Very strong. No one could make him do anything.

ISAAC *(Carefully)*: Did someone make you do something?

BOO-SENG: No, but. You know, my marriage to your mother was arranged. We meet and then we decide to marry. Just one time. Very different, huh? Okay, you are okay, we marry. That's how it was.

My friend . . . he didn't understand. He said I was being coward.

But I said to him: You want to choose what you want to be, but that is not for our generation. You and me—we are just laying foundation. That's all. Just laying foundation.

ISAAC: Sure.

BOO-SENG: Isaac? Maybe when we get home, I could buy you another guitar.

ISAAC: I thought you said it was a waste of time.

BOO-SENG: It is, but road is almost done. You did interview. Once you get in, then that is big job finished. So you deserve something you want. A reward. A new guitar. A better one. But not too expensive.

ISAAC: That's uh . . .

Thanks.

(Pause.)

Hey, Dad?

You know, Jimmy and I were talking. And . . . it sounds like he's under a lot of stress, you know. School. Swimming.

Anyway, I thought maybe, maybe he should stop doing so much.

BOO-SENG: Busy is good.

ISAAC: Yeah, but the swimming takes up a lot of time, don't you think?

BOO-SENG: Jimmy love to swim.

ISAAC: But that's the thing, Dad, I don't think he does—

BOO-SENG: What do you know? You never love anything in your life. Jimmy love to work hard. Like me. That's why he is honor student. All-city-

ISSAC AND BOO-SENG: champion in 100-meter backstroke

BOO-SENG: *and* 200-meter IM—

ISAAC: All I'm saying is, what's the big deal if he takes some time off swimming?

BOO-SENG: How's he going to go to college if he doesn't swim?

ISAAC: Jimmy's smart, he'll get some money like I did—

BOO-SENG: I mean a *good* college, not state.

ISAAC: Look, I just want him to be happy, don't you want him to be happy?

BOO-SENG: Jimmy is happy.

ISAAC: How do you know? Have you asked him?

BOO-SENG: **I don't have to ask.**

ISAAC: Right, 'cause you know us *so* well.

BOO-SENG: I don't have to ask Jimmy because Jimmy is very honest, clear.

ISAAC: And I'm not?

BOO-SENG: No. Always act one way, then another—

ISAAC: Like when?

BOO-SENG: Many time.

ISAAC: Name one.

BOO-SENG: Family Day.

ISAAC: What?

BOO-SENG: Family Day.

ISAAC: **And again: what?**

BOO-SENG: **Bring Your Family to Work Day.**

ISAAC: Okay, that was like five years ago.

BOO-SENG: *I* remember. I remember I bring my son, my son who I am SO proud of to work. Straight-A student. Rank number

two in class—could've been number one but you didn't work
hard enough. I introduce you to my co-workers and then I turn
around and what do I hear?

    They're saying, "Hey, Isaac, how you understand your father?
His English is so bad!" And you laugh and say, "I know. But
lucky for me, I am fluent in bad Asian accents."

ISAAC: I didn't—it was the first thing that popped into my head—

BOO-SENG: You laugh at me so my co-workers will like you?

ISAAC: I was sixteen, I was an asshole, what did I know?

BOO-SENG: No respect, always the same, you never think before you
    talk, just like your—

ISAAC: **At least she talked.** She wasn't a **FREAK** who holds things
    in for like **five fucking** / years

BOO-SENG: **Put on brake.**

    I said, PUT ON BRAKE.

(Isaac pulls over.
    Boo-Seng gets out of the car and slams the door shut.
    He walks away from the car, trying to cool himself off and
calm down.
    Jimmy has been awake and listening.)

JIMMY: Isaac?

    What just happened?

ISAAC: I don't know, we were just talking and then—

JIMMY: What did you do?

ISAAC: What did *I* do?

JIMMY: Dad?

(He starts to get out of the car and go towards Boo-Seng.)

BOO-SENG: Jimmy, **stay in the car.**

(Jimmy retreats. He hits Isaac on the shoulder.)

JIMMY: What is wrong with you? Why do you do this?

ISAAC: Do what?

JIMMY: You make him, like, implode. Why can't you just leave him
    alone?

ISAAC: I was trying to help *you*, you little asshole.

JIMMY: Who says I need your help? All you ever do is make things
    worse.

ISAAC: Man, who the fuck made it Pick on Isaac Day?

JIMMY: Dad. Dad. C'mon. Get in the car. Please.

(Boo-Seng walks over to the driver's side.

He opens the car door and Isaac flinches. He motions to Isaac to get out.)

ISAAC: What?

(Boo-Seng gestures even more furiously.

Isaac hits the steering wheel hard and then gets out. Boo-Seng sits in the driver's seat.

Isaac walks away from the car. He takes a moment and then opens the back door of the car.

To Jimmy:)

Get out.

Take the front.

I said, TAKE. THE FRONT.

(Jimmy gets out and gets into the passenger side as Boo-Seng starts the car. He burns rubber and they're off.)

16.

Boo-Seng remembers his wife. She's a little drunk.

She is speaking in Korean but we understand her in English. There is no trace of an accent.

BOO-SENG *(As his wife)*: Please stop yelling, you're giving me a head-ache. And it's your fault anyway: you should've hidden your beer better. It tastes awful, by the way, I don't know how you can drink it. God, I hate how cheap you are.

You should hide your letters better too.

(She holds up the brochure. It is new.)

It looks very pretty. I'm sure you'll have a wonderful time. Of course, it's not as beautiful as Hawaii, but it's a lot closer isn't it? Who knew you had such a burning desire to see . . . Colorado.

(*She throws the brochure down.*)

I don't want to fight. I am too tired. So I am not going to tell you not to go. If you want to go see him, go. You're a free man. You have a choice.
    But, husband. I do have some news. I saw my doctor.

(*She puts her hand on her left breast.*)

It is bad.
    And it has spread.
    So tell me.
    What would you like to do?

17.

A small park in Durango, Colorado.
    It's a beautiful, clear day. The light is sun-dappled.
    Jimmy and Boo-Seng sit on a bench.

JIMMY: God, I am *so* glad to be out of that car.
    So is this it? Is this what you wanted to see?

(*Boo-Seng looks around.*)

What are you doing?

BOO-SENG: Trying to imagine. What it was like. In the past.

(*They sit in silence.*)

JIMMY (*Looking off*): Wish he'd hurry up. How much you think the tickets are, huh, Dad?
BOO-SENG: Jimmy?
JIMMY: . . . Yeah?
BOO-SENG: Do you like swimming?
JIMMY: . . . Sure.
BOO-SENG: You don't do it because I . . . make you do it?
JIMMY: No, Dad. Why're you asking?
BOO-SENG: Well. Isaac said.
JIMMY: What. What'd he say?

BOO-SENG: That you don't like swimming so much.

JIMMY: Let's talk about it later, okay, Dad? When we get home.

BOO-SENG: Because you know, it's important. It will help you for college. I can't . . . I can't anymore.

JIMMY: What're you talking about, Dad?

BOO-SENG: I thought . . . I thought my accuracy will protect me. That I do a good job, no one else can do such a good job. But accuracy is not enough. Twenty years and then gone.

JIMMY: What do you mean, gone?

BOO-SENG: I mean gone. Like my watch. *(He bares his naked wrist)* What I've done. What I am. All gone.

(Isaac enters.
He looks a little stunned. He slowly sinks onto the bench.)

ISAAC: There're . . . no more tickets. The last train left three hours ago. They only run two a day. And we missed the second. We missed it.

(He starts to laugh helplessly.)

But get this? They were sold out anyway! Turns out you have to make a reservation months in advance. Reservations, can you believe it? This stupid train is so popular that apparently you have to make reservations! Who knew? Girl at the ticket office looked at me like I was an idiot when I asked for tickets for the next train. She's like, "What do you think this is? Grand Central?"

BOO-SENG: No train?

ISAAC: That's right, Dad. No train.

BOO-SENG: Tomorrow?

ISAAC: No. They're sold out till next month.

BOO-SENG: I didn't know . . .

ISAAC: Obviously.

BOO-SENG: I didn't know.

ISAAC: What kind of person doesn't *plan* this kind of thing, doesn't at least LOOK UP the—

JIMMY: Isaac, lay off—

ISAAC: NO. I can't believe I fell for it AGAIN. But you were like, oh, please, Isaac, a family trip, it'll be fun— *(To Boo-Seng:)* **What a fucking waste of time.**

JIMMY: Stop yelling at him!

ISAAC: I mean, what kind of moron, what kind of / *loser*
JIMMY: I mean it, Isaac. LAY OFF.

(*He pushes Isaac away from Boo-Seng and Isaac pushes Jimmy back, hard.*)

ISAAC: God, the way you kiss his ass.
JIMMY: You're the one who's a loser, Isaac.
ISAAC: You're such a fucking daddy's boy, Jimmy.
JIMMY: You're the one can't even show up for your own stupid—
ISAAC: SHUT UP.

(*Pause.*)

All right. You want to go there? Okay, fine. Let's go. Let's fucking go. Dad: I didn't go to my interview.
JIMMY: Isaac.
ISAAC: No, Jimmy, it's okay. It's been eating away at me ever since I got back, so let's just throw it out there. I did not go to my interview.
BOO-SENG (*To Jimmy*): What is he talking about?
JIMMY: He did go, he did, he just—
ISAAC: No, Jimmy. I didn't. I didn't go.
BOO-SENG: What?
ISAAC: I'm saying I lied, Dad. About all of it.
BOO-SENG: You didn't go . . . ?
ISAAC: Why does everyone make such a big—I'm never going to get in, doesn't anyone see that but me?
BOO-SENG: But it was ARRANGED. All you had to do was show up—
(*He stops himself*)
ISAAC: Wait, wait—what did you just say?
    You mean the interview, right? You arranged just the interview, *right*?

(*A long pause.*)

Nice, Dad.
BOO-SENG: What.
ISAAC: Way to teach your boy some ethics.
BOO-SENG: What ethics?! You think other people don't have help? Some guy his father donate new science building, you think

that is more fair? The one time I can help you, I do it, I help you. What's wrong with that?

ISAAC: Help me? Is that what you think—

BOO-SENG: Everything I do is to help you. But you never appreciate, never once. Ever since you were small, so selfish. Jimmy: *he* is my son.

ISAAC: Right. Your champion.

BOO-SENG: He is a winner. What do you do?

ISAAC: Nothing, Dad. I watch porn in hotel rooms, okay? **That's what I do.**

A winner. Hear that, Jimmy? You're a winner.

Maybe Dad doesn't understand what he's dealing with here. Shall we enlighten him?

JIMMY: Isaac.

ISAAC: Oh, come on. Let's all be truthful. Honest. Why, not, I've been honest.

So come on, Jimmy, don't you have something to share?

JIMMY: ISAAC.

ISAAC: Maybe Dad would wanna see some sketches—oh, excuse me, "figure studies."

JIMMY: Dad, just ignore him—

ISAAC: What, you only like the truth when it comes to *me*?

JIMMY: Shut up.

ISAAC: Doesn't it get cramped in there? In that dark, lonely closet?

JIMMY: I said, SHUT UP.

(*Jimmy hits Isaac as hard as he can.
Isaac buckles and goes down.
He is clearly in pain.*)

BOO-SENG: What are you doing? STOP IT.

ISAAC: Fuck. That hurt.

(*Jimmy stands over him, fists clenched.
He is bigger and stronger than Isaac has ever realized.*)

JIMMY: I'm not so little anymore, Isaac. And I'm only going to get bigger.

So you better be careful. You better watch your fucking back.

(*Isaac slowly, painfully stands up.*)

ISAAC: Stupid me. I thought we were going to be honest.
　　All right.
　　You win.
　　I'll shut up.

　　(They sit on the bench.
　　　Silence.)

　　So now what?
JIMMY: We're going home.
ISAAC: After all that . . .
JIMMY: Well, we're not going to wait around for a month, are we?
　　I'm tired.

　　(He gets up.)

　　Come on. Let's go. You heard me. Let's go.
BOO-SENG: Yes. Let's go.

18.

The Red Angel appears.

JIMMY: Every now and then, the Red Angel still dreams about it.
RED ANGEL: If I close my eyes, I can see it: the burning house.
JIMMY: One second the window seemed high above him and then
　　suddenly
RED ANGEL: I'm gripping the frame, twenty feet off the ground.
JIMMY: He looked in the room and saw his parents, huddled in a cor-
　　ner. He picked up his father with one hand and with his other,
　　he grasped his mother around her waist.
RED ANGEL: They were as light as children. When did they become
　　so light?
JIMMY: As the house crumbled around them, he stepped onto the
　　windowsill.
RED ANGEL: I put one foot out into the darkness
JIMMY: and jumped.

　　(The Red Angel is in flight.)

　　His wings beat in the darkness around them.

RED ANGEL: My family. My father. My mother. Me.

JIMMY: Below, all the neighbors were gathered around,

RED ANGEL: all of the people I'd grown up with my whole life.

JIMMY: And when the Red Angel finally touched down, shaky from his first flight.

RED ANGEL: I looked around this crowd of people

JIMMY: their faces glowing red from the fire

RED ANGEL: and I saw nothing but fear on their faces.

JIMMY: They crowded in on him as the house burned and they raised their fists and picked up whatever their hands could find—

(*The Red Angel cries out.*
    Silence.)

It turned out that the place where the wings met his back was more delicate than he had realized.

(*The Red Angel's wings are gone.*)

After he healed, he left the town.

RED ANGEL: You wouldn't even look twice at me now.

JIMMY: He's just a guy with some scars on his back.

RED ANGEL: And when I need to go someplace,

JIMMY: he just puts one foot out into the darkness	RED ANGEL: I just put one foot out into the darkness

RED ANGEL: and walk.

(*The Red Angel walks away.*
    The car. Jimmy is in the passenger side. Isaac is driving. Boo-Seng is asleep in the back.
    Jimmy opens his window.)

ISAAC: What're you doing?—I've got the AC on.

(*Jimmy takes his notebook out. He opens it and then begins ripping sheets out of it. He tears the sheets up and throws them out the window.*)

Stop it. Jimmy. Don't.

(*Jimmy keeps tearing up the paper and throwing it out the window.*)

Jimmy, not the—

(*Out goes the plastic bag with the photo inside.*
Out goes more paper until the whole notebook's gone and Jimmy's hands are empty. He rolls the window back up.
Silence.)

19

Home.
The lights are off. The door opens and Isaac, Jimmy and then Boo-Seng come through the door.
Isaac turns on a light.
All three sit, exhausted. Wordless.
They sit for a long time.

ISAAC: I'm going to bed.

(*He stands up.*)

I'll call the school tomorrow, okay, Dad? See if I can reschedule. I'll uh. Tell them I had food poisoning. Bad sushi or whatever. Okay?
    G'night.

(*He leaves.*
Jimmy and Boo-Seng sit together.
A long silence.)

BOO-SENG: He never says sorry. He never just says sorry.

(*Silence.*)

JIMMY: Maybe I'll be a doctor.
BOO-SENG: Is that what you want?
JIMMY: Sure.

(Silence.)

BOO-SENG *(To himself)*: I want . . . to do something good before I die.

(Silence.)

JIMMY: Dad?
I love you.

(Jimmy leaves.
Boo-Seng goes to the answering machine. There's a message on it. He listens to it.
It's the voice of an older man, speaking in Korean. It is Boo-Seng's old friend in Hawaii.
Boo-Seng looks at the brochure of Durango.
In his room, Jimmy sits at his desk but does not draw.
In his room, Isaac holds the guitar. He plays a few chords. It's the beginning of a song—the same one we heard at the beginning of the play.)

END OF PLAY

Julia Cho's plays include *The Language Archive*, *The Piano Teacher*, *Durango*, *The Winchester House*, *BFE*, *The Architecture of Loss* and *99 Histories*. Her work has been produced at the Public Theater, the Vineyard Theatre, Long Wharf Theatre, Playwrights Horizons, South Coast Repertory, New York Theatre Workshop, East West Players, The Theatre @ Boston Court, Theater Mu and Silk Road Theatre Project among others. Honors include the 2009–2010 Susan Smith Blackburn Award, the Barrie and Bernice Stavis Playwriting Award, the Claire Tow Award for Emerging Artists and the L. Arnold Weissberger Award. An alumna of the Juilliard School and NYU's Graduate Dramatic Writing Program, Julia is a member of New Dramatists.

Satellites

Diana Son

Author's Statement

I grew up in a small town in a small state that aside from a couple things I can't think of right now, had little to recommend it. No theatres, no galleries, no places to hear live music . . . For fun, my friends and I would go to the Kmart behind my house and have each other paged. "Diana Son, please come to the front desk, your friends are looking for you." When they built a Best Western next to the Kmart, we would sneak in and ride the elevators all the way to the top! It was a thrill to see things from that vantage point. *The*

fourth floor. My husband doesn't let me tell this story anymore, he says it's not funny.

But one major thing my artistically-bereft hometown had going for it was that it was racially diverse. Or at least, bi-verse. My neighborhood and schools were almost equally black as white. My first friends were black, the daughters of Airmen who came home from work in crisp blue uniforms and changed into khaki shorts and Hawaiian shirts. We played hopscotch, tag and, yes—I have to admit it—cowboys and Indians. At school, at the doctor's office, the supermarket, the mall, African Americans were part of my daily life. I'm not going to say it was a paradise of racial harmony but the predominant culture was Middle Class American, and black and white families subscribed to the same values. Safe neighborhoods, good schools, church on Sundays. We were the only Korean family around and my parents were fierce assimilators, so with our perfect English and our Sears-bought clothes, my brother and I fit right in. We rode big wheels on the sidewalk, threw eggs on Mischief night and had sleepovers at our friends' houses. It wasn't paradise but it was pretty sweet and I never, ever, thought about, heard of or experienced any Korean vs. African American tension.

For that, I had to move to New York City. Yes, my beloved New York, with its theatres, galleries, music clubs, vibrant street life and the million other things to recommend it. I came here as a freshman at New York University and while I was preoccupied finding my way around the big city, meeting new friends, and feeling otherwise overwhelmed and exhilarated—I realized that, overnight, black people disappeared from my life. My dorm and liberal arts classrooms were populated with a wide variety of white people—New Yorkers, Southerners, West Coasters, Jews . . . even Europeans, my god, she speaks real French!—and a very conservative-seeming bunch of Asian Americans. I had dyed-blonde hair and a new wavey wardrobe and the pre-med crowd stared at me like I was on fire. The few African Americans I met at NYU were either wealthy and sophisticated or urban and inaccessible. I missed my black friends who were, well, like me. Which I guess you would describe as pretty unremarkable so far, but aspirational.

This was in the 80s and there were a couple of landmark events that brought to my attention the tensions between Koreans and African Americans—which is centered on the **disproportionately** large number of Korean-owned businesses based in African American neighborhoods. The first event was a boycott of Korean-owned businesses in Harlem and the second was the L.A. riots. I'm going to admit to you right now that I just had to google those events. Because the truth is, I'm not a political person and I never studied or truly understood the social conditions that led to those events. What I remember is seeing images on the news of angry African Americans clashing with angry Korean Americans, sometimes violently, sometimes fatally, and hearing voices on both sides articulating painful and ugly stereotypes and accusations which would leave me feeling a jumble of emotions that is best characterized as anguish. This subject was and continues to be one that is very, very painful to me.

Prior to *Satellites* and with the exception of my short, early play *R.A.W. ('Cause I'm a Woman)* which is about sexual stereotypes of Asian American women, I had written plays in which the roles were not race-specific. It has always been my hope that the roles were universal enough to be cast without regard to race and it was and still is my commitment to cast as many actors of color as I, in collaboration with my director, can. When my most produced play *Stop Kiss* was published, I included the author's note: As this play takes place in New York City, the cast should reflect the ethnic diversity of New York City. However, over the years, as the play went on to be produced hundreds of times in theatres big and small, I would be sent a press clipping or a link to an online review and saw that most of the productions did not take my broad instructions to heart. There have been tons of productions of *Stop Kiss* with all-white casts. Or, with white actors in the lead roles and actors of color in the smaller roles. Unlike our premiere production which featured Sandra Oh and Kevin Carroll in lead roles. Now, I'm sure that many times there were practical reasons why that happened. Small cities, towns or universities have smaller acting pools. They couldn't find the right actor. And as an advocate of color blind casting I will be the first to tell you that if you do not take the **extra** time and effort to audition as many actors as you can, and end up casting an actor of color who is **not right** for the role, you are doing a disservice to the actor, the play and the whole idea of color blind casting.

But, in my experience, if you put in that extra time and effort, and look beyond the usual pool of actors the casting director, theatre, director, playwright have become comfortable relying on, you can and will find a talented actor of color who is right for any role you are casting. And my assumption, when I see my or other people's plays cast with exclusively white actors when the text does not specifically demand it, is that people in positions of power were lazy.

So, after *Stop Kiss*, I decided that my next play would be race specific. Which was an ambitious and tricky mandate for myself considering my life has not been race specific. But I try in every play to do something I've never done before, so I decided to make the lead characters a married couple in which the wife was Korean American and the husband was African American. And I gave them a new baby and put them in a crumbling brownstone in a newly gentrified (i.e., formerly African American) neighborhood in Brooklyn and set them with the task of figuring some shit out. At the time, my husband, young son and I were living in a perfectly nice brownstone in Clinton Hill, Brooklyn, and I found the dynamics between the newcomers and old-timers intriguing. There was tension on the block. But it wasn't exclusively racial. Even though my household was Caucasian/Asian and many other newcomers were white, there were also a number of new homeowners that were African American. I would go to block association meetings where my black neighbors would talk about getting rid of "the element" that could be found hanging around outside the corner bodega at all times of the day and night. Meanwhile, I was the friendliest of any of my neighbors with the ringleader of "the element," a lifelong resident of the block. Izzy talked to me about his romantic troubles, brought toys for my son, and sold drugs. He lived in a brownstone with at least half of his twelve siblings and many of their children, some of whom were adults. Our block was split about 50/50 between new residents and old, black and white and I was practically the only Asian person around. For the first time since I came to New York City some (cough cough) years ago, I was living in a neighborhood that, at least demographically, resembled the one I grew up in. But in character, it was very different. Very very different. And I found it all pretty fascinating.

People assume *Satellites* is autobiographical but I could make a long list of things that happen in the play that never happened to me, or people that are in the play but aren't in my life. And my husband, who is a doting and enthusiastic dad to three sons bristles at the thought that anyone thinks he is similar to the anxious and questioning Miles. Let me set the record straight on that one. But I did envision Nina as having a similar upbringing as mine. I can see her in her backyard playing politically incorrect games with her two best pals; see her wandering to Kmart's sports department as Pam and Rhonda stifle laughs at the customer service desk and report her missing; and I can see Nina and those girls riding the elevator all the way to the fourth floor of the Best Western motel, taking in the view . . . and wishing they could go higher.

Production History

Satellites premiered in 2006 at the Public Theater in New York City (Oskar Eustis, Artistic Director; Mara Manus, Executive Director). It was directed by Michael Greif. The set design was by Mark Wendland. The costume design was by Miranda Hoffman. The lighting design was by Kenneth Posner. The composer was Michael Friedman. The sound design was by Walter Trarbach and Tony Smolenski IV. The production stage manager was Martha Donaldson. The cast was as follows:

NINA	Sandra Oh
MILES	Kevin Carroll
ERIC	Clarke Thorell
KIT	Johanna Day
MRS. CHAE	Satya Lee
REGGIE	Ron Cephas Jones
WALTER	Ron Brice

Characters

NINA, mid-thirties, Korean American, an architect and new mother
MILES, mid-thirties, African American, an unemployed dot-com casualty and new father
ERIC, late-thirties, Caucasian, Miles's brother, an entrepreneur
KIT, late-thirties, Caucasian, Nina's business partner, an architect
MRS. CHAE, mid-fifties/early-sixties, Korean from Korea, a nanny
REGGIE, early/mid-forties, African American, the king of the block
WALTER, any age, any race, a tenant in the brownstone

Setting

Various rooms in Miles and Nina's unrenovated Brooklyn brownstone.

Time

Now.

Note

The symbol (.) denotes a barely perceptible (and yet perceptible) pause where a character chooses not to say something.

Un-italicized text within parentheses, such as (this), indicates the word/s not spoken when a character is cut off.

A forward slash (/) indicates overlapping text. The next character begins speaking at this point.

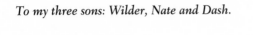
To my three sons: Wilder, Nate and Dash.

Scene 1

Late night/early morning—they've bled into one another. Nina, still tender from a C-section, bounces her two-week-old newborn as best as she can and pats her back, trying to soothe the crying baby.

NINA: Okay, sweetie, I'm trying, I'm trying— *(Reacting to harder crying)* I'm sorry it hurts so much, I never knew gas could be so painful and hard to get out—

(Nina pats harder.)

You know, if only it were this hard for adults to fart, riding the subway would be a much pleasanter (experience.)—

(We hear the tiny pop of a baby passing a puff of gas. Nina reacts with the pride of a mother who's just watched her daughter win Olympic gold. The baby makes a happy, gurgling sound.)

You did it! Oh, I'm so happy for you!

(Nina holds the baby in front of her to look at her face. She gives her an encouraging little shake.)

My little champion!

(The baby starts to cry again. To herself, out loud:)

Holy shit, don't shake the baby. I'm such a fucking—

(She puts the baby back over her shoulder.)

Mommy didn't mean that, sweetheart, Mommy wasn't shaking you, Mommy was vibrating—

(Miles walks in, wearing pajamas.)

MILES: Sorry I didn't hear you guys, I was out cold. Did she want to nurse?

NINA *(Not ironic)*: No, she wanted to watch *The Godfather*. Did you know that *The Godfather* is on every night? On different channels at the same time. If you turn on your TV after midnight, you have no choice but to watch *The Godfather*.

MILES: You want to watch it now?

NINA: Why don't you take her, so I can go back to bed.

(Nina carefully puts the baby in Miles's arms. The baby starts to cry harder.)

Look at her, Miles, chocolate skin, almond eyes . . . she's the best of both of us.

MILES: . . . I hope so.

NINA: What do you think about hiring a Korean woman to be her nanny? So she could speak Korean to her.

MILES *(Distracted by crying baby)*: Is that important to you?

NINA: I just started thinking about it. I can't speak Korean so she's not going to hear it from me.

MILES: Alright, sounds like a good idea. *(Re: baby)* You want to take her?

NINA: Why don't you try singing a song? Like a lullaby or something—

MILES *(Sings)*: "The eensy-weensy spider went up the water—"

NINA: That's not soothing.

(A bang from the apartment above.)

MILES: Aw, come on, man.

NINA: Fucking asshole. *(To upstairs neighbor:)* My baby has gas, man, I'll kill you, motherfucker.

MILES: Hopefully we'll close on the house next month, and finally be able to move in.

NINA: It's impossible to have a baby in this cramped little tenement. We've outgrown this apartment, this whole neighborhood.

MILES: Remember when we used to have wakes for our friends who moved to Brooklyn?

NINA: They're laughing at us now. Still, as much as we paid, it'll be worth it.

(The baby wails, the neighbor bangs on the ceiling again.)

MILES: You'd better take her.

(Nina opens her arms. The baby quiets down a little.)

NINA: What should I sing?

(Miles thinks a beat.)

MILES: "Hush little baby—"

(Nina joins in, a beat behind, singing what Miles sings.)

MILES AND NINA: "Don't say a word, Papa's gonna buy you a mockingbird . . ."

MILES: "If that—"

NINA: "When that—"

MILES AND NINA: ". . . mockingbird won't sing, Papa's gonna buy you a—"

(They look at each other, unsure what the rest of the words are. Finally—)

NINA: I can look up the words, I found this website that has the lyrics to all the—

MILES *(Sings, cues Nina)*: "Rock-a-bye—"

(Nina joins in.)

MILES AND NINA *(Singing)*: "—baby, on the treetop. When the wind blows, the cradle will rock. When the bough breaks, the cradle will fall—"

(Nina stops, thinks about the words.)

MILES *(Still singing)*: "And down will come baby, cradle and all."
NINA: We are never singing that song to her again.
MILES: Why not?
NINA: The baby falls, Miles, the baby falls and the cradle falls on top of it. What kind of lullaby is that?

Scene 2

Miles and Nina's brownstone. It's dark, lit by a standing lamp near the kitchen. The living room blends into the kitchen, a stairwell leads to the bedrooms above, another connects to the garden level office below. Many moving boxes are piled on the floor, some opened, most not. There is very little furniture. Miles carries in a box as Nina comes down the stairs.

NINA: I just got her down. Miles, that box belongs in the kitchen. It says "Kitchen" on it.
MILES: It doesn't matter. I've been putting things wherever there's room.
NINA: Well, I've been putting everything exactly where it's/gonna go—
MILES: But I haven't. We'll deal with it later.

(Nina grabs an end of the box, starts pulling towards the kitchen, Miles pulls it back.)

NINA: You know we won't. Half of these boxes are going to be sitting in our living room for the next year and a half because we're not going to have the time or energy to/move them later.
MILES: We'll move them tomorrow. Or next week . . . or next month, it doesn't—
NINA: No, we're not. We'll get used to them being there. We'll start putting things on them, like our feet when we're sitting on the sofa. Or our drinks, they'll become end tables. We'll choose the paint color for the walls by whether or not it matches the boxes. You know we will.
MILES: No, we won't.
NINA: How many years did we use a plastic shopping bag hanging on the front doorknob as a garbage can?

(Miles makes a dismissive sound.)

Seven years. I bought us our first trash can on my thirtieth birthday because I couldn't stand it anymore. Miles, please, let's just move the goddamn box to the kitchen. I need to finish here and go downstairs to—

MILES: Stop bossing me around.

(Nina starts to pull him towards the kitchen again, Miles resists. She stops in her tracks when she feels a cutting pain. She drops her half of the box.)

NINA: Ow, motherfuck.

(Miles sets the box down, walks over to her, helps her to sit onto a nearby box.)

MILES: Honey . . . you shouldn't be doing all this. You need to stop pushing yourself so much.

NINA: I'm not pushing myself, Miles.

MILES: So, what—I am?

NINA: There's no one else to help us. We've burned through all the friends who offered to . . . let's just finish. After I'm done here, I have to go downstairs and help Kit work on the site plan.

MILES: You're gonna work tonight?

NINA: Kit's been carrying my weight for the past month.

(Miles starts to massage Nina's shoulders.)

She's been working on the Tillman job and on the Barcelona competition. Not to mention she set up the whole office by herself.

MILES: Yeah, well, Kit can do that. She has the time. You should just . . . take it easy, you know? Relax a little.

(Miles touches Nina's breasts. She wriggles out of his reach.)

Hey!

NINA: I'm sorry . . . honey, it's just . . . these aren't mine anymore.

MILES: Nina, I've been keeping it all to myself for the past four months.

NINA: What're you—counting?

(Miles tries to nuzzle her.)

MILES: C'mon, the baby's asleep.

NINA: I can't believe I just told you everything I have to do tonight and you want to have sex?

MILES: Yes, I want to have sex! Remember sex? It's how we made the baby and got ourselves into this mess in the first place.

NINA: That's seductive.

(Miles lets go of her hand, walks away angry and rejected.)

MILES: I'll get the rest of the boxes myself. You just . . . relax.

NINA: I don't have time to—

MILES: You need to/relax—

NINA: I'm not relaxing!—

(Eric runs into the house, shuts the door behind him. His jacket pocket is torn. Miles and Nina look as surprised to see him as he is to see them.)

ERIC: Two fucking guys just chased me for four blocks. They took my iPod and backpack, they had a gun!

NINA: Eric! Where did you—

MILES: Are you okay? You want me to call the cops?

ERIC: Yeah, no, it's okay, I just—

(He walks over to the window, looks out.)

MILES: Where was this?

ERIC: Like a block from the subway, by the projects. All of a sudden, these two (.) guys came up from behind me and ripped my iPod out of my pocket—

(Nina examines at Eric's pocket.)

MILES: Did they get your wallet?

ERIC: No, I have a hole in my pocket so it drops down into the lining of my coat. They grabbed my backpack, and then I just . . . took off. I just kept running until I saw Rosa Parks Avenue.

NINA: How'd you know how to get here?

MILES: You want a glass of water or something? A beer?

ERIC: In a minute, I just— *(Changing gears)* Hi, how are you?

(Eric kisses Nina on the cheek.)

NINA: I'm fine.

(Miles and Eric embrace, clap each other on the back.)

MILES: I thought you were in Malaysia.
ERIC: I just got off the plane. I'm fucking lagged.
NINA: Where are your bags?
ERIC: I put them in a mini-storage near the airport.

(Looks around.)

Get a load of this place. What's the deal?
MILES: . . . This is . . . our house.
ERIC: This is outrageous, man, your other apartment was like a dorm
    room. How many floors is this?
NINA: Four. We converted the garden level into an office for me and
    Kit so, we're only living on this floor and the one above.
ERIC: That where the bedrooms are?
NINA: Yes.
ERIC: So how many are there?
NINA: Three. We use the third bedroom as a family office.
MILES: My office.
ERIC: Sweet, man. Mom and Dad said it was nice but I didn't expect
    it would be like this.
MILES: Why, what'd they say?
ERIC: Don't sweat it, Miles, they liked it. They were just more into
    the baby. Where'd you put the baby?
NINA: She's upstairs sleeping.
ERIC: Can I get a peek at her?
MILES: Sure.
NINA: I don't think it's a good idea.
ERIC: How old is she, a month?
MILES: Six weeks.
ERIC: Is she sleeping through the night?
NINA *(On the verge of tears)*: No!
MILES *(An apology)*: The baby gets up every couple hours to nurse.
    Nina's up all night.
ERIC: I noticed the moving van out front. You guys need a hand?
MILES: You don't have to, man, you must be exhausted.
ERIC: Getting mugged got me pumped. Let's do it.

(Kit walks upstairs carrying a pizza box.)

KIT: Your pizza came, they rang the bell downstairs.

MILES *(Turns to Eric)*: Let's eat something first. *(To Kit)* Kit, you've met my brother before, haven't you? This is Eric.

(Kit extends her hand.)

KIT: Not yet, but I've heard the stories.

ERIC: Uh-oh . . .

KIT: You've been bitten by a rattlesnake and lived to tell the tale, and you sold the Dalai Lama a laptop.

ERIC: His Holiness is addicted to Tetris.

KIT *(To Nina)*: Nina, I've started regrading the site plan.

NINA: I told you I'd pitch in with that.

KIT: We've got to finish this by tonight. We should be cutting out shapes for the model by tomorrow.

NINA: We will. I'm going to work all day tomorrow.

ERIC *(To Kit)*: Are you guys doing a charette?

MILES: Listen to you and your "charette."

ERIC *(To Miles, a frequent joke)*: Just because I didn't go to Columbia, like some of us in the room—

MILES *(Looking at Kit)*: All of us, actually.

(Nina's mobile phone rings. Miles and Eric help themselves to pizza.)

NINA *(To Kit)*: Audrey Tillman.

KIT: Why's she calling you?

NINA *(Into phone)*: Hello? Yes, Mrs. Tillman . . . no, I wasn't at the jobsite today but Kit was—

(Nina looks at Kit, who nods, yes, I was, everything was fine.)

No, the carpenters are going to fill that in . . . It's going to look exactly as we discussed. *(Brightens)* Oh, yes, thank you. She's six weeks old, she's just— *(Mrs. Tillman could give a fuck)* I'll make sure Kit takes a look tomorrow morning. Thank you, Mrs. Till—

(Mrs. Tillman has hung up.)

KIT: Why didn't she call me? I'm the one whose been holding her shriveled little liver-spotted hand for the past two (months.)—

(The baby starts crying upstairs. Nina reacts as if she's been electrically jolted.)

NINA: You guys, go ahead, eat. I'll bring her down when I'm done nursing her.

KIT: I guess I'll be working by myself after all.

(Eric hands Kit a slice of pizza on a plate.)

ERIC: Here you go.

(He goes to the fridge to get her a beer. Miles touches Kit consolingly.)

So, do you live in Brooklyn too?

(Eric hands her a beer.)

KIT: Ha! Thanks. Noooo. Look, Brooklyn's great, it's beautiful and cheaper, but . . . I want to be able to drop off my dry cleaning, go to a gallery opening, see an eight-hour Hungarian movie, then drink overpriced green apple martinis—all within a block of my apartment.

ERIC: That's what's great about New York, right?

(Suddenly, we hear a smash—the sound of glass being shattered and falling on the floor.)

MILES: What the—

(Kit grabs a flashlight, they see glass pieces on the floor and a jagged hole in the window.)

ERIC: Shit, man—

MILES: What just happened?

(Kit walks towards the window, surveys the debris. Finds a rock, picks it up.)

KIT: It's a rock. Someone just threw it at your window.

(Miles walks over, Kit shows him the rock.)

MILES: Why would someone do that?

ERIC: You've got a stereo, TV, all kinds of computer equipment . . . people in this neighborhood probably saw all that gear and thought Puffy was moving in.

KIT: Or, maybe they weren't trying to steal anything. Maybe they were just trying to send you a message. *(Goes for phone)* Want me to call 911?

(Nina walks a few steps downstairs.)

NINA: Miles? What was that, what broke?

MILES: Stay upstairs, honey. There's broken glass down here.

(Nina, holding the baby, walks down, sees the broken glass on the floor.)

NINA: What the fuck! Who broke my fucking window?

MILES: I'm checking it out, don't worry. Go back upstairs where it's safe.

(Nina ignores him, keeps walking.)

NINA: It's going to take weeks to get a replacement glass . . . what are we supposed to do with a fucking hole in our house for three fucking weeks?

MILES: I don't know. Just take the baby upstairs, okay? *(To Eric)* Her first word's gonna be fuck if Nina keeps—

NINA: What?

MILES: Just please take the baby upstairs.

(She goes upstairs.)

KIT: You should call the cops, Miles.

(Beat.)

MILES: I don't want to do that. *(Beat)* We're new here. I don't want people to get the wrong impression.

KIT: What would that be?

MILES: I don't want to dwell on this. The most important thing to do is cover up that hole.

KIT: Home Depot's open twenty-four hours. You can buy a four-by-eight piece of plywood and some hardware to anchor it to the wall.

ERIC: I'll go. Will you come with me so you can show me?

KIT: I'll get my jacket.

(Miles shakes his brother's hand.)

MILES: Thanks, man. Can you believe this happened?

(Eric looks out the window, at the sky.)

ERIC: It's a full moon. Maybe it's a sign of good luck. Getting all the bad things over with first.

MILES: Or it's a sign that moving my family here is the biggest mistake of my life.

(Kit comes back with her jacket, she and Eric walk out, leaving Miles alone and feeling it.)

Scene 3

Early morning. Miles tries to set the plywood into the wall, manual labor is not his forte. A man walks by on the street, Reggie, his clothes not quite clean, his hair in need of a comb. He stops in front of the broken window. The hole still uncovered.

REGGIE: Oh, shit! What happened, man?

(Miles looks at Reggie.)

MILES: What happened? Somebody smashed the window.

REGGIE: And you ain't hardly even moved in yet—that ain't a way to welcome a brother to the neighborhood.

(Miles—a small reaction to "brother.")

MILES: It's not exactly a pie on the stoop, is it?

REGGIE: That's what I'm saying! You done a lot of work on this house, man.

MILES: Not really. I mean, we bought a door and . . . we put glass in the—

REGGIE: We got all kinds of people up in here now, building new condos and renovatin' these old brownstones . . . You see that house over there? Two homosexuals bought that, fixed it up to historical accuracy, and all that. I'm glad you came to the neighborhood, man. What you do, you a lawyer or something?

MILES: I'm . . . an interactive producer.

REGGIE: A producer! You know Biggie grew up two blocks from here, right? I used to send that punk to the store to buy me Milk Duds.

MILES: Actually, I produce websites for corporate clients. But, I like Biggie.

REGGIE: I'm glad you came to the neighborhood, man. This glass was custom-made, wasn't it?

MILES (*A little surprised*): Yeah, it was.

REGGIE: 'Cause 'round here all the brownstones have one seventy-two-inch window or two thirty-six-inch ones. That was the style in the 1870s when most of these buildings was built. But this one here is eighty inches, only one like it. I know they charged you a lot of money for that piece of glass.

(*Miles waits to see where Reggie's going with this.*)

Mm-hm, a lot of money.

(*Reggie nods gravely.*)

MILES: You seem to know a lot about my house—

REGGIE: I got a guy I can go to—he'll cut that glass for you cheaper than you paid for.

MILES: Thanks, but my wife's got her sources. She's an architect so she has reliable (vendors.)—

REGGIE (*Insistent*): Listen, man, you don't know me. But, I'm telling you— (*Extends his hand*) I'm Reggie, I live across the street from you, I lived on this block for—matter of fact, I was born on this block. I'm forty-two years old—I got three grown kids, they live with they moms, but everybody 'round here know Reggie. If you need something, I'm your boy.

(*Nina walks downstairs carrying the baby.*)

NINA: Miles, you take the baby. Kit's going to be here any— *(To Reggie)* Hi, I'm Nina.

(She can't offer her hand because she's holding the baby.)

REGGIE: Alright.

MILES: This is Reggie, he lives across the street.

REGGIE *(To Miles)*: Like I said, you make up your mind, you come to me.

(Miles, feeling awkward, turns to Nina.)

MILES: Oh, I should tell you, Reggie mentioned that he, uh, he has a glazier that he recommends.

NINA: He's done work for you?

REGGIE *(A nod)*: Mm-hm.

NINA: Do you have his card or can you give me his phone number?

MILES *(To Nina)*: I thought you would want to use Frankie again.

NINA: I'll call Frankie, but if this guy's in the neighborhood—

(Reggie sees someone offstage.)

REGGIE: I gotta talk to this—Hey, Mo! You need to settle up with me, son. *(To Miles)* Look, I'm a go get my boy's card and you talk to him. Whatever you want, he'll do it.

NINA: Thanks, Reggie. *(To Miles)* I don't know what kind of work this guy does, I'm just saying let's get a price from him.

MILES: Doesn't it seem weird to you, this guy who's always hanging out on the corner, coming up first thing in the morning, telling us, "I got a guy who can fix that for you . . ."

NINA: So?

MILES: And where were those guys last night? They're always out there, doing whatever they're doing, selling whatever they're selling, but last night—they're not there. Where were they?

NINA: What—you think Reggie or one of those guys broke the glass?

(Miles gestures—I'm just saying.)

. . . I don't think Reggie did it. Why would he do it?

MILES: Maybe he gets a fee. Whenever Reggie finds some sucker to give this guy business—

NINA: And what's the deal with your brother? He tell you how long he's gonna stay?

MILES: No. But he usually stays a week or two—you have a problem with that?

(Nina turns to the baby for unconditional love.)

NINA: Look, she's dreaming. Look at how her expression changes every couple seconds. *(Narrating the baby's thoughts as she goes from a smile, to a frown, to tears, to a smile again)* Flowers . . . car alarms . . . mmm, Mommy's nipples . . .

(Eric comes downstairs.)

ERIC: Alright, let me see her. *(Looks at baby)* She's beautiful.

NINA: She's the perfect mix of the both of us, don't you think?

ERIC: She's herself. You, on the other hand, seem to have turned into a completely different person. Didn't I just hear you talking baby talk?

NINA: I was giving voice to her thoughts.

ERIC: Can I hold her?

(Nina hesitates.)

MILES: Of course, man.

NINA: Just—make sure you support her neck.

(Nina gingerly hands the baby to Eric.)

ERIC: Ohmigod, it's so much responsibility. If I don't hold her right, her neck will break off.

(Miles goes to get a camera.)

MILES: Hang on a second, let me take a picture of you two.

NINA: Miles—don't put him on the spot.

ERIC: I don't mind.

(Eric smiles for the camera. Miles clicks the shutter. Nina responds to the sound of the downstairs door being opened.)

NINA: Shit, Kit's here. I'd wanted to get a head start before she showed up. Miles, take the baby.

MILES: Eric's got her.

NINA *(To Miles)*: You said you'd watch the baby today—

MILES: I will. But, just today. Remember I have an interview at Poseidon tomorrow—

(Nina heads downstairs.)

ERIC: You guys don't have a nanny?

MILES: Not yet. But we'd better soon, because I can't go on interviews if I'm stuck here taking care of the baby.

ERIC: Look at you man, you've got a wife, a kid, a house . . . Not just any house, a Brooklyn brownstone.

MILES: Yeah, but it needs a lot of work, man. I mean, this kitchen is like, from *Sanford and Son*. This linoleum floor . . . I was gonna fix it but then we ran out of money.

ERIC: What do you mean you ran out of money—look at this place, you're swimming in bucks.

MILES: Look at this place, exactly. I don't even want to tell you how much we paid for it. I had to cash in the last of my stock options for the down payment. If it weren't for the income we get renting the top floor apartment, we couldn't afford to live here.

ERIC: There's another apartment?

MILES: On the fourth floor. Eventually, we hope to take it over but right now we need the money.

ERIC: You've got something set aside, I know you, Miles. You've probably got ten thousand dollars in quarters all rolled up and stuffed inside a pair of tube socks upstairs.

MILES: Dude, InTech laid me off six weeks before the baby was born. Nina's the only one making a steady check now—

(Eric holds the baby with one hand, undoes his pants with the other.)

ERIC: Check this out. This is what I got for spending three months in a tropical Asian paradise.

(Eric's pants crumple around his ankles, revealing small piles of blue currency rubber-banded around each leg.)

MILES: What the hell are those?

ERIC: Ringgits. I sold hot dog carts to street vendors in Kuala Lumpur. This is my take home. Thirty thousand ringgits. Which is about ten thousand U.S. dollars.

MILES: What're you, waiting to deposit them in Chicago?

ERIC: Oh. Did I say I was going back to Chicago? My building went co-op so they kicked me out. How are the rents in this neighborhood? Think I could find a one-bedroom in the six-hundred-to-seven-hundred-dollar range?

MILES: Aw, no, man, maybe three years ago but now—

ERIC: Fucking yuppies coming in, jacking up the rents so that even a guy like me can't afford to live in the ghetto.

(*A smile, he pats Miles on the back.*)

MILES: It isn't exactly the (ghetto.)—

ERIC: I'm just kidding, man.

MILES: I know it's still rough around the edges, but, it's got a good history. A lot of families have been in these brownstones for six or seven generations. You've got teachers, artists, musicians—Biggie grew up a couple blocks from here.

ERIC: Okay, I get it.

MILES: It'll be good for Hannah to grow up around (.) . . . all kinds of kids.

ERIC: It's a great place to start a business. What does this neighborhood need?

MILES: We have to drive two neighborhoods over to get organic milk.

ERIC: What else?

MILES: You know—pasta sauce, good cheese, bread . . .

ERIC: So, a place where you can buy upscale groceries, sit down and get a good cup of coffee, and—meet other people like you in the neighborhood.

MILES: Sounds good, man, I hope someone opens one.

ERIC: Why not you?

MILES: The thing I need to do right now is get a job. Bring some money into this house. Starting a business costs money.

ERIC: That's what investors are for.

MILES: Plus, it's risky.

ERIC: Man, don't you know you're taking a bigger risk waiting around for the right position to open up in the right company. Starting a business gives you control. Look, I've got these ringgits. We can use them to get us off the ground.

MILES: Okay, I'll . . . think about it, man.

(Walter, the tenant, walks down the steps and out the door. He tries not to notice Miles and Eric, standing there in his underwear with the ringgits. He heads up the stairs.)

ERIC: Who the hell is that?

MILES: That's the tenant, Walter.

ERIC: He walks through your house to get to his apartment? That is weird, man. Come on, let's take a walk around the neighborhood. Scope out some old storefronts. I'll carry the baby.

MILES: We can't leave with the window like that.

ERIC: It'll be fine. We'll be back in ten minutes.

(Miles picks up the BabyBjörn.)

MILES: You want to wear the Björn?

ERIC: No, man. I don't want that thing. Think about it—two dudes walking down the street with a mixed-race baby in a BabyBjörn? It's not like people are gonna guess we're brothers. I'll just carry her like this, okay?

(Eric holds Hannah in the football hold.)

MILES: She hasn't made a peep this whole time, she likes you.

ERIC: Of course she likes me, man. I'm crazy Uncle Eric. She needs me.

MILES: For what?

ERIC: To be everything you're not.

(They exit.)

Scene 4

Nina, holding Hannah, sits across from Mrs. Chae, who is dressed neatly and paying a little more attention to Hannah than Nina.

NINA: I didn't expect to have to go back to work so soon. The good thing is I get to work at home—unlike other working mothers who have to go to their midtown (offices.)—

MRS. CHAE (*Korean accent*): Yes, I know. My daughter is lawyer and she (works.)—

NINA: But, most working mothers get three months maternity leave and I have to start working after only six weeks. My partner and I have made it to the finals in a major design—

MRS. CHAE: These days, woman has to work. My daughter says—

NINA: —A major design competition for a new arts center in Barcelona.

(She looks to Mrs. Chae for approval, signs she's impressed. She gets none. Clearing throat:)

Arts Center in Barcelona. It's an international competition and only four groups made it to the final. It's an honor and a huge—

(Mrs. Chae makes clicking noises at the baby.)

Anyway, the deadline is in six weeks so that's why I need a nanny to start right away—

MRS. CHAE: Can I hold her?

(Nina unconsciously hesitates.)

NINA: Yes, of course, just—be careful of/her (neck.)—

MRS. CHAE (*Soothing to Nina*): I know . . . I know . . .

(Mrs. Chae takes the baby, while saying in Korean, "Oh, look at you, you're such a pretty girl." This unexpectedly touches Nina.)

Your mommy and daddy must be very happy.

NINA: I think my dad liked her, it's hard to tell.

MRS. CHAE: But your mommy, she was so proud.

NINA: No, Mommy's dead.

MRS. CHAE: Tsk tsk tsk. You take care of baby, your mommy suppose take care of you.

(This moves Nina again. The baby makes a sound. Mrs. Chae immediately soothes her by patting her on the back and saying a few words in Korean.)

NINA: She's smiling at you.

MRS. CHAE: Babies love me. And I love the babies too. The family I worked for before? Husband got the new job in Ohio. They ask me to move with them, "Please, nanny, come with us." But I cannot go. I have my family here. I have a grandson, did you know?

NINA: Oh, how old is he?

MRS. CHAE: My daughter, she work at big law firm, they have daycare center in building. I told my daughter, "I quit my job to take care of him, he's my grandson." But she say, "Mommy, don't be selfish, I want him near me."

NINA: Her name is Hannah, did I tell you?

MRS. CHAE: I think maybe you name her Hannah *(Pronounces it huh-NAH)* because she's first one born.

NINA: Actually, we just liked the name. And it's HA-nah, not huh-NAH. That would be weird, wouldn't it? Naming her "number one"?

MRS. CHAE: You know Huh-nah?

NINA *(Counts in Korean, pronunciation shaky)*: Hana, tul, set . . .

MRS. CHAE: Oh. Because when you tell me you don't speak one word of Korean, I think you don't speak one word.

NINA: I do know one word. I know "hana." Actually, I can count to ten, my parents did teach me that. I just don't know how to say . . . eleven or twelve. I don't know any Korean lullabies, or how to say "koochie koo—"

MRS. CHAE *(Starts to sing; insert first couple lines from a Korean Lullaby)*: Your mommy sang this to you.

NINA *(Moved, wishing she weren't)*: Yes, I think she did.

MRS. CHAE *(Looking at Hannah)*: She has the curly hair.

NINA: Yes, from my husband. I'm thrilled.

(Mrs. Chae looks at the baby again.)

MRS. CHAE: She looks like . . . your husband?

NINA: I don't know. My family thinks she looks like my husband and my husband's family thinks she looks like me.

MRS. CHAE: Your husband . . . he is . . . architect too?

NINA: No, he's uh . . . he's a computer guy.

(Miles hurries in.)

MILES: I'm sorry I'm late, the interview went long—

NINA: So, it must've gone really well. What did they—

MILES: I'll . . . tell you later. (*To Mrs. Chae*) Hi, I'm Miles.

(*He goes to shake Mrs. Chae's hand, she bows.*)

NINA: Oh, uh, Miles, this is Mrs. Chae. Mrs. Chae, this is my husband Miles.

MRS. CHAE (*Not skipping a beat*): Congratulations. She is beautiful baby.

MILES: Thank you, thank you.

MRS. CHAE: So, you don't mind? Nina says she want the Korean nanny to speak Korean to Hannah. You don't worry?

MILES: No, I—I think it'd be great. I think it'd be wonderful for Hannah to understand Korean. You thought I might be worried?

MRS. CHAE: Maybe some American parent don't want the child to get confused or handicapped.

MILES: No, no, I think it's totally a good thing.

(*Mrs. Chae looks at Hannah, then Nina and Miles.*)

MRS. CHAE: She is lucky baby.

(*Miles smiles, puts his arm around Nina.*)

MILES: Hey, why don't I take a picture of you three together?

(*Miles gets his camera.*)

NINA: Um . . . Miles? It's a little premature—

MILES: It'll be nice.

(*Nina stands next to Mrs. Chae, not quite committed. Mrs. Chae holds Hannah closer and smiles into the camera.*)

That's great.

(*Flash. The doorbell rings. Nina turns to Mrs. Chae.*)

NINA: Thank you for your time. Let me walk you to the door.

MRS. CHAE: Should I call you tomorrow?

NINA: I'll call you, thank you.

MILES: You guys look great together!

(She opens the door to let Mrs. Chae out, sees Reggie.)

NINA: Oh, hi Reggie. Um, come on in.

(Mrs. Chae leaves as Reggie comes in carrying a large, ornate chandelier.)

REGGIE *(To Miles)*: Check this out, man. I just bought it for fifty bucks, I sell it to you for seventy-five.

MILES: Where did you get that?

REGGIE: I told you, I bought it. *(Looks at their ceiling.)* I see you got a hook where one used to be. All you got to do is slip it on. You got a ladder?

MILES: Listen, Reggie, thanks but, we don't want to buy that.

REGGIE: It ain't gone be that hard, here—

(He hands it to Miles, who reluctantly takes it. Reggie moves some boxes underneath the hook.)

I could probably reach it like this.

MILES: Can you get down, please? You're stepping on some fragile electronic equipment.

REGGIE: You got some computer stuff in here?

MILES: Can you just come down?

(Reggie steps down.)

REGGIE *(To Miles)*: So, I talked to my boy over at the glassworks, I told him it was a eighty-inch window and he says he can do it for fifteen hundred dollars.

NINA *(To Reggie)*: Oh. Did you get his card? 'Cause I should talk to him about some details.

(Reggie digs through his pockets.)

REGGIE: I got his card, I got his card, here—

(He hands her a folded piece of paper then turns back to Miles.)

But if you want to pull the trigger on this, tell me. I'll set it up for you. Even with my fee, you ain't paying what you'd pay if you walked in there yourself.

(Miles looks at Nina.)

MILES: Your fee. That's part of the fifteen hundred.

REGGIE *(Goes to fridge)*: Oh, shit. You still got that fridge? That ugly-ass fridge been here since the seventies.

(Reggie opens the fridge.)

MILES: Do you mind?

REGGIE: You know, I been in your house before. Yeah, I been in here before. Had some good times up in here, man. The night of the blackout, 1977, city was coal-black. People were running around crazy, smashing store windows, grabbing up anything they could get—bananas, turntables, diapers . . . Me and my friends climbed through that window, lay down on our backs, and looked straight up, man, saw stars we never get to see—the constellations. Aquila the eagle; Cygnus the swan; Hercules the warrior—he took on the labors, man. He brought down the lion, the hydra, Cerberus, himself. After the riots is when the monsters took over this neighborhood—drug dealers, gangs, robbers. Hercules should've stuck around, we coulda used him. But when the power came back on, all the stars faded away.

(Miles hands Reggie the chandelier.)

Scene 5

The office. There are two drafting tables and stools, a desk with a computer and printer. Kit and Nina are building the landscape their model will sit on. Kit finishes gluing on a layer of gator board and is waiting for Nina to cut out more shapes. Meanwhile, Nina is looking for something.

KIT: Nina, I'm ready for more shapes. What're you doing, what're you looking for?

NINA: A green and yellow receiving blanket. It was mine when I was a baby. I have this picture of my mom holding me in it . . .

(Their office phone rings. Kit checks the caller ID.)

KIT: Don't get it, it's Mrs. Tillman. She's called three times already.

NINA: Not about the wall again.

KIT: The first two calls were about the wall. The third call was about the bathroom. She said the light made the wall tiles look "too shiny." I am so sick of these overly-entitled, ignorant, tantrum-throwing rich people.

NINA: Me too. I just want to be one.

KIT: I want to be in a whole new league. Get the hell out of residential work, be rid of these idiots forever.

NINA: I wonder what Mrs. Chae is doing to try to soothe her.

(Kit listens, hears nothing.)

KIT: Hannah's not crying.

NINA: She is, they're upstairs in the bedroom.

KIT: You're saying you can hear them two floors above? I can't hear anything.

NINA *(Standing up)*: I'm gonna go up there and offer to nurse her—

KIT *(Also standing)*: Nina, don't. Just . . . leave her, it's disrespectful. If the baby really needed you . . . or your breasts . . . the nanny would bring her down here. I don't even think she's crying.

NINA: I hear her. Being a mother has given me superhero powers. And Hannah—Hannah can smell me from twenty feet away.

KIT: You measured?

NINA: I read it and I tested it. And her crying—it triggers my milk. I was in the bathroom yesterday and she started crying, and milk shot out of my nipples. Smacked right into the back of the door. Sometimes my milk attacks her.

(We hear Hannah crying. Mrs. Chae has brought her downstairs to the living room. Nina looks at Kit.)

KIT: No, Nina, concentrate. We blew the first two months of our deadline already. We have six weeks to do what all our competitors have had four months to do. I didn't mean blow.

NINA: I couldn't stand up—

KIT *(To Nina)*: I know, honey.

NINA: Any woman who has a planned C-section is a fucking moron.

KIT: I like the image of the doctor grabbing your intestines by the handful and piling them on your stomach, then shoving them back in after she gets the baby out. You know, I think you've broken some kind of sacred code of silence by telling me the details of your horrible birth experience.

NINA: Are you afraid to have a baby now?

KIT: Hell yeah! Not that it's an option right—

(Eric comes downstairs, puts a set of keys on Kit's desk.)

ERIC: Thanks for letting me borrow these, Miles made a spare set for me.

KIT: No problem.

ERIC: Hey, you know that radio station you told me about? I tuned into it this morning. They play some great music.

KIT: I figured since you lost your iPod . . .

ERIC: I appreciate it. Well, I'll leave you gals to your work.

(Eric heads upstairs.)

NINA: What the hell was that about? You loaned him your keys?

KIT: Yeah. What's wrong with that?

NINA: I don't want him getting too comfortable. I don't want him to be here at all. Eric is not the kind of person Miles should get into business with.

KIT: Why not?

NINA: He's never done anything legit, he's never had a proper job . . . and he's never been able to commit to a relationship.

KIT: That was unsolicited.

NINA: Stream of consciousness. The thing is, I think Miles is using Eric and this business as a way of avoiding having to spend time with the baby.

KIT: If you think that there's some guy out there who's going to do more than what Miles is doing . . . you're nuts.

NINA: Fucking Joe.

KIT: You think Joe's a shit because he wouldn't marry me after six years, but I think Joe's normal. Every guy in the world is like Joe. You've had it lucky Nina, you don't know—

NINA: How hard it is out there? It's hard in here. This is hard.

(Beat.)

KIT: Last night, I went to a Salvadoran restaurant with this guy. I kept telling him in a nice way "It's not El Salvadorean food. It's Salvadoran." But all night he kept saying "I've never had El Salvadorean food before," "I have to tell my friends I went to an El Salvadorean restaurant."

NINA: Sounds like another online loser. Where was the restaurant?

KIT: Deepest Queens. To get there we had to take the Z train. The Z train to Jamaica Center. Then we had to walk twelve blocks to get to this little piece-of-shit restaurant that served the most heavenly pupusas made on the planet.

NINA: You bring some back for me?

KIT: No. Hot off the griddle—the crust was crisp and toothsome and when you bit into them the cheese and pork oozed out—

NINA (*Putting out her hand*): Stop—

(*Kit reaches into her desk, pulls out a bag of pupusas, tosses them to Nina.*)

KIT: They're not going to be as good cold, but—

NINA: Love.

(*Miles comes downstairs.*)

MILES: Nina, have you seen my camcorder?

NINA: What? No.

MILES: I know I put it on the bookshelf yesterday, but now I can't find it. I wanted to shoot some video of Hannah on her first day with Mrs. Chae.

NINA: You know what, Miles, I want you to spread the word that this office is off-limits to anyone who doesn't work here.

MILES: What—?

NINA: We're on a serious deadline here.

KIT: Yes, and it's ticking away every minute that you stand there arguing with your (husband.)—

MILES: This office is part of my house, Nina—

NINA: Our house. But, Kit and I pay rent here.

MILES: You have to throw that in my face?

NINA: This is our space, Miles, and I don't want anyone else down here.

MILES: That is so—

(*He storms off.*)

NINA (*Calling after him*): Except Hannah and Mrs. Chae! They're still allowed to (come.)—

(*The office phone rings.*)

KIT (*Into phone*): Hello? What?! Javier, I told you twice before I left last night those pipes had to be flush with the I-beams—Alright, look, just tell Mrs. Tillman to put her ass on ice, I'll be there in an hour. (*Off his reaction*) I'll take a cab, but I'm in fucking Brooklyn.

(*She hangs up the phone, dials another number.*)

NINA: Want me to call a car service?

KIT: I'm already doing it. (*Into phone*) Yeah, can I get a car at 127 Rosa Parks Avenue? Thanks.

NINA: I'll finish the shapes for the foundation by the time you—

(*Mrs. Chae walks downstairs carrying the crying Hannah.*)

MRS. CHAE: I'm sorry, Nina, I try give her pacifier, I try my finger, I play nice music—

NINA (*Looks to Kit*): Can you try taking her for a walk outside? Could you try that?

MRS. CHAE: Okay, yes, okay. I'm sorry I interrupt—

NINA: It's okay.

(*Nina looks at Hannah, feeling she might lose her resolve, she turns away. Sound of a car horn outside. Mrs. Chae starts to leave, Hannah cries harder. Kit grabs her bag.*)

KIT: That's my car. If you finish the layers by the time I get back, we might be able to stay on schedule.

(*One quick look at Nina, who continues working, then Kit's out the door. When Nina hears the door close, she stands up. She starts for the stairs—then stops, starts—stops . . . then runs upstairs.*)

Scene 6

Afternoon. Living room. There are fewer moving boxes—the place looks more settled. The window is still broken, a piece of plywood has been anchored to the wall to cover it. Reggie walks in carrying two boxes of ceramic tiles and sets them down on the kitchen floor, near another open box of a different shape. He can't resist looking into the other box. Miles walks in carrying another two boxes, sees Reggie.

MILES: Can I help you, man?

REGGIE: I see you got a Xbox. I can get you some games that go with it real cheap. They still in the plastic, let me show you what I got—

(*He starts for the door.*)

MILES: It's alright. I don't have time to play games these days.

REGGIE: They factory sealed. They ain't no cheap-ass Chinese—

(*Oops. Reggie does a quick scan for Nina.*)

MILES: She's not Chinese. And if they're meant to be sold in a store, how'd you get them?

REGGIE: I got a guy, he works in a Circuit City. He say sometimes they order twenty-five copies of a game, they get twenty-six.

MILES: So, they're stolen.

REGGIE: How's it stolen, the store ain't paid for it!

MILES: If you take something from a store without paying for it, you stole it!

REGGIE: Man, who lives like that?

MILES (*Trying to get rid of him*): Yeah, right, thanks for your help, Reggie, I can get this from here.

REGGIE: You got ten more boxes out there.

MILES: I can handle it.

REGGIE: Where you gone lay them tiles down anyway, the kitchen?

(*Miles hesitates, he knows where this is going.*)

MILES: I've got it all taken care of.

REGGIE: That will look nice, man. But you gotta take up all that linoleum, then you gotta patch up the holes and put something smooth down to glue the tiles to—you can't do all that by yourself.

MILES: Well, I have the time right now so I think I'll be alright.

REGGIE: We done did this in my mom's house in the eighties, man, I'm telling you—you gone need some help. Pulling that old stuff off piece by piece—ain't nothing for that but a pry bar. I don't mind an honest day's work. You hire some guy in the phonebook, he gone charge you two bills a day. I'll do it for half.

(*Nina, wearing the baby in a sling, walks in carrying plastic bags loaded with groceries in both hands.*)

NINA: What's this—you bought tiles? How much did they cost?

(Miles glances at Reggie, wants to get rid of him. Miles reaches into his pocket and hands Reggie a five-dollar bill.)

MILES: Here you go, man, thanks.

(Reggie looks at the money, doesn't take it.)

REGGIE: That's alright. We do it another way.

(Reggie heads out the door. Miles, embarrassed, puts the money back in his pocket.)

MILES: Eric paid for the tiles, says it's his housewarming gift to us.
NINA: Miles, take the baby. You haven't held her since yesterday.
MILES: No, I don't want to wake her.
NINA: What about your interview this morning?
MILES: I went.

(Opens a box of tiles.)

Look, I got those tiles that you circled in the catalog—
NINA: Miles, how'd it go?
MILES: I don't want to take a job that I'm going to resent going to every day. You know what I really want to do.
NINA: Open a store with your brother? Miles, we make fun of your brother and his ridiculous schemes.
MILES: This isn't a scheme, it's a good idea.
NINA: I don't trust your brother, Miles. I'm sorry, but I don't. He doesn't have the experience—
MILES: He has tons of experience!
NINA: He's never opened a business here. He just goes to these Western-worshipping little Asian countries with his all-American good looks and he bamboozles them. He sells them shit.
MILES: How can you talk like that about my brother?
NINA: You don't need your brother. If you really want to start a business, then why don't you start something yourself?
MILES: Start a business—what business, with what? I don't have any ideas—
NINA: Look what Reggie does, Reggie doesn't have anything but he's out on that street corner, paying attention to what's going on, looking for opportunities—

MILES: I'm not one of the guys on the corner, Nina. Are you telling me to stand on the corner with the rest of the unemployed black guys?

NINA: No.

MILES: This store is my idea. It's how I want to present myself to the community. A lot of these families living in these brownstones, they stayed committed to the community during the rough times. And now people like us are moving in and I want to be connected to their history. I don't want to be the intruder. I want to bring something.

(*Mrs. Chae walks in. Miles and Nina brighten like schoolchildren.*)

NINA AND MILES: Good morning, Mrs. Chae.

(*Mrs. Chae makes a beeline for the baby.*)

MRS. CHAE: She's asleep? You give me whole sling. This way you can work and I can keep Hannah while I do her laundry. And I do your laundry too.

(*Mrs. Chae picks up a few stray pieces of dirty clothing lying around.*)

NINA: Oh, you don't have to do that.

MRS. CHAE: I do this for my daughter too.

(*Mrs. Chae starts picking up stray laundry from around the living room.*)

NINA: . . . Huh. Do you . . . cook for her too?

MILES: Nina—

MRS. CHAE: Yes, of course. She and husband spend every weekend at my house. I cook a lots of food—chap chae, bulgogi, kimchee chigae—then Sunday, pack it up and they take home.

NINA: Man, I haven't had home-cooked Korean food in a long, long—

MRS. CHAE: You like the Korean food? Even the stinky kimchee?

NINA: I love kimchee. But I used to have to sneak it because my mom wouldn't let me eat it. She'd say, "You'll never have an American boyfriend."

MILES: Unless he also eats kimchee. (*Re: laundry*) Let me get you something for that.

(*He heads upstairs.*)

MRS. CHAE: Your mommy want you to have American boyfriend?

NINA: That's all we had where I grew up. Except for this one Filipino boy.

MRS. CHAE: I see. That's why she don't teach you the Korean language.

NINA: I don't think she knew I'd live in a place where I could speak Korean every day. Where every time my local Korean deli got a new cashier, I'd have to explain no, I'm not Japanese, I'm Korean, I just can't talk to you.

MRS. CHAE: If you want, I teach you the Korean words I speak to Hannah.

NINA: That would be amazing.

MRS. CHAE: That way you both learn together. And maybe someday I make kimchee for you. You work hard all day. You spend evening with Hannah instead of cook, clean and do laundry, eh? Hannah misses the mommy.

NINA: Do you think?

MRS. CHAE: She love the mommy and daddy. She talk about you all the time.

(Miles comes downstairs with a laundry bag.)

MILES: Here you go, you can put things in here.

MRS. CHAE: Oh, thank you, Miles. Such a good husband, hm? My husband, he never touch the laundry, never change the diaper, but Miles . . . he does so much.

(Mrs. Chae touches Miles's cheek, then goes upstairs. Eric opens the front door. Pushes in half a dozen large pieces of luggage.)

MILES: You need a hand with that, man?

(He goes over to help.)

NINA: What's going on, Eric?

ERIC: Miles was running out of clothes that fit me. Plus it was costing me twenty-one bucks a day to have this stuff in storage.

NINA: You took all of this to Malaysia?

ERIC: I was there for three months. I wanted to have my options.

MILES: I don't know if all that's gonna fit in the upstairs office.

ERIC: What about the basement? I don't need to put my hands on all this stuff every day. A bunch of these bags can go downstairs.

NINA: How long do you plan on staying here, if you don't mind my asking?

ERIC: To get a store off the ground could take a year. But, I don't have to stay here the whole time—

MILES: Where else are you going to stay?

ERIC: I can get a sublet—

NINA: It's just that we're still trying to get settled here—

MILES: I don't want you to do that, man. You're family.

NINA: Miles—

MILES: I asked him to stay here and help me launch the business. The least we can do is offer him a place to stay. We have the room—

NINA: No, we don't. That's supposed to be our office—

MILES: You have your office downstairs. The upstairs is my office and I say Eric is welcome to stay.

ERIC: I'm sorry, Nina, if I'd've known you were against me staying here, I wouldn'ta brought all my shit—

NINA: This isn't personal, Eric, you just happen to have shown up at a time when we're . . . we're still trying to figure things out ourselves and . . . I just need to put my family first.

MILES (*To Nina*): Eric is family. (*To Eric*) Come on, man, let's get these things upstairs.

Scene 7

Night. Eric sits at Nina's desk, Kit stands with her coat on, she's just come into the office.

KIT: Does Nina know you're down here?

ERIC: No, she's asleep. Why?

KIT: Well, she said she didn't want anyone else down here anymore.

ERIC: Oh—

KIT: Anyone except for me, her, Mrs. Chae and Hannah, of course . . . which only leaves you and Miles.

(*Eric turns to the computer.*)

ERIC: I didn't know, I'll close my document right now.

KIT (*Stopping him*): So—what were you working on? Something to do with the store?

ERIC: I was drafting a proposal. Miles scoped out a great location. So, what do you think of our idea?

KIT: S'pretty good. Neighborhood's changing . . . yuppies love their pesto and their lattes, I know I do.

ERIC: You know, I don't know why Miles never had the idea to run his own business before.

KIT: It's a lot of extra work. And it doesn't always pay off. You know this.

ERIC: I just wonder if Miles leans on Nina too much. If she ends up holding him back. Because Miles—

(*They hear a sound from the floor above.*)

I should get out of here—

KIT: Go on.

ERIC: Miles can do anything, man.

KIT: He's smart and hardworking, he's creative—

ERIC: What? He's way more than that, man. Miles came into the world a four-pound, undernourished, heroin-addicted, premature little bird you could hold in the palm of your hand.

KIT: Miles was a heroin baby?

ERIC: His birth mother was some junkie, shot ten bags of dope to induce her labor. Then after she gave birth, she snuck out of the hospital. My parents adopted him when he was still in the pediatric ICU.

KIT: I've known Nina and Miles for fifteen years, I've never heard that story.

ERIC: Ask Nina. When Miles was a kid, he had to go to physical therapy, occupational, speech . . . he rode the little special ed bus to school with the retards. And then in the fifth grade, pow! He just shot up and shot out. Next thing we knew he was doing karate, playing piano . . . writing code on the Commodore computer I got for Christmas.

KIT: Wow, a commodore. Your parents were cutting edge.

ERIC: All I did was play Pong on it so they ended up giving it to him. That's why I say Miles can do anything. And it's just . . . weird to come here and see him so . . .

KIT: Well, getting laid off right before you have a baby isn't exactly an ego booster.

ERIC: Guess not.

KIT: I've watched Nina and Miles's relationship for a long time. They try to pass the power back and forth between them, but one person always ends up holding the ball. That's true with most relationships, it's even true with two women.

(Beat.)

ERIC: This is so embarrassing.

KIT: What?

ERIC: I'm such an idiot.

KIT: Why?

ERIC: Are you gay?

KIT: No!

ERIC: I thought . . . because you said two women—

KIT: I'm talking about my friends Stephanie and Laura.

ERIC: Okay, good.

KIT: Why would it have been embarrassing?

ERIC: I don't know. Listen, I should go. I'm in your way.

KIT: I can still do my work with you here.

ERIC: I know. But, I'm not sure I can.

Scene 8

Office. The sound of scraping and prying from above—Miles and Reggie working on the floor. Kit and Nina work on the model—they are gluing on a cantilevered roof onto its beam. Kit applies the glue as Nina balances the top-heavy roof piece.

NINA: Your birthday already? What's today's date?

KIT: The third.

NINA: I completely lost track of time—okay, Thursday, your birthday. Is it— . . . are you gonna turn (forty?)—

KIT: Let's not touch on that.

NINA: Okay. Okay, what do you want to do? Do you want me to throw you a party?

KIT *(Re: roof)*: Press down harder on this side.

NINA: Dinner with a bunch of our friends?

KIT: No.

NINA: Kit, you gotta ring it in. Your fortieth—

KIT: Do not speak the number.

NINA: You can't do nothing.

KIT: I don't want to do nothing. I want to go out to a nice, quiet dinner, just you and me. We can go to that new French place on Smith Street. You can be home in time to nurse Hannah.

NINA: You sure you don't want to go somewhere fabulous in Manhattan?

KIT: With you constantly checking your watch, worried that your breasts are going to explode?

NINA: I guess you're right. (*Kit finishes, leaves Nina holding the newly glued-on piece.*)

KIT: So, Hannah being such a big baby and all, I was wondering— were you a big baby?

NINA: Normal. My body was skinny but my cheeks clocked in at about a pound each.

KIT: Miles must've been a big baby, then, huh?

NINA: Mm . . . no.

(*Kit, having hoped for a longer answer, fishes for more.*)

KIT: Have you ever seen pictures of him as a baby?

NINA: I have a picture of him when he was about a year old in my desk.

KIT: Can I see it?

NINA: Uh . . . sure. It's in my top drawer.

(*Kit opens Nina's top drawer, sifts around to find it. Looks at it.*)

KIT: Well. Looks like a perfectly healthy one-year-old to me. Perfectly healthy.

(*She puts the photo back, goes to her desk, silently kicking herself for believing. Nina watches her, unsure what this is about.*)

NINA: Actually, a normal one-year-old should weigh about twenty pounds and Miles only weighed seventeen.

(*Kit turns to Nina—enthused.*)

KIT: Tell me more.

NINA: His mom said he was a fussy eater—

(*Kit's disappointment is visible.*)

KIT: . . . Right.

NINA: He wouldn't drink milk or eat cheese which are good sources of fat.

(*Nina looks at Kit, trying to read her reaction.*)

KIT: That makes sense.

(*Beat.*)

NINA: Plus, he was addicted to heroin for the first two months of his—
KIT: Yes!
NINA: You're in love with Eric! He told you about Miles. That's Miles's big secret.
KIT: It came up in conversation.
NINA: Pillow talk.
KIT: Eric and I haven't even gone out yet, let alone slept together.

(*Half beat.*)

NINA: Don't trust him, Kit.
KIT: What do you resent so much about Eric? Has he ever hurt you or Miles?

(*Beat.*)

NINA: He's never there when it counts, you know, he didn't even come to our wedding. Then out of nowhere, he just swoops in and inserts himself into our lives.

(*Mrs. Chae carries downstairs a tray with two bowls of soup.*)

MRS. CHAE: It's lunch time for the hardworking woman. (*She means "women"*)
NINA (*Smelling, just saying it fills her*): What is that? Seaweed soup?

(*Mrs. Chae places a bowl on Nina's desk.*)

MRS. CHAE: Mi yuk guk. I write it down for you. Very good for the mommy after delivering the baby, because it has iron and protein. Good for you now because of the breastfeeding. You need the strength.
NINA: Thank you! I'll have it as soon as—

(*Mrs. Chae places another bowl in front of Kit.*)

MRS. CHAE: Good for you too, because it also helps to make the baby.

(*Kit gently pushes the soup bowl away from her.*)

KIT: Hmmmm . . . . Thanks . . .

(Mrs. Chae notices. So does Nina, she's embarrassed.)

MRS. CHAE: Your husband don't want the children?
KIT: My husband . . . right. He says he's not ready.

(Nina flashes her a look.)

MRS. CHAE: You cannot wait for him. The man is never ready for the
   children, he is still his mommy's baby. But, having the child will
   make him a man.
NINA: You can still eat it, Kit, the soup won't impregnate you.
MRS. CHAE *(To Nina)*: If you like, I teach you how to make it.
NINA: God, I would love that.

*(Nina looks at the soup, she still can't move her hands. To Mrs.
Chae:)*

Would you mind moving that a little closer to me?
MRS. CHAE: Of course.

*(Mrs. Chae does so. Nina leans her head down, without moving
her hands, trying to get her mouth close enough to the bowl. She
manages a sip.)*

NINA: Mm, smells fantastic.

*(She blows on it. Mrs. Chae watches Nina struggle to drink the
soup.)*

I'm dying to eat it but I can't move my hands until the glue—

*(Mrs. Chae picks up the bowl, scoops up a spoonful of soup and
blows on it before offering it to Nina.)*

MRS. CHAE *(In Korean)*: Eat well.
NINA: Oh, gosh, um—

(Nina takes a sip of soup.)

Mm, that's delicious.

(Mrs. Chae continues to feed Nina.)

MRS. CHAE: Soon it will be Hannah's paek il. We must have a big party.

NINA: Paek il? What's that?

MRS. CHAE: Paek il is for one hundredth day because back in old times, when a baby did not die by one hundred days, we have a big party. We say now she will live long life.

(Mrs. Chae feeds Nina another spoonful.)

KIT: Where's Miles's camera when you need it?

NINA: Gosh, I really appreciate this but . . . you don't have to feed me.

(We hear Miles and Reggie's voices in disagreement.)

MRS. CHAE: It's okay. Hannah is sleeping and I am in the way upstairs. Miles and his brother are working so hard.

NINA: Eric's helping?

MRS. CHAE: Yes.

(Nina looks at Kit.)

NINA: I thought he was going to the realtors—wait a second. Who do you mean by Miles's brother?

MRS. CHAE: The man, his brother. The one who's helping him.

NINA: Is he black?

MRS. CHAE: Yes.

NINA: That's not Miles's brother.

MRS. CHAE: Oh—

NINA: You met his brother. Eric. Eric's his brother. Reggie's . . . just some guy who lives on our street.

(Kit notices Nina's tone of voice.)

MRS. CHAE: Oh, I see . . .

(A beat. Nina's uncomfortable.)

Miles is adopted?

NINA: Yes.

MRS. CHAE *(A Korean sound)*: Oh . . . *(Tsk tsk tsk)* Such nice parents.

NINA: . . . They're nice because they're white people who adopted a little black baby?

(Kit tastes the soup.)

KIT: Mmmm, Mrs. Chae, this is good. What kind of seaweed is this?

MRS. CHAE: We call it mi yuk.

NINA: Because actually, I think Miles's parents were—they did things that were kind of . . . like raising him in an all-white neighborhood, sending him to schools where he was the only black kid—

KIT: I thought you liked your in-laws—

NINA: Miles was teased a lot. The reason he'll be emotionally enslaved to Eric the rest of his life is because Eric would beat the shit out of kids who picked on him.

MRS. CHAE: But Miles grew up so nice. Clean and smart, handsome.

NINA: Did you just say (clean.)—

KIT: Mrs. Chae, you mentioned your daughter has a child Hannah's age. Maybe he and Hannah can have a playdate! *(To Nina)* It'd be good for Hannah to have another kid she can speak Korean to because . . . you don't really have Korean friends . . .

MRS. CHAE *(Hesitates)*: I don't think—

NINA: What—you're afraid your daughter won't let him come because Hannah's black?

KIT: Nina—

MRS. CHAE: Hannah is not black. If you look at her, maybe you cannot tell. People cannot tell the daddy is black. She is just beautiful baby.

(Miles walks in through the outside door.)

MILES: Nina, I've got to use your computer for a minute.

(He sits at her desk, launches a web browser.)

NINA: Why can't you use your computer upstairs?

MILES: I told Reggie I was going to the hardware store to get something. I hid a little webcam so I can watch him. Mrs. Chae, do you mind staying down here for a few minutes?

KIT: Watch him do what?

MILES: Steal from me.

MRS. CHAE *(A Korean expression of shock)*: Aigu.

NINA: Miles, you have no reason to think that Reggie stole your—

MILES: The man openly offered to sell me stolen goods, Nina. This is what he does. He insinuates himself into people's homes, and then he takes things he can sell. The gentrification of this neighborhood is the best thing to happen to him in years.

(*Miles checks the web browser.*)

See that—look, he's looking in one of our boxes. I put my portable DVD player in there on purpose.

(*Nina looks.*)

NINA: This is wrong. I'm going upstairs to tell him—

KIT: Nina, don't let go of that—

(*Nina starts for the stairs. Kit rushes to the model to grab the roof. Miles goes after Nina.*)

MILES: Nina, stay. I want to catch him.

NINA: You've set up a trap.

KIT: Look at it this way. If he doesn't take anything, you'll have won.

NINA: You approve of this?

KIT: No, but I admit I'm on the edge of my seat.

(*Miles looks at the browser.*)

MILES: He's looking around . . . he's walking towards my iPod . . . he's picking up a pry bar—

(*We hear the corresponding sound on the ceiling.*)

And . . . he's pulling up the linoleum off the kitchen floor.

NINA: I am so embarrassed, Miles.

MILES: Well, someone took my camcorder.

NINA: You should go up there and apologize.

MILES: I'm not going to apologize. But I will let him keep working for us. And keep my eye on him.

(*Miles goes out the front door.*)

MRS. CHAE: Can I . . . go upstairs now?

NINA: Yes.

(Mrs. Chae goes upstairs, Nina takes over the job of holding down the roof from Kit. Kit goes to her desk.)

KIT: Do you want . . . me to feed you the soup?
NINA: No, I don't want it anymore. Do me a favor and throw it away.

Scene 9

Living room. The next day. Reggie holds one end of a tape measure while Miles pulls the rest across the length of the floor.

MILES: One-hundred-and-thirty-five inches. Divided by two, that's sixty-seven-and-a-half inches.

(He walks to that number on the measuring tape, then makes a mark on the floor.)

So this is the center of the room.
REGGIE: Why you doing this the hard way? All you have to do is start at this wall—

(Walks to the border between kitchen and living room.)

—get your tiles going across, then whenever you run into your fridge or your stove, you just cut the tile to fit. That's it.
MILES: No, if you do it that way then that's the only line that will look like full tiles. It's better to start in the center. That way I can distribute the error factor around the periphery of the room.

(After a beat.)

I'm going downstairs to ask Nina to take a look at—
REGGIE: Man, why do you have to—

(Miles turns to him.)

Alright, alright, I get you, man. Now, I get you. I ain't never been married yet so I wasn't feeling you before, but now I am.
MILES: What?

REGGIE: 'Cuz I notice how you talk to your female, see what I'm saying. 'Cuz you always saying "I gotta ax Nina this," or "I can't 'til I ax Nina—" and I've been thinking, "What is this brother, henpecked or some shit?" But now I know that's how you do her to do you right. I'm'a try that shit myself.

MILES: Man, Nina's done this before.

REGGIE: I done this before! I keep telling you!

MILES: Nina's done this hundreds of times before. Not just once in her mother's house. Anyway, why are you still living in your mother's house?

REGGIE: She getting old, she need somebody.

MILES: Yeah, but, you never moved out, right? So, who's taking care of who?

REGGIE: I got four brothers and three sisters, seven nephews and eight nieces, we all there.

MILES: All living in that house?

REGGIE: We family, man. We got seventy-seven years history in that house. Ain't no yuppie gone come up in here and buy us out.

(Eric walks in.)

ERIC: I tracked down the owner of the diner, he's this Hasidic guy who hangs out with his buddies in this bakery in Williamsburg. I made an appointment for Friday so you can meet him.

(Reggie starts arranging the tiles the way he wants them. Not gluing them, just placing them down to make a point.)

MILES: Awesome.

REGGIE: "Awesome, dude."

ERIC: The landlord said another party approached him about the space last week. They want to open a tea lounge.

MILES: A tea lounge? Who around here is going to go to a tea lounge?

REGGIE: I would. I drink tea.

ERIC: To get an edge on these guys, I think we should put down a deposit. Are you ready to do that?

REGGIE: He gone ax his wife.

MILES: It's your money. If you want to be that aggressive—

ERIC: That's how you compete, little brother. You have to be fierce, you have to use that big brain of yours to think—how do I get the advantage? What idea can I come up with that no one else could.

MILES: I can do that.

ERIC: I'm gonna go to the bank tomorrow, convert my ringgits.

(*Eric heads for the stairs just as Walter comes down. Once again, he goes straight out the door, without acknowledging anyone. Eric gives Miles a look—weird. As Eric goes upstairs, Nina comes up from the office. Reggie, having placed a few rows of tiles on the floor, seizes the opportunity.*)

REGGIE (*To Nina*): Mommy, look at this here. How this looks? You walk into the room, you see one solid line. That's the way to do it.

NINA: You're . . . right, Reggie. That is . . . a way to do it. But—

REGGIE: You hear that? She said I'm right. She said I'm right and she know more about this than you. But you ain't never said nothing like that.

MILES: Oh, Nina's your hero now?

NINA: Miles—

MILES: I've been telling you since the minute I met you that she's an architect. But you keep treating her like she doesn't know anything.

REGGIE (*To Nina*): Is that true? That ain't true. You the one who act like I don't know anything. I done did this before and you ain't. But you gotta be like one of them new niggas who always think—

(*The baby starts crying upstairs. Nina can't decide whether to get the baby or stay with Miles.*)

MILES: No, man. No. I'm not any kind of nigger. You hear me?

REGGIE: Man, I ain't mean it like that. Over here when somebody say new nigga we mean somebody who turn they nose up at something 'cause it ain't new or good enough—

MILES: I don't care what you say it means, man. I don't want to hear it in my house.

(*The baby's cries become jagged and intense. Nina can't take it anymore, goes upstairs to soothe the baby.*)

REGGIE: Man, you all new niggas to me, buying up these here brownstones for a million dollars when they done sat here for decades all boarded up—shit, city couldn't give these buildings away.

MILES: Don't try to give me that back in the day bull (shit.)—

REGGIE: This house that you living in now been abandoned so long it had a tree growing out of it—right through the roof. When we was little kids, we called it the tree house—

(Walks to window.)

We used to climb through that window and sit under the tree—

(Points to a spot on the floor.)

Right here—and smoke cigarettes, kiss, party, you name it. This was our house.

MILES: Man, don't try to make it sound like it was better back in the old days 'cause I know this house went on to be a shooting gallery and a crack house before the city took it over.

REGGIE: I ain't saying it was better. Shit, I got shot walking down my street just going to buy some chicken wings at the Chinese restaurant. So I ain't saying nothing 'bout no back in the day. All I'm saying is—this is the way you do your tiles, son. You get them going across, ain't nothing else to worry about.

MILES: Reggie, man, if you want to help, I'll pay you. But we're gonna do it the way I want it. Okay? It's my house now.

(Beat.)

REGGIE: Alright. *(Checks watch)* I gotta go check on my girl, wake her ass up otherwise she ain't gone get to work—

(He goes out the door. Nina comes downstairs carrying Hannah.)

NINA: Miles, is everything okay?

MILES: Where's Mrs. Chae? Why isn't she here taking care of the baby?

NINA: I told her to come in a little later this morning, I wanted to talk to you about her. I think we have a problem.

MILES: What're you talking about? She seems to be working out great.

(Eric hurries downstairs carrying a pair of boxer shorts.)

ERIC: This is fucked up, man. This is out of line, this is fucked up.

MILES: What's going on, man?

ERIC: My ringgits are gone.

MILES AND NINA: What?

(He holds out his boxer shorts.)

ERIC: I hid the money in here—I folded these up and put them underneath the mattress in the sofa bed—not the most inventive hiding place, I admit, but I figured we were all family here.

MILES: Man, what is going on around here?

ERIC: You got a lot of new people coming in and out of this house. The tenant passes by all our bedrooms to get to his floor. He's got a lock on the door to his apartment, but all our rooms are wide open. Maybe he took your camcorder. What do you know about that guy?

MILES: Not much.

ERIC: If you ask me—you guys need to close ranks. Clean house. How much is he paying in rent?

NINA: Twelve hundred a month.

ERIC: I could pay that. Or close to that. I've got some money in the bank, plus I've built in salaries for me and you in the business proposal.

(Nina looks at Miles—you're not going for this, are you?)

MILES: We can't just kick him out, we gave him a two-year lease.

ERIC: I should be part of this community too. It'll be good for the profile of the business.

MILES: We'll see what we can do to make that happen, man.

NINA: We will?

ERIC: Let me go upstairs and have another look.

(He goes upstairs.)

NINA *(To Miles)*: We need twelve hundred for the upstairs apartment. I cannot meet our mortgage payments without—I can't take it on, Miles. I can't have one more thing on my back.

MILES: It's not going to be on your back. Eric said he's going to pay rent.

NINA: No, he's not. Eric came here with the intention of getting us to give him a free place to live.

MILES: He just got off a plane! He came here to meet the baby.

NINA: We haven't seen or heard from him in months—

MILES: That's usual for him.

NINA: Then on the day we move in, he shows up at our doorstep with no place to live. He comes up with this business idea, says he's got the money to get it started, gets you all riled up about it, then all of a sudden—the money's gone. He never had the money, Miles.

MILES: You never saw it, but I saw it.

NINA: He probably bought it at a party store with a pack of tropical drink umbrellas. What bothers me the most, Miles, is that we've always laughed at your brother . . . together, we've indulged him, we'd listen to his stories and wink wink at each other knowing that it was all a big show . . . but now I look over at you, and you're rapt. You're like a kid listening to his con-man uncle and hanging on every word.

(Hannah starts to cry.)

MILES: You really think that I'm that gullible?

NINA: I think you're . . . vulnerable, I think you think you're cast out in some way . . . and that your brother's going to bring you in. But you're not cast out. Hannah and I are your family, now. Why don't you hold her, maybe she'll stop crying if you do.

(Nina tries to hand Miles the baby. He doesn't take her.)

MILES: No, she won't. She only cries harder.

NINA: Only when she senses your fear. Just focus on how much you love her, and she'll calm down.

MILES: You know she's going to reject me.

NINA: No, she won't.

MILES: She only wants you. I don't have anything she needs.

NINA: Miles, take her—

MILES: No, you want me to fail. You want me to.

(He storms off. Nina turns to Hannah.)

NINA: It's okay, sweetie, Daddy loves you. Daddy loves you.

Scene 10

Office. Kit is working, Nina is nursing Hannah.

KIT: Nina, you can't take time away from work to look for a new nanny. I won't let you.

NINA: It won't take that long this time, I'm not going to hold out for a Korean woman. I'll take anyone who isn't going to poison my baby with racist thoughts.

KIT: I think you're blowing this whole thing out of proportion.

NINA: I'm not. I know that as sure as someday Hannah's going to fall off her bike and scrape her knee, that someone is going to call her a chink, and a nigger—

KIT: Cover her ears!

NINA: I can't stop it. I can't protect her from it—I can't stop it from happening to me as a grown woman. Last month, I was standing in the front lawn of my childhood home, where I used to play cowboys and Indians, and ride my banana seat Schwinn, and eat Creamsicles from the ice cream man, and some teenager shouted from a car, "Go back to Vietnam—"

KIT: It's horrible, it's embarrassing, but I still think that's completely different from what Mrs. Chae—

NINA: My whole bright idea about hiring a Korean nanny was to give Hannah a reason to be proud to be Korean. I thought if she could, I don't know, speak the language, have some sense of belonging—it would help those names bounce off of her. We had the same reasons for wanting to raise Hannah in a mostly black neighborhood.

KIT: Look, you guys are making great choices for her—

NINA: No, we're not, we're failing in every way. The Korean nanny's denying her blackness, the black neighbors are throwing rocks through our window . . . Miles won't hold our baby and . . . I see how hard you're working and I'm trying my best—I know I'm not pulling my weight—but I swear I am giving this everything I have left. And all I ask from Miles, all I want him to do . . .

(*A beat for Nina.*)

. . . is to be in it with me.

(*Nina covers her mouth to hide that she's crying—something she saw her mother do.*)

KIT: Hey—

(*Kit walks over to Nina.*)

NINA: But instead, he wants to know when we're going to start having sex again. And I can't—I swear, Kit, I don't have anything left to give.

(*Nina hides her face by nuzzling Hannah.*)

KIT: When we're in Barcelona, I'm gonna take you to this fantastic little tapas place I read about. We'll eat little plates of fried octopus eyes and beef snout on toast while we watch them build our building.

(Nina nods but aims all her need at Hannah, kissing her, holding her close. Kit goes to touch Nina supportively, but Nina has closed the circle—there's only room for her and her baby. Kit stands up, walks back to her drawing table. She draws for a minute.)

NINA: Eric tell you about the missing money?

KIT: I heard about it.

NINA: What do you think? Do you think someone really stole it?

KIT: I think a ghost took it. I think that first night when your window got smashed, the ghost of all the neglected communities past—who couldn't get the city to fix their sidewalks, or keep their electricity going on hot days, let alone provide them with a local source of organic half-and-half—wafted in here and is trying to spook you into leaving.

(Kit puts something down on the table, Nina picks it up—a matchbook from a restaurant.)

NINA: What's this?

KIT: It has the restaurant's name and address on Smith Street. The food was good, you and Miles should go there some time.

NINA: What? Ohmigod. Oh please God, please please please let it not be—

KIT: It's new, so it's not that crowded yet. They let me sit for a while.

NINA: You waited for me? Why didn't you call?

KIT: I have some dignity, you know.

NINA: Why didn't you remind me during the day!

KIT: Just, let it pass, Nina.

NINA: No, it's totally my fault. I can't believe I forgot to show up for your fortieth birth (day.)—

KIT: Just stop talking about it, okay? I don't care that you didn't show up, I don't care. I ate dinner, went to a bar, I fucked a guy in the bathroom—it was perfect. The best birthday ever. All I want from you, Nina, is for you to do your work. Fucking do your work. I can't finish this model by myself, not with less than six weeks left. I waited for you, Nina, I could've started two months ago without you, but you told me to wait.

NINA: I shouldn't have done that. It's just—I never . . . it's like this feral—this animal drive to take care of my daughter. I can't even apologize for it, it fucking feels right.

KIT: So you shouldn't be trying to work.

NINA: I want to work. I don't want to be a stay-at-home mom. I know it doesn't add up, okay? But I still love my work.

KIT: Look, Nina, you're a good mom—my mom, she took Dexatrim when she was pregnant with me because she didn't want to get fat. And I—I don't think women should have children if they're not going to be like you. But this work is all I have and I fucking want to win this competition.

NINA: I do too.

KIT: Don't say that.

NINA: I know it doesn't make sense to you—

KIT: Nina, I'm forty years old, I already don't have what I thought I would have by now but I know I can make beautiful buildings. It's not fucking fair for you to hold me back. Between Mrs. Tillman's unreasonable demands and your constant distractions, we're way behind already.

NINA: I'll take care of Mrs. Tillman.

KIT: No, you won't.

NINA: When she calls today, tell her I'll meet her at the house.

KIT: That's nice of you to finally offer, but Mrs. Tillman isn't going to call today because I told her we quit.

NINA: What—?

KIT: This morning, she insisted I go all the way to the Upper East Side just to show me some dust from the living room had "penetrated" her bedroom. And I just—I fucking had it.

NINA: You quit—you— . . . you quit before she finished paying us?

KIT: Now we can focus on the model.

NINA: Kit—how could you do that to me?

KIT: We need to concentrate on the model.

NINA: Mrs. Tillman is my livelihood. That money is what my family lives on.

KIT: We split the money but I do all the work.

NINA: I designed the plans with you. I did my share until the baby was born.

(Nina thinks a beat, looks at the baby, then picks up her bag. Calling upstairs:)

Mrs. Chae? *(To Kit)* I'm going to apologize to Mrs. Tillman.

KIT: Go ahead.

NINA (*Yells*): Mrs. Chae! (*To Kit*) I'm getting this job back, Kit.

KIT: Fine, you can run up there every time a nail gets hammered in crooked.

NINA: Mrs. Chae!

(*Mrs. Chae rushes downstairs.*)

MRS. CHAE: Sorry, Nina, I could not hear you.

NINA: I need you to take Hannah right now.

MRS. CHAE: Yes, yes, I will take.

(*Mrs. Chae reaches for the baby, says in Korean, "It's okay, baby, Mommy is very busy so Grandma will take care of you."*)

NINA: What did you just say?

MRS. CHAE: Hm?

NINA: What did you say to her?

MRS. CHAE: I say you are very busy, so I will take her upstairs—

NINA: Did you call yourself "halmoni"?

MRS. CHAE: . . . Yes?

NINA: Grandma?

MRS. CHAE: In Korean language, a child will call any woman my age—

NINA: When I come back, we need to talk.

(*Nina flies out the door.*)

KIT: I'm sorry—

MRS. CHAE (*Consoling herself, but aiming it at Hannah*): It's okay, it's okay, I know everything will be okay.

(*Mrs. Chae heads upstairs as Eric walks in through the front door. He walks up to Kit, stands close to her.*)

ERIC: Hey.

KIT: Hi.

ERIC: Now I know why you take a car service, it's a bitch to get here from your house by train. Do you feel hungover?

KIT: Eric, I don't have the money.

ERIC: You didn't get to stop by the bank on your way in?

KIT: No.

ERIC: Well, you still have a couple hours—

KIT: I'm not going to loan you any money. I'm sure both of us said things last night that we don't intend to follow through on. We were drunk, we were having a good time—

ERIC: You called me up, lured me to that restaurant with your sob story—

KIT: I invited you to join me, you ordered the most expensive thing on the menu, I picked up the tab . . . everything that happened after that was fun, but it wasn't worth five thousand dollars. You're just going to have to tell your brother you never had the money.

ERIC: I had the money. I had it until last night.

KIT: Well, I'm sure you'll find a way around it, Eric, you're fast on your feet.

Scene 11

Living room. Miles comes downstairs in a suit and jacket—he's missing a tie. He starts looking through some boxes, pulling out kitchen utensils from one box, winter clothes from another . . . Eric comes downstairs wearing a dress shirt and tie.

ERIC: You look sharp, man.

MILES: I'm looking for my ties—

ERIC: You don't need a tie, you look crisp without one.

(Miles lifts a box off the top of a stack and looks in the box underneath it.)

MILES: I want to make a strong appearance, those tea lounge people probably wear thrift store T-shirts and flip-flops.

ERIC: Don't bring up the tea lounge unless he brings it up first. As far as I know, they haven't put down any money so we'll be on even ground.

(Miles pulls his camcorder out of a box.)

MILES: My camcorder . . . that's what I did with it. I put it in here after Reggie came in with his chandelier and was roaming all over the place.

ERIC: Well, alright. That's great.

(*A beat.*)

MILES: So, if my camcorder was never stolen . . . what happened to your ringgits?

ERIC: I don't know, man.

MILES: Eric . . . tell me straight up. Were those ringgits real?

ERIC: Of course they were real.

MILES: Where are they, man, I don't believe Walter took them.

ERIC: Oh, I think he has them.

MILES: Eric—

ERIC: What you want to do is watch his checking account. You have all his information from his credit report, right? Watch his account for the next couple weeks and you just might see a big deposit show up.

(*Beat.*)

MILES: Then, what, he's going to tell me he's moving out?

ERIC: Could be.

MILES: Is that what you did with the money, Eric? You wanted me and Nina to think Walter stole it, but really you paid him so he would move out?

(*Beat.*)

ERIC: I offered it to him, yeah.

MILES: Man—that money was supposed to be for our business.

ERIC: You want me to commit to this business but what're you doing for me? You own this whole brownstone, but you'd rather price-gouge a stranger than give your brother a home.

MILES: We're not making decisions right now based on preference—we need to make ends meet.

ERIC: You always make ends meet, Miles. Why're you acting like you don't know that everything's gonna turn out your way—it always does.

MILES: You think things just snap into place—?

ERIC: Nina's gonna win her competition, the store's going to be an instant success, Hannah's gonna be the poster baby for the new Benetton campaign . . . you're going to have it all, like you always do—why do you have to deny me a piece of it?

MILES: Man, I've earned what I have. This is what I've always worked for. But you've been flitting around the world, cobbling together

this little job with that one, never building anything, never dig-
ging roots, and now you're looking at me and saying "I want
some of that"?

ERIC: You don't think I want a house, a steady career and a family? What do you think I am, a circus performer? A pirate? Of
course I want those things but I've never been able to work for
them because I'm not allowed to have what Miles has. Miles
is the super baby, the poor little black boy left on our doorstep
who goes on to save the town and my job in life is to make sure
I never overshadow him.

MILES: Mom and Dad gave you every chance they gave me. They cut
everything straight down the line.

ERIC: I can see why you'd want to remember things that way, but
they weren't. You were always the golden boy, the miracle . . . I
could never live up to it, Miles.

MILES: Did you try? All you had to do was try.

ERIC: What, you think because I'm white, because I know who my
biological parents are, because I can walk down the street of our
hometown without some old lady calling the cops—that every
door in the world is open to me? They're not, Miles. The doors
are for you.

MILES: You want what I have? Do you know what it is like for me
to look at my baby, and see her brown skin, and curly hair, and
long eyelashes and know she got them from me—but I don't
know who I come from? What am I giving her? What have
I passed on? I don't know. Maybe there's some disease that
skips a generation, and I've given it to her. Or maybe my great-
great-grandfather was a Civil War hero, but I'll never be able to
tell Hannah about it. All I can do is take her to Mom and Dad's
house in Indiana, where Mom can explain every little tchotchke
and how it was handed down to her . . . and dad can break out
the family albums going back seven generations—but when she
looks at those people in the photographs, she won't see herself,
she won't see me.

ERIC: You think I see myself in those old pictures? All I see are a
bunch of old people in stiff suits who had sixteen children and
were half-dead from lung cancer by the time they were our age.

MILES: That's how you make it hard for yourself, Eric. Trying to
invent yourself from scratch.

ERIC: You did. But I can't, no matter how hard I've tried.

(Nina walks upstairs, notices the camcorder.)

NINA: You found the camcorder.

MILES: . . . Yeah.

NINA: Where was it?

MILES: . . . Where I put it.

ERIC: I'm gonna go to this meeting, man.

NINA: Miles, I want to fire Mrs. Chae this afternoon.

ERIC: If you want to catch up with me . . . (*Eric leaves.*)

MILES: Why?

NINA: I just need you to trust me on this.

Scene 12

Living room. Mrs. Chae crosses the room to get to the door, Miles sees her.

MILES: Mrs. Chae, are you leaving?

MRS. CHAE: Yes.

MILES: You left your lunch—

MRS. CHAE: Not my lunch. It's jap chae for you and Nina. You have it for dinner.

(She heads for the door.)

MILES: You'll still be with us for two more weeks, right?

MRS. CHAE: I am old woman with nothing to do. Husband is dead, no job, what I'm going to do?

MILES: I—I don't know what to say, you've been wonderful to Hannah . . . but—

MRS. CHAE: I try so hard, I want to make you and Nina happy. What have I done so wrong?

(Nina walks upstairs from the office, having overheard the last part. Mrs. Chae takes a step towards her.)

Nina—

(Without thinking, Mrs. Chae speaks to Nina in Korean:)

Nina, you're such a good girl, hm? Give me another chance. I'll do everything right.

NINA: I don't understand you.

MRS. CHAE: You are good girl, such a good mommy, hm? Best mommy. My daughter, she hire the British nanny to take care of my grandson. She tell me she don't want Mommy to take care of grandson. She don't want grandson to speak the bad English like Mommy. Kyung Soon say when she was little girl, she speak the English like Mommy, go to school and say "preejing," it's "preejing" outside. And children laugh, laugh.

NINA: . . . Pleasing?

MRS. CHAE: So cold, it's preejing and Kyung Soon come home and say, "Mommy, you are dummy. You are such dummy!"

MILES: . . . Kids can be rough.

MRS. CHAE: So, she hire another nanny, not me. British nanny take care of my grandson.

NINA: You said your daughter has her son in daycare at her firm?

MRS. CHAE: Now I am telling you. British nanny comes at seven o'clock in morning, stay until eight o'clock at night. Then, Tibetan nanny comes on weekend, so Kyung Soon and husband can play golf.

MILES: She has two nannies?

MRS. CHAE: Yes.

MILES: That's a lot of nannies.

NINA: So . . . you've been lying about all of that?

MRS. CHAE: I tell you the truth now. Before, I wanted you to hire me, I see nice family, two good parents—happy baby . . . I wanted to be in this house, I wanted to be in this (family.) . . .

(Miles turns to Nina.)

MILES: Nina, maybe firing her isn't the right thing to do.

NINA *(To Mrs. Chae)*: I know people like you. Some of my mom's friends, they came to this country in the sixties, people taunted them, told them their food stank, their faces were flat, called them gook, chink, chingaling—

MILES *(To Nina)*: Whoa—

NINA: Made them feel like shit for what, for walking down the street, for sending their kids to school, for starting a business. For that they got beaten up, their stores got vandalized, right?

MRS. CHAE: . . . Yes. My husband and I had a gift store in Yonkers. Somebody paint all over the windows.

NINA: So what did you do?

MRS. CHAE: We cleaned the windows. My husband and I scrubbed the paint off with our hands—

NINA: You went looking for someone you could feel superior to. And you picked black people.

MILES: Nina, I think you need—you need to take a step back.

NINA: It makes me mad, it makes me ashamed of being Korean, fucking racists.

MILES: Mrs. Chae is new to this country, she's from another generation . . . I don't like what she said to Hannah but I don't think she's a racist—

NINA: Bullshit. My mom was all those things and she never said anything like that. Even in that shitty little town we lived in. Mrs. Chae is from Queens, she has no excuse.

MILES: Well, she'll learn—

NINA: Who taught my mom—nobody. It was in her heart.

(Half beat.)

MILES: Oh, I get it. I get it now, Nina. It's like you hired Mrs. Chae to be your mom. And you fired her because she's not.

NINA: Geezus, Miles, is it too much to ask you to take my side?

MILES: Side—!? What do you want this to be, Nina?

NINA: I want you to . . . I want you to defend me.

(Miles looks at Mrs. Chae, who has kept her head down, turns back to Nina.)

MILES: Nobody's attacking you!

NINA: That's not the point.

MILES *(To Mrs. Chae)*: Excuse her, Mrs. Chae, Nina's under a tremendous amount of press(ure.)—

MRS. CHAE: She is working very hard.

(Moves towards Nina, who turns to Miles.)

NINA: Don't fucking apologize for me.

MILES: You just said you wanted me—

NINA: Not to apologize, I want you to—Christ, if you think I'm being unreasonable—

MILES: Yes!

NINA: Then, fucking . . . hold me or something.

MILES: You're not making me want to hold you.

NINA: I have to do something—?

MILES: Well, you're not making me feel like it—

NINA: So, making all the money for the family doesn't qualify me for a hug?

MILES: Why d'you—

(*Looks at Mrs. Chae.*)

Why d'you have to say that?

NINA: Because I'm tired of having to tiptoe around your ego. My work is totally stressful, I'm not giving the baby the time I want—but at the end of the day, I don't get to vent to you. If I say anything about the pressure that is fucking crushing me—you think I'm trying to make you feel bad.

MILES: So, what, you're discounting the fact that most of the down payment for this house came from cashing in my stock options?

NINA: I'm not counting money, I could give a shit about the money, Miles.

MILES: This is obviously about money, you resent me for not being able to provide for my daughter. Look at this house—it's crumbling down around us. We can't afford to fix it, we can't afford to live in it. This is no way to raise a baby. We never should have . . . we were not ready to have a baby.

(*Kit walks upstairs.*)

KIT (*To Nina*): Is everything okay?

NINA: You're blaming me because we have a healthy, beautiful baby?

MILES: No, I'm blaming you because we have a baby that I don't deserve.

NINA: All she needs is for you to love her, Miles.

MILES: It's not enough.

(*The doorbell rings. Reggie appears on the other side of the broken window.*)

REGGIE: Hey yo, son, I got the guys with the glass, they gonna install it.

NINA (*Looks at Miles*): Now? They were supposed to have come at two, here they are at six-thirty.

MRS. CHAE: That's Korean time.

MILES: You deal with this, Nina, I'm—

(*He heads upstairs.*)

NINA *(Calling after him)*: You're what?

(Miles continues upstairs. Nina looks at Mrs. Chae.)

Fuck him, man, fuck all of you. I had this perfect, precious baby and all anyone wants to do is blame me for how she's changed our lives. Of course she's changed our lives. What was so fucking good about them before?

(Reggie knocks on the front door then opens it.)

REGGIE *(To Nina)*: Yo, mommy, they gone have to take the rest of that old glass out first. So I'm'a have to put some drop cloth down there so you don't get no glass shards on the floor.

NINA: Okay, Reggie.

(A beat.)

REGGIE: I'm'a go to the hardware store, so, you gone have to hit me so I can get the drop cloth.

NINA *(Handing him a twenty)*: Here.

REGGIE: I'm'a need sixty.

NINA: Sixty dollars for drop cloth?

REGGIE: Okay, forty.

NINA: I don't have forty dollars, Reggie.

KIT: I have forty dollars.

(Reaches into wallet.)

Oh, no, I don't.

NINA *(To Mrs. Chae)*: Do you have any money?

MRS. CHAE: Sorry.

NINA: Just—fuck it, Reggie.

REGGIE: Alright, thirty dollars, I'll get the cheap stuff.

NINA: Forget it—forget the whole thing. Tell the guys they have to come back another—

(Smash. The sound of the workmen smashing the glass to make way for the new window.)

Goddamnit—!

REGGIE: What the fuck! Stupid motherfucker!

(He heads for the door. Another smash. Nina releases a sound—something between a growl and a war cry. She picks up a pry bar and walks to the window and starts smashing the glass as Kit and Mrs. Chae watch. Reggie, on the other side, backs up. Nina takes several whacks at it until there's little window left. The sound of Hannah crying. Nina takes a breath, her demeanor changes. Mrs. Chae also responds to the sound. They both head for the stairs—)

NINA *(To Mrs. Chae)*: I'll get her.

(She just gets to the stairs when Miles appears at the top of the stairs holding the baby.)

MILES: I got her.

(He walks downstairs towards Nina. Knows the words.)

"Hush little baby, don't say a word. Papa's gonna buy you a mockingbird. If that mockingbird won't sing, Papa's gonna buy you a diamond ring."

(He meets up with Nina.)

You want me to teach you the rest of the words?
NINA: Yes.
MILES *(Sings)*: "If that diamond ring turns brass."

(Nina repeats after him as they walk towards the window.)

NINA *(Sings)*: "Turns brass."
MILES *(Sings)*: "Papa's gonna buy you a looking-glass."
NINA *(Sings)*: "—looking glass."
MILES *(Sings)*: "If that looking glass gets broke—"

(They stop at the window. They look out into the street for a while. We start to hear the sounds of the neighborhood. Indeterminate voices in conversation. A basketball being bounced, music from a car stereo.)

NINA: You know what I think that rock coming through our window was?
MILES: What?

NINA: A meteorite. A chip off of some billion-year-old comet that came crashing through here to let out all the ghosts, all the stories, all the history . . . To let us know . . . we can make up the words ourselves.

(The sounds from the street swell as Nina and Miles look out.)

END OF PLAY

Diana Son is an award-winning playwright, a writer/producer for television and a screenwriter. Her plays *Stop Kiss* and *Satellites* premiered at the Public Theater in New York City and her work has been produced at theatres like the Oregon Shakespeare Festival, Seattle Repertory Theatre, Woolly Mammoth Theatre Company, Delaware Theatre Company, BRAVA, Geva Theatre Center, People's Light and Theatre Company, in addition to many others. *Stop Kiss* won the GLAAD Media Award for Best New York Production and was on the Top 10 Plays lists of the *New York Times* and other major publications. Diana also won the Berrilla Kerr Award for playwriting. *Stop Kiss* is published as a trade paperback by the Overlook Press and produced at hundreds of theatres nationally and abroad. Her play *BOY* premiered at La Jolla Playhouse under the direction of Michael Grief and her play *Fishes* was produced by New Georges in New York City. Her short play *R.A.W.* (*'Cause I'm a Woman*) premiered at the Ohio Theatre in New York City and has been anthologized in a number of collections.

Diana has been a writer/producer for the television shows *Blue Bloods, Southland, Law & Order: Criminal Intent* and *The West Wing*, in addition to writing a number of TV pilots for CBS and A&E. Also, she's written screenplays for Showtime, Fine Line and Robert Greenwald Productions. Diana has taught playwriting at the graduate level at the Yale School of Drama and the Dramatic Writing Program at New York University. She is a member of the Dramatists Guild of America; Writers Guild of America, East; Women in Theatre and is an alumnus of New Dramatists.

She lives in Brooklyn with her husband and three sons.

Rice Boy

Sunil Kuruvilla

Author's Statement

In May 2008, the artistic staff at the
Stratford Shakespeare Festival staged
a reading of *Rice Boy* to better see the
play as they considered it for production, giving me an opportunity to revisit
a work I had been away from for years.

I wrote the first draft in 1996 when
I left home to study playwriting in the
States; after numerous revisions, the
play was produced in 2000, and other
productions followed. Initially, I wrote
Rice Boy without ambition, to just
combat homesickness. A product of
ache, *Rice Boy* is a collection of love
stories that struggles with the transitory
essence of home, memory and affection, the south Indian ritual of
creating kolams (intricate patterns of rice powder that disappear
within hours) is at the core of the story. The people in the play find it
difficult to accept the kolam's message: all things are impermanent
and should be celebrated for being so. But they try.

The story is set in Waterloo, the place where I grew up and
now live, and Kochi in South India, a place I spent some childhood
summers. Character, dialogue and images sped into my head as
I wrote—the call of the Fish Seller, the aroma of the Harmony
Lunch restaurant—a play of memory and invention.

Minutes into the Stratford audition of the play, I found myself
making notes in the script, cringing at the bad writing. Fortunately
for me, the theatre decided to include the play in its season, and
I was able to make an old play new. One of the big changes I made:
the grandmother in the play has been replaced by a grandfather giv-

ing the story a sad symmetry as now three generations of men in the same family have lost the women they love and are devastated.

I don't know why my work on this play continued to be speedy (but on others goes slowly). Certainly my collaborators played a role throughout. I have worked with Mark Bly, Liz Diamond, Chay Yew, Iris Turcott, Robert Blacker, Guillermo Verdecchia, and many others to build the story. I am proud and humbled as I like what the script is now but know that I did not write it by myself.

Acknowledgments

Lisa Kuruvilla.

Robert Blacker, Mark Bly, Lisa Channer, Liz Diamond, Des McAnuff, Iris Turcott, Guillermo Verdecchia, Chay Yew, the Canada Council for the Arts and the Ontario Arts Council.

Production History

Rice Boy received its world premiere in October 2000 at the Yale Repertory Theatre in New Haven, Connecticut (James Bundy, Artistic Director; Victoria Nolan, Managing Director). The director was Liz Diamond. The set design was by Tobin Ross Ost. The costume design was by Cameron Lee Roberts. The lighting design was by Matthew Richards and the sound design was by David Budries. The stage manager was Rachana V. Singh. The cast was as follows:

TOMMY	Wayne Kesserman
FATHER	Sean T. Krishnan
TINA	Angel Desai
AUNTIE	Shaheen Vaaz
UNCLE	Sanjiv Jhaveri
GRANNY	Yolande Bavan
SERVANT GIRL	Anita Gandhi
FISH SELLER/CLERK/UMBRELLA MAN/NUT SELLER	Ajay Naidu
MR. HARRIS/MENNONITE FARMER	Colin Lane

Rice Boy's West Coast premiere was in April 2001 at the Mark Taper Forum in Los Angeles, California (Gordon Davidson, Artistic Director; Charles Dillingham, Managing Director). It was directed by Chay Yew. The set design was by Victoria Petrovich. The costume design was by Joyce Kim Lee. The lighting design was by José López and the sound design was by John Zalewski. The cast was as follows:

TOMMY	Ravi Kapoor
FATHER	Subash Kundanmal
TINA	Lina Patel
AUNTIE	Meera Simhan
UNCLE	Shelly Desai

GRANNY	Noor Shic
SERVANT GIRL	Purva Bedi
FISH SELLER/CLERK/UMBRELLA MAN/	
NUT SELLER	Ossie Mair
MR. HARRIS/MENNONITE FARMER	Christopher S. Wells

Rice Boy's Canadian premiere was at the Canadian Stage Company (Martin Bragg, Artistic Producer) in Toronto, Ontario in March 2003. It was directed by Micheline Chevrier. The set design was by Deeter Schurig. The costume design was by Judith Bowden. The lighting design was by Elizabeth Asselstine and the sound design was by Don Horsburgh. The stage managers were Alison Peddie and Jennifer Kowal. The cast was as follows:

TOMMY	Zaib Sheikh
FATHER	Sean T. Krishnan
TINA	Imali Perera
AUNTIE	Deena Aziz
UNCLE	Sanjay Talwar
GRANNY	Zohra Segal
SERVANT GIRL	Pragna Desai
FISH SELLER/CLERK/UMBRELLA MAN/	
NUT SELLER	Anand Rajaram

Rice Boy was revised for a production in the 2009 season of the Stratford Shakespeare Festival (Des McAnuff, Artistic Director) in Stratford, Ontario. It was directed by Guillermo Verdecchia. The set and costume design was by Jessica Poirier-Chang. The lighting design was by Robert Thomson and the sound design was by Thomas Ryder Payne. The stage manager was Brian Scott. The cast was as follows:

TOMMY	Araya Mengesha
FATHER	Raoul Bhaneja
TINA	Anita Majumdar
AUNTIE	Deena Aziz
UNCLE	Sanjay Talwar
GRANDFATHER	Sam Moses
SERVANT GIRL	Asha Vijayasingham
FISH SELLER/CLERK/UMBRELLA MAN/	
NUT SELLER	Anand Rajaram
MR. HARRIS/MENNONITE FARMER	Jonathan Purdon

Characters

TOMMY, twelve, boy

FATHER, Tommy's father

TINA, seventeen, Tommy's cousin

AUNTIE, Tina's mother

UNCLE, Tina's father

GRANDFATHER, father of the Father and the Uncle

SERVANT GIRL, ex-wife of the Fish Seller

FISH SELLER

CLERK

UMBRELLA MAN

NUT SELLER

MR. HARRIS

MENNONITE FARMER

One actor can play Fish Seller, Umbrella Man, Clerk and Nut Seller. One actor can play Mr. Harris and the Mennonite Farmer.

Setting

1975. Canada and India. Both places exist on stage simultaneously, with scene shifts indicated quickly by light and sound (not by set changes). At times, the sounds of the countries mix—we hear the Nut Seller's sad call in India blend with the winter gusts of Canada. When Tommy doesn't appear in a scene, the audience should feel he is still watching from the shadows. When not involved in the action, the Indian characters drift on and off stage, sometimes assisting in the mechanics of the play—one might hand a milk carton to Tommy. Most times, they just watch. But always they haunt the boy.

Note

The dialogue in parentheses is unspoken; it appears only to give the actor some context as to what is said aloud.

A forward slash (/) indicates overlapping text. The next character begins speaking at this point.

For Isaac.

Act One

Summer. Kochi, a city in Kerala, India. On the front porch of Uncle's house, Tina kneels on the floor, trying to make a kolam—a pattern made from rice powder. The girl's legs are bent awkwardly—they don't work; the trolley she uses to travel the house is nearby. Auntie stands above her, watching. The Servant Girl enters carrying two cups of coffee, handing one to Auntie, keeping one for herself.

At a distance:

Six months later. Winter. Kitchener, a city in Ontario, Canada. Tommy, in a winter coat, sits in a tree as his father, in a dhoti, sleeps on the kitchen counter, covered by a blanket. The boy watches the scene in India, remembering his cousin. As Tommy moves in the play between Canada and India, he always wears his winter coat.

FATHER: I'm awake, sir.

(No response.)

Come in the house, boss!

(No response.)

Hullo, leave the tree alone!

(No response.)

What's wrong with you? Six months we've been back and you still just sit like a stick in the branches. Do you hear what I'm meaning, Tommy?

(No response.)

Leave it and come. Take care of your father. Hey! Mister Stupid!

(No response.)

If we were in India. There, children listen to their parents. Idiot! Say something!

(Tommy finally looks at his father.)

TOMMY: Did you go to work today?

(No response.)

Did you go to work today?

(No response.)

You said you were going to.

(No response.)

All you do is sleep.

(No response.)

Hey!

FATHER: You shut up! What are you talking!

TOMMY: All you do is sleep!

FATHER: I'm tired! It's the time change.

TOMMY: We came back six months ago! You're going to lose your job again.

FATHER: Show respect! Is this the way a son talks to the father? If we were in India, I could spank the skin right off your hand. So hard I could thrash you! Here—I'd get arrested.

TOMMY: Why do you keep sleeping on the kitchen counter?

FATHER: I'm sad!

TOMMY: Why?

FATHER: Why!

TOMMY: Mom died ten years ago!

FATHER: What did I just say? You come down from the tree and you rub my head!

(Tommy climbs down from the tree and steps through the window, into the kitchen.)

So disrespectful.

(Tommy starts to massage his father's head. Father takes his son's hand and smells.)

Your mother's hand. It smelled like this skin. The gold sari she'd wear to church. Bright as a flag. We'd come home and I'd unwrap her. Going in circles, moving away from her body and then in the end, moving close. Rolling on the ground. Silk in the mouth. The taste like hair. But then mister, you would start to cry and she would have to go to you.

(Father gazes around the kitchen.)

Everywhere I look, our problems are there.

(Father stands, goes to the fridge, studying a math problem written on its front door.)

This was the last one we ever did together. Complex numbers.

TOMMY: What happened to Tina?

FATHER: Your mother was so smart.

TOMMY: I know. What happened to Tina?

FATHER: Tina talk, Tina talk. Talk about your mother.

TOMMY: When summer comes, we should go back and look for Tina.

FATHER: No sir, we stay right here. It was a big mistake to go last summer.

TOMMY: We should do camping then. Or Algonquin Park. African Lion Safari. Do what normal people do. Mini-golf. Water ski.

FATHER: Those are Canadian things.

TOMMY: That's okay.

FATHER: I can't do those things.

(Father returns to the counter.)

TOMMY: You could sign me up for power skating tomorrow. Or get me some Ponys. Or North Stars. We should use our car more. We should use our car!

FATHER: Gas, mister!

TOMMY: You keep saying that. All my friends do.

FATHER: Friends!

TOMMY: The people in my class.

FATHER: Then say that. But don't call them friends, you don't have friends.

TOMMY: You need to drive me to school.

FATHER: Why? What's the problem? You're not special—you take the bus like everyone else.

(Beat.)

What you need to do, you need to find me a new job. That's your job for me.

(Father slumps.)

TOMMY: You should go back to Kitchener Datsun. I liked the courtesy van.

FATHER: That's why they told me to go, mister—they found out I was giving too many rides to you. Your fault.

TOMMY: No. It's because you kept missing work.

FATHER: I hate the Pepi's Pizza. I come home and take shower but the cheese smell is still there. Che! I burn so much incense trying to get rid of it but it's on my socks, even.

TOMMY: I like when you bring garlic bread home for me.

(Beat.)

When you get fired, your next job should be Rockway Fish and Chips.

FATHER: So lousy these jobs. I am a math professor!

TOMMY: Not anymore.

FATHER: Hey—so many years I worked at that university. So hard I worked.

TOMMY: But you stopped going to class!

FATHER: What about you! Did you go to school today?

TOMMY: Yes.

FATHER: You're lying. Are you lying?

(Father studies Tommy.)

TOMMY: What?

(Father lies back on the counter.)

FATHER: You're going to fail your school again. Three times you're going to do grade seven. I know it.
TOMMY: Stop saying that.
FATHER: Dummy. Just cut a banana, pour some oil.

(Tommy takes a milk carton from the fridge and starts to read the side panel.)

What if tomorrow I go to the farmer's market and buy you a goat? A big, healthy one. We can kill it in the basement. No stink. We'll open the windows and use the fan. You can make me a nice curry.
TOMMY: The boy on the milk carton. He's from St. Jacobs.
FATHER: And some bean thoran.
TOMMY: He's got a Levi's jean jacket.
FATHER: All those kids are dead.
TOMMY *(Still transfixed by the lost-boy notice on the milk carton)*: You think so? Doug Harris.
FATHER: You wash my boxer pants?
TOMMY: Yes.
FATHER: And my banyan?
TOMMY: Yeah.
FATHER: I hope you ironed my shirts. I don't like when it's rough.

(Silence.)

Come. Give a bedtime story. You need to talk to me more, keep me awake. All I do is sleep.

(Tommy moves to the phone book, starts searching.)

TOMMY: He's from St. Jacobs. That's so close.
FATHER: Useless! You don't talk when I ask or give banana chips or rub my head—

(Strains to look at Tommy.)

I have an M.Sc. from I.I.T. and Ph.D. from Poona—Both were full tuition and scholarship, mister.

(*Beat.*)

Come here, I said.

(*Tommy moves closer to his father.*)

You need to take care of me more. That's your job, okay? Full-time hours.

(*Beat.*)

When you were a crybaby and the dirty diapers were there, who did it? That was me. Your mother was gone.

(*Silence.*)

Next month is tax time—you have to do it. I'm too tired this year.

(*Tommy just stares at his father. Growing uncomfortable, the man curls in a ball.*)

What?
TOMMY: I'm deciding.
FATHER: Mister Smarty Shorts. What deciding?

(*Silence.*)

TOMMY: This is the last time I'm ever going to see you.
FATHER: Che—! Leave me alone!

(*Father kicks at the boy. Tommy puts the milk carton in the pocket of his winter coat, then goes back to the phone book, tearing out the page he was looking at before.*)

TOMMY: I'm running away.
FATHER: Wife, are you watching all this? How did this happen to me?

(*Silence.*)

I keep thinking about you. More and more. I see so much in the dark. The brain remembers most at night.

(*Father continues to lie on the kitchen counter as Tommy steps outside. The boy watches Tina, Auntie and Servant Girl work on the rice pattern.*)

AUNTIE: No. First you have to put the dots then you connect. Fingers into rice powder. Powder onto the floor.

(*Tommy exits, wandering the Canadian countryside with his milk carton. He meets a Mennonite Farmer.*)

TOMMY: You're a Mennonite. You wear black and don't believe in electricity.
MENNONITE FARMER: Look at you. I've never seen a brown fella before.

(*Tommy preens as the Mennonite Farmer inspects him up close.*)

TOMMY: When I see nice pictures in a magazine, I eat them. I scoff bottles of jam from Central Meat Market and drop them from the bridge near my house.
MENNONITE FARMER: I sat in a car once. No one knew.
TOMMY: I take Mrs. Timlock's bras when she hangs them on the line.

(*Beat.*)

At school, the kids chase me with a skipping rope and try to hang me from a tree.
MENNONITE FARMER: At night. When everyone's sleeping . . . (*Whispers*) I have a radio.

(*Beat.*)

I know all the words to "Papa Was a Rolling Stone." Do you like the Temptations?

(*Tommy races up a tree by the side of the road. The Mennonite Farmer is trumped. Impressed.*)

What do you see?
TOMMY: A big field. Snow.

MENNONITE FARMER: What else?

TOMMY: That's all.

MENNONITE FARMER: No, keep looking. I was born on this farm, that house right there. My whole life, I've never gone past that road.

(Silence.)

What do you see?

(Silence.)

It's my tree.

(Tommy returns to the ground.)

Where do you live?

TOMMY: Kitchener.

MENNONITE FARMER: You should go. Your parents must be worried.

TOMMY: My mother's dead. She died long time ago in India. She was swimming in the river behind the house where she grew up and she drowned. She swam there every day when she was a girl, but she forgot where the dangerous spots were. No, it's okay—don't look sad. I don't remember her.

MENNONITE FARMER: What about your father?

TOMMY: He used to be a math professor. My mom was, too. They figured out problems on the kitchen wallpaper together—it's all still there. The university fired my dad a few months ago.

MENNONITE FARMER: Why?

TOMMY: He's dead too, now. My dad was walking on the side of the road and got hit by a truck. Snowplow. Because he didn't use his car.

(The Mennonite Farmer is speechless.)

I see the psychologist every morning at school, but she hasn't fixed me yet.

(Beat.)

Which way to Kitchener?

(The Mennonite Farmer points left. Tommy goes right.)

MENNONITE FARMER: You're going the wrong way. You're headed toward St. Jacobs—Hey!

(The Mennonite Farmer starts to follow Tommy. The boy pauses.)

What's your name?
TOMMY: Tommy.
MENNONITE FARMER: Maybe I'll come with you, Tommy.
TOMMY: No—You'll wreck everything.
MENNONITE FARMER: I won't.

(Awkward silence.)

TOMMY: You can walk with me but then you have to go.

(Continued silence as the Mennonite Farmer thinks it over. Finally:)

MENNONITE FARMER: No. Go by yourself.

(Tommy exits. The Mennonite Farmer crosses to the tree, climbs up, and starts to gaze into the night.
The opening scene of the play continues: Auntie and Servant Girl watch Tina design a kolam. Tommy sees them.)

TOMMY: The brain does remember more at night.

(Tommy steps close, watching, remembering:)

AUNTIE: No. Your fingers have to go into the rice powder. Then the powder has to go onto the floor. Water onto the floor, finger into the rice powder. Powder onto the water.
SERVANT GIRL: Tiny swirls.
AUNTIE: Soon, you will be doing this every morning. Like the other wives in the village. Show her.

(Servant Girl gives her coffee cup to Tina and starts to design. Tommy leans close to inspect.)

So tired but you still have to get up. Your husband just sleeps. You get the water and grind the rice to make powder. You clean the porch and then you start.

SERVANT GIRL: Your husband dreams dreams as sweet as sandalwood.

AUNTIE: Finally, he wakes up. He looks for a moment then just goes right through your design.

SERVANT GIRL: The powder that touched your fingers sticks to his feet.

(Tina tries to design with Servant Girl.)

AUNTIE: The wind comes. And the ants.

SERVANT GIRL: Magic.

AUNTIE *(To Servant Girl, gesturing with her coffee cup)*: I keep telling you: you put too much sugar. I can't drink it.

(Beat.)

No Tina, watch her. Just sit.

TINA: Mother. You don't do this.

AUNTIE: You know why. Keep watching.

(Auntie exits, taking her coffee cup into the house.)

TINA: My fingers don't work. I'll never get a husband.

SERVANT GIRL: You'll be alone, forever, maybe.

TINA: Don't say that.

(Grandfather enters, brushing his teeth using his finger and charcoal.)

GRANDFATHER: Where's your grandmother?

TINA *(Exasperated)*: Tsssst.

GRANDFATHER: What?

TINA: You keep forgetting.

SERVANT GIRL: Your wife died a few months back. That's why I lie in front of your bedroom at night. To keep you from leaving.

TINA: You don't see her and you step on her. She wakes up hurt then tells you Grandma is dead.

GRANDFATHER: I'm hungry.

(Servant Girl exits into the house.
Tommy continues to stare at Tina. Suddenly, Auntie runs from the house, through the design, straight to Tommy. The woman grabs the boy's ear, twisting it, pulling him through the design into the scene.)

TOMMY: Auntie!

AUNTIE: You come inside and go pop!

TOMMY: I want a toilet.

AUNTIE: You haven't had a bowel movement since you got here!

TOMMY: No, I'm okay.

AUNTIE: Do pop!

TOMMY: It's just a hole in the ground!

AUNTIE: You don't have to sit. Just bend.

TOMMY: I want toilet paper.

AUNTIE: Learn to use water. Clean with your hand.

TOMMY: I want Canada.

AUNTIE: You're going to pop open. Listen!

TOMMY: Let go of my ear—you're paining me!

(Tommy breaks free and scales a coconut tree.)

AUNTIE: Come down.

TOMMY: India. All I do is sit under the fan and read *Reader's Digest*.

AUNTIE: Come down.

TOMMY: I hate this place. I want a hot dog!

AUNTIE: Enough, Tommy!

TOMMY: You're not my mother.

AUNTIE: Yes I am. Every woman in this village is your mother. You respect them and you listen. Where's your father?

FATHER *(Offstage)*: I am here.

(Father enters, stepping from the house onto the porch.)

How am I?

(Father steps close to Auntie and smiles a big smile.)

Is there pepper in my teeth? I should have come back long ago. The breakfast, I forgot how wonderful! What's happened?

(Answering his own question.)

Up in the tree.

AUNTIE: Make him come down. He needs to go pop.

TOMMY: No, I went this morning.

FATHER: He's lying.

AUNTIE *(To Father)*: Do something.

FATHER: Tommy!

(Tommy remains in the tree.)

You see what he does? —Study! Do your worksheet!

(Tommy remains in the tree.)

AUNTIE: Che—! *(To Tina:)* Where's your father?
TINA: Shopping, Mother.
AUNTIE *(To Tommy)*: We're going to push your stomach until you explode! Grandpa. You watch him. Make sure he doesn't fall. Only monkeys climb coconut trees!

(Auntie exits.)

FATHER: Uppa, the servant girl is making your egg. One bull's eye.
GRANDFATHER: And Bombay toast?
FATHER: Yes. Bombay toast.
GRANDFATHER: Don't fall.

(Grandfather exits into the house. Father looks at Tommy. A few beats. The man doesn't know what to do. He quickly exits into the front yard.)

TOMMY: Who are you?
TINA: Your cousin. You don't know that?
TOMMY: Your name?
TINA: I'm getting married.
TOMMY: How old are you?
TINA: How old are you?
TOMMY: Twelve.
TINA: Ha! I'm seventeen. Eighteen almost.
TOMMY: Your legs are weird.
TINA: They don't work.
TOMMY: I can see everything from up here.
TINA: What do you see?
TOMMY: The fish seller is riding his bicycle. Some men are pushing a taxi. A boy is running beside a tire, slapping it with a stick.
TINA: What does the river look like?
TOMMY: I don't know. Water.
TINA: No, look.

TOMMY: It's dirty.

TINA: Keep talking.

TOMMY: Your mother is running. I could slip.

TINA: Go higher.

TOMMY: I've never climbed a tree before. They aren't this big in Canada.

TINA: Are people swimming?

TOMMY: Some.

TINA: How many? Count.

TOMMY: Four. Four men.

TINA: How far is it from here?

TOMMY: I'm tired.

TINA: No, describe. Keep going. What do the houses look like? Are they different from this one? You can be my eyes. How wide is the road? What do the buses look like? And the trucks? They paint big names on the front, don't they? I've heard them drive by all my life.

TOMMY: You've never seen a truck!

TINA: I've never left this house.

TOMMY: Stupid Girl!

TINA: Read the trucks. Tell me what you see.

TOMMY: Vymol . . . Raju . . . Georgie . . . Simon . . . Saju . . . Lisa. I always look for "Tommy" but I haven't found one yet.

TINA: Find "Tina."

TOMMY: There's no "Tina." The trucks have boy names.

TINA: You found "Lisa."

TOMMY: I'll find "Tommy" before I find "Tina." First one wins.

TINA: You could lie. I wouldn't know.

TOMMY: You have to just believe me. I'm goalie for the Montreal Canadiens.

TINA: That hammering sound. Are the women cutting into trees?

TOMMY: I play hockey for the Canadiens.

TINA: Are the women putting up coconut shells?

TOMMY: Guy Lafleur writes me letters.

TINA: They're collecting rubber. It comes from the tree.

TOMMY: Like maple syrup.

TINA: You must have seen it the last time you were here. All I see are rubber trees.

TOMMY: I don't remember the last trip.

TINA: Your mother died. You don't remember that?

TOMMY: I was too little.

TINA: Stupid Boy.

TOMMY: I can see the whole world. What can you see?

TINA: Stop talking.

TOMMY: I see the sari store, the water fountain, the post office.

TINA: Stop it.

TOMMY: I see chickens running through the church. I see the powder factory and butcher shop. I see your mother talking to some man. Can you see the powder factory? Smart Girl, what can you see?

TINA: Blood.

TOMMY: Where?

TINA: On the ground. You're dripping.

TOMMY: My nose is bleeding. Get me a Kleenex!

TINA: Get it yourself.

(Tina sits on her cart and rolls herself into the house.)

TOMMY: Don't go. I want to drip on your head. Ugly turtle. Straighten your skirt, you almost showed me your legs. I don't want to get sick.

(Tommy remains in the tree.
Grandfather enters, holding a plate of breakfast. Servant Girl follows him.)

GRANDFATHER: Good—you didn't fall. Where's Tina?

TOMMY: In the house.

GRANDFATHER: I heard you talking. Good boy, Tommy. She's usually so shy.

(A bicycle bell sounds. The Fish Seller enters, walking his bicycle. He opens his basket.)

FISH SELLER: Kingfish, Uncle?

GRANDFATHER: What else?

FISH SELLER: Take some trout.

GRANDFATHER: No.

FISH SELLER: Trout, Uncle.

GRANDFATHER: What else?

FISH SELLER: I don't catch the fish, Uncle, I just deliver them. Keri-mean?

GRANDFATHER: No.

FISH SELLER: Tilapia?

GRANDFATHER: No.

FISH SELLER: River fish?

(Servant Girl glances at Fish Seller's basket.)

GRANDFATHER *(To Servant Girl)*: River fish?

SERVANT GIRL: Che—!

FISH SELLER: Butterfish?

GRANDFATHER *(Disdainfully)*: Butterfish.

FISH SELLER: Shrimps is there.

GRANDFATHER: Smelts?

FISH SELLER: No.

GRANDFATHER: Pomfret?

FISH SELLER *(Simultaneously sucking his cheek, blinking his eyes, shaking his head, meaning "no")*: Tisk.

GRANDFATHER: What else you have?

FISH SELLER: The net catches what it catches, Uncle.

GRANDFATHER: Not today.

FISH SELLER: Don't go, Uncle. Take a look.

GRANDFATHER: Come back tomorrow. Bring kingfish. Big ones.

FISH SELLER: Small ones are tastier, Grandpa.

GRANDFATHER: I'm not some boy. Stop your nonsense.

FISH SELLER: Try, buy, you'll like.

GRANDFATHER: I'm going.

FISH SELLER: Pay me tomorrow.

GRANDFATHER: I'm going inside.

FISH SELLER: Show your sons. Go get them.

GRANDFATHER: They're not here. Good-bye.

FISH SELLER: Go bring them.

GRANDFATHER: They're not here.

FISH SELLER: Ask them.

GRANDFATHER: Hey! Fish seller.

FISH SELLER: I'm sorry.

GRANDFATHER: I'm nice to you but now you're bothering! You're bothering bothering too much.

(Grandfather exits into the house. Servant Girl shakes her head disdainfully at the Fish Seller, then quickly exits into the house. Fish Seller repacks his fish in newspaper but leaves one on the porch. He speaks to Tommy aloft in the tree.)

FISH SELLER: The coalition government got me a new bicycle seat. Next month, when the communists come to power, I will get my own store with a refrigerator. I won't have to hurry when I work, afraid my fish will spoil. I will sit in my little store and you people will come to me.

(Pause.)

Boy. Who are you?

(Grandfather returns, pouring coffee from one glass to another to cool, then giving the drink to the Fish Seller.)

Pray for a majority government. God listens to old people.

GRANDFATHER: No he doesn't.

FISH SELLER: She doesn't listen to me.

GRANDFATHER: Next week we'll need lots of fish.

FISH SELLER: Are you dying?

GRANDFATHER: Not a funeral. A wedding.

FISH SELLER: You're getting married, Grandpa?

GRANDFATHER: Tina. There's a boy in the city. My sons and I are meeting the family in a few days.

(Fish Seller hands the coffee back to Grandfather.)

FISH SELLER: Please, Grandpa, not today. My stomach is paining again.

GRANDFATHER: You come tomorrow.

FISH SELLER: Maybe.
BUY BUY!
FRESH BIG FISH!
BUY BUY!
FRESH BIG FISH!

(Fish Seller rings his bicycle bell as he rides away. Servant Girl runs onto the porch.)

SERVANT GIRL *(Shouts at the Fish Seller)*: If you were still my husband, you'd wear nice shirts!

GRANDFATHER: Take your fish.

(Servant Girl takes the fish left for her on the porch and exits into the house. Grandfather starts to drink the coffee. Father enters in dhoti and undershirt, carrying a newspaper.)

FATHER (*Gesturing to Grandfather*): Tommy, what do you think? Are
    we the same?

TOMMY: No.

FATHER: What if I put a moustache?

(*Father lies on the porch face down.*)

We're the same.

(*Grandfather lies on the porch beside Father, also face down.*)

Tommy. Walk on my back.

GRANDFATHER: No. You walk on mine.

FATHER: I'll give you money.

TOMMY: How much?

(*Tommy climbs down from the tree.*)

FATHER: Five rupees.

TOMMY: How many dollars is that?

FATHER: Do something! My back hurts.

TOMMY: Stop sleeping on the floor at night.

FATHER: I don't fit in the bed anymore. It's the same one I had when
    I was a boy.

(*Tommy steps on his father's back but doesn't walk. Father turns
to Grandfather.*)

It's strange to be back.

GRANDFATHER: It's good that you came.

FATHER: I'm not alone anymore.

GRANDFATHER: I'm so alone now.

FATHER: Everywhere I look. I can see my wife.

GRANDFATHER: You need to keep me company. Stay longer.

TOMMY: I have school.

FATHER: Only in September.

TOMMY: There's no one to play with.

FATHER: Tina.

TOMMY: She's weird.

FATHER: So are you. Walk!

(*Beat.*)

I would be better with moustache, no?

(Tommy steps off of his father.)

TOMMY: (Give me) the money.

(Father searches his pockets: no money. He extends a book of matches toward Tommy.)

FATHER: Be careful. Matches aren't for children.

(Tommy takes the matches. Grandfather holds out a coin. Tommy takes it.)

TOMMY: What is this?

FATHER: What should I do with him? Tell me.

GRANDFATHER: How?

FATHER: You wanted to buy me a sewing machine. That was your dream for me. To be a tailor. I studied and got scholarship. Look what I did for you. Your house is a good house. My son? My son is a stupid. Maybe we should move back here.

TOMMY: Forever?

FATHER: What do you think? One year?

TOMMY: No!

FATHER: Hey—you don't talk like that.

TOMMY: I'm not moving.

FATHER: There's a boys' school here.

TOMMY: No!

FATHER: I'm the father! You have to do what I say. I haven't decided yet.

TOMMY: You tricked me!

FATHER: You see how he talks? That's how they talk in Canada!

TOMMY: Is this why we came? I have my rights!

FATHER *(Amused)*: Oh yes!

TOMMY: Did you sell our house? What about my room? The Ping-Pong table!

FATHER: Listen you—nothing's happened. I'm just thinking. You do your pop yet?

TOMMY: Yes.

FATHER: Truth?

TOMMY *(Gesturing with coin)*: How much is this?

FATHER: You're rich! Rich man, I need a loan!

(Grandfather and Father laugh at Tommy. Servant Girl enters, motions to Father. The man rises, goes into the house. Few beats. Tina slides onto the porch. Tommy proudly holds up his coin. Father returns.)

In the bathroom, did you go pop on the floor? Yes or no?

TOMMY: No.

FATHER: Tell the truth.

TOMMY: No.

FATHER: Who was it then?

TOMMY: I don't know.

(Silence.)

FATHER: Show your underwear.

TOMMY: What?

FATHER: Just tell the truth. You won't be in trouble.

TOMMY: It wasn't me.

FATHER: You missed the hole and got the floor, so what? Don't lie. Just say it. You're not in trouble. I promise.

TOMMY: I didn't.

(Father grabs Tommy, wrestles roughly with him, trying to look down the boy's pants.)

FATHER: Stop!

TOMMY: Stop! Dad!

FATHER: Show me!

TOMMY: Okay!

FATHER: Just say! —Say or show!

TOMMY: I said okay! Please!

FATHER: Show the underwear!

(Grandfather grabs Father.)

GRANDFATHER: Stop now.

FATHER *(To Tommy)*: What's wrong with you?

(Suddenly, Uncle runs onto the porch from the street.)

UNCLE: It was amazing. The bus was driving then it turned and hit the pole. We pushed forward then fell back. It was quiet for a moment then screaming. The children and a goat. It stumbled up and down the aisle, one of its legs was broken. The bus was tilted on its side and we moved forward, climbing over the seats. The driver wasn't drunk. He was dead. Heart attack. We were near the medical center—some of us ran to get a doctor, some stayed back. Running, running, out of breath. We got back and the bus was empty. The driver's fingers were chopped off, blood all over the steering and the dash. He was just sitting there in his underwear. That goat-shit bus. They took everything. Watch, rings, necklace, even his socks. An ugly, ugly sight. I hope you never, never have to see something like that. You want to go see? It's still there.

(Father eagerly stands to join his brother.)

GRANDFATHER: Did you get your new tie?
UNCLE: My God! I left it on the bus.
FATHER: Wait, let me put on a shirt.

(Father runs inside the house to get a shirt.)

UNCLE: Hurry!

(Uncle waits for Father. Few beats. Then exits, Grandfather following. Father returns to the porch holding a shirt.)

FATHER: What's happened? They went!
UNCLE *(Offstage)*: No!
GRANDFATHER *(Offstage)*: Idiot, hurry!

(Father exits in Uncle's direction. Tina looks at Tommy.)

TINA: When I get married I won't have to see these people ever again.

(Ashamed, Tommy dashes away. Tina moves to the edge of the porch, wanting to leave as well, frustrated that she can't. Few beats. Auntie returns, happily tossing an apple into the air then catching it. She smiles, pats Tina on the head, then playfully slides the girl on her trolley into the house as if she were a toy.
On the road, Tommy continues to run, almost hitting the Fish Seller.)

FISH SELLER: Almost hitting! It's my road, not yours—Slowly! Careful!

(Back home: Auntie saunters onto the porch, her hair still wet from a shower. She sees a bowl of rice powder. The woman picks it up and blows, sending dust into the air.)

FATHER *(Offstage)*: Simon Something?
UNCLE *(Offstage)*: Kutty.
FATHER *(Offstage)*: Yes. Is he there?
UNCLE *(Offstage)*: No.
FATHER *(Offstage)*: What about Matthew Thomas? The teacher.
UNCLE *(Offstage)*: Gone.

(Uncle and Father enter the front yard, both covered in dirt. Uncle carries a bright shopping bag.)

FATHER: And the other teacher? Thomas Matthew.
UNCLE: Same. He is no more.
FATHER: The pretty one. Mary Abraham?
UNCLE: Terrible what happened to her. She's fat now.

(The men step onto the porch.)

AUNTIE: Where were you? Always playing.
UNCLE: Where were you?

(Tina wheels onto the porch.)

AUNTIE: You know where I was.
UNCLE: I can see. You look happy.
AUNTIE *(Defiantly)*: I am, yes.
UNCLE: For you.

(Uncle extends the shopping bag. Auntie doesn't take it.)

AUNTIE: What have you done?

(Uncle opens the bag, takes out a new, beautiful, green sari.)

UNCLE: To wear for the wedding.
AUNTIE: Take it back.
UNCLE: For the wedding. Just (take it).
AUNTIE: I don't want it.

(Uncle puts the sari back in the bag, resting it on the porch.)

UNCLE: I'm going to leave it. Until you take it. I know what you like.

(Auntie exits. Uncle pats Tina on the head then enters the house. The sari remains on the porch. From the street, Tommy enters. Father sees his son.)

FATHER: I'm still upset, mister.

(Father enters the house. Tommy avoids looking at Tina. Silence.)

TOMMY: What?

TINA: Nothing.

TOMMY: I saw the bus . . . You want me to tell you?

TINA: Say.

TOMMY: It was smashed up.

TINA: And the driver?

TOMMY: What about him?

TINA: What did he look like?

TOMMY: I don't know.

TINA: Describe.

TOMMY: He was gone.

TINA: You didn't see anything.

TOMMY: Broken window.

TINA: That's nothing.

TOMMY: I licked a cow.

TINA: What?

TOMMY: On the way back. The one by the fence.

TINA: No you didn't.

TOMMY: When Grandpa was milking it. I did.

TINA: No.

TOMMY: I really licked the cow. I lie all the time but not now. Cows taste the same way dirty underwear smells.

(Tina laughs.)

TINA: Lick mine.

TOMMY: You lick mine.

TINA: No!

TOMMY: I can.

TINA: You won't.

TOMMY: Give it and see!

(Tina pulls her underwear out from under her dress. She holds it out then pulls it back. Tommy suddenly grabs the underwear. Long pause. He moves his tongue toward it and holds the pose, the underwear just inches away.)

TINA *(Incredulous)*: Sho—! What are you doing!

(Tommy touches the underwear with his tongue.)

Aaaaaah!
TOMMY *(Overlapping)*: Aaaaaah!

(Beat.)

Pick something else!

(Silence.)

Pick! I can do anything!
TINA: Some night. You should steal a sari from my mother's closet.
TOMMY: What else?
TINA: Go to the station and tie it to the back of a bus. Do that one.

(Tina points to the sari Uncle left on the porch for Auntie.)

TOMMY: I'll make it drag on the road, all the way out of town.
TINA: Have you gone to the ocean?
TOMMY: Not yet.
TINA: I hear it sometimes.

(Beat.)

You're crazy.
TOMMY: I can go for you. To the ocean.
TINA: Yes. And the rice paddies. And the banana trees. You can be my legs.
TOMMY: Okay.
TINA: My life on this patio has been so small—I've never been afraid of anything. Give it—

(Tina holds out her hand. Tommy returns her underwear. The girl wheels away into the house. Tommy exits. The sari Uncle got Auntie remains on the porch. The boy walks the Indian country-side.)

TOMMY: I walk in the rice paddies. The minnows and the tadpoles nibble at my legs. The rice plants scratch like puppy's teeth. The roots wrap around my ankles and I sink into the mudsuck up to my shins. The water snakes come close and I have to splash my hands to keep them away. Stuck deep until the fish seller pulls me free.

(Tommy continues to walk and gaze.)

The banana trees. All I see is green. The green is darker than the leaves on the coconut tree but lighter than the frogs that come onto the porch at night to cool off.

(Tommy stops walking.)

There's more to say. *(Inhales deeply, holds his breath, exhales)* But how?

(Tommy walks, coming upon Auntie and Servant Girl washing clothes at the side of the river. From a distance, he watches them slap the garments against rocks. Their saris are rolled up to the knee. Bare feet. Water splashes. They stop, inspect their work, then slap again. Over and over, start then stop. Rhythmic music.)

SERVANT GIRL *(Gesturing with a green sari in her hand)*: Is this the one Uncle got for you? No.
AUNTIE: That's an old one.
SERVANT GIRL: Looks the same.
AUNTIE: A man's shirt. Easier than a sari.

(Servant Girl trades with Auntie, giving her the sari, taking the man's shirt. The girl starts to slap hard. Auntie puts down the sari and picks up another man's shirt. Auntie flails as angrily as Servant Girl. Each tries to outdo the other, then Auntie concedes, watching Servant Girl's violent, long solo. The girl stops, exhales.)

SERVANT GIRL: My body feels wonderful.

(Tommy walks, nearing the porch. Father and Uncle smoke beedies, the sari Uncle got Auntie still on the porch. The boy hides, then approaches mischievously.)

UNCLE: I was surprised. I asked you to come and you said yes.

FATHER: The great mathematics professor.

UNCLE: Why you say it like that? You are.

FATHER: All I have is three sections. Three sections is nothing.

UNCLE: Get more.

FATHER: They won't give me. Because of my accent. The students can't follow.

(*Beat.*)

So hard I've worked—I sit on every committee. The sipes are lazy. Eight-thirty is too early for them. I take all those classes.

UNCLE: You should come back to India and teach at the college.

FATHER: There is nothing for me here.

UNCLE: It's no money, but still. You should do it.

FATHER: Maybe.

UNCLE: Where's Tina?

FATHER: Inside.

UNCLE: And the boy?

FATHER: Don't know. I need to talk to you.

UNCLE: There's something I need to tell you.

FATHER: You can give some advice about Tommy. He does so many lies.

UNCLE: That's how children talk.

FATHER: No, but he failed this year—he has to repeat! What should I do? He's a Stupid. Maths even! In September, he has to do grade seven again.

(*Beat.*)

He kept saying he was doing good, but each time the report card would come—terrible! I was supposed to be signing his test papers when he failed. All year he was just putting my name! His teacher called me for a meeting and I said, "He's doing good, no?" She laughed at me. How can this be?

(*Silence.*)

I'm thinking he should go to the boys' school here. The headmaster was your classmate, no? We'll move back for one year. What do you think? I don't know.

(No response.)

What do you think?

UNCLE: After Tina gets married, my wife is going to leave this house. Yes.

FATHER: Brother, you talk nonsense.

(Tommy grabs his father's package of beedies and returns to his hiding spot, continuing to hear everything.)

UNCLE: Long time ago, my wife would bring lunch to me at the talcum factory. I don't stay in my office. I work with the men. In the big room they smash rocks into powder. We all look the same in the dust—gray. I would stand quiet and make my wife find me by my smell, my sweat. She'd move among the men, sniffing at the neck until I was there. We would eat fish curry and rice from the tiffin, the spices lifting into our face, stinging the tongue. I touch her nose with mine, roll one way against her face, then roll the other way, leaving a white mask on her skin. But after Tina was born she stopped bringing me food. When my wife makes love she grips the head of our bed. I dusted powder onto the wood one morning before I left for work. I came back in the evening and saw the marks of her fingers. I walked into the pepper field behind our house and lay on the ground until I could stand up again.

(Beat.)

Our mother moved into the house to help care for Tina. My wife was no longer alone during the day. She started bringing me lunch again. Just as before.

FATHER: Hey—Tommy! What are you do—Go inside, do your worksheet! *(To Uncle:)* See what I'm meaning!

(Tommy exits, entering the house. Father turns back to Uncle.)

Who was the man?

UNCLE: Our doctor. I go to him when I'm sick. He looks into my eyes. He touches my body. All these years he's made me feel better.

FATHER: Get a new doctor!

UNCLE: He's the best in the village! He lives close by. He knows our family. My wife will go to him after the wedding. The only time

I kiss my wife is on the shoulder when she sleeps. Sometimes, the neck.

FATHER: Your pain is like mine.

UNCLE: Bigger. A place changes but you still see what was there before. Maybe I will stay here. Maybe I will move away. I don't know.

FATHER: Should I go to the river?

UNCLE: Why?

FATHER: No?

UNCLE: What are you talking?

FATHER: I don't know.

UNCLE: I want you to listen. This boy for Tina. We'll see him tomorrow. May God give us a good marriage.

(*Uncle stands, walks to the bushes to urinate. Father follows. He doesn't urinate. Just stands beside his brother.*

From inside the house Tommy steps onto the porch with the women, helping to bring mats for night prayers. The boy goes to Tina.)

TOMMY: Something's wrong with your parents.

TINA: My mother is leaving when I get married. She told me.

TOMMY: You're not upset?

TINA: I'm tired of all that. Did you go to the ocean?

TOMMY: The rice paddies.

TINA: And the banana trees?

TOMMY: Yes.

TINA: What was it like?

TOMMY: You want me to. But some things can't be described.

TINA: Try.

TOMMY: No, you have to see for yourself. The way it smells.

TINA (*Dismissively*): Just go.

(*Silence.*)

My life will change when I get married. I will finally leave this house.

TOMMY: What if I show you? What if I take you to the bus station? You can tie your mom's sari.

TINA: What?

TOMMY: At night, we can go to the city. When the others are sleeping. I'll roll you. We can go after prayers.

TINA: No one will know?

(*Tommy shakes his head. Tina grabs the new green sari on the porch, hiding it under her skirt.*)

TOMMY: You don't have to wait until you get married.

(*Tina smiles. Father and Uncle enter, sitting on the mat.*)

I'll be the husband. We should just run away.

(*Father gives Tommy a quick pinch and twist to quiet him.*)

FATHER: Prayers.

(*All sit on the floor, one Bible to share. Uncle notices that the green sari is no longer on the porch. He smiles at Auntie. She, too, notices the sari is gone. She nods approvingly then starts to read from the Song of Solomon.*)

AUNTIE: My lover is an apple tree. The finest in the orchard. I am seated in his much-desired shade and his fruit is lovely to eat.

(*Father takes the Bible and starts to read.*)

FATHER: Oh feed me with your love—your raisins and your apples, for I am utterly lovesick.

(*Tina giggles. Tommy giggles. Father slaps the boy on the head then continues to read.*)

His left hand is under my head and with his right hand he embraces me.

(*Father hands the Bible to Tina and she starts to read.*)

TINA: Here he comes, leaping upon the mountains and bounding over the hills. My beloved is like a gazelle or young deer. /Look, there he is behind the wall now, looking in at the windows.

(*Grandfather joins Tina, reciting from memory.*)

GRANDFATHER: /Look, there he is behind the wall now, looking in at the windows. (*Remembering his wife*) —Sho!

(Uncle takes the Bible. Scans. Then starts to read.)

UNCLE: My beloved says to me, "Rise up, my love, my fair one, and come away for the winter is past and the rain is gone . . . Arise my fair one. Come run away with me."

(Father takes the Bible from Uncle, giving it to Tommy.)

FATHER: Read, Tommy.

TOMMY *(Quickly)*: How sweet is your love, my darling, my bride, and how much better it is than mere white wine, and the perfume of your love is more fragrant than all the richest spices, and your lips, my dear, are made of honey.

FATHER: —Slowly!

TOMMY: Yes, honey and cream are under your tongue and the scent of your garments is like the scent of the mountains and cedars of Lebanon.

(Servant Girl sighs. Tommy plugs his nose, trying hard not to laugh. Suddenly:
Blackout. The always-present power strikes. Voices in the dark:)

FATHER: Che! Electric-company fucks!

AUNTIE: Pray, Tommy.

SERVANT GIRL: Should I go?

GRANDFATHER: Wait. Let's see.

(Pause. No light.)

SERVANT GIRL: Should I go?

GRANDFATHER: Wait.

AUNTIE: Pray, Tommy.

SERVANT GIRL: I'll go.

AUNTIE: Yes. Go get the torch.

TOMMY: I'll go.

FATHER: Wait here.

TOMMY: Ow!

AUNTIE: Grandfather?

GRANDFATHER: Right here.

UNCLE: What's this?

AUNTIE: What?

UNCLE: Who's this?

AUNTIE: What?

UNCLE: Who's this? Who am I touching?

AUNTIE: Your wife!

UNCLE: I'm sorry.

FATHER: How much longer?

GRANDFATHER: Don't get up.

TOMMY: You don't have to hold my foot.

AUNTIE: Pray, Tommy.

TOMMY: What for?

(Sound of a slap.)

FATHER: Just pray—Don't get smart!

GRANDFATHER: Don't get up.

TOMMY: Owww! Shit!

SERVANT GIRL: Sorry.

(Servant Girl returns with a weak oil lamp.)

TOMMY: Who stepped on my hand?

AUNTIE: Where's the torch?

SERVANT GIRL: I looked for it.

GRANDFATHER: Useless creature.

AUNTIE: Pray for Tina.

TOMMY: Who stepped on my hand!

FATHER *(Tiredly)*: Just leave it.

TOMMY: I want to know!

AUNTIE: Pray for the wedding. Pray, Tina.

UNCLE: Big girl.

(Silence.)

GRANDFATHER: Tina?

AUNTIE: What?

GRANDFATHER: Where's Tina?

TOMMY: Let go of my foot!

AUNTIE: That's my foot.

SERVANT GIRL: Where's Tina then?

UNCLE: Tina?

FATHER: Where could she go?

AUNTIE: Tina!

GRANDFATHER: Tina Girl!

(Lights up as electricity returns. Tina sits quietly.)

AUNTIE: You heard us talking.

GRANDFATHER: Tina.

AUNTIE: When we say something, Tina, talk back. Don't just sit there.

TINA: I don't want to talk.

TOMMY: She's just quiet.

AUNTIE: Quiet, Tommy.

UNCLE: You're getting married but I can still slap you.

AUNTIE: Go for a walk. I'll make you a tea when you get back.

(Blackout.)

FATHER: What's happened? Again!

AUNTIE: Pray, Tommy.

TOMMY: God: please make the boys' school catch on fire—

FATHER: Hey!

TOMMY: —Jesus name, amen.

UNCLE: Tina?

(Silence.)

Tina?

(Silence.)

Say something, Tina!

TINA: You can stop. I hear you.

AUNTIE: Good girl.

(Lights up. A beat. Blackout. In the dark:)

FATHER: Che-da! Fuck's sake!

(Lights up.

Later: Grandfather sleeps in his bed. Servant Girl sits on the floor in the bedroom doorway beside an oil lamp, brushing her long hair. She lies on her mat and turns off the lamp. Few beats. The lamp comes on again. Servant Girl sits and starts to brush her hair again. Lost in thought. She smells the brush then caresses her lips. As if being touched by another. She turns off the lamp and lies down. Few beats. Grandfather rises, Servant Girl stirs.)

SERVANT GIRL: Grandpa.
GRANDFATHER: Bathroom.

(Grandfather exits, arriving at Father's bedroom. The old man rouses his sleeping son.)

Help me.

(Sleepy Father follows Grandfather.)

FATHER: Is this a nightmare? What are we doing?
GRANDFATHER: Come to the road. Where should we go? This way.

(Grandfather and Father walk on the road.)

FATHER: I need to ask you: what should I do with Tommy? What did you do with me?
GRANDFATHER: Your mother did everything.
FATHER: What did she do?
GRANDFATHER: She keeps running away, wanting me to find her.
FATHER: When I was a boy you wanted to buy me a sewing machine. That was your dream for me. To become a tailor. Instead, I studied and got scholarship. Look what I did for you—your house is a good house. My son? My son is a Stupid.

(Beat.)

I'm going to put him in the boys' school here. We'll stay one year and see. He needs more discipline.
GRANDFATHER: You take me back to the States with you.
FATHER: I live in Canada.
GRANDFATHER: Same thing.

(Beat.)

I'm going to surprise you! I'll buy a ticket and just come.
FATHER: I remember so many times being with my wife on this road. Right now, she could just come walking—I feel like that.

(Grandfather moves to the side of the road. Father starts to follow him.)

GRANDFATHER: No. You look over there. It's so dark.

FATHER: Who are we looking (for)?

GRANDFATHER *(Calling sweetly)*: Vud-day.

(Grandfather keeps looking.)

FATHER: Hey . . . Uppa!

GRANDFATHER *(Calling sweetly)*: Cuppa.

FATHER: Hey!

(Grandfather pauses.)

Umma is dead.

(Silence.)

You understand what I'm saying?

GRANDFATHER: Close your eyes. Close them.

(Father closes his eyes. Grandfather pinches him hard.)

FATHER: Hey! What for?

GRANDFATHER: To make you cry. *(Beat)* When a fisherman goes missing, the wife brings the children to the water and makes them cry. To make him come back.

FATHER: You! Don't be foolish. She's gone. You keep thinking about her—you have to stop. Help Tommy. He's still alive. Are you listening?

GRANDFATHER: Look. Five minutes, even?

(Silence.)

I lost my wife. Y'eh-Da—help me find her.

FATHER: This way. Come.

(In the city, the Nut Seller roams the street, selling cashews. Tina sits on her cart, tying the beautiful green sari from the porch onto the bumper of a bus.)

NUT SELLER: Sweet sweet. Sweet nuts. Sweet sweet. Sweet nuts. Sweet sweet. Sweet nuts.

(Tommy runs to Tina.)

TOMMY: Did you tie it tight?

TINA: EEEE! I don't want to let go. I want to hold on and get pulled away.

TOMMY: In Canada? When it snows? I hold onto the back bumper of the school bus and slide like I'm waterskiing.

TINA: I've never seen so many people in one place!

TOMMY: This is really the first time you've ever left your house?

TINA: This is the first time I remember. My parents carried me around when I was a baby, but then I got big and had to stay at home. This is more than Christmas presents!

NUT SELLER: Sweet sweet. Sweet nuts. Sweet sweet. Sweet nuts.

TOMMY: What else you want to do, wife?

TINA: I want to do everything.

TOMMY: We have to be back before the others wake up.

TINA: I don't want to practice the rice pattern anymore. I want to go down that street. Don't be a baby.

TOMMY: I'm not.

TINA: Have you ever tasted beer?

TOMMY: Yes.

TINA: Indian beer?

TOMMY: I want to.

TINA: Buy from that man.

(Tommy starts to push the cart, to take Tina with him.)

Stop. You can leave me.

(Tommy stops pushing.)

TOMMY: No, wife, come with me.

TINA: I'm fine, Tommy.

TOMMY: You want one?

TINA: No.

TOMMY: Drink something.

TINA: There's a restaurant. The Anjali. I want to go and have a milk-shake in a big glass.

TOMMY: What flavor?

TINA: Doesn't matter.

TOMMY: You've never had a milkshake?

TINA: Hey stupid, I have. But not in a big glass. All the home glasses are little.

NUT SELLER: Sweet sweet. Sweet nuts. Sweet sweet. Sweet nuts.

TOMMY: We can come back tomorrow. Every night until you get married. Tie your shoes, wife.

(Tommy bends to tie Tina's shoes.)

TINA: Don't touch. I can do it.

(Tina ties her own shoes.)

TOMMY: Look at my fingers . . . Look!

(Tina doesn't.)

They're all yellow.

(Finally, Tina glances at Tommy's hands.)

I helped Grandfather pick curry leaves.

TINA: Filthy.

TOMMY: My fingers are blue in Canada. I pick blueberries for Mr. Timlock. You could come back with me and make lots of money. He gives a quarter a carton. The other kids put milk bags on their shoes, but I don't care about mud. Tell me to do something—
    (Grabbing dirt) You want me to eat it!

TINA: Stop talking, just pull.

TOMMY: You have to frown the whole day. If you smile, Mr. Timlock will see all the purple on your teeth from the blueberries.

TINA *(Starts rubbing out their marks on the ground)*: This way, no one can follow us. Pull, I said.

(Tommy grabs the rope tied to the front of the cart and starts to walk, like a horse pulling a carriage. Tina continues to trail her hand in the dirt. Gesturing with her dirty hands:)

I'm same as you now. —Faster.

(Tommy starts to spin in circles.)

—What are you doing?

(Tommy continues to spin.)

Tommy!

(*Tommy stops spinning and falls to the ground.*)

TOMMY: I'm dizzy. Everything's going in circles.
TINA: Why?
TOMMY: Because I'm dizzy.
TINA: What's dizzy?

(*Tommy spins Tina on her cart. Both collapse on the ground.*)

I'm dizzy.
TOMMY: No more India.
NUT SELLER: Sweet sweet. Sweet nuts.

(*Tina sets herself back on her cart.*)

TOMMY: You don't want to see the bus go with the sari?
TINA: No. Let's go to the cinema.
TOMMY: We have to be careful. Indira Gandhi steals people at night
   and gives them operations so they don't have children.
TINA: She won't do that to us. Just the poor people.

(*Tina starts to slowly wheel herself away. Tommy moves to push
her.*)

I can do it. Get a branch. Rub our marks off the ground.

(*Tommy follows behind, dragging his feet, erasing their trail.*)

Husband, hurry—Pull your wife.

(*Tommy runs to his cousin, starts pulling her again.*)

TOMMY: You should come back with me to Canada.
TINA: Go faster!
NUT SELLER (*Offstage*): Sweet sweet. Sweet nuts. Sweet sweet. Sweet
   nuts.

(*On the road, Servant Girl searches for Grandfather. Fish Seller
enters, walking his bicycle. The two see each other and stop.*)

FISH SELLER: Yes. Hello.
SERVANT GIRL: Fine. How are you?

FISH SELLER: Yes. How are you?
SERVANT GIRL: Good, how are you?
FISH SELLER: I'm glad.

(Silence.)

My new bicycle seat. It's too hard. My body aches when I work.

(Beat.)

It will get better.
SERVANT GIRL: Have you seen Grandfather?
FISH SELLER: Gone again?
SERVANT GIRL: I can't just stand and talk with you.

(Servant Girl exits.
      Back home, Tommy and Tina approach the house.)

TOMMY: We're late.
TINA: Doesn't matter.
TOMMY: Your mother's going to be waiting with the rice.
TINA: She can do the pattern. I'm tired.
TOMMY: Talk softly.

(They enter the porch. Grandfather startles them—he has just
been sitting quietly.)

TINA: Grandpa! What are you doing?
GRANDFATHER: I'm going to bed.
TINA: What's wrong?
GRANDFATHER: I went looking for my wife. Calling her name, getting
      upset, but then I found her. All is better. She has a place in the
      cemetery.

(Grandfather exits.)

TOMMY: Good night, wife.
TINA: Sleep.

(Father enters.)

TOMMY: Morning!

(Tommy and Tina tense—have they been caught?)

FATHER: Tina. Just now! You remember my wife?
TINA: Maybe.
FATHER: No, the place you're standing. She picked a flower and put it in your hair. The two of you would be right there.

(No response.)

No, you remember that. Every morning she did it.
TINA: It was too long ago.

(Tina and Tommy enter the house. Few beats. Tommy comes back.)

TOMMY: We should stay longer.
FATHER: You have school.
TOMMY: Only in September.
FATHER: Why are you asking? You don't like it here.
TOMMY: No, I do now.
FATHER: Always lying.

(Tommy exits.)

No, no, come talk—Tommy! Come back to me!

(Back in Canada: from his winter coat Tommy pulls out the page he tore from the phone book and the milk carton. He starts to read the side panel.)

TOMMY: Doug Harris. St. Jacobs, Ontario. Twelve years old. Blond hair, blue eyes. Four feet, eight inches. One hundred pounds. Last seen September 1973.

(Tommy digs a hole, burying the milk carton in the snow. He stands, pauses, then strides toward a front door. He knocks, then waits. Mr. Harris opens the door.)

Mr. Harris? I don't have blond hair or blue eyes. I'm taller than four feet, eight inches, and bigger than a hundred pounds, but I can be your son. All you have to do is feed me and buy me new socks when I get holes instead of making me put tape. And car rides. In the car wash. I won't have to do your taxes or pay the phone bill because you want to just lie there. You can teach me to throw a spiral and how to do oil changes in the driveway. This driveway. I'll be proud to eat with you at the A&W instead of making you do drive-through, and people won't stare at us when we buy our groceries at Zehrs. I can take peanut butter and banana for lunch, instead of rice and dahl, and my sweaters won't have curry smell. My mitts won't get put in the toilet ever again, and I won't get kicked on the school bus when I try to sit down. I have to stand the whole way. Every morning the driver calls me Hot Chocolate and everyone laughs. Can you just drive me and pick me up? Please! —You use your car, right? You can pay for gas?

(No reaction.)

It's been more than a year. I don't think Doug is coming back.
MR. HARRIS: Come inside.

Act Two

On the porch, Tina, bored, gathers rice powder in her palm, and blows. Auntie enters.

AUNTIE: Stop. Properly! Show.

(Tina starts to design a kolam.)

You look tired. Are you getting enough sleep?

TINA: Yes.

AUNTIE: You're getting better. Bend your fingers like this. You have to be a good wife. It's hard to see what you're doing when you're so close. You have to look from above.

(Auntie goes to the floor and starts to design.)

You like what I'm doing? I would make such big patterns—I covered the whole porch. You need a wedding sari. Tomorrow, we'll go downtown to the sari stores. You've never left this house. Don't be scared.

TINA: I'm not.

AUNTIE: Good girl.

(In the bathroom, Uncle and Father cradle Tommy over the hole in the floor so that he doesn't have to squat.)

TOMMY: I'm flying. A crow. Look out below.
FATHER: The stink.
UNCLE: Finish.
TOMMY: One more.
FATHER: —Tommy! Oh.
UNCLE: Are you finished?
TOMMY: No.

(Pause.)

UNCLE: Finished?
TOMMY: Okay.

(Pause.)

Wipe please.

(Father and Uncle look at each other. Neither moves.)

Wipe please.
UNCLE: You're the father.
FATHER: You be the father!
TOMMY: Wipe.
    Wipe!
    WIPE!

(Fish Seller enters the front yard on his bicycle. On the porch, Servant Girl tries to read her palm. Grandfather is asleep.)

SERVANT GIRL: At night you would sleep with your fingers in my hair. My hair is clean now. No more fish smell.

(Silence.)

Talk.
FISH SELLER: I have come for the wedding.

(Servant Girl gently nudges Grandfather awake then exits. Fish Seller takes out a notebook.)

Kingfish, Uncle?
GRANDFATHER: Correct. How many will you bring?

FISH SELLER: Three hundred.

GRANDFATHER: No.

FISH SELLER: Four?

GRANDFATHER: Correct. And you will bring them when?

FISH SELLER: The day before. In the morning.

GRANDFATHER: Early morning.

(Fish Seller starts to leave. Stops.)

FISH SELLER: They're not making curry.

GRANDFATHER: I think so.

FISH SELLER: No. You must tell them to fry.

GRANDFATHER: Why? No.

FISH SELLER: It's more work but tastes much better.

GRANDFATHER: Curry will do.

FISH SELLER: Sorry. You must fry.

GRANDFATHER: No.

FISH SELLER: What?

GRANDFATHER: I bought the curry leaves.

FISH SELLER: Use masala. Paprika. Coriander.

GRANDFATHER: They will make a curry and use tomato, onion and cumin.

FISH SELLER: You will use chili powder and turmeric and you will fry—Give me your word.

GRANDFATHER: It's too much work.

FISH SELLER: Hey—they're still my fish. I don't have to sell.

GRANDFATHER: What?

FISH SELLER: That's right.

GRANDFATHER: All right, fried, fried—Che!

FISH SELLER: Sign my sheet?

(Fish Seller takes a form from his pocket.)

It's a petition. We want to start a union.

GRANDFATHER: No.

FISH SELLER: We need one. The coolies at the railway station, you see how they work, but still they make more than us. Why? They have a union.

GRANDFATHER: No, I said. You need to listen.

FISH SELLER: But why? People can change the way they live.

(Silence.)

GRANDFATHER: You show me where.

(*Fish Seller points to a line on the sheet.*)

FISH SELLER: Right here. Just your name. Please, sir.

(*Grandfather takes the pen but doesn't write. Suddenly realizing the problem, Fish Seller takes Grandfather's hand in his and signs his sheet for the old man.*)

GRANDFATHER: Thank you. Take it.

(*Fish Seller takes his sheet from Grandfather both men pleased. Servant Girl enters.*)

FISH SELLER: Sign for a union?

(*Servant Girl signs his form.*)

SERVANT GIRL: I remember how you brushed my hair. What is it you remember? Something.
FISH SELLER: The ice is melting. My fish are starting to smell. (*Hands her a fish*) Take.
        (*To Grandfather:*) Tell the ladies: fresh oil. And don't leave them long.

(*Fish Seller starts to ride away. Then stops, turning back to Servant Girl.*)

I remember taking lessons at the post office. And finally being able to read the newspaper to you. But you fell asleep. This is what I remember. That first time.

(*India. Dusk. A soccer field. Father and Uncle in shirt and tie kick a soccer ball, Tommy following behind. Drinking from coconut shells, the men are drunk from toddy. Tommy is sober.*)

UNCLE: Nice house.
FATHER: Nice car.
UNCLE: Nice wife.
FATHER: Nice daughters.
UNCLE: Nice Alsatian.

FATHER: A very Christian family.

UNCLE: None more so.

FATHER: Very important.

UNCLE: Very important.

FATHER: We share the same values.

UNCLE: Definitely. Kick.

(Father kicks the ball weakly to Uncle.)

FATHER: How long have you been looking?

UNCLE: Few months maybe.

FATHER: He's a nice boy.

UNCLE: Pass.

(Father passes the soccer ball.)

FATHER: A quiet boy. Strange.

(Tommy suddenly disappears. He has fallen into a ground-level well.)

Like Tina.

UNCLE: No, he's better. He went to a school. He can't run, but he can walk.

FATHER: They'll be happy. I hope so.

UNCLE: All we can do is try.

TOMMY *(Offstage)*: Dad!

FATHER: The boy didn't smile.

UNCLE: His mind is fine.

FATHER: He didn't say anything.

UNCLE: He can talk.

TOMMY *(Offstage)*: Dad!

FATHER: I worry.

UNCLE: We'll live close by. We'll watch over.

FATHER: But who was that man in their kitchen?

UNCLE: The one with the red tie?

FATHER: Him. Yes.

TOMMY *(Offstage)*: Hey!

UNCLE: It's not who you think.

TOMMY *(Offstage)*: Hey!

FATHER: Who do I think?

UNCLE: You think the bad-luck tailor.

FATHER: Yes! The bad-luck tailor. I remember the bad-luck tailor. There is still the bad-luck tailor!

UNCLE: If he says hello to you, a bus hits you. He told the butcher he liked his haircut. The poor man doesn't leave the house for a week. He finally goes to work. The first day back, he cuts off his thumb!

FATHER: Don't look at him.

UNCLE: Don't shake his hand.

FATHER: Don't scratch his dog.

UNCLE: Don't pinch his wife.

FATHER: Don't let her pinch you.

UNCLE: He brings bad luck wherever he goes.

FATHER: He's part of our family now? Fools!

UNCLE: No, no. I thought so, too, but we're lucky. That was one of the boy's uncles. He just looks like the bad-luck tailor.

FATHER: The bad-luck tailor is still alive.

UNCLE: Still downtown.

(Beat.)

Don't go to his store. Never.

FATHER: How does he survive?

UNCLE: We put money under his door so he doesn't drop by.

(Silence.)

Is this marriage a good thing?

FATHER: This is good.

UNCLE: I don't want to go home.

FATHER: I can't live here.

UNCLE: No, you're going to teach at the college.

FATHER: How? The river goes right through the campus.

UNCLE: Why are you scared of the river?

FATHER: Everywhere I look I remember things. I know it will do something if I see it again.

UNCLE: There's nothing there. Go see.

(Silence.)

Come live with me. In my empty house.

FATHER: You come to Canada. My empty house.

UNCLE: What empty house, you have the boy.

(Beat.)

What about the boys' school?

FATHER: Let me just sit.

UNCLE: Meet the headmaster. Decide.

(Uncle belches loudly.)

FATHER: I can leave Tommy with you. You can take him one year.

UNCLE: Just put him in the YMCA school. He can live there.

FATHER: A child should be with family, not strangers.

UNCLE: If we're going to talk like this then no more talking.

(Uncle tries to drink from the coconut shell. Empty.)

No more toddy.

(Uncle puts the empty coconut shell on his head. Father does the same. Then he belches.)

More drink, Tommy.

(Silence.)

Where's the boy?

FATHER: Dammit.

UNCLE: What's wrong?

FATHER: He's hiding. Tommy! I'm too drunk.

UNCLE: Where is he?

FATHER: Hiding. Tommy!

UNCLE: Where are you, Boy?

FATHER: Tommy!

UNCLE: Tommy!

FATHER: Che—Tommy!

UNCLE: Nephew!

FATHER: Nephew!

(They come upon the well.)

Tommy?

(Father and Uncle peer into the depths.)

UNCLE: Do you see anything?

FATHER: Are those eyes?

UNCLE: I can't see.

FATHER: Tommy?

TOMMY: I fell in the well.

UNCLE: —My God!

FATHER: Are you hurt?

TOMMY: No.

FATHER: Is it deep?

TOMMY: No.

FATHER: You're okay. We'll get some rope.

> (*Father and Uncle collapse to the ground.*
>
> *Grandfather enters, surveys the scene, then sits on the ground. Tommy climbs out of the well. The old man nods tiredly, drunkenly, then lies on the ground.*
>
> *Tommy walks home. Tina is designing a rice pattern on the porch.*)

TOMMY: I met your husband. You're not pretty but still. He's terrible.

> (*Silence.*)

What do you want to know?

> (*Silence.*)

TINA: Can he walk?

TOMMY: Yes.

TINA: Does he have hands?

TOMMY: Yes.

TINA: I'll make him pull me like I make you.

> (*Uncle and Father enter the porch.*)

UNCLE: The boy is like you. Quiet. His face is ugly but his hands are nice. You'll have children. Don't worry. They won't come through you. The doctor will cut them from your stomach like he cut you from your mother. Your children will be better than you. Strong. Healthy. Smart. They'll take care of you. I'm going to sleep.

> (*Uncle exits.*)

FATHER: Did you tell her? He failed this year. He has to repeat.

(*Father exits. Offstage:*)

He's Mister Grade-Seven Repeater. Tell that.

(*Beat.*)

You should be studying! Fractions!

TINA: Where should we go tonight?

TOMMY: I don't care.

TINA: I'm tired of downtown.

TOMMY: Then don't go. I'll go by myself.

TINA: We should take the train to Madras. Or Kottayam. I want to read the news on state television. Every day the producers drive around Kerala and pick a girl to read that night. Maybe she's waiting at a bus stop. Maybe she's selling mango pickle by the side of the road. Sometimes the girl makes so many mistakes. But everyone sees her that night. Why not me? My face is pretty enough. You wouldn't see my legs behind the desk. I'm going to wander the streets until I get picked.

TOMMY: You need me. I could trick you and leave you in the city. You'd get in so much trouble.

TINA: So would you.

TOMMY: Not as much as you—you're older! I'd tell them you made me take you and you didn't want to come home.

TINA: You wouldn't do that. You like me too much. You're a Stupid.

TOMMY: I'm not going to tell you when, but one night, I'm just going to leave you there. I'm not a Stupid.

GRANDFATHER: Leave her.

(*Grandfather steps onto the porch. Tina goes into the house.*)

You have to be nicer, Tommy. Tina's wedding is coming. She will be gone soon. You will think of all the times you said bad things to her.

(*Night. Tina sits on the beach. Tommy runs to her, pants rolled up; he's been running in the ocean. Neither talks as they listen to the water.*)

TOMMY: In Canada. At recess. The children chase me with a skipping rope and try to hang me from a tree.

TINA: Teach me to swim. I want to be a fish and just swim away!

TOMMY: No.

TINA: Husband.

TOMMY: You need legs.

TINA: I can still.

TOMMY: You'll drown.

(Tommy stands, starts to exit.)

TINA: Where are you going?

TOMMY: To pee.

TINA: Do it here.

(Tommy pauses.)

Show me. Why not?

TOMMY: Because I have a boner. You gave me a boner.

(Tommy exits. Tina hides.
Long silence.
Tommy returns. No Tina.)

Hey.

(Tommy searches.)

Hey!

(Frantic, Tommy runs to the water's edge.)

Hey!!!

(Tina re-emerges from the shadows.)

TINA: Here.

(Tommy grabs Tina's hair, starts to pull.)

Ahhh!

(Tommy keeps pulling.)

Stop!

(Finally, Tommy lets go.)

TOMMY: You don't do that!
TINA: Okay.
TOMMY: You have to stay with me all the time.
TINA: Take me home.

(Tommy pulls Tina. A long, silent journey. Reaching home, Tina goes inside the house. Tommy sits on the porch. Father enters from inside the house.)

FATHER: I've decided something:

(Father slaps Tommy.)

I don't know all the bad things you do, so every once in a while I'm going to just give a quick paddock. You'll probably deserve it. You're up early.
TOMMY: I was reading the Bible.
FATHER: It hurts to stand up.

(Father lies on the porch, his back to the floor. Few beats. Father stands.)

Hurts to lie down.

(Father sits.)

Rub my head.

(Tommy massages his father's head.)

Give me a slap.

(Tommy slaps his father's head then rubs vigorously. Grandfather enters. Seeing Tommy and Father, Grandfather sits in front of his son. Father starts to massage his father as Tommy continues to massage him.)

Harder, harder.

(Tommy rubs harder.)

GRANDFATHER: Yes!

(Father rubs harder.)

FATHER: You're not doing anything!

(Tommy rubs even harder.)

GRANDFATHER: Do it!

(Father rubs even harder.)

FATHER: Shake my bloody head! See if you can!

(Tommy rubs harder still.)

Make me stop thinking!

(Suddenly, Tommy stops massaging Father. Father stops massaging Grandfather.)

What?
GRANDFATHER: Enough?
TOMMY: Enough. What about the boys' school? Yes?
FATHER: You think we can live here?
TOMMY: We can live here.
FATHER: I'm going to see. I'm going to take shower.

(Father stands.)

GRANDFATHER: Are you meeting the headmaster?
FATHER: The river.
GRANDFATHER: Why you want to go? The river is the river.
FATHER: It's like a cut. The Band-Aid has been all this time. I should keep it covered but I want to go see if there is blood still or skin. I don't know. You come with me Tommy. After my shower.

(Father exits.)

TOMMY: Where's Tina going to live?
GRANDFATHER: With her husband. His family.
TOMMY: The house we went to, yes?
GRANDFATHER: That's right. Close by.

(In the backyard, the Servant Girl carries two buckets of water. Tina follows, dragging herself on the ground. Servant Girl takes off Tina's top, leaving her naked from the waist up. Servant Girl dips a plastic cup into the bucket, then wets Tina's hair.)

SERVANT GIRL: Your hair isn't as nice as mine. Mine's thicker. I have beautiful hair. Clean. No smell. Everybody tells me. I walk in the town and the shopkeepers beg me to cut it off. They'll give lots of money. Close your eyes.

(Servant Girl starts to lather.)

Che—I forgot the towel. Wait here.

(Servant Girl exits. Tommy enters. He's been watching from the bushes. Tina's eyes are still closed. Tommy starts to shampoo. Tina immediately opens her eyes and turns, discovering her cousin is washing her hair. She covers her breasts but lets him continue. Tommy lifts Tina's hands in his, bringing them to her head. The two lather her hair. Both are transfixed. Tommy reaches for the plastic cup to rinse, but Tina hands him the shampoo bottle—she wants more. Sound of Servant Girl approaching. Tommy runs away.)

Good girl. All by yourself.

(Father steps from the shadows of the house, fresh from a shower. The man is dressed in black. He has seen everything between Tommy and Tina. Father darts toward Tommy, then stops. He starts to dart away, but Tommy sees him.)

FATHER: Hey—what's happened? Watching!

(Both are embarrassed, flustered.)

I'm the father, okay. That means I'm always there. So you have to do good things, not bad things. Just—you stay here and do your worksheet.

(Father exits quickly.
*   At the sari store, a Clerk works disinterestedly, casually throwing saris around Tina as Auntie and Servant Girl instruct. Tommy saunters in, holding an umbrella. He watches.)*

AUNTIE: That one.

SERVANT GIRL: No, that one.

AUNTIE: No.

SERVANT GIRL: That one.

(Trying to find the sari the women are pointing to.)

CLERK: This?

AUNTIE: Higher—No—That one—Not that one, that one. That one. This one!

(Auntie reaches out and grabs the sari she's been wanting.)

CLERK: Omigod!

SERVANT GIRL: You're wasting our time!

(The Clerk swirls more saris around Tina's shoulders.)

AUNTIE: No. Try that one.

SERVANT GIRL: No, Auntie, not for a wedding.

AUNTIE: What then?

CLERK: This one.

SERVANT GIRL: Mine had thin gold lines. Give one like that.

(Clerk throws some saris.)

More color.

(Clerk throws brighter saris.)

More color.

AUNTIE: That's too much.

(Clerk throws lighter saris.)

Too bright.

(Clerk throws lighter saris.)

Too bright.

(Clerk keeps throwing.)

Too bright.

SERVANT GIRL: Too light.
    No.
    No.
    Che—No!

(Clerk stops throwing, shrugs his shoulders.)

TINA *(Holding a green sari)*: I like this one.
AUNTIE: Bring all your red ones.
SERVANT GIRL: Red with gold border.

(Clerk leaves.)

AUNTIE: He's useless. How are you, Tina?
TINA: Fine.
AUNTIE: You like the city?
TINA: Yes.
AUNTIE: Do you, Tommy?
TOMMY: Yes.

(Clerk returns with a stack of saris.)

SERVANT GIRL: Bring the bride some drink.
CLERK: You want chai?
AUNTIE: She's a child! Bring a soft drink.
CLERK: Limca, Thums Up, Campa Cola?
AUNTIE: Choose, Tina.
TINA: Bring a Goldspot.
CLERK *(Annoyed)*: Tisk.

(Clerk leaves.)

AUNTIE: So quiet, Tina. Can be excited.

(Silence.)

    Tina.

(Tina sits glumly.)

    Tina!
TINA: What?

AUNTIE: What?

(*Servant Girl throws some saris around Tina, drowning the woman in color.*)

SERVANT GIRL: Color,
     color,
     swim,
     swirl,
     drown.

(*In the city, an umbrella repairman sits on the street. Tommy approaches in shorts, carrying an umbrella.*)

TOMMY: How much to fix?

(*The umbrella repairman inspects Tommy's umbrella.*)

UMBRELLA MAN: You have nice legs.
TOMMY: Thank you. I think it's the spring.
UMBRELLA MAN: Maybe. Yes. It's the spring.
TOMMY: How long will this take?
UMBRELLA MAN: No time. Wait.

(*As the Umbrella Man works:*)

     Like a girl's. You shave them?
TOMMY: No.
UMBRELLA MAN: I love these legs.
TOMMY: Your hands are greasy!
UMBRELLA MAN: It's good you brought your umbrella in. The floods will start soon.
TOMMY: How much will this cost?
UMBRELLA MAN: Twenty-five rupees.
TOMMY: Ten.
UMBRELLA MAN: Ten, Boy!
TOMMY: My grandpa said ten.
UMBRELLA MAN: Fifteen.
TOMMY: My grandpa gave me ten.
UMBRELLA MAN: Get more.
TOMMY: Five.
UMBRELLA MAN: Five now!
TOMMY: Five and you can feel my legs.

(Silence.)

UMBRELLA MAN: Naughty boy. Okay.

(Umbrella Man caresses Tommy's legs.)

TOMMY: How much for your whistle?

(Tommy points to a whistle around the Umbrella Man's neck.)

UMBRELLA MAN: Ten rupees.
TOMMY: Five.
UMBRELLA MAN: Five and you feel my legs.
TOMMY: What?
UMBRELLA MAN: Feel my legs.
TOMMY: Give me the whistle.

(Umbrella Man hands Tommy the whistle. The boy blows.)

UMBRELLA MAN: It works.

(The boy blows the whistle again.)

Feel.

(Umbrella Man stretches out his legs and closes his eyes. Tommy rubs, intermittently blowing the whistle.)

UMBRELLA MAN: Slow.

(Later that evening, in the family room, Tina and Auntie watch the news.)

AUNTIE: She's pretty.
TINA: She's a Stupid.

(Auntie turns off the television.)

AUNTIE: Today, at the sari store, you should have been excited. You can be. Your marriage won't be like this one. Eventually you will be unhappy, but not in the beginning. You will understand all that I'm saying when your marriage becomes like mine. These are the ingredients: Passion. Respect. Admiration. If you have two in a marriage, it's enough. Just one, you talk like brother and sister. None, you just have silence. This is what I have with your father. But if you are lucky to have three, it's—I don't know what. This is what I have with the doctor. He's the smartest man. Don't make that face—we are together because of you.

TINA: Yes, yes—you saw him so much when I was born because I was so broken.

AUNTIE: Don't talk like that.

TINA: You don't have to tell everything.

AUNTIE: I'm trying to help you, but that's okay, you be stupid.

TINA: I'm sorry, then.

AUNTIE: You need to talk nicer to me. The doctor writes books. What does your father do? Every evening, he just sits and looks at the sky. What is he thinking? My whole life, I have been stuck in this place!

(Silence.)

Something is so wrong with me. What I just said? Yes, I think about leaving your father, but then sometimes my legs can still turn like yours. Why is that? Your father is nothing!

TINA: I don't know.

(Silence.)

AUNTIE: Long time ago. Before you were born. I would take lunch to your father at the talcum factory. One day I went but he wasn't there. The men said he had to go for a meeting so I left the tiffin. The next day, same thing. What meeting? I went to the perfume store to buy more soap and I saw him rush by the window. So fast, just by himself. He crossed the street and went into the cinema. I bought a ticket to surprise him. Up and down the aisle I walked, looking, trying to find him. I went to the balcony. He was there sitting with his accountant. She was an old woman, so dark, so ugly. Yes, she was taller than me, but I'm a short thing. So loud it was, people shouting at the movie, but the two of them were just there, not even talking. And they were having ice cream. Like a little boy. Your father doesn't take ice cream! I went straight to the woman's house and told her husband. That night he broke her arm—the neighbors had to run for the police. The woman wouldn't say what happened but her husband did.

That family stayed some time then moved away. Your father cried and told me sorry, but I just laughed at him—he could only get an old woman. Ann was her name. I knew because they weren't talking. And the ice cream. I am a very smart woman. You father doesn't rush, always keeps me waiting.

(Auntie turns the television back on. They watch and then giggle.)

You're right. She's a Stupid.

(Night. Uncle sits on the porch. Father enters and sits.)

UNCLE: The beautiful sari I bought my wife. She will wear it at the wedding and look so . . . . She still loves me a little.

(Silence.)

FATHER: I went to the river.
UNCLE: And what?

(Silence.)

Say.

(Silence.)

Say!

(Silence.)

You can't describe it, even?
FATHER: No.
UNCLE: The river is nothing.
FATHER: Maths is nothing.
UNCLE: Whenever I dream about my wife, I only see the back of her head. Always leaving.
FATHER: I walked to the edge and looked right into the water. I saw something. What do you think? What did I see?

(Silence.)

Just me.

(Beat.)

I lay there so long I fell asleep. Like a Stupid. What was I hoping? I don't know.

UNCLE: Soon. I will lose my daughter then my beautiful wife will go.

FATHER: No, you listen. All this time you had someone. I don't want you to talk. Just let me be alone.

(Silence.)

UNCLE: What about the headmaster? Are you going to see him or no?

FATHER: No.

UNCLE: Don't say that.

FATHER: I built your house. My first winter in Canada, instead of buying winter coat, I sent money. The other professors said I was crazy, why was I just wearing my sweater! I told them I was too hot all the time. Every paycheck I gave more than I kept. All that I did for you, but you won't take the boy one year even.

UNCLE: Leave him then.

FATHER: Don't say it that way. You should want him more.

(Silence.

Next morning, at the back of the house, Tommy is surrounded by dead chickens. He picks one up as Uncle approaches. The man cleans his axe, his clothes covered in blood.)

TOMMY: This one's the winner. Look how far.

UNCLE: That one's still twitching.

TOMMY: It went running like this—

(Tommy runs a delirious, erratic pattern.)

UNCLE: You want to kill one?

TOMMY: Can I!

(Uncle hands Tommy the axe then holds a chicken.)

UNCLE: Quick and strong. Watch my fingers.

TOMMY: Count me down.

UNCLE: One, two, three—CHOP!

TOMMY: CHOP!

(Tommy swings the axe. Uncle lets go of the chicken. The headless bird drops. No big run. Auntie enters, sees the execution and freezes, eyes wide.)

That's not fair. Mine didn't run.
UNCLE: Go again.

(Uncle holds another chicken.)

One, two, three!

(Tommy swings the axe. Again, the bird just drops.)

TOMMY: Run! Do something!

(Tommy kicks the bird. Uncle slaps Tommy.)

UNCLE: Show respect!
TOMMY: It should do something. It didn't even twitch.
UNCLE: Go wash.
TOMMY: We're not finished.
UNCLE: You have kidneys on your neck.

(They notice frozen Auntie.)

TOMMY: What's wrong with Auntie?
UNCLE: I didn't see her coming.
TOMMY: What's wrong?
UNCLE: She goes stiff if she sees an animal get hurt.
TOMMY: How long does she stay like this?
UNCLE: Not long. Few hours. Leave her. Pick up the chickens.

(Uncle stares at his wife.)

So still. Beautiful.
TOMMY: Can she see us?
UNCLE: No.
TOMMY: Give her a kiss like Sleeping Beauty. You can be the prince. Wake her up.

(Uncle hesitates then kisses his wife on the lips. No reaction. She remains frozen.)

I'll get the doctor.

UNCLE: No!

TOMMY: Why not?

UNCLE: She's fine. Help me.

>*(Tommy helps Uncle gather the dead birds.*
>
>*At the front of the house, Servant Girl steps onto the porch. Seeing a newspaper, she turns the pages, glancing at the pictures. Fish Seller enters the front yard, delivering buckets of fish. He sees her with the newspaper.)*

FISH SELLER *(Laughing)*: Reading!

SERVANT GIRL: You stink!

FISH SELLER: I'm hot.

SERVANT GIRL: Your hands are filthy!

FISH SELLER: I'm going to rub your skin.

SERVANT GIRL: Get away from me!

FISH SELLER: You used to lie on top of me. You forget that?

SERVANT GIRL: The way you'd lick my body and wouldn't stop—Che! Like a lizard!

FISH SELLER: Your tongue.

SERVANT GIRL: Your tongue.

FISH SELLER: My finger. With your smell.

SERVANT GIRL: Your smell.

>*(Beat.)*

I remember all that.

>*(Silence.)*

FISH SELLER: I have to work.

>*(Fish Seller exits. Servant Girl sags. Suddenly, the Fish Seller returns.)*

Tonight.

SERVANT GIRL: What? —Where?

FISH SELLER: You know where.

>*(Fish Seller exits quickly.*
>
>*At the back of the house, Auntie remains frozen from seeing the massacre of the chickens. Tommy's father just sits on the ground, watching her. Slowly, she thaws.)*

FATHER: Okay?

(Auntie nods. Sits.)

Sure?

(Auntie nods.)

Funny stuff.

AUNTIE *(Touching her forehead)*: Hurts.

FATHER: I need you to do something for me. Because I don't have a wife. I want you to tell Tommy about his body. And yours. Say the differences, and what you can do and cannot. Understand? This is the mother's job, not the father's, so you can do it . . . Right. Good.

(Silence. Tommy enters, watching from a distance, unseen.)

You want me to rub your head?

AUNTIE: How?

(Father starts to rub Auntie's temple.)

I miss your wife.

FATHER: About my wife. Don't say anything.

AUNTIE: I know you went to the river. Your brother told me.

FATHER: When she was a girl, everyday she swam there.

AUNTIE: She forgot the dangerous spots.

(Father keeps rubbing in silence. Finally:)

FATHER: The smell of the water. Same as when she drowned. Like dirt. Boys still play with cups. Women still wash their babies. Somewhere, she is there still. I just want her body. Feel her teeth. Pull the wet hair away from her neck. One last time, touch her ear. I should've never come back. Too many things are coming into my head now. Not just how she lived. How she died.

(Beat.)

Most men feel fifty percent. I feel ninety. Ninety-five. When she died, I kept her toothbrush and hairpins. I slept with her socks. I would run my hand through the shag hoping one of her toenails would jump up. I had to be brave and stop all that. For the boy. All these years there was nothing, but I've started to dream about her again. That's me. Lots of feeling. I'm hundred percent.

AUNTIE: What's "shag"?

FATHER: Shag rug. Oh, very expensive.

(Beat.)

I told all my dreams to her. Last night, I dreamt I was a cow.

AUNTIE: A cow!

FATHER: Yes! The one that always stands by the fence. I was in the field, eating fresh mango, and all of you were inside the house having a party—you were people, not cows—I was the only one. The rains started coming and the mudslide happened and I was shouting for help but no one came running. I got pulled away to the river but not the other cows.

AUNTIE: The cow was eating a mango?

FATHER: I was a person but still an animal.

(Suddenly, for a moment, Father's massage turns to a caress of Auntie's hair. The two quickly pull away from the other.)

And—When the wedding is over you should just stay with your husband, okay, and not the doctor.

(Auntie exits quickly. Father moves to exit as well, but stops when he sees Tommy. A charged moment but the boy doesn't fully understand why.)

TOMMY: What?

FATHER: I'm the father, okay, not you. I watch you, you don't watch me.

(Beat.)

You just think about you, not me, okay. I know more than you.

(Father exits quickly.
From inside the house, Tina slides onto the porch, her hair in a kerchief. Tina starts to design a rice pattern. Tommy approaches, hiding something in his hand.)

TINA: You smell different.

TOMMY: I was running in the cinnamon field. I bought you a present.
TINA: What?

(Tommy reveals a whistle. He blows it then hands it to Tina.)

TOMMY: Blow.

(Tina blows the whistle. Tommy takes the whistle back and blows. He hands it back to his cousin, who blows again.)

Like kissing.
TINA: The women are inside frying fish. Then they will make chicken curry. Then dahl and rice. Eight hundred guests are expected tomorrow. They will sit in the garden. The children will run then hide in the folds of their mother's saris. The men will smoke beedies, the richer ones, Charminars. They will drink toddy and Kingfisher. It will be sunny. The bride hasn't met her husband yet. He has been told about her legs but she knows he will still be disappointed when he sees her. He will think her ugly. In time, he will learn how to move around her body, but he will always touch her as if she is a bird. He will keep her in the house. I am Miss Tina. This ends our broadcast.

(Tina undoes the kerchief and covers her face, as the television is covered by the tablecloth to protect from dust.)

I want to show you my legs.
TOMMY: Are they bad?
TINA: Yes.

(Tina raises her skirt to reveal her damaged legs.)

TOMMY: I knew they were ugly but not this much.
TINA: Touch them. Try.

(Tommy forces himself to touch her legs.)

No one else will ever do that.
TOMMY: Your husband.
TINA: I need to take rest.
TOMMY: Let's go somewhere special tonight.

(No response.)

TINA: Go by yourself.

TOMMY: No, it's our last time.

(Tina turns away and lies down, her back to Tommy.)

TINA: Where will you go?

TOMMY: I'm not telling.

TINA: You can tell me in the morning.

TOMMY: No. You'll always wonder where I went but you'll never know.

(Tommy exits.
In the kitchen, the women prepare food. Lots of activity. Uncle enters.)

SERVANT GIRL: Leave!

UNCLE: Show me how to make what we eat.

SERVANT GIRL: Why? I'll cook for you.

UNCLE: But when you're gone someday? What then?

SERVANT GIRL: Uncle! Don't worry!

UNCLE *(To Auntie)*: What are you making?

AUNTIE: Porotta. Get flour. Get a bowl.

SERVANT GIRL: Someone should make a song about turmeric.

(Auntie hands her bowl to Uncle.)

AUNTIE: Touch with your hands. Mix with me.

UNCLE: This is all you put?

AUNTIE: Oil is there. And some salt.

(Auntie takes his hand in hers.)

Touch with your fingers. Keep it warm or it will spoil.

(Uncle and Auntie knead together.)

UNCLE: She's so happy today.

AUNTIE: More than happy.

UNCLE: Why?

AUNTIE *(Hushing Uncle)*: Shhhh—

UNCLE: What?

AUNTIE: She's meeting her fish seller tonight.

UNCLE: Finally.

AUNTIE: Big secret. Don't say anything. —Happy ending.

UNCLE: My nose— (*Showing his messy hands*) Scratch me!
AUNTIE (*Showing her messy hands*): Same as you.
UNCLE: Please!

(*Auntie leans forward, scratches Uncle's nose with hers, rolling one way then the other.*)

AUNTIE: Better?
UNCLE: Better.

(*Night. Tina sits on her bed under a mosquito net. Auntie and Servant Girl enter.*)

TINA: What is it, Mother?

(*The women sit on the bed and put their hands under the covers, touching Tina's body.*)

AUNTIE: Tomorrow night, your husband will touch you here.
SERVANT GIRL: Here.
AUNTIE: Here.
SERVANT GIRL: Here.
AUNTIE: Here.
SERVANT GIRL: For a brief moment, it will feel wonderful.

(*The women giggle. Uncle appears at the door.*)

UNCLE: Are you coming to bed?
AUNTIE: I was going to sleep beside Tina tonight.
UNCLE: Yes. It is your last night to be with her.

(*Uncle starts to exit.*)

AUNTIE: No?
UNCLE: What?
AUNTIE: Yes?
UNCLE: Yes or no?
AUNTIE: Pick.
UNCLE: You pick.

(*Uncle exits. Auntie remains.
     In the city, the Nut Seller roams the street. Tina rolls in. Then Tommy enters, coughing as he smokes five beedies at one time.*)

TOMMY: Lookkk a mee!

(*Tina looks but says nothing. Tommy spits out the beedies.*)

NUT SELLER: Sweet sweet. Sweet nuts.

TOMMY: You want cashews?

TINA: No.

TOMMY: You want a Cadbury's?

TINA: No.

TOMMY: You're not saying anything.

NUT SELLER: Sweet sweet. Sweet nuts.

TINA: I want to be quiet.

TOMMY: Why did you change your mind and come to the city if you're going to be like this? We've wandered all over, the places we always go to, but you're not having fun. What happened, wife? You don't like me anymore?

NUT SELLER: Sweet sweet. Sweet nuts.

TOMMY: You should've just stayed home, then. Why did you even come?

TINA: Why did you show me all this?

TOMMY: What?

TINA: If I had never left the porch. If I had just stayed where I'd always been.

TOMMY: We can go back then.

TINA: You go first. I've never come home by myself. I want to see if I can. I should do something on my own once in my life.

TOMMY: I'm not leaving you.

TINA: Stupid, I'm leaving you. Tomorrow morning I get married.

TOMMY: When I go to the boys' school I can come visit you.

TINA: Go. Start the rice pattern for me.

TOMMY: You like your husband more than me?

TINA: Go home, Tommy. Wait for your bride.

NUT SELLER: Sweet sweet. Sweet nuts.

TOMMY: You're going to get hurt.

TINA: Trust me.

TOMMY: I don't like you. You always get what you want.

(*Tommy exits. Nut Seller starts to follow him.*)

NUT SELLER: Sweet sweet. Sweet nuts.

TOMMY: No.

NUT SELLER: Take.

TOMMY: No, I said!

NUT SELLER: You take!

TOMMY: Fuck off!

(Frightened, Tommy runs away. He comes across Grandfather just sitting at the side of the road.)

GRANDFATHER: I am glad of one thing: that my wife is the dead one, not me. The most pain I have ever felt is now. At the end of my life. Why did God make it like this?

(Late at night. In a field. Servant Girl stands in a beautiful sari, flowers woven in her hair. Sound of footsteps. Tommy runs past her, not seeing her. Silence. Sound of more footsteps. Fish Seller enters, wearing a crisp shirt and tie.)

FISH SELLER: Hello.

(Servant Girl smiles, then looks away. The two glance at each other, nervously keeping their distance.)

Weddings are hard work. I brought so many fish today.

SERVANT GIRL: Your shirt looks nice.

FISH SELLER: I did it.

SERVANT GIRL: How?

FISH SELLER: With an iron.

SERVANT GIRL: No you didn't!

FISH SELLER: Yes, I bought one.

(Fish Seller sits. Still at a distance.)

It's so quiet.

SERVANT GIRL: And the sad trees. And the lovely smell. I remember coming here with you so many times.

(Servant Girl sits. Still at a distance.)

FISH SELLER: It's so hot. The mosquitoes are here still. I thought they would be gone by now. It wasn't like this before.

(Silence.)

I brought so many fish today. Hundreds.

(Beat.)

I also had my other customers. My new bicycle seat is too hard.
My body aches when I work. What about you?

SERVANT GIRL: How?

FISH SELLER: You say something.

SERVANT GIRL: What should I say?

FISH SELLER: Anything.

(Silence.)

How are you?

(No response.)

I said, "How are you?"

SERVANT GIRL: I know.

FISH SELLER: Should we go?

SERVANT GIRL: No.

(Silence.)

FISH SELLER: You want me to comb your hair?

SERVANT GIRL: I liked how you did that.

FISH SELLER: No you didn't.

(Silence.)

Give your brush.

SERVANT GIRL: I didn't bring one.

FISH SELLER: Oh.

SERVANT GIRL: What you could do . . . You could just touch my hair.
If you want.

FISH SELLER: No.

(Fish Seller sniffs his fingers.)

No.

(Silence.
    Servant Girl looks at her palm.)

Always with your hand. What does it say? Can you read?

(Silence.)

Days like today. I'm tired, yes, but what will I think about when I lie in bed? I won't think about cinema songs or Vijay Amritraj. So many tiny lives—we have to be bigger than we are. The ache in my hands and my feet—I like it. Makes me do more. I don't think how children on the bus spit in my hair when I ride in the city, and the scooters squeeze me off the road. I just keep going. Further and further. I never think about what's over. All the times people have hurt me are gone. Now, wishes and dreams are just there. Human beings have desires, yearnings—I see so clearly, now. The things that aren't there—that's what people really are. That's what I think. What do you think?

(Silence.)

That's what I think.

SERVANT GIRL: Good night then.

FISH SELLER: Okay.

(Servant Girl turns away, not wanting to show that she has started to cry. She stands, starts to exit.)

Wait—

(Servant Girl stops. Fish Seller stands. Long pause. Fish Seller shakes his head. Servant Girl exits. Fish Seller sits then slumps.
Back home, early morning. Tommy sits on the porch, asleep. Suddenly, Auntie runs onto the porch. She is wearing the green sari she washed at the river.)

AUNTIE: Have you seen Tina?

(Grandfather runs into the front yard.)

GRANDFATHER: She's not at the grave.

(From inside the house, Servant Girl runs onto the porch.)

SERVANT GIRL: She's not inside.

(Continuing to search, the women come and go. Tommy just watches them.)

AUNTIE (*Offstage*): Did she get this idea from you, Tommy? To run away.

(*Grandfather, Servant Girl and Auntie return to the front yard. They sit defeated. Uncle enters.*)

HUSBAND: Why did I sleep beside you!

UNCLE: The guests know something is wrong.

SERVANT GIRL: Where's the groom?

UNCLE: Crying in the taxi. His father punched me.

(*Beat.*)

A good marriage. A healthy baby. I want to feel these things. All the people see the same thing: failure as a husband. Now, failure as a father.

AUNTIE: Don't wait, serve the food. People are laughing at us.

(*Beat.*)

She's just doing a trick. She'll come back when everyone's gone. If she didn't want this marriage, she should have just told us—What?

UNCLE: That's not the sari I bought for you.

AUNTIE: No.

UNCLE: You were supposed to wear it today.

AUNTIE: How?

UNCLE: You couldn't even do that one thing.

AUNTIE: You took it.

UNCLE: What are you talking?

AUNTIE: I don't have it.

UNCLE: You took it!

AUNTIE: Quiet.

UNCLE: I don't have it.

AUNTIE: Whisper!

UNCLE: Just, find it and put it. For good luck. To make Tina come back.

(*Silence.*)

Have I lost my daughter?

AUNTIE: You still have your wife. The doctor is laughing.

(In Canada, Tommy lies in Doug Harris's bed. Mr. Harris sits beside him, eyes closed. Slightly creepy.)

TOMMY: Where's my mother? Mr. Harris?

MR. HARRIS: She's not here anymore.

TOMMY: Did she die?

MR. HARRIS: We're divorced. Stop talking.

TOMMY: What do you do?

MR. HARRIS: I'm with Kitchener Hydro. I go into people's backyards to read the meter. I looked in hundreds of windows to see if you were inside. I don't want to know where you've been. Never tell me. You're back now. That's all that matters.

TOMMY: Open your eyes.

MR. HARRIS: I repainted the whole house. I did the basement and the kitchen and the family room. But when I got upstairs. I couldn't do your room. Can you smell the paint from downstairs?

TOMMY: You want me to tell you a bedtime story?

MR. HARRIS: No.

TOMMY: I can't sleep.

MR. HARRIS: Try.

(Tommy rolls over.)

No—Doug sleeps on his back.

TOMMY: Turn on the lights. I'm not tired yet.

MR. HARRIS: You can't keep talking.

TOMMY: Let's do something. Let's go outside.

MR. HARRIS: No.

TOMMY: We can look at the Christmas lights.

MR. HARRIS: I wasn't going to put them up this year but I forced myself. Yes. Let's go outside and look. Promise not to talk?

(No response.)

Good boy.

(In India, Fish Seller enters the front yard, carrying a banana-leaf plate full of fish.)

FISH SELLER: Congratulations, Grandpa! The fish is excellent! I told you.

GRANDFATHER: She's the one.

FISH SELLER: I remember.

SERVANT GIRL: You taught me: only put tiny spice. Don't make the fish chicken or beef. Let the fish be fish.

FISH SELLER: I remember our wedding.

SERVANT GIRL: Just eat.

(Fish Seller eats a bit of fish.)

FISH SELLER: I do. Even your fingernails. They were red that day. Same with your toes. And the way—

(With her fingers, Servant Girl picks fish from the Fish Seller's plate and feeds him, filling his mouth.

In Canada, Tommy stands in front of a tree. Mr. Harris calls from offstage.)

MR. HARRIS: Close your eyes, Doug. Ready?

(The Christmas lights come on. They shine oddly, the string of lights only placed halfway up the tree. Mr. Harris joins Tommy.)

Just like we always do. It was hard doing it myself.

TOMMY: Looks dumb.

MR. HARRIS: I couldn't go higher—you weren't here to hold the ladder.

(Mr. Harris exits and returns with a ladder.)

Hold the ladder.

TOMMY: I want to climb up.

MR. HARRIS: Quiet! You can't be my son if you're going to keep talking. You don't sound like Doug so just hold the ladder.

(Tommy holds the ladder as Mr. Harris climbs up to extend the lights higher in the tree. He returns to the ground.)

You want to climb up? I'll hold. Go on. You can see Kitchener. The library. Kmart. Canada Trust.

(Tommy climbs to the top and looks toward Kitchener.)

Tomorrow we'll go to the farmer's market. Haven't been there for a while. I'll buy a tray of apple fritters and we can go to the Siskins game. After the hockey, we'll have cheeseburgers at Harmony Lunch. Our clothes will smell like fried onions. For supper we'll do the buffet at Mei King or wiener schnitzel at the Schwaben Club or the Black Forest. Eh—stupid me, eh, I forgot: the father-son Christmas dinner is this weekend at church, came back just in time. Everyone will be there. They'll be surprised to see you.

(*Silence.*)

Maybe you should come down.

(*Tommy climbs down the ladder.*
In India, the family continues to just sit.
In Canada, as Tommy returns to the ground:)

For a few minutes you made me feel better.

(*Mr. Harris starts to fold up the ladder.*)

TOMMY: No—

(*No response.*)

    Keep trying.
MR. HARRIS: What's your name?
TOMMY: Doug.
MR. HARRIS: Your real one.
TOMMY: Doug.
MR. HARRIS: Stop.
TOMMY: It is!
MR. HARRIS: Don't say that.
TOMMY: I'm Doug!
MR. HARRIS: Then just go. Leave, Doug, and don't come back! Thank you.
TOMMY: You're welcome . . . but where should I go?
MR. HARRIS: No clue.

(*Mr. Harris exits, leaving Tommy standing by the lit-up tree. Tommy is suddenly in the dark as Mr. Harris has unplugged the Christmas lights.*)

AUNTIE: Children run away. But then they come home.

(*In Canada, Tommy walks. He comes upon an odd sight. He moves closer, gazing up: the Mennonite Farmer he met earlier in the evening is high in a tree.*)

MENNONITE FARMER: Isaac? Oh—hello—it's you! I thought you were my boy. He was here before, trying to get me down. His mother, too—shouting at me, watching and waiting. I see so much. I never realized. I don't want to go home. How was your night? Did you get to St. Jacobs? Who are you again? Johnny? Tommy?

(Tommy keeps walking.

In Canada, in the kitchen, as at the top of the play, Tommy's Father continues to sleep on the counter. Grandfather enters and whispers in his ear.)

GRANDFATHER: A nightmare: the handsome man and his beautiful wife go to the river to swim but only one returns to shore. People hear you screaming and come running with torches. You cover yourself with one hand and with the other you point. The men dive deep as you crawl in the dark trying to find your pants. The women wrap you in your wife's sari then sit in the dirt with you until morning. Your clothes hang in the tree where you left them. You change. Your beautiful wife is never found. She sunk to the bottom of the river. Or was carried to the sea. Or is she in Cape Comorin eating beef biryani in a five-star? Maybe she's in Mysore sucking on a mango seed as she swings in a hammock? Your beautiful wife walks in the Nilgiris, wiping the soap from another man's ear. The two of them talk about the problems in your marriage when they stop kissing. Your wife always cut the top of your head off when using the camera so you took the pictures. Every photo in the house is of her. You hide them in a box downstairs. Years later, your pipes burst. The basement floods. You stand knee-deep in water as your wife floats on the surface—hundreds of pictures. She smiles up at you as you worry about the carpet.

(Beat.)

Y'eh-Da—Get up! You lost your wife. Go find your son!

(Startled, Father wakes and sees Grandfather.)

FATHER: Hullo, Tommy—Hullo hullo hullo!

(Outside, Tommy arrives home. He goes to the front door and is about to knock. But he steps away, going back deep into the yard. He lies on the ground.)

TOMMY: I know where babies come from. I've got little seeds inside of me. I'm going to plant one right here. Come summer, I'll have a baby. A new Tommy. Good Tommy. Someone Canadian. You'll grow up and take care of me. You won't want to. Too bad, idiot, I'll just make you.

(*Tommy tries to dig deep but can't. Angrily, he hits the frozen ground then unzips his trousers. He rubs into his hands, grinding against but unable to penetrate the soil.*
Father opens the front door and steps into the yard, wearing boots and a winter coat, carrying a flashlight. Grandfather also steps from the house, following behind. Father walks then sees Tommy humping the snow.)

FATHER: Hey! What's happened? Doing sex now!

(*Tommy punches the frozen ground. The characters from India move closer, then sit, watching father and son.*)

Go inside.

(*Tommy starts to follow his Father to the house. The man stops, turns to his son.*)

TOMMY: What?
FATHER: You're not an animal, you're a human person. You can't just do what you want. You have to stop yourself. Always!

(*Beat.*)

What's wrong with you?
TOMMY: I want a new father.
FATHER: Same. And a new son.
TOMMY: One I don't have to look after.
FATHER: What kind of pervert, sex maniac—?
TOMMY: I'm tired of taking care of you!
FATHER: You don't!
TOMMY: I found a new dad tonight.
FATHER: What happened then?
TOMMY: Nothing. He didn't want me.
FATHER: Nobody wants dirty types.
TOMMY: I'm going to keep looking.

FATHER: Good. You do it.

TOMMY: Someday, I'll just be gone.

FATHER: Like Tina. She's your hero?

TOMMY: Like your wife.

FATHER: That's what you want? To be dead like them?

TOMMY: It's not for sure.

FATHER: Yes.

TOMMY: There was no body.

FATHER: Talk inside.

TOMMY: Tina could still be somewhere, sliding.

FATHER: What do you want me to say? You want me to give happy ending? Okay, Tina arranges shoes and gives slippers when people go into the Taj Mahal. She lives in Vellore and has rosewater ice cream for breakfast. Every day, your mother makes a jasmine ponytail. —Horse puckey.

TOMMY: We should go back and look for them.

FATHER: What, you're going to come and go until you find them?

TOMMY: Put me in a school over there. I could look Saturdays and Sundays. Every day after class.

FATHER: Che—I'm not going to just put you. We have to be together.

(Beat.)

You have to think they're gone. You have to just kill them.

(Silence.)

We have to kill all of them. Or we'll just go point A to point B. Then back to A and back to B and back and forth. Always in between. Living nowhere.

(Father stares at Uncle.)

Maybe Uncle watches the news each night, hoping to see his daughter. Then one day he gets kicked in the stomach by a cow. Auntie runs to get the doctor but it is too late.

(Uncle and Auntie exit.)

Make something up. Think that they're dead or they'll be there forever. Is that what you want?

(Tommy stares at Grandfather.)

When you get older, you stop thinking. All you do is remember.
TOMMY: Grandfather dies. Because he's old.
FATHER: One morning he just keeps sleeping.

(Grandfather exits.
Father stares at Servant Girl. She's reading her palm. He looks at Fish Seller.)

The Servant Girl and the Fish Seller never get together. She always thinks about him brushing her hair again but then the communists come to power.
TOMMY: The man waits and waits for the government to buy him a fridge.
FATHER: Instead, they give him a boat. He moves to the port.

(Tommy stares at Fish Seller.)

TOMMY: In that old boat, the poor old man starts sailing.
FATHER: To Ceylon. To make some money.
TOMMY: But he never gets there.
FATHER *(Impressed with the make-believe)*: Good.

(Fish Seller exits.)

TOMMY: The Servant Girl doesn't know this. She tries not to, but she keeps on waiting for the Fish Seller to come back to her. She thinks of him praying for kingfish. And that he throws all the mermaids back into the sea.

(Servant Girl exits.)

FATHER: What about Tina?

(No response.)

Tina gets hit by a lorry.
TOMMY: Mother got eaten by a shark, then.
FATHER: Fine. We're the same: boys without girls.

(Beat.)

You tell good lies, Tommy.

TOMMY: You too.

FATHER: When you grow up, you can be story writer. Or sell carpet.

TOMMY: You could do that: sell carpet.

FATHER: No. I will be a math professor again. With tenure this time, and I will work hard again. I have been as big a Stupid as you, maybe. Maybe you are stupid because of me even! Ache makes the body go slow, but I'm going to stop the lying and doing nothing.

(Tommy starts to spin in circles.)

Hey—What are you doing? —Tommy!

TOMMY *(Shouting to the sky)*: Good-bye, wife!

(Father doesn't spin but he shouts to the sky.)

FATHER: Good-bye, wife! Gone for good! —Done! —Finally!

(Father continues watching Tommy spin. Then starts to spin himself.)

The world is flipping! Spinning! Zigzag! Can you see me, Tommy?

(Father and Tommy stop spinning, each trying to focus on the other. Dizzy, Father kneels, then lies on his stomach, motionless.)

Aaaaaah, help me. My head is paining . . . Idiot, hey!

TOMMY: You're still the same.

FATHER: No. I came looking for you. That's something.

(Suddenly Tina enters with Auntie and starts to design a rice pattern. Tommy sees his cousin and moves closer. He kneels, still dizzy, still haunted. Father rolls onto his back.

Softly, continuing to lie on the ground, staring up at the sky:)

Can you see me, wife? —Hullo.

AUNTIE: Your pattern only has to stay a little while then it can just go. No problem.

(Tommy watches Tina continue her pattern.)

TOMMY: Please go away.

END OF PLAY

A finalist for a Governor General's Literary Award, Sunil Kuruvilla graduated from the Yale School of Drama's playwriting program. His work has been produced at many theatres including the Stratford Shakespeare Festival, the Yale Repertory Theatre, the Mark Taper Forum, the La Jolla Playhouse and the Canadian Stage Company. Sunil has had many outstanding teachers including Robert Blacker, Mark Bly, Liz Diamond, Alistair MacLeod, Donald Margulies and the late Anthony Minghella. His awards include the Truman Capote Literary Fellowship and the ASCAP (American Society of Composers, Authors and Publishers) Foundation Cole Porter Award. He has been generously and steadily supported by the Ontario Arts Council and the Canada Council for the Arts. Sunil lives in Waterloo, Ontario, Canada with his beautiful wife Lisa and their beautiful son Isaac.

The Square

Bridget Carpenter, Ping Chong,
Constance Congdon, Kia Corthron,
Maria Irene Fornes, Philip Kan Gotanda,
Jessica Hagedorn, David Henry Hwang,
Craig Lucas, Robert O'Hara, Han Ong,
José Rivera, Diana Son, Alice Tuan,
Mac Wellman and Chay Yew

Artist's Statement

by Lisa Peterson,
Co-Creator and Director
of *The Square*

I met Chay Yew in 1995,
when we were both headed
for new jobs at the Mark
Taper Forum. It was
a golden time for new
play development in Los
Angeles—there was still
plenty of foundation funding for experiments in new work, and the
Taper alone hosted half a dozen new theatre labs, each focused
on creating work within a specific community of artists. I was the
Taper's Resident Director and also organized the Writers' Workshop
for mid-career writers. Chay arrived and founded the Asian Theatre
Workshop, and *The Square* was one of his first big and wonderful
ideas. We'd been knocking around various ideas for a collaborative
piece that could bring together a mix of the amazing playwrights
that we were in contact with. We talked about not only advocacy
for the Asian American playwrights, but also about multiplicity and
culture clash; we were intrigued by the challenge of asking people to
think in a bigger way about being Asian in America, and about what
culturally-specific theatre really is. We wondered what the boundaries of this kind of theatre might be. And so we invented a game.

Chay and I had both read a very interesting review of an avant-
garde performance in Germany that basically recreated a day in
the life of a city park. We began to imagine a large play that took
place in one corner of a park in Chinatown. We had in mind a real
place—Columbus Park in lower Manhattan—but we liked to think
of our fictitious park as being anywhere in Chinatown, U.S.A. Many
American cities have a Chinatown of one size or another, and they

are these intense crossroads of immigrant experience and urban necessity, of history and of culture. We made a list of remarkable Asian American playwrights that we knew: David Henry Hwang, Philip Kan Gotanda, Ping Chong, Han Ong, Diana Son, Jessica Hagedorn, Alice Tuan and Chay Yew himself. Then we made a list of writers who were not Asian American, but who we thought might love the idea of taking part in a group experiment, and who had unique voices that would pop out as part of a mosaic: Maria Irene Fornes, Connie Congdon, Kia Corthron, Craig Lucas, Mac Wellman, Bridget Carpenter, José Rivera and Robert O'Hara.

Once we had our diverse group of sixteen writers, Chay and I developed the rules of the game. Building off the multiple meanings of the word "square," we made up a kind of four-sided structure. The evening would be made up of sixteen very short plays. There were four possible periods that the play could inhabit: 1880, 1920, 1960 or 2000 (which at the time was the very near future). Each play could have between one and four actors in it. Each play would center around one of four themes: History, Change, Chaos or Tradition. Each play would have a mix of Asian American and non-Asian American actors in it. Finally we assigned a period, a theme, a cast size and a racial makeup of that cast to each of the sixteen writers *randomly*, drawing their assignments out of a hat. To spark the writers' ideas, we supplied them with observations from Columbus Park: photographs, a map, a timeline, a historical sketch. Happily, we found we had chosen a group of writers who liked games, and who found that our rules gave them a kind of freedom. Often this is true in art—the more circumscribed the form, the more intense the personal expression. Poets love to try their hand at sonnets because they're so strict, composers work in strict form all the time, as do dancers and choreographers and architects. In theatre, sometimes we lose sight of the old forms, because we've moved so far beyond them—the days when Greek drama were limited to two actors and then (an innovation!) three actors—those days feel so far away. But we still like games, and strict forms. The writers began to send us five-minute plays that took place in this Square, as various in style and tone as the playwrights themselves.

Chay and I arranged a mosaic out of those short plays. We imagined a day in the life of an urban space, though that day happened across one hundred and twenty years. We had chosen periods because of the pleasing math: each period was separated from the others by four decades. But also we knew that each period we chose had particularly juicy historical elements. The 1880s was a time of mass immigration to the United States from various Asian countries; the great Depression hit in the 1920s; in the 1960s, the idea of civil rights came alive in the U.S.; and 2000 contained all the dread and hope of the approaching millennium. Throughout, we heard insistent rhythms and discerned recurrent themes. *The Square* grew into a choral piece animated by intersection, interruption and provocative juxtaposition. A character from one play could reappear, walking through another piece from a different moment in history. Motifs recurred. Tasting blood. Blind men. The snip, snip of a pair of scissors. The painful and sometimes comic struggle to learn English. The erotics of master-servant or doctor-patient relationships. Gay sexualities. Attraction, identification, hostility, alliance—among people of different races and class positions. These become metaphors for a larger existential and historical horizon of immigration and racism, of loneliness and love, of the (im)possibility of connection.

So we quilted the sixteen plays together, and did a production for the Taper, using a wonderful warehouse space at the Actors' Gang. We produced it very simply, with a company of ten actors, each playing several roles. We created a square of space in a large dark room, and used a few benches and chairs and artifacts to move from period to period. Many of the plays ended up feeling like hauntings, as if the ghosts of the inhabitants—Asian and non-Asian—of this invented Chinatown were passing not only in front of the audience, but criss-crossing past each other, brushing the hems of other times and sensing the loneliness and the oddity of being strangers in a strange land.

In 2001, we were invited by Ma-Yi Theater Company to remount *The Square* in New York, at the Public. We were planning to fly to New York to start rehearsals on September 12; instead, we gathered in a coffee shop in Silverlake and stared at each other in shock at what had happened to Manhattan, wondering when and how we would be able to get there. When we were finally able to begin rehearsals, we went with the cast down to Lower Manhattan, to the Chinatown park that inspired the play, and breathed in the acrid air.

The Square is an expression of multiple points of view, and I think that's what always made it so amazing. We were interested in the idea of one lovely thing made by many different minds and perspectives. Not only is every little story unique, it's the tone and style of each wildly different writer, bumping up against the others, that makes it provocative. *E pluribus unum*: out of many, one.

Production History

The Square was originally commissioned by the CTG Mark Taper Forum's Asian Theater Workshop (Gordon Davidson, Artistic Director/Producer) in Los Angeles, California.

The Square premiered in 2000 at the Mark Taper Forum in Los Angeles (Gordon Davidson, Artistic Director/Producer; Charles Dillingham, Managing Director). It was directed by Lisa Peterson, and conceived by Chay Yew and Lisa Peterson. The set design was by Rachel Hauck. The costume design was by Joyce Kim Lee. The lighting design was by Geoff Korf. The sound composition was by Nathan Wang. The production stage manager was Erika H. Sellin. The cast was as follows:

Marcus Chong	Elizabeth Ruscio
Dennis Dun	Barry Del Sherman
Arye Gross	Elizabeth Sung
Emily Kuroda	Jodi Thelan
Soon-Tek Oh	Tamlyn Tomita
Saundra Quarterman	Greg Watanabe

The Square received its New York premiere in 2001 at Ma-Yi Theater Company (Ralph B. Peña, Artistic Director; Jorge Z. Ortoll, Executive Director). It was directed by Lisa Peterson, and conceived by Chay Yew and Lisa Peterson. The set design was by Rachel Hauck. The costume design was by Christianne Myers. The lighting design was by James Vermeulen. The sound design was by Fabian Obispo. The production stage manager was Wendy Ouellette. The cast was as follows:

David Wilson Barnes	Michael Ray Escamilla
Joel de la Fuente	Fiona Gallagher
Saidah Arrika Ekulona	Wai Ching Ho

Jennifer Ikeda
Ken Leung
Hamish Linklater

Ching Valdes-Aran
Henry Yuk
Janet Zarish

Characters

Twelve actors. Three Asian males, three asian females, two Caucasian males, two Caucasian females, one black male and one black female.

Setting

A square in Chinatown, New York City.

Note

The use of a forward slash (/) denotes where the next character begins an interruption or an overlap.

Act One

MY OLD HABIT OF RETURNING TO PLACES PART 1

Mac Wellman

OLD WOMAN:
> My old habit of returning to places
> is the only thing I understand.
>
> (*Pause.*)
>
> All I can recall at the start of my long
> journey is a box of matches. I lit the first
> match when I was a young girl in Shantung;
> They gave me too much salt and vinegar.
> Every night I would go outside, count
> all the stars, eighty-seven, eighty-eight,
> eighty-nine, just like that. I had no
> trouble except too much vinegar and
> also too much salt. I think about all
> this because my family are all gone now.
> Some of them have turned into pigs. So,
> out of respect for them I am going
> as far as I can from Shangtung, where
> I was born, and from Shanghai, where

I went to study, and from Singapore
where my family immigrated in the sixties.

I can't tell the difference between one
day and the next so all I want to do is
sit down for a while and take off my shoes
and rest my little feet. See up there,
up there in the sky? I know the names
of all the stars, and I have walked down
the whole length of the Milky Way looking
for a place where I might put down my
packages. Put down my packages and rest.
That's why I have returned here. Come
back to China. Here. China. The
habit of returning to places is the
only thing I understand.

UNTITLED

Han Ong

FIRST MAN: Bah Yah
SECOND MAN: Bay
FIRST MAN: Baah
SECOND MAN: Bay
       Ay
       Ay!
FIRST MAN: Hey!
SECOND MAN: Bay
FIRST MAN: Beh
SECOND MAN: Bay
FIRST MAN: Beh
SECOND MAN: Bay
FIRST MAN: Beh
SECOND MAN: Good
       Is good
FIRST MAN: Goo! Goo!
SECOND MAN: Yard

FIRST MAN: Yar!

SECOND MAN: YarD

FIRST MAN: YarT!

SECOND MAN: Bay-yard

FIRST MAN: Beh-Yaht

SECOND MAN: Street

FIRST MAN: Steeh

SECOND MAN: Treet

FIRST MAN: Tweet

SECOND MAN: Treet

 Not tweet

 Tweet is bird

FIRST MAN: Burr fligh

SECOND MAN: Not bird

FIRST MAN: Not burr?

SECOND MAN: You not bird

 Bird fly

 You not fly

 You stay

FIRST MAN: Me stay

SECOND MAN: Stay here

 Bay-yard

FIRST MAN: Beh-Yaht

SECOND MAN: You are on Bay-yard

FIRST MAN: Burr fligh

 back to China

SECOND MAN: No China

 Bay-yard forever and forever

 Bay-Yard

(Third Man comes up.)

 How arr yoo?

THIRD MAN: Yoo do what-what?

SECOND MAN: Day off

THIRD MAN: What?

SECOND MAN: No working

THIRD MAN: Oh! Offt day

SECOND MAN: Yes

THIRD MAN: Offt day offt day me no offt day! So la-zee!

SECOND MAN: No no

 Day off me teach

No
I teach
I teach English!
Make some mo-nee
send back to home
FIRST MAN: Chi Nah Beh-Yaht
Beh-Yaht Chi Nah
THIRD MAN *(To First Man)*: Engleesh engleesh
no important
FIRST MAN *(To Third Man)*: Importat!
THIRD MAN: only know: work
FIRST MAN: Wurr wurr!
THIRD MAN: Work hard
Only know: no feel lone-lee
FIRST MAN: Me lone-lee yes!
SECOND MAN: Good!
Lonely
Short
English short always drop long
and heavy ting
No long ting in English
No heavy ting in English
Chinese all long and heavy ting
but English dif-rent
Just lonely not lone-leeeee
Right?
Yes is right
FIRST MAN: Yes lone-lee

(First Man looks at Second Man.)

THIRD MAN: Bah!
Me go work!
You stand here
Like sky you own
Like rain you drink
FIRST MAN: Beh-Yaht Steet
SECOND MAN: Street
THIRD MAN: No Use!
SECOND MAN: Good-bye
FIRST MAN: Goo Bai!
Bah-Yaht Steet

(A spotlight isolates the First Man. He is holding the sheet of paper.)

FIRST MAN: My dear wife
    the days are long but
    worthwhile I am working
    so hard so hard that
    at night I fall fast
    asleep despite the thickness
    of the car sounds like
    a third language that I
    have still to learn. Every day
    I am paying someone to teach
    me because to learn
    is to improve and to improve
    is to make more money.

    Here is some

(He begins to rip the sheet, turning it into money-confetti.)

    for you
    and the boys
    Here is money for the gods
    of our house.

(Throws confetti into the air. His Dear Wife appears.)

    Dear Wife:
    The tree in our yard
    a mere sapling when
    you left now gives
    shadow during the summertime
    and the boys in their own eyes
    are no longer boys. They
    look at me and I am learning
    every day
    that when I talk
    I am only speaking
    to a wall uttering the
    language of the dead
    I hope they will not think
    to join you I couldn't bear

that loss but nobody listens
It is only tradition after all:
Men leave
when opportunity calls. We are
respecters of tradition. Like
fidelity. I hope you remember

(Dear Wife disappears. First Man is back with Second Man. The street sign now says Mott.)

SECOND MAN: Mott

FIRST MAN: Mott

SECOND MAN: Good!

FIRST MAN: Everee-deh I learn

SECOND MAN: Learn what?

FIRST MAN: In English drop heavy
      drop long tings
      No more Chi-neees
      Is all dif-rent

SECOND MAN: Good
      Mott

FIRST MAN: Mott is good!

SECOND MAN: Street.

FIRST MAN: Treet!

SECOND MAN: Good!

FIRST MAN: Lonely!

SECOND MAN: Very good!

FIRST MAN: Not lone-leee
      Lonely!

SECOND MAN: Yes

FIRST MAN: Lonely lonely lonely!
      Lonely Bay Yart
      Lonely Mott
      Lonely Bow Ree

SECOND MAN: Bowery

FIRST MAN: Bow Ree Lonely
      Everee-wehr lonely
      Hah hah! Me learn! Yes!

THE OLD CHINESE MAN

Philip Kan Gotanda

BETH: We see a park. A normal, every day park in Chinatown, New York, U.S.A., with the usual assortment of characters and activities, pigeons and dogs.

We notice an old Chinese Man, sitting at a park bench, off to the side. He sits there quietly. There's nothing special about him. In fact, you normally hardly notice him. He's the old Chinese man you always see. He could be someone's grandpa, someone's uncle, someone's father. Alone. Old. Lonely.

Today like every day he's feeding the pigeons. He seems to be taking meditative pleasure in the act. We see one pigeon, then a few more gathering

A young couple enter. A Chinese woman in her mid-twenties and a Caucasian man of the same age. She's American, born to hard-working Chinese immigrant parents and, though proud of her cultural heritage, she's spent her entire life distancing herself from that world, creating a persona that is very, very American like all of her friends at college.

He on the other hand is the boy next door. Athletic, handsome, with a big, gregarious attitude. He loves his fiancée's oriental features, her oriental culture and her Americanized hybrid of a psychology that at once makes her familiar and yet unknown.

GIRL: I loved that movie, I simply loved it. I want to see it again and again . . .

GUY: Doesn't your uncle own a noodle shop on Mott or something?

GIRL: And when Nino Castelnuovo kissed Catherine Deneuve, ahhh . . .

GUY: Maybe we can get some egg rolls or something . . .

GIRL: Sit, come on, sit, sit . . .

(Girl grabs Guy over to bench.)

Kiss me.

GUY: What?

GIRL: Kiss me like that. The way he kissed Catherine Deneuve . . .

GUY: Okay . . .

GIRL: Okay . . .

BETH: Now the couple have begun to kiss. Long, wet, romantic osculations. The old Chinese man has now stopped feeding the pigeons and only stares at the couple. The woman looks up and notices the old Chinese man staring at them. She tries to return to the embrace but the old Chinese man's staring is now making her very uncomfortable.

The woman knows that he's staring at her for being with this white man. For daring to bring him to a public park in Chinatown. For daring to kiss him in public. For daring to show that she loves this American boy, for turning her back on the old ways, for trying to be a Bak Guay.

But this Chinese old man is like her parents, like her uncles and aunts, like her Popo and Gung Gung, whom she loves but knows will never understand her need to be all-American (even though somewhere in her heart she knows that she can never be truly an American like everybody else, but it's a tiny voice that's speaking this and she knows she's strong enough, willful enough to block it out) because this is where she lives and that is what she is and wants to be and not some FOB eating stinky food, wearing unfashionable clothes with rice bowl haircuts, on the arm of some Chinese boy whose black hair and short stature and yellow skin and slanty eyes can never be like her fiancé's, can never be like everybody on TV, like everybody that's important, sexual, powerful, dangerous, normal, real, American.

The dog charges in after the pigeons who scatter every which way. The commotion unsettles the woman and her fiancé, while the old Chinese man remains implacable, continuing to stare at them. The woman grabs her fiancé and pulls him away.

After they leave, the pigeons and dog have settled in elsewhere in the park, the old Chinese man slowly gets up. It's been a long day and his bones are getting stiff, his stomach restless. Maybe a good bowl of juk. He puts on his hat and reaches into his pocket . . .

As he makes his way off. The dog runs up and barks a friendly good-bye to him, a pigeon flies over to see if he's got any more food. The end.

THE AUDITION

Maria Irene Fornes

LEE: What?

HIROSHI: . . . No work for Asian actor.

(His head rolls from side to side.)

What can Hiroshi . . . do?

(He sobs. Lee shakes his head in sympathy.)

. . . No acting for poor Hiroshi . . . poor Hiroshi . . . poor Hiroshi . . . no bride for Hiroshi either!!! No job! No bride! Nothing here for Hiroshi!!! What to do!!!

(He crumples the newspaper pages as the huffing increases. He starts crying. Hiroshi starts to calm down. His head hangs close to the paper. As he reads the following, he gradually becomes saddened again. His crying subsides.)

"Young unmarried woman wants to marry young man in good position." Why young!! Young!!—Young!! Young woman wealthy wants to marry young man wealthy? Why not marry poor old man? Marry poor old man!!!!

LEE: You would marry for money?

HIROSHI: Not for money. I love her if she's rich. —Not you?

LEE: No.

(Pablo enters. Pablo does a step-hand-word greeting. Lee and Hiroshi mirror this.)

Hello, Pablo.

PABLO: Did you start?

LEE *(With Chicano accent)*: We're waiting for you. *(Handing Pablo a script)* This is the scene.

(Lee puts on the ranchero hat.)

PABLO: Let's see.

HIROSHI: Would you have coffee.

PABLO: Yes, please.

(Hiroshi takes off the saucer covering the third cup and places the cup on the saucer. Pablo points to Hiroshi.)

You play Don Fermin. *(Pointing to Lee)* You play Francisco.

HIROSHI *(As Don Fermin with a Japanese accent)*: "You are crumb. I would like for you to live long long long long after me, to give chance for people to see what crumb you are." *(Shaking his hands at the wrists as if casting a spell)* "I want you to live longer and be miserable and ugly, get skinny and skinnier on bone and miserable and ugly more and more the longer you live. Bum. The longer you live the uglier you get. I curse that."

(Pablo signals Lee to read with a large arm gesture.)

LEE *(As Francisco with a Chinese accent)*: The longer I live the more beautiful I am, you lousy patron of the chingada. And the more beautiful I am the more I am pleasure to world and more even pleasure to me. And more pleasure to girl. More show me fine. You crumb—I aristocrat. Look at my hat. Fine hat. You ugly bum. I beautiful. Like movie star.

HIROSHI *(As Don Fermin)*: That-is-it. *(To imaginary person:)* Rogelio!

(He stamps his foot.)

Bring in wild mad dog to eat alive this hijo de la chingada.

(He stands.)

(As Don Fermin:) Good-bye for you at standing on two feet. Now for you only crawl. Now girls only kiss all my inch when I turn every year more handsome. Not you. You less.

LEE *(As Francisco)*: You ugly fat balloon shaky like little worm. I is handsome, beautiful man of the girls. I am handsome and I fly. I look down to spit at you.

(Pablo takes the script from Lee and looks at it.)

PABLO: Okay. That's good. Now—you want me to coach you?

(Hiroshi and Lee nod and grunt.)

You want the Mexicano, Ranchero, Chicano or Cholo accent?

(They both make a grunting sound. This time they don't understand what Pablo is talking about.)

Or Cholo? —This is Ranchero. *(Using the particular wording, intonation, facial gestures and body movement of traditional Ranchero while Hiroshi and Lee observe with deep concentration)* You little snaky eye. You ugly fat balloon. Shaky little worm. I is handsome, beautiful man of the girls. Ha!

(Hiroshi and Lee discuss the pros and cons of this style, each speaking in their language. Pablo waits till they are finished. They nod to let him know they are finished.)

This is Mexicano.

(Pablo performs the same line with Mexican immigrant accent. Hiroshi and Lee repeat the discussion process.)

This is Chicano.

(He performs the same line using the mode and manner of Chicano speech. Hiroshi and Lee repeat the discussion process.)

This is Cholo.

(He performs the same line using the mode and manner of Cholo speech. Hiroshi and Lee repeat the discussion process. They then turn to Pablo.)

HIROSHI: We like the Cholo.
PABLO: All right . . . Let's go!!!
HIROSHI: It used to be that there were roles for Asians . . . then no more Asians. One day I see Mexican movie. "Rancheros," lovely "señoritas," horses, songs, good leading man. I look close. Leading man is Japanese actor good friend of mine. —He wears ranchero hat, and he's Mexican. I too can be Mexican. Same.

(He shows his face.)

Same. —My friend in Mexico looks good with big hat. —I look good with big hat. *(Pointing to Lee)* He looks good with big hat. So we're okay. He played Mexican so can we. You teach us how. We do it. You get two percent.

(Masks on.)

LEE AND HIROSHI: I have suffered . . . too much . . . since I am . . . among you.

JADE FLOWERPOTS AND BOUND FEET

David Henry Hwang

BETH: Ni hao ma?

(Pause; she listens to the tape.)

Ni hao ma?

(Pause.)

Wo de ming ze shi state-your-name-here. Oh. Beth Williams. Wait. Williams Beth.

(She reverses playback.)

Ni hao ma?

(Pause.)

Wo de ming ze shi Beth—shit!—Williams Beth.

(Mei-Li enters, a Caucasian in her mid-thirties, black hair in pigtails, dressed in a cheongsam, carrying a large purse.)

Wo de ming ze shi Williams Beth.

(Mei-Li sits beside Beth, who hasn't noticed her entrance. Still repeating from the recorder:)

Ni de ming ze shi shen me?

(Pause.)

Ni de ming ze shi shen me?

MEI-LI: Wo de ming ze shi Kwok Mei-li.

(Beth sees Mei-Li, whips off her headphones.)

No, no, don't tell me—
MEI-LI: What?
BETH: *You're* Mei-Li Kwok.
MEI-LI: Yes. And you are the woman from Amazon Dot Com Publishing?
BETH: Williams Beth. I mean, Beth Williams.

(They shake hands.)

You claim to be the author of *Jade Flowerpots and Bound Feet?*
MEI-LI: Yes. I *am* the author. That is my book.

(Beth rises to her feet.)

BETH: Well—thank you so much for agreeing to meet me. I was very impressed by your writing, though I'm afraid A-Dot-C will not be able to accept your work for publication. Please do think of us the next time you have a manuscript, I will be happy to read anything you write. Good day.

(Beth starts to leave. Mei-Li rises to her feet.)

MEI-LI: I know what you're thinking. I wrote in my book that because of my mixed-race heritage, many in the Asian community do not accept me as Chinese.
BETH: Well, you can add to that some in the non-Asian community as well.
MEI-LI: Ms. Williams, I am of Asian ancestry. And every word in that memoir is the absolute truth.
BETH: Oh come now, my dear. No memoir is the absolute truth. Any author who wants to tell the truth writes fiction.

(Mei-Li pulls from her purse an old photo.)

MEI-LI: This is a picture. Of my great-grandmother—Chiao. She is the one who was sold as an eleventh wife, beaten first by her husband, then by her seven sons—one for each day of the week—and finally, when she dared to associate with a Christian missionary, thrown down a well. Miraculously, she crawled out, only to be bayoneted by invading Japanese soldiers. She survived those wounds, but then, during the cultural revolution, she was sent to the countryside and made to pull carts loaded with oxen. Wherever she may be today, somehow I know in my heart . . . she is still suffering.

BETH: Yes, yes—very moving story . . .

(Looks at picture.)

MEI-LI: "Her feet were crushed with stones . . . and still she would not cry out."

BETH: I loved that chapter. Brought a tear to my eye.

(Hands back the photo.)

You could've gotten this anywhere, it doesn't prove a thing.

MEI-LI: But—I *am* Kwok Mei-Li!

BETH: All right—if you're determined to put me through this—luckily for you, I respect good writing—let's see your driver's license.

MEI-LI: I . . . don't drive.

BETH: Okay, then your social security card.

MEI-LI: Oh, c'mon—no one actually keeps those things—you write the number down someplace, and—

BETH: Bank card, universal phone card, gas bill—anything with your name on it.

(Pause.)

You expect me to believe you don't carry a credit card?

MEI-LI: Okay, okay, I . . .

BETH: Uh-huh . . .

MEI-LI: Kwok Mei-Li, I admit, it's more my Chinese name—

BETH: Exactly.

MEI-LI: It seemed more appropriate to use it for my—you know—my nom de plume.

BETH: So what name do you go by regularly?

MEI-LI: You mean, in white America?

BETH: If you insist.

MEI-LI: Ashley.

BETH: Ashley—what?

MEI-LI: Ashley . . . Winterstone.

BETH: Really?

MEI-LI: But . . . I tend to think of that as my slave name.

BETH: Whoa, I'll give you credit, you've come more prepared than most.

MEI-LI: Most?

BETH: This happens about twice a month. Why do you think A-Dot-C instituted a policy of meeting all multicultural authors face-to-face?

MEI-LI: Twice a month?

BETH: Last month, we had four. This all dates back to '96, when they discovered some poems attributed to a Japanese A-bomb survivor had actually been written by a white academic in Ohio. I called him in for a meeting just to set eyes on the dumbass. But A-Dot-C didn't really start to worry until last year. That was when—well, you must have heard about the case . . . it wasn't exactly hushed up very effectively.

MEI-LI: I have to admit—I saw or read all of his plays and felt certain they were written by a Chinese man.

BETH: Yes, one of the most effective uses of makeup in theatrical history. At any rate, the rash of copycat authors that followed threatened to undermine the authenticity of all our ethnic publications. So—I hope you can understand why we've had to resort to such rigorous security checks.

MEI-LI: Of course. When I read a work by an Asian American author, I expect it to be authentic.

BETH: Look, we can't sell you as an Asian woman—we can't put your picture on a book jacket—

MEI-LI: Why not?

BETH: Mei-Li, are you going to force me to—?

MEI-LI: In my cheongsam, with my pig tails—maybe if you took a full body shot—or if I stood with my back to the camera—?

BETH: I'm sorry, you're making me do this.

(*She grabs Mei-Li's hair, pulls off a black wig, revealing blond hair beneath.*)

MEI-LI: Give that back to me! This is so unfair.

BETH: It's just business.

MEI-LI: People have always assumed just because I'm blond, that I couldn't possibly be Chinese. Lots of Eurasian children are blond—even some with only one white parent. With me—a quarter Chinese—it's entirely possible that I could look as I do and still be authentic.

(Pause.)

BETH: All right, Mei-Li. if you're absolutely determined to pursue this to the finish—

MEI-LI: Absolutely.

BETH: We have a procedure for just such occasions.

(Two Medical technicians enter with a syringe and rubber band for blood-taking.)

MEI-LI: What's that?

BETH: It takes blood samples. Are you really willing to submit to scientific verification?

MEI-LI: Just out of curiosity, what percentage Asian does an author have to be to receive the A-Dot-C seal of authenticity?

BETH: One-eighth. We consider any figure lower than that to be statistically random.

MEI-LI: Where'd you get the number one-eighth?

BETH: Honestly? Out of thin air. But a major corporation has to draw the line someplace, doesn't it?

(Pause.)

MEI-LI: You know . . . has it ever occurred to you—that even a work written by someone who's one hundred percent non-Asian might be authentic? Or, that one written by a full-blooded Asian might not be? What if the book by the non-Asian was better?

BETH: Don't try and make my life more confusing than it already is.

MEI-LI: What does "authentic" mean anyway? For instance, let's just say—what if we weren't real people, what if we were fictional characters, would we be authentic?

(Pause.)

BETH: Not if we were written by a man.

(A Medical Technician pricks Mei-Li's upper arm with the needle.)

MEI-LI: Ow!

BETH: Look the other way—it always makes life easier. *(As the Medical Technician draws blood)* In the end, Mei-Li, we simply have to draw a line somewhere, to hold back the tides of anarchy. After all, it is the duty of those in power to maintain order.

(The Medical Technicians watch her blood fill the vial.)

EXAMINATION

Craig Lucas

DR. TSANG: Cough.

(A cough.)

Again.

(A cough.)

Okay.

(Dr. Tsang walks away from the patient and makes some notes on the chart.)

You can pull your pants up.

(Very slowly Eric stands, making a great fuss of adjusting his underwear, his belt, his privates, going as slowly as a person could possibly go with this rather quotidian task. It goes on and on and on. Finally, Dr. Tsang looks over at him.)

DR. TSANG: Are you still trying to pull up your pants? All right. I want to do some blood studies, check your cholesterol.
ERIC: I'm HIV-negative.
DR. TSANG: Check for hepatitis. Are you having safe sex?
ERIC: Sometimes I . . . have oral sex without a condom.
DR. TSANG: Uh-huh.
ERIC: I really like the . . .
DR. TSANG: You don't have to justify yourself to me.
ERIC: But surely you have a theory.

DR. TSANG: Statistics seem to show a certain level of transmission through oral sex, but we don't know if those people are reporting truthfully, I can't help you with this one. It's a very personal decision.

ERIC: What do you do?

DR. TSANG: . . .

ERIC: I mean . . .

DR. TSANG: I think it's best for you to make up your mind on this. It's a quality of life issue, finally.

ERIC: I agree. I couldn't live without . . .

DR. TSANG: I understand.

ERIC: Is that what you feel? You couldn't live without . . . ?

DR. TSANG: I . . . I'm sorry, but what makes you think I'm gay, Eric?

ERIC: Just a hunch. I mean, you're very masculine, but . . .

DR. TSANG: Why are you leaving Dr. Giordano?

ERIC: He took too many vacations, the doctor I had before him had no answering machine, you could only call during business hours, or in an emergency. But when I went to Giordano I told him I didn't care finally what the future of medicine was going to be, I wanted a doctor I could call on the weekend if I was upset or paranoid about something, I wanted great care and I would pay for it. Oh, do you take Empire Blue Cross Blue Shield?

(A nod.)

But then he started working for this drug company up in Connecticut and only having office hours on Tuesdays and his secretary wouldn't say where he was and he changed his home number, blah blah blah . . . but I wanted to stay with a gay doctor, so I heard about you.

DR. TSANG: Who recommended you again?

ERIC: Can't remember.

DR. TSANG: I don't make, in this community, I don't make a particularly loud noise about my sexuality. Most of my patients are Chinese, some are gay, but a certain amount goes unsaid.

ERIC: I understand.

(Dr. Tsang looks at his chart.)

DR. TSANG: You're still using Proventil?

ERIC: Yeah, I haven't had any real bouts with it.

(Dr. Tsang gives him some samples of a new inhaler.)

DR. TSANG: Try this.

ERIC: Oh, okay, great.

DR. TSANG: And you're still on the Prilosec?

ERIC: Yeah.

DR. TSANG: Coffee, chocolate—

ERIC AND DR. TSANG: alcohol—

ERIC: I know. I've eliminated the alcohol.

(Pause.)

I try not to eat too late. Do you have a boyfriend?

(Pause.)

DR. TSANG: Not at the moment, I'm dating.

ERIC: Wanna have dinner?

DR. TSANG: Uh, Eric . . . I can't, it isn't

ERIC: Kosher.

DR. TSANG: To date my patients.

ERIC: Right, but you could find me another good doctor if we had a nice date, or two, or ten.

DR. TSANG: Yes, I—

ERIC: I think you're really handsome.

DR. TSANG: You are—not unattractive yourself, Eric.

ERIC: Very politic.

(Pause.)

DR. TSANG: Are you an exhibitionist, is this what you do?

(Headshake.)

ERIC: Never. I knew somebody who dated you—

DR. TSANG: Who?

ERIC: Cuong Huang.

DR. TSANG: Mmm.

(Pause.)

How do you know Cuong.

ERIC: We were in the same fraternity at Brown. I ran into him.

DR. TSANG: Where? No, don't tell me.

(*Pause.*)

ERIC: He told me why it didn't work out—the music you like, how much time you like to spend at home, reading, quiet, how you save your money, how difficult it is for you to . . .

DR. TSANG: ????

ERIC: Express your feelings sometimes. Everything he said was a problem I thought, I've waited my whole life to meet a guy like that. Your interest in the arts.

DR. TSANG: Ah.

ERIC: How much you liked my opera.

(*Pause.*)

DR. TSANG: Is this our first date?

ERIC: I hope so.

(*Pause. Dr. Tsang starts to laugh.*)

DR. TSANG: Do you want me to refer you to someone else or do you want to see how we do on date number two before you reject my medical skills in favor of my . . . reported others.

(*Pause.*)

ERIC: IIII—

(*A middle-aged Asian couple, Tsang's mother and father, appear in the doorway; one of them is holding a large paper bag. The following is in Cantonese:*)

DR. TSANG: Is something wrong?

MOTHER: We brought you some soup.

DR. TSANG: Soup? I'm working.

MOTHER: I know when you take your lunch.

DR. TSANG: You can't, I've asked you not to just show up here like this, it's very unprofessional.

MOTHER: Well, we'll leave it for you.

ERIC: (*English:*) Hi. I'm Eric Toller.

DR. TSANG: (*English:*) This is my mother and father. (*In Cantonese:*) This is my patient, Eric Toller.

(Nods, murmurs.)

ERIC: What kind of . . . what did you bring, it smells good?

DR. TSANG: It's from their restaurant. *(Cantonese:)* You have to go home, I'm not taking lunch today.

MOTHER: What?

DR. TSANG: No lunch, not today. I'll call you. Tonight.

MOTHER: Yes.

FATHER: All right.

DR. TSANG: Good-bye.

(They try to give him the soup.)

No, I won't have time. Take it.

ERIC: I'll / take—

DR. TSANG: Stay out of it.

MOTHER: Good-bye.

(They exit. Short pause.)

DR. TSANG: Sorry.

ERIC: 's okay.

DR. TSANG: No, it's not. That makes me so . . .

ERIC: What?

DR. TSANG: . . . it's complicated.

ERIC: I'd like to hear.

(Dr. Tsang picks up the phone, pushes a button; into the phone:)

DR. TSANG: Is anyone waiting? . . . All right, five minutes.

(Pause.)

I can't understand them, they can't understand me.

ERIC: That's . . . isn't that a sort of de rigueur for parents and children.

DR. TSANG: No, I mean, I don't speak their language, I never learned Cantonese, they've never learned English.

ERIC: How is that possible? You just spoke to them.

DR. TSANG: I can say the most basic of things, observe the most basic rules of formality, understand enough of what they are trying to tell me, but we are complete strangers.

ERIC: I'm sorry, I don't . . . how is that possible?

(Pause.)

I'm sorry.

DR. TSANG: I don't expect you to understand.

ERIC: But I'd like to.

DR. TSANG: You can't.

(Pause.)

ERIC: When did they come to this country?

DR. TSANG: When I was five. From Hong Kong. Six brothers and sisters, I was the oldest, the first to learn to speak English.

ERIC: You must have spoken some Cantonese at that point, more.

DR. TSANG: All my friends spoke English. We were saved from a life, I would, now, by this point, I would be selling trinkets on the street.

ERIC: And look where you . . . I mean—

(Pause. Eric glances out the window.)

Look, there they go across the square.

(Pause.)

DR. TSANG: They told me I couldn't do it. Whenever I said I wanted to try something, debating society, learning French, going to college, medical school: "You'll never be able to do it." They're terrified at any moment everything is going to go away. I have never hugged my father. If you tried to hug my mother she would recoil and think you rude.

ERIC: They know you're gay?

DR. TSANG: I don't know what they know.

ERIC: They . . . they love you, they brought you food.

DR. TSANG: They want to be connected to me, I'm the only one who has stayed here, everyone else has moved away, we're all . . . we love them, but . . .

ERIC: You're embarrassed by them.

DR. TSANG: No. I feel nothing.

(Eric makes a buzzing noise.)

ERIC: No, sorry. You're furious at them?

DR. TSANG: Why would I be furious? They've done everything for me.

ERIC: Everything except love you.

DR. TSANG: They've loved me the only way they knew how, trying to
protect me. Protect me from having anything, from believing . . .

(Pause.)

ERIC: Are you in therapy?

(A nod.)

Me, too.

(Pause.)

Does it help?

(A shrug. Dr. Tsang is on the verge of tears. Beat.)

I'd like you to refer me to another doctor.

(Pause. Which stretches on. They smile at each other.)

MY OLD HABIT PART 2

Mac Wellman

OLD WOMAN: See these shoes?
I bought these very fine shoes on Orchard Road
at C.K. Tang's. Very good shoes. And the
only thing I understand is my old habit of
returning to places. Up there in the sky no one
knew who I was.

My husband talks to his car. My only son
is a devil who works in a factory of other
devils. They make devilmoney by changing people
into noodles and dim sum. Devilnoodles and
devildimsum. All devil stuff. All this scares
me. That's why I want to come home.

That is why the only thing I can remember is my
old habit of returning to places. Places
like this. The land of radishes. The land
of rice. The land of salt. The land of vinegar.
So far away, and yet so near I can still smell
the fabrics.

All I want is to take off my shoes and rest
a little. Will someone take me home?

(Pause. She carefully removes her shoes.)

YOUNG MAN: This is Mister Huang. He is angry at his car. I don't
know why he is angry at his car. Although, he is rich, he is a
person without conscience.

(The Old Man scowls.)

He says his surname is not Huang, so please don't call him Huang.

(They exchange looks.)

Okay, okay. Sorry.

(More looks.)

You shouldn't drink too much wine.

(The Old Man scowls, points to the car.)

He says: You are completely mistaken. *That (Pointing to the car)*
is not my paternal uncle; he is my music teacher. Unintentionally
he lost my hat; he bought me a new one. A strong country can
become weak; a weak country can become strong, he says. He
also says: You and he are also individuals. By "he" he means
the car.

(The Old Man scowls.)

He says: The water of the Yellow River flows very swiftly. He
says: This place is really very bright. *(To Old Man:)* No one can
understand the meaning of life, old man.

(The Old Man is suddenly wistful, a faraway look in his eye.)

The Golden Gate; the city by the Golden Gate.

(Pause. He looks and sees Something in his mind.)

A stone house; the great stone face; a heart made of stone.

(Pause.)

People like long life; they do not like short life. The silvery waves of the ocean are very pretty. A dead horse does not eat grass. I don't know what inanimate objects are.

(Pause. To us:)

The old man passed away last night.

(The Old Man scowls at us, at the car.)

He says: I am an individual.

(Pause.)

He says: You all, and him *(Pointing to car)* are also individuals.

(Pause.)

You see: he is a silly old man. And all he is thinking is silly old man thoughts. He is angry with the car because he thinks it is an individual, like you, like me. He is silly. just look at him. He thinks his car is not behaving responsibly by not starting.

(Pause.)

(To us:) I like to speak to him, but not knowing his surname I don't know what to call him. It is not Huang; I was wrong. *(To Old Man:)* Please, tell me your name; I wish to write you a letter tomorrow. He says: Unexpected success is very expendable. Human society is made up of individuals; therefore that which belongs to individuals also belongs to human society. Young people should rely on their own conscience and talents. I have

lost that nameless book. *(To us:)* I am going to tease that silly old man. *(To Old Man:)* You shouldn't drink too much wine.

OLD MAN: Who is the magistrate in this district?

YOUNG MAN: His name is elephant.

OLD MAN: The elephant is a very large animal.

YOUNG MAN: Why do you stand there doing nothing?

OLD MAN: I was studying at home this morning when I heard someone call me by name. The result of indolence is failure.

YOUNG MAN: Why do you stand here doing nothing?

OLD MAN: Can you see what it is on the horse's back? Yes I can. It is the carcass of a dog. That woman is carrying a small child in her arms.

YOUNG MAN: You are talking the wrong words as before.

OLD MAN: My country produces a lot of copper and tin. The Yellow Emperor lived centuries before Confucius. I have lost that nameless book.

YOUNG MAN: Silly old man, you drink too much wine.

(The Old Man wistful once more.)

He says: I see the silvery waves on the ocean in the moonlight. I see the girl with the very short hair. I see a man with white eyebrows. A noseless cow; a toothless dog.

(Pause.)

The nose is above the upper lip. The tongue is in the mouth. My car is very old. Very old. The trains are going to the East. Yesterday I bought a new car. One cow; one calf.

(Pause. He turns, scowls at the car. The Young Man whispers eerily, speaking the Old Man's innermost thoughts, slowly:)

Does the man have a dog? A sheep? A cow? A little dog does not see the two calves on the mountain. There are two gates at the foot of the mountain. Do dogs have hands? Do dogs have feet? Are dogs men? No, dogs are not men.

(Scowling Old Man turns, grabs car.)

HANDSOME

Diana Son

Mrs. Lillian Baldwin sits on a bench in the town square. Chee Kwan runs to catch up with her, carrying several shopping bags. He wears Chinese servant clothes and has a long queue that runs down his back.

CHEE KWAN: Teacheress! I sorry, so sorry.

MRS. BALDWIN: Oh, Chee Kwan, there's no need to apologize. Of course you should buy things you need for yourself. Now sit down and show me what you bought. A toy to send home to your precious daughter? A hair ribbon for your lovely wife?

(Chee Kwan pulls out a large pair of scissors, the size of garden shears.)

Father in heaven!

(Chee Kwan snaps them open and shut.)

CHEE KWAN: *(Imitating the sound)* Clik!

MRS. BALDWIN: What do you intend to do with those?

CHEE KWAN: Teacheress, I want to cut off my queue.

MRS. BALDWIN: No, no, Chee Kwan. They only cut off the queues of the Chinese who are criminals. Those men are marked for a reason.

CHEE KWAN: Not short like the bristles of a brush but . . . dignified . . . handsome. Like your husband and Dr. Sullivan and Professor Mead.

MRS. BALDWIN: No, dear boy, you don't understand. You shouldn't cut off your queue any more than you should wear Western clothes. God made you a Chinaman and that was no mistake. You are industrious beyond any other people, patient under trial, cheerful under burdens, literary, pious—knowing your people as well as I do I say it is no wonder that the Creator has made one third of the human race after the Chinese pattern and less than seventy million Americans.

CHEE KWAN: How many handsome Chinamen you know?

(Pause.)

MRS. BALDWIN: The Father of this country wore a queue—

CHEE KWAN: President Washington? He is ugly worse than Chinaman.

MRS. BALDWIN: Many of our finest young ladies wear their hair in queues these days. Look around the square.

(Chee Kwan turns so that his queue is facing her.)

CHEE KWAN: Cut it for me, yes? You do / it.

MRS. BALDWIN: Chee Kwan, if you cut off your queue, you can't go back to China. The Manchus—

CHEE KWAN: Why should the Manchus control me even here?

MRS. BALDWIN: You have to go back to get your family. You've always talked of doing it.

CHEE KWAN: I send them money.

MRS. BALDWIN: You can't expect your wife to travel alone with your daughter, you know better.

CHEE KWAN: I don't want them here.

MRS. BALDWIN: It's a difficult time for the Chinese in America, I know, but I will help you and your family.

CHEE KWAN: Why would you?

MRS. BALDWIN: Because I am fond of your people, haven't I shown that to you?

CHEE KWAN: I am fond of you.

(Pause.)

MRS. BALDWIN: And I of you, Chee Kwan, you are a gentle, courteous—

CHEE KWAN: I want to be handsome for you.

MRS. BALDWIN: —and diligent in your Christian studies.

CHEE KWAN: I am Christian for you.

MRS. BALDWIN: I marvel at your humble, wonderful prayers praising God for the beauties of this world and the wonders of his grace—

CHEE KWAN: You have touched me.

MRS. BALDWIN: Thank you, Chee Kwan—

CHEE KWAN: In my sleep. You come up to my bedroom and you touch me.

MRS. BALDWIN: I have a great deal of affection for you of course. You're a tender nanny for my beloved little boy.

CHEE KWAN: You move the shirt away from my breast and look at me. Blow on my chest. And touch it.

MRS. BALDWIN: You are speaking of the time you had that terrible cold. You wouldn't let me call Dr. Sullivan so I snuck into your room and rubbed a salve on your chest. You were better the next day but you never knew why. I'd have thought you'd notice the smell of mint but—

CHEE KWAN: You come several nights a week. In your bedclothes after Mr. Baldwin is asleep.

MRS. BALDWIN: Now that is a lie.

CHEE KWAN: And you rub your lips against my cheek.

MRS. BALDWIN: I won't hear any more of it.

CHEE KWAN: I wait for it.

MRS. BALDWIN: Be silent.

CHEE KWAN: But I am embarrassed to kiss back. I feel ugly and Chinese.

MRS. BALDWIN: No, Chee Kwan, no. You're beautiful.

(*Pause.*)

I love your hair. I want to see it unbraided and hanging long around you. Trickling down onto your hairless chest. I want to eat it.

CHEE KWAN: (*Turned on*) American Woman—

MRS. BALDWIN: You cannot cut your hair.

CHEE KWAN: Yes I must.

MRS. BALDWIN: Darling don't.

CHEE KWAN: I will never go back to China, to the Manchus, to my family and wife. I stay here with you.

MRS. BALDWIN: We can meet in the carriage house every afternoon while Peter is napping and Mr. Baldwin is still at work.

CHEE KWAN: I will wear Western clothes.

MRS. BALDWIN: You could wear suits of Mr. Baldwin's that he's outgrown.

CHEE KWAN: Yes.

MRS. BALDWIN: I'll have them taken up and in.

CHEE KWAN: That would be very handsome.

MRS. BALDWIN: I think it will be.

(*Chee Kwan hands her the scissors.*)

CHEE KWAN: Cut it and I'll be free from everyone but you.

(*Mrs. Baldwin takes the scissors and pinches them at the base of his queue. She rears up as if she were about to press, then pulls them away. Chee Kwan turns to her.*)

Darling—?

(Mrs. Baldwin hands him the scissors.)

MRS. BALDWIN: Do me first.

CHEE KWAN: What?

MRS. BALDWIN: *(Turns so her long hair faces him)* Cut my hair, cut me bald.

CHEE KWAN: No, my little dove.

MRS. BALDWIN: Yes. I don't want to be beautiful to anyone but you.

CHEE KWAN: But, you are beautiful to me, my darling . . . as you are.

MRS. BALDWIN: Signifies, Chee Kwan, do you know what that means?

CHEE KWAN: Your long hair signifies great beauty to me.

MRS. BALDWIN: Cutting your queue signifies an enormous commitment to me. Leaving your family, defying your culture. I want to show the same commitment to you.

CHEE KWAN: *(He takes her hands and kisses them)* Devoted, courageous woman . . . I like your hair the way it is.

MRS. BALDWIN: But don't you see what it'll say. With short hair I'll be free of everyone but you.

CHEE KWAN: But I will be handsome with short hair.

(Mrs. Baldwin takes the scissors from Chee Kwan. Without ceremony, she cuts off his queue. She hands it to him)

MRS. BALDWIN: Pick up those bags, look at how much time I've lost waiting for you. The next time you want to buy things for yourself, you can make a separate trip into town. Mr. Baldwin will be home in two hours. I want you to make his favorite for dinner tonight.

CHEE KWAN: Elizabeth, my dove—

MRS. BALDWIN: No, roast lamb.

(She starts off.)

Hurry along, now. Chop chop—

(Chee Kwan picks up the bags as she exits. He looks after her then the opposite way deciding which path to follow. He starts off after Mrs. Baldwin.)

SCISSORS

Chay Yew

A: Mister Richard?

B: Building.

A: Mister Derek.

B: Bridge.

A: Manhattan?

B: Brooklyn.

A: Ah I see. Missus Mathilda?

B: Gunshot wound.

A: Temple?

B: No. Mouth.

A: Fitting end. That one always had big mouth.

B: Yes. Remember how she ordered you around to fetch her things—

A: "Boy, fetch my mink stole—"

B: "Boy, fetch my smelling salts—"

A: "Boy, fetch my necklace—"

B: "Boy, fetch my husband—"

(*A and B laugh. Beat.*)

A: Mrs. Mathilda dead. Sometimes there is God.

B: No, not God. Stock market.

(*Pause.*)

A: You?

B: What do you mean?

A: Stock market.

(*Pause.*)

B: I'm fine—

A: What do you mean "fine"—

B: I'm fine—

A: Sir, is there something I should know?—

B: You don't have to call me "sir" anymore.

A: Habit.

B: I know, George.

A: George not my name.

B: I gave you that name.

A: Because you never can remember my real name.

B: No I can't. What do they call you here?

A: Nothing. They no speak to me here. I stranger here.

(Silence, except for the snip snip of the scissors.)

You invest?

B: What are you talking about?

A: Stock market. You invest?

(Pause.)

B: Yes.

A: And?

B: I'm fine. The company's—unscratched.

A: I no worry about you. But your children. Monsters. They never listen to you. Always try to take away your company—

B: Everything's fine. I'm fine. Stop nagging, Okay?

A: Okay.

(Silence, except for the snip snip of the scissors.)

B: Look, in fact, I made out like a bandit in the crash. To celebrate, I went straight to Beau Brummel and bought myself a new red suit. I'm wearing it right now.

(A feels B's black suit.)

A: Red suit?

B: It's the latest fashion to Charleston in.

A: What is this Charleston?

B: A dance in four/four time. It's the rage all over the world.

A: Dancing at your age?

(B hums a rapid melodious tune and pretends to dance the Charleston while sitting down.)

(Laughing:) Stop! Stop! Stop! You getting senile!

B: You should see the suit! It's dapper!

A: I blind. *(Beat)* I would love to see you dance Charleston.

B: It's quite a sight.

A: Maybe you teach me Charleston.

B: Sure. I can teach it to you.

A: We can do it here.

B: Where everyone can see.

A: It will be quite a sight.

(Silence, except for the snip snip of the scissors.)

How they treating you? The monsters.

B: Like a child. Can't do this. Can't do that. The only thing they allow me to do, on my own, is to take the tram here every Sunday—

A: The tram? You say Harold take you—

B: Did I say the tram? I meant to say that they allow me to use the driver on Sundays. I am getting senile. How about your monsters?

A: The same. They work too hard. Sometimes I help out at their provision shop on Bayard Street. What little I can. I know they want me out of way. They say "Ah Pa, you spend whole life working, now time for you to relax, slow down." Which mean you too old, you blind, get out of way. Funny, these children first need you all the time. Now suddenly, they don't need you anymore. If I relax, slow down, I will die.

B: I know the feeling.

(Silence, except for the snip snip of the scissors.)

A: They looking over here again?

B: Yes.

A: You know, I give them something to talk about. Blind Chinaman cutting kwai loh's hair in middle of Columbus Park.

B: You don't have to cut my hair.

A: I need to.

(Silence, except for the snip snip of the scissors.)

B: You know, I go to sleep hearing this.

A: Hearing what?

B: This. The snip snips of your scissors. The tiny snip snips. Precise. Clean. The endless restless murmur of metal blades. It immediately comforts me. Forces me to surrender my body, my soul, to the serenity of the snip snips. Makes me drift away from this world. Surface in another quite unlike this one.

(Snip snip of the scissors.)

Snip snip. Snip snip. Can you hear it? What sounds do you sleep to?

A: Yelling, laughing. Drunk people in saloon across the street. Click clack click clack sound of mahjong tiles next door. Screaming screaming. Children running up down up down the road.

B: You know you can come back and live with me—

A: Silly fool. Your monsters, my monsters won't like. A Chinaman living with you. It upset their world.

B: I can speak to them.

A: You don't understand. It no longer our world.

(Silence, except for the snip snip of the scissors.)

B: Oh, listen. Do you need any money? I've got some—

A: I okay.

(B digs into his pockets, fishes out a wallet and takes out some money.)

B: Here take some—

A:I say I okay—

B: Take it—

A: No—

B: I want you to have it—

A: I have enough. You keep it.

B: Take—

(A slaps the bills out of B's hand. A immediately goes down on his knees feeling the ground for the money. B looks at A for a beat. B helps A to pick up the money. A finds the money and thrusts the bills back to B's hands. A and B resume their routine. Silence, except for the snip snip of the scissors.)

I'm sorry.

A: It's okay.

B: It's not. I always—

A: I know.

B: I just want you to be—

A: I know.

(A pats B on the shoulder. Silence. A resumes cutting B's hair. Suddenly A winces in pain.)

Ouch!

B: What's wrong?
A: Cut myself.
B: Let me see.

(*B takes A's hand into his own.*)

A: It's okay.
B: Let me take a look at it.
A: It's okay. Really.

(*B places his mouth over A's cut, licking his wound tenderly. A is still.*)

They looking.
B: They are not looking.
A: I see them looking.
B: Let them look.
A: I live here. You don't.
B: Iron.
A: What?
B: Your blood. It tastes like iron.

(*Slowly B withdraws his mouth from A's hand. A's hand makes a slow and deliberate study of B's face.*)

A: You getting old.
B: Is that a fact?
A: I miss feeling your face.
B: Yes.
A: Different, but yet still same. The same.
B: They're looking.
A: Let them look.

(*A slowly retrieves his hand and starts cutting B's hair again. Silence, except for the snip snip of the scissors. B looks at his watch.*)

What time?
B: About five.
A: Five.

(*Silence, except for the snip snip of the scissors.*)

B: I should get going.

A: So soon?

B: I've got a board meeting early tomorrow morning.

A: Board meeting?

B: Correspondences to catch up on. Product meetings to organize. So on and so forth.

(Silence, except for the snip snip of the scissors.)

A: You should stop working. At your age. Work yourself to—

B: I know. I know.

(Silence, except for the snip snip of the scissors.)

There's Harold.

(B waves to no one. Everyone in the park looks at him bewilderedly.)

He's waving to me. It's time to go.

(B calls out to no one.)

In a moment, Harold!

A: Harold the driver?

B: Yes.

A: Harold still working for you?

B: Yes.

A: Really?

B: Really.

(Pause.)

A: Call him over.

B: Some other time.

A: I want to say hello to him.

B: Some other time.

A: No, I want to—

B: I said some other time!

(Pause.)

A: Okay. Some other time.

(*Silence.*)

B: See you next week?
A: Yes. Of course.

(*Silence.*)

B: Sunday?
A: For another trim.
B: Yes.

(*Silence.*)

A: Sunday.
B: Sunday.

(*A and B don't move.*)

kismet, in a square on a wedding day in spring

Bridget Carpenter

JIN-HE:

HATS!
ART HATS FOR SALE!
I'VE GOT A HAT FOR YOU! CHECK IT OUT! BELIEVE IT!
WEAR YOUR ART!
My mother's not here right now.
She's upstairs. She has an apartment across the street, over-looking the park.

Today's her wedding day.
This is a bridesmaid hat. I made it.

My mom's getting married and I'm the bridesmaid.
That is fucked up.
You see that sculpture over there? The hollow steel square?
My mother made that.

Yeah, it is. It is beautiful. Everyone loves it.
I asked her what it meant once, and she said,
(*Imitating mother:*) "Ohhh . . . square's waiting to be filled . . . all the time."
My mother, the fifty-two-year-old Korean flower child.

"Today is beautiful, yeees? Ohh yes! And this week is a good week, early this week I meet new people, new neighbor, very nice, very nice, his name is Andeee Warhol!!! You know Andeee Warhol?" I say, yes, I know of Andy Warhol. And she says, "I make him some coffee and we have a nice talk, and we talk about DRUG CULTURE! You know about Drug Culture?" I say, yes, I have heard about drug culture. And she says, "And then Nico come over, you know Nico?" Not personally. "And his other friends come over, and one friend give me marijuana and you know what?" What, mom. "I try it! It make me laaaugh!"

God.
She tries everything, it makes her laaaaugh.

Destiny.
That's my mother's name. Destiny.
Her name before was Unyun.
"But on the day I get married, I'm Destiny now! Your mother is your Destiny!"

Warhol's up there taking pictures. He's going to make a silk-screen for a wedding present. I guess he's really particular about his wig, and he got mad. I just wanted him to try it on for a second. People need to be open to experience art.

My mother came here in her teens to marry my dad, who was some ancient neighbor of her parents. When she was sixteen she got shipped off to the States. Like a care package. She got married, no questions asked, and she got pregnant, no questions asked, and then he died. And then she had me.

So my mother's this newcomer to New York City and she doesn't speak the language and she can't read English and she has a baby and she's living with my dead father's sisters, who hate her.

And she becomes a cleaning woman. For Betty Parsons.

Yeah, that Betty Parsons.

Betty owned this gallery and represented Jackson Pollock, and de Kooning, and Stills, and Rothko. And my mother was, like, de Kooning's maid. And eventually my mother moved to the Village, and she learned to read, and she raised me, and—you wouldn't believe it unless you were sitting right in front of it— she became an artist. But not an artist like any of them. Not like the men. My mother looked at their art, and she said, "Ooohh, so many lines," And she took out almost all the lines, and she painted squares.
Just squares. Four lines each. Clean. Simple. Sharp right angles: four of them. That's all. And she painted squares for a long time, and people started to notice those clean four lines, all of them connected. And people started buying her squares. And then she started welding squares. My mother, the Korean widow; my mother, the flower child; my mother the artist; my mother the welder.

They installed it here in the park last summer. Everyone came; the mayor came, Andy Warhol and everyone from the Factory came and everyone from her first husband's family came—even the sisters who hated her—and we all drank champagne and looked at my mother's square.

When I ask her why squares, she says, "Four lines!" And I say, well, you know, but isn't "four" unlucky . . . I mean, isn't the number four related to death . . . and she says, "But you begin with four lines, and then there is what you put inside! So that not unlucky, that's verrry lucky, because there are so many other things inside four lines!

She titled that square "Jin-He."
That's my name.

Have you ever realized you're happy, while you're happy? Not remembered it, but understood it at the time?

Me either.

But I was watching my mother from across the room, my crazy fearless mother, and I suddenly felt her blood running like quicksilver through my own veins. And I saw her, Destiny, my mother, my ma with her enormous smile, and I felt certainty descending upon me, warm, like the morning sun. And watching her, I had a flash—of something, of euphoria maybe.

Anything can happen. That's what I thought; that's all. But it seemed so large. I wanted to come outside and sit and look at the square. Waiting to be filled.

Anything is possible. Isn't it? Don't you think?

Act Two

EXCERPTS FROM THE DIARY OF
A CHINESE ENVOY

Ping Chong

ASIAN MALE: May 12th

Bright with sunshine

Went by carriage at seven in the evening to a theatre some five li away to attend an excellent performance about a journey beneath the sea. The effects at different levels—moonlit isles, a swim through fishland, dragon fairies—were incredibly well contrived. I was transported.

WHITE FEMALE: May 16th

Clear

We arrived in Washington, the capital of the United States, at five in the afternoon at the Metropolitan Hotel on Pennsylvania Avenue, where we stayed. The men servants and maids are descended from Africans brought over 200 years ago. They have shining black faces, silvery white teeth and thick wiry hair. They are called blacks by the Westerners. For as soon as the British acquired America in the early sixteenth century they set about supplying its under-developed vastness by means of cheap African slave trade, paying as little as one foot of figured silk a head.

ASIAN MALE: June 6th

> Hot, then thunder

> I am told shaking hands, brushing cheeks and kissing are exchanges of civility by making bodies come together. When Westerners meet friends or relatives they touch their hands to their lips instead. I have also heard that the way to kiss requires making a chirping sound. In the Western language it is called "qiasi." Those who do not know how to translate say the sound is like fish drinking water, but this is wrong. When immoral men and women encounter each other on the street, they suck the back of their own left hand and suck the five fingers of their right hand. After sucking they put the fingers on the left palm and blow toward the other as they part smiling. Such behavior, I am told is wanton in the extreme.

ASIAN FEMALE: June 20th

> Light rain

> Drove some way in the evening to see a sham-black show. Nine white men disguised themselves as blacks and lined up on stage playing strange dissonant music to accompany stranger songs. The rain cleared at once, a radiant moon.

ASIAN MALE: June 21st

> Dull with overcast

> I have heard that Americans have an unofficial form of punishment known as "lynching" with which to treat blacks. It started with a farmer named Lynch. Because he had been offended by a black, he suspended him from a tree to wait for the police officers to arrive, but the black man died before they came. So his name has been used for this ever since. Recently another common practice is burning black people to death. Whenever a black has committed an offense a mob will be directly gathered and burn him without going through the courts.

ASIAN FEMALE: July 18th

> Sunny and shining

> Recently the treatment of blacks in America has been carried over to the yellow people. When a cobra is unable to release its poison fully it vents its rage by biting wood and grass. Afterwards, no one touches the poisoned branches will escape death. We the yellow people, have we touched its dead branches? Of the Americans, the more calculating ones are alarmed at the entrepreneurial spirit of the Chinese. They have fanned the flames of bigotry successfully shutting out our people from all but the

most menial work. Are we to be the new American slaves now that the blacks have been freed?

ASIAN MALE: July 20th

Clear, light rain at 1:30

At Western dinner parties men and women usually attend together (contrary to Chinese custom), but you may not sit next to your wife. There may be someone you know well who will sit with her to convey his respects, or wives may politely talk to each other as an expression of attentiveness. If you find yourself seated next to a female guest, when the meal is over you should say to her, "I am honored by ma-dam's kindness; may I be permitted to take your arm?" If she gives you permission, use your right hand to hold her left arm and accompany her to the living room. If she wants to stroll, walk slowly with her. If she wants to sit down, you should take her to a chair; after she is seated, she will thank you and you should then bow politely in return and step away. If you want to leave, you must wait until all the female guests have left before you can thank your host and say good-bye . . .

MY OLD HABIT PART 3

Mac Wellman

OLD WOMAN: Have you seen my son—? He has my shoes, very nice satin pumps. I got them on Orchard Road at C.K. Tang's. Why are you looking at me that way? They are very nice shoes and my son is a hoodlum. Or worse.

(*Shoes get taken.*)

Have you seen my son—? He has my shoes, very nice satin pumps. I got them on Orchard Road at C.K. Tang's. Why are you looking at me that way? They are very nice shoes and my son is a hoodlum. Or worse.

THE SPOT

Robert O'Hara

BLACK WOMAN: what you sayyo name was?

ASIAN WOMAN: ming.

BLACK WOMAN: I ain't never heard of nobody named ming.

ASIAN WOMAN: I ain't never heard of nobody named shakella.

(Silence.)

BLACK WOMAN: I know five people on my block named shakella . . . same as me . . .

ASIAN WOMAN: my grandmother and cousin are both named ming.

(Silence.)

BLACK WOMAN: well listen *ming* I'm holding this spot right here for some friends . . . we been waiting to see the reverend dr. speak for a year and a half now . . .

ASIAN WOMAN: same as me

BLACK WOMAN: what you mean same as you?

ASIAN WOMAN: I'm holding this spot also . . . my friends waiting for the reverend dr. as well . . .

BLACK WOMAN: well the two of us can't hold this same spot

ASIAN WOMAN: why not?

BLACK WOMAN: why not? . . . I don't know how they do it over there in them slant eye lands but it ain't *communal* or whatsinever *over here* . . . it ain't share and share alike *over here* . . . this my spot and my friends are expecting me to be holding them a large enough spot for all of them to fit . . .

ASIAN WOMAN: what's a slant eye land?

BLACK WOMAN: you know *(She slants her eyes)* slant eyes . . . china or hawai'i or whatsinever

ASIAN WOMAN: hawai'i american

BLACK WOMAN: they still slant eyes

ASIAN WOMAN: so what you call africa? . . . *big lip land?*

(Silence.)

BLACK WOMAN: you lookin for a fight?

ASIAN WOMAN: just holding my spot . . .

BLACK WOMAN: I don told you this ain't yo spot.

ASIAN WOMAN: we share.

BLACK WOMAN: we don't share *over here*!

ASIAN WOMAN: why do you keep saying *over here*? what's *over there*?

BLACK WOMAN: over *here* is americans over *there* where you come from is *slant eyes*

ASIAN WOMAN: so brooklyn is *slant eyes too*?

(*Silence.*)

BLACK WOMAN: is you looking for a fight *lady*?

ASIAN WOMAN: no fight. just my spot . . .

BLACK WOMAN: *MY spot! dammit!*

(*Silence.*)

and you don't come from no damn Brooklyn

ASIAN WOMAN: how you know? you live in my house with me and my husband?

BLACK WOMAN: you live in brooklyn?

ASIAN WOMAN: yes. where do you live?

BLACK WOMAN: noneya

ASIAN WOMAN: where's noneya?

BLACK WOMAN: noneya bizness . . .

ASIAN WOMAN: you live at a bizness?

BLACK WOMAN: it ain't none of yo bizness where I live at

ASIAN WOMAN: I answer your question. you should answer mine . . .

BLACK WOMAN: I come from brooklyn lady . . . okay . . . but I was talking about where you was *born* when I said you don't come from brooklyn . . .

ASIAN WOMAN: born in brooklyn.

BLACK WOMAN: you was what?

ASIAN WOMAN: born and raised in brooklyn . . . prospect park . . .

BLACK WOMAN: bullshit.

ASIAN WOMAN: I never saw a bull shitting in prospect park?

(*Silence.*)

BLACK WOMAN: you fucking with me ain't you . . .

ASIAN WOMAN: no fuck women. I like men. I'm married . . .

(*Silence.*)

you fuck women?

BLACK WOMAN: WOMAN IS YOU CRAZY WILL YOU PLEASE LEAVE ME ALONE?!!!

(*A black officer appears.*)

officer!!! officer!!!

(*Officer comes over to women. Officer approaches Asian Woman.*)

excuse me officer but I'm the one called you over this woman here is harassing me when all I'm trying to do is wait quietly here for a few hours until my friends show up . . . could you please tell her something please . . .

(*The Officer kisses Asian Woman.*)

ASIAN WOMAN: hey honey . . .
BLACK WOMAN: you gotta be kiddin me . . .
ASIAN WOMAN: shakella meet my husband . . . ben
OFFICER: nice to meet you shakella

(*Silence.*)

you can speak to me if you like . . . I understand english
BLACK WOMAN: I ain't got nuthin to say to you
ASIAN WOMAN: but you were so talk-talk earlier?

(*Silence.*)

(*To Officer:*) honey do you think they might let me use the rest-rooms over there . . .
OFFICER: ask officer michael over there to open one of the port-o-potties . . .
ASIAN WOMAN: save my spot.

(*They kiss. Asian Woman leaves. Silence. The Black Woman glares at the officer. She rolls her eyes and looks away.*)

BLACK WOMAN: that's the problem with the black man today.
OFFICER: what is that?
BLACK WOMAN: don't give a damn about his own people . . . I could understand a white woman . . . I wouldn't like it . . . but I could

understand it . . . BUT a slant eye? they ain't got no kinda shape
. . . knock-kneed short and—

OFFICER: slant eye?

BLACK WOMAN: don't play dumb nigga you know what I'm talking
about . . .

(Silence.)

OFFICER: what if I were to tell you that I asked that nice asian woman
to come over here and find out your name for me because
I wanted to come over and ask you out on a date later on after the
rally . . . would you understand me then?

(Silence.)

BLACK WOMAN: that's not true . . .

OFFICER: that's the problem with the black woman today . . .

BLACK WOMAN: what is that?

OFFICER: don't trust the black man enough . . .

(Silence. The Asian Woman comes back.)

BLACK WOMAN: *ming* is this yo husband or not?

ASIAN WOMAN: you like him?

BLACK WOMAN: it ain't about what I like or don't like . . .

(The Asian Woman and Officer kiss strongly.)

that's nasty

ASIAN WOMAN: you like him?

BLACK WOMAN: no I don't like him!

ASIAN WOMAN: you *like* him!

*(Silence. The Officer goes to the Black Woman. Pause. The
Officer kisses the Black Woman. Asian Woman smiles.)*

OFFICER: you *like*?

BLACK WOMAN: what is it with you two? is this some type of—

ASIAN WOMAN: you know what they say about black men . . . look
here at his *hands*

(The officer holds his hand out to Black Woman.)

and his feet.

(The officer shows his bare feet to the Black Woman.)

OFFICER: nice huh?

BLACK WOMAN: I've seen black feet and black hands before.

ASIAN WOMAN: but have you seen *asian* feet and hands . . . ?

(The Asian Woman shows her hands and bare feet.)

BLACK WOMAN: y'all need help . . . professional help . . . and quick
 . . . by the way . . . I think you kissing me I could get you fired
 for—

ASIAN WOMAN: show us your feet.

BLACK WOMAN: what?

ASIAN WOMAN: come on show us your feet . . .

BLACK WOMAN: No!

OFFICER: we showed you ours

ASIAN WOMAN: *FEET!!! FEET!!!*

OFFICER: FEET!!! FEET!!!

BLACK WOMAN: Shut up!

ASIAN WOMAN AND OFFICER: *FEET FEET FEET FEET!!!!*

*(Violently, the Black Woman takes off her shoes and shows them
her bare feet.)*

hands!

*(The Black Woman sticks her hands out to them . . . the Asian
Woman takes one hand while the officer takes the other . . . they
begin massaging her hands.)*

BLACK WOMAN: what the . . . hey . . . mmmhhhmmm . . . that feels
 good . . .

ASIAN WOMAN *(Asian)*: ancient chinese secret . . .

(They start rubbing the Black Woman all over her body.)

BLACK WOMAN: what is this?

OFFICER: free love.

ASIAN WOMAN: wanna come home with us . . . ?

BLACK WOMAN: no I—

ASIAN WOMAN *(Asian)*: we love you long time . . .

BLACK WOMAN: why are you speaking like that?

ASIAN WOMAN: you no like?

BLACK WOMAN: no . . . I mean yes . . . I like but . . . I've never . . . I don't think I should . . .

ASIAN WOMAN: we make big lip slant eye babies . . .

BLACK WOMAN: *people can see!!!!*

(*They stop.*)

ASIAN WOMAN: you know what they say about asian women? wanna see? we have *tight*—

BLACK WOMAN: *NOOOOO!!!!!*

(*Silence.*)

ASIAN WOMAN: ssshhhhhhhh you wake up whole neighborhood

OFFICER: I'll go see if anybody's coming . . .

(*Officer exits. Silence.*)

BLACK WOMAN: I can't believe I let you guys do that to me . . .

ASIAN WOMAN: believe it.

BLACK WOMAN: what is the world coming to?

ASIAN WOMAN: shit.

(*Silence.*)

BLACK WOMAN: why are you here?

ASIAN WOMAN: I tell you . . . I'm waiting for spot to hear reverend dr. . . . why you here?

BLACK WOMAN: same as you *MARTIN LUTHER KING RALLY!!!*

(*Silence.*)

ASIAN WOMAN: martin luther king not speak here.

BLACK WOMAN: yes he will

ASIAN WOMAN: this chinatown

BLACK WOMAN: I know . . . and he's speaking here tomorrow . . .

ASIAN WOMAN: no he spoke here this morning . . .

BLACK WOMAN: no he didn't . . .

ASIAN WOMAN: yes he did . . .

BLACK WOMAN: no he—

(*The Black Woman stops herself and checks her pocket . . . she reads a flyer and realizes.*)

shit!!!

ASIAN WOMAN: that's what the world is coming to . . . I told you it's coming to—

BLACK WOMAN: you let me wait here all this time

ASIAN WOMAN: you let yourself wait here . . .

BLACK WOMAN: you knew I had the dates wrong

ASIAN WOMAN: I knew you wanted your spot and didn't want to share

BLACK WOMAN: why didn't you tell me I had the dates *wrong*?!!

ASIAN WOMAN: you never ask . . .

(*Silence.*)

BLACK WOMAN: slant eye.

ASIAN WOMAN: big lip

BLACK WOMAN: gook

ASIAN WOMAN: spook

BLACK WOMAN: oriental!

ASIAN WOMAN: colored!!

BLACK WOMAN: chink!!!!

ASIAN WOMAN: nigger!!!

(*They begin to fight. A voice off stage is heard.*)

VOICE: *Scene!*

(*The women stop fighting . . . house lights come up. The women start looking toward the audience where they see the origin of the voice . . . it is the Officer.*)

OFFICER: so how do you *feel*?

(*Silence.*)

SHAKELLA: I don't know I mean . . . I think I'm okay . . .

MING: yeah . . . it was strange there for a minute but . . .

OFFICER: but what? . . .

SHAKELLA: are people really like that? . . .

MING: worse.

OFFICER: she right . . . you have to be prepared for just about anything . . . and I mean ANYTHING when you're undercover . . . we have to be able to infiltrate any group and bring back as much information as possible on those white folks black folks yellow folks . . . and you have to be able to stand your ground when someone comes up to you . . . we chose you two because you're like beacons . . . you will attract a large number of curiosity seekers wanting to know what you're doing—some of them may be nice in one breath and sexual predators in the next . . .

MING: how was my accent?

OFFICER: it was good . . . that's your secret weapon ming . . .

SHAKELLA: the feet thing threw me for a second . . .

OFFICER: that's why I came in . . . I *wanted* to throw you . . . that's the nature of improv . . . anything can happen . . . okay . . . show me your weapons . . .

(The women pull out guns, hidden in their clothing and/or purses.)

good . . . that's the last resort . . .

MING: why won't the president acknowledge our division? . . .

OFFICER: the climate isn't right for him to be aware of two special agents being women and minority

MING: what about you? . . .

SHAKELLA: yeah you're *black*

OFFICER: you just think I'm black . . . this washes of with soap . . .

(Silence.)

if I showed you my true identity . . . nations would fall . . .

SHAKELLA: they did a good job on your feet and hands . . .

OFFICER: we try . . .

MING: but why can't we practice with *real racists*?

OFFICER: they're all busy . . .

(The women look at each other.)

ming?

MING: yes sir?

OFFICER: how about this time you start . . . same park . . . same time . . . but in the next round I want you to be the aggressor . . . provoke as much racial animosity as possible . . . shakella you have to be prepared to take it . . .

SHAKELLA: I can take it . . .

MING: we'll see about that . . .

OFFICER: okay . . . agents . . . to your *mark* . . .

(*The women go back to their original places . . . the houselights go out . . . silence.*)

ASIAN WOMAN: this my spot . . . get lost . . .
BLACK WOMAN: can't we share? . . . share the same spot? . . .

PEDIATRICS

José Rivera

PETE *(To the Girl)*: We're not gonna hurt you.
MIKE: Wanna bet?
PETE: Shut up. Don't scare her.
LIZZY: Let's cut off her hair and tie it around her neck and see if she dies the way a normal human dies or maybe their hearts are made all different and they don't got souls like we do.
PETE: They got souls, you *stupid*. As long as she's baptized she's got a soul.
MIKE: You been baptized?
GIRL: I'm lost. The streets are badly designed. The buildings all look the same. I can't read the signs!
LIZZY: What a noise!

(*Lizzy does a grotesque imitation of the Girl's Chinese.*)

MIKE: Baptized is the holy water pissed on your head and the water burns up the devil's ass and the devil evacuates your body and you get cleansed and shit.
PETE *(To Mike)*: You are *emphatically* a barbarian!

(*Lizzy repeats her incomprehensible imitation of Chinese.*)

GIRL: I don't speak that language! I know you're mocking me! I know that!
MIKE: It's not a baptized creature this yellow girl. I can tell. There's devil prints in her black eyes. The devil's footprints marking his territory and his bride.

PETE (*To Mike*): How did I become friends with you?

GIRL: I'm sorry I can't speak with you yet! Find someone who understands!

LIZZY: It would be worthwhile examining her vocal chords. See if they vibrate left to right or what?

PETE: Don't listen to these macabre morons, they don't have no learning and they were raised by cockroach parents.

LIZZY (*To Pete*): I'll kick your ass for that!

PETE: Get yourself some civilization, Lizzy!

LIZZY: You just wanna touch her thing!

PETE: Do not!

LIZZY: Stick your little finger up her pizza pie!

(*Lizzy and Pete box.*)

MIKE (*To the Girl*): Okay, you're unbaptized, you get whammed by a truck, body sent flying into a ditch, heart stops, soul flies outta your nostrils—*then* what? Heaven? What's heaven in your yellow mind? What's up there? God? You have a God in your universe? Jesus Christ? Who says hello to you your first day of your new afterlife? Who do you pray to? Who watches your actions and counts your sins? You have sin? Or do you unbaptized mothers have blanket immunity to kill and rape and lie and rip off customers at the laundry?

(*Lizzy socks Pete in the nose. He falls, bleeding.*)

PETE: Hooker!

LIZZY: Sissy!

PETE (*Touching his bloody nose*): That's called *bloody* you hump!

LIZZY: I'm the boss on this street. I say we take the lost soul over here and *dissect* her. See what her anatomy is *like*.

PETE: No, Lizzy . . .

LIZZY: Shut up. This is my street. All of you are visitors on my street.

GIRL: Don't touch me!

LIZZY: Can it, whore. Who's got a knife? Who's got a KNIFE?

MIKE: I don't have it on me.

LIZZY: Go *get* it!

MIKE: You're fulla shit, Lizzy!

(*Lizzy boxes Mike.*)

PETE *(To Girl)*: I'm not trying to tell you what way to live your own life. But first. Try to understand me. Maybe you can read my thoughts and hear them in your mind translated in your language. Don't know. I hear you people have mystical powers. So if you ever did: use them now and understand me. Go away. That's all. Go away. This city is not for you. We cut the Italians and they *look* like us! We're fierce. We're only children and you should see our folks! Go away. Take the ship back to China. Load up all your tea and your laundry and set sail for home, all right? Understand? UNDERSTAND?

(Lizzy whacks Mike and he falls.)

MIKE: The girl is terrifying!
LIZZY: Go get your knife.
MIKE: All right, all right.

(Mike goes.)

PETE: Lizzy . . .
LIZZY: Shut up. I just want to *experiment*. I just want to see what color her blood is. I just want to see it running down the street. We draw a line, Pete. A line in blood up and down this street. That line says, don't cross. Don't move here. Don't sell your evil trinkets to our people. Don't bring diseases. Don't hypnotize us. Don't come.
PETE: It's not yellow, it's red. Look.

(The Girl has cut her hand with a small knife. She holds her bleeding hand up to Lizzy.
Mike returns with a knife.)

GIRL: This is as far as you will get. This is as close to my heart as your fingers will go.
LIZZY: How did she understand me?
GIRL: I'll kick your ass next time you even look at me!
LIZZY: Mike, the knife.
MIKE: I changed my mind.
LIZZY: Let's see the *knife*.
MIKE: I changed it, I said!

(Lizzy speaks to Mike in her incoherent Chinese-speak during Pete's speech.)

PETE (*To the Girl*): You made your point. Put your blood away. Go home. Turn out your lights. Close your eyes. Listen for thieves. Protect your babies. Don't trust us. Hundreds of years will pass and nothing will change. You're determined to ruin everything for yourself. It must be really bad where you're from. Famine and pestilence everywhere. What did you expect from us? Open arms and a pat on the back? Marriage? I'd marry you. I'd marry a girl that looked like you.

LIZZY (*To Pete*): You're just a fucking pig.

(*Lizzy takes the knife from Mike and cuts her own hand.*)

MIKE: Oh Jesus . . .

LIZZY: Now we're even! Now we're even!

MIKE: What an insane Polack!

LIZZY (*Singsong*): Pete's gonna marry the China girl! Pete's gonna marry the China girl!

MIKE: Pete's gonna marry the China girl! Pete's gonna marry the China girl!

PETE: I never said I would! I never said I would!

(*Mike and Lizzy dance around Pete and the Girl.*)

GIRL: *I wasn't supposed to be walking! I was curious! I was tired of working! I heard there was a park!*

(*Lizzy starts kissing Mike.*)

LIZZY: Put your hand on my thing, Mikey!

MIKE: I'll bite your tongue off, harlot!

(*Laughing, Mike and Lizzy run away, but not before Lizzy kicks the Girl in the ass.*)

GIRL: I told my mother I would only be a few minutes: I want some air mother! I can't breathe in here! She said only a minute! I looked for the park, for something green. And I got lost. The streets are badly designed and I got lost.

PETE: I never said I would marry a China girl. I never said that.

(*Pete holds out his hand. The Girl gives Pete her bloody hand. Pete puts a finger into her blood. Then he puts the bloody finger into his mouth.*)

MY OLD HABIT PART 4

Mac Wellman

YOUNG MAN (*Fiercely*): Come on, silly old man. We'll take you to the hospital; to the benevolent society; to the Home for Old People; to Belleview; come on, come on, old man, let's go.

(*But the Old Man fears the worst, and resists.*)

OLD MAN: My son's a devil, worse than a devil!

(*In a puff of smoke the Young Man changes into a full-blown Chinese-demon and pushes the Old Man into a cage, takes him offstage. A chorus of minor devils sings and dances.*)

CHORUS:
She lit a match, and she lit another match.
She struck a fourth match and saw her
grandmother.
She was afraid her grandmother would
leave her soon. So she lit a whole
bunch of matches in order to make her
grandmother stay longer.
Then she saw a great smile on her
grandmother's face.
The two of them went to live with god.
She was dead on New Year's Eve.
Her corpse lay near the house corner.
There was a smile on her face,
a great smile.

(*Thunder.*)

SILENT MOVIE

Jessica Hagedorn

Thunder.

EMMA: I told you. We should've waited.

LUCY: No way. Tonight's our only chance.

EMMA: We're in deep shit now. Dear God. Why'd I listen to you? You're just a—

LUCY: What? Yer l'il dumb maid? *(Pause)* Oh, Emma. Stop.

EMMA: Stop? The rain won't stop. And then what?

LUCY: Then nothing. We ain't goin' back.

EMMA: That's right. It's flooding pigshit out there and I'm stuck in this Chinatown shithole with you and can't go home—

LUCY: Because you're high. Face it Emma. You're too high, and it's okay, and you're never goin' back.

EMMA: He'll find us.

LUCY: Shut up. You said he'd be away till tomorrow. *(Pause)* He ain't found us yet, has he? Hasn't figured any of it out, and it's been a whole year.

(Laughing softly.)

EMMA: Don't tell me to shut up. You're getting just a wee bit too cocky, dear. *(Pause)* I know he knows. He's known all along—

LUCY: You're high.

(A series of low, urgent knocks at the door startles them both.)

(Mutters to herself:) What the fuck.

EMMA *(Frantic)*: Oh Jesus shit. Mother of Mary. I knew it.

(Emma backs up against the wall terrified.)

What shall we do, Lucy?

LUCY: Will you calm down?

(Lucy struggles off the pallet, then crawls slowly to the door and speaks in a hoarse whisper. Knocks end.)

Uncle Wong? Is that you? *(Pause)* Everything okay! We're getting ready to go, promise! Soon as . . . soon as the weather changes . . . soon as the sky goes from gray to black . . . *(Pause)* There. He's gone, Emma.

EMMA: It's not the Chink I'm worried about.

(Lucy offers her the pipe.)

LUCY: Here. Better than your damn whiskey.

EMMA (*Hysterical, knocking the pipe out of Lucy's hand*): Are you listening to me? It's not that harmless old man I'm worried about. It's my husband! Don't you understand he wants to kill me? And you! You!

LUCY (*Stone-faced*): Don't ever do that again.

EMMA: I'm sorry, Lucy.

(*Emma gets on her knees and crawls around in the dark to find the pipe, which she cautiously hands back to Lucy.*)

I'm sorry—

LUCY: Don't ever.

(*Lucy refills the pipe, offers it to Emma. Her tone softens.*)

I think you need to slow down and refresh yourself, Mrs. Hanlon.

(*Emma lays on the pallet next to Lucy and reluctantly takes a deep toke. She watches while Lucy snorts cocaine.*)

EMMA: That powder's evil. I hate when you get so damn arrogant.

LUCY (*Amused*): Yeah? And I hate yer damn whiskey breath. And whiskey sweat.

EMMA (*Agitated again*): Oh, Lucy, sweet Jesus. Let's get out of here. We'll find another way out of town. We will—

LUCY: You just jumpy, that's all. Rain'll let up soon. It's early—nothin' to fret about. We'll get away soon enough. We're halfway there, ain't we? We'll be outta this shithole, soon as the sky . . .

(*Emma nods off to sleep.*)

Dream a while. Yeah. That's it. (*Pause*) I hate you sometimes. Hate havin' to make it all better for you, the way I always do, like I'm expected to. You pay me enough, I s'pose. And you trust me. (*Pause*) I love you too, Mrs. Hanlon. Stupid pitiful Emma. Beautiful Emma. But we can't stay here forever darlin'. Too dangerous. Uncle Wong will most definitely be back. We make him nervous, don't we? I hate the way he scurries around after takin' our . . . your money. Can't wait for us to leave! He's worse than a girl.

(*Lucy shouts at the door, waking Emma briefly. Emma drifts back into sleep.*)

IKNOWYOU'RETHERE,YAOLDGEEZER!EAVESDROPPIN'
AND PEEPIN' AT US!

(She grabs rubber straw and pokes it through keyhole.)

ARE YOU PLAYIN' WITH YOURSELF AGAIN? I CAN HEAR
YOU GASPING AND WHEEZIN' IN CHINESE! *(Mocking
and mimicking:)* "Hurry, hurry missee. Don't want no trouble.
Why you no get stuff from Uncle Wong and just take home? Go
home missee! No safe here! No safe here!" *(Laughing. To audience:)* She likes goin' to the pictures. That's how it all started.
The big shot husband had no time, but she had all the time in
the world.

(Emma sits up, disoriented.)

EMMA: Come with me to the pictures.

*(Emma gazes out at the audience as if she is watching a movie. As
she and Lucy speak, flickering, unfocused images from the 1919
D.W. Griffith film* Broken Blossoms *are projected on the wall
behind them.)*

LUCY *(To audience)*: Sure, I said. Anything to get outta cleanin'
that mansion of hers. I made my eyes real big and round, like
this—

*(Images of Lillian Gish as the movie version of Lucy Burrows, in
the squalid hovel she shares with her father. She is on her knees,
tearfully wiping her angry father's shoes as he stands there glower-
ing at her.)*

(Demonstrates:) —"Swell, Mrs. Hanlon. I've never been to the
pictures"—
EMMA: Poor thing.
LUCY: Off we went to the Bijou. What a dumb picture. I couldn't
wait to get out of there. *(To Emma:)* Please, Mrs. Hanlon.
EMMA: It's beautiful. Let's sit through it, again. Please, Lucy. Think
of it like a beautiful, scary dream.
LUCY: No thanks. I come from a family of lunatics, and I think you're
just like them, Mrs. Hanlon.
EMMA *(Bursts out laughing)*: You're a funny dear. Why don't you call
me Emma?

(Emma stares at her, then kisses her impulsively.)

Forgive me.

    I must truly be out of my mind. Please, dear. Don't tell any-one. I promise I'll never do it again.

LUCY: Then I'll do it. *(Pause)* Emma.

(Lucy kisses Emma.)

EMMA: I know this place where we can be alone. You ever been to Chinatown?

LUCY: Sure. Once or twice.

EMMA: I grew up there, before the Chinks moved in.

LUCY: I thought you were rich.

EMMA: My husband's rich. *(Pause)* I know this place on Baxter street, right by where I was born. We'll have fun.

LUCY: Fun. *(Dryly)* I don't know the meaning of the word.

EMMA: I'll show you.

(A thunderclap explosion. Terrified, Emma makes a move to bolt and run, but Lucy stops her. They struggle until Emma finally gives up, exhausted and resigned. The two women stare at each other for a moment, the sound of rain pouring down. Emma sheds her cloak.)

Dance with me again.

LUCY: Sure.

(As Lucy and Emma make love in the dark, specific clips from Broken Blossoms *are projected on the walls, but clearly this time. The entire room is bathed in these black and white images. The images are not shown in order, and can be repeated: Richard Barthelmess in his obsequious, effeminate pose as "The Chink," his taped eyelids perpetually downcast. Lillian Gish as the abused Irish girl, Lucy Burrows, cowering in terror from her brutal, drunken father, played by Donald Crisp. The Chink attempting to kiss the terrified White Girl, then suddenly pulling away from her in shame. The White Girl's immense look of relief. Her sub-titles which read: "What makes you so good to me, Chinky?" The enraged Drunken Father killing his daughter. The Chink shoot-ing the Father, then carrying the White Girl's limp body back to his curio shop. The grief-stricken Chink kneeling on the floor by*

*the bed on which the White Girl's corpse lies, then stabbing him-
self to death in glorious slow motion.)*

EMMA *(Disengaging herself from Lucy)*: Good. The rain's stopped.
We can go.
LUCY: What's the hurry? *(Teasing)* You're hurtin' my feelings, Mrs.
Hanlon.

(A sound outside the door.)

Not again.
EMMA *(Nervous)*: Is that you, Uncle Wong?
LUCY *(Taking another hit of cocaine)*: He don't understand English.

*(The door is kicked open by a brawny, fiftyish white man dressed
in an elegant suit, overcoat and hat. He points a gun at Emma.)*

EMMA *(To man)*: I knew you'd find us.

*(The man shoots Emma. She collapses. He shoots her a second
time, then a third. Meanwhile, Lucy has pulled her own revolver
from under the pallet. She points it at the man. The man, aiming
his gun at her, hesitates.)*

LUCY: Go ahead. You'll either die with me—or die first. *(She shoots.
Soft and tentative:)* Uncle Wong? Where are ya, old man?
(Pause) Ah, Mother of God, he got you too.

*(Lucy gets dressed quickly. She rummages through the dead
man's pockets and takes his wallet. She starts to take his gun,
then changes her mind. Kneeling down next to Emma's body, she
runs a hand gently over Emma's open eyes, to close them. Lucy
snatches her gun, Emma's spilled money, and, after snorting the
last of the precious cocaine, takes what's left of the opium. She
stuffs everything into the carpetbag and starts to leave, then turns
back once more to survey the room. Emma's luxurious cloak lies
on the floor. Lucy scoops it up and wraps herself in it. She slowly
backs out the door.)*

ANCHOR ARIA

Kia Corthron

Crash. A skillet falls from the ceiling. Agnes is under the covers in a bed.

AGNES: Margaret Sanger

(A cute stuffed dog. As it falls from the ceiling, sound of ferocious, even rabid, bark-growling.)

Mary Pickford

(A paper smiling man-in-the-crescent-moon falls.)

Mamie Smith

(Moon hits the floor with a cymbals clash.)

Blues! Did I vote? We got the vote, women, we got the vote, I vote?

(She starts to cough. Then quickly clamps her hands over her mouth, suppressing the coughs. Then removes her hands.)

I got the key.

(Sound from outside: clanging bell like an old fire engine.)

President Warren G. Harding. "Fuck the League of Nations!"

(The rocking horse rocks. Sound: a real horse's clip-clop. Agnes smiles.)

My daddy rode it. My daddy, cowboy like all the rest. Black like all the rest. He hit 'em: Montana. Kansas. Oklahoma. Daddy say "We stay 'til the weather turn or the cross burn." Then: we move on.

(From outside: a siren.)

Speakeasies.

(Chinese opera music. Agnes is a strict teacher before her class:)

Three hundred years ago today, they set foot Plymouth Rock set foot 1620—

(*A piano falls from the ceiling, cutting off the opera music with a splash, followed by bubbling water that continues under Agnes's speech. A strange light on Agnes, who stands up and walks down the bed, steps off the foot, continues walking directly downstage until at some point she will start walking backwards, back up onto the bed and finally under the blanket again.*)

My mother, born a Tanka southeast China and Tanka is a boat-person

(*A ship, held by strings, comes down the ceiling, swinging back and forth a few times in the air, before being pulled back up.*)

and there's Tankas born, live and die on the boat their whole lives never set foot land Muuchin Mother Muuchin My mother born a Tanka, born on a boat, her parents born on a boat, her grandparents from north China and went southeast with the blessing of *no one*, they go southeast now they boat people 'til my mother take a boat crost the Pacific meet a black man then come me.

(*Thunder, lighting, rain outside.*)

Ain't goin'! I ain't goin' to school today!

(*An umbrella falls from the ceiling onto Agnes's bed. Agnes opens it over her head.*)

Congress pass Chinese Exclusion Act. Congress don't pass anti-lynching bill.

(*It starts to rain inside, on Agnes's bed.*)

My mother likes the free agent cowboy wife life. She the first to say it "MOVE!" We in Texas "MOVE!" Oklahoma "MOVE!" Callyfornia "Lotsa Chinese here. They hate Chinese MOVE!" She a Tanka. Boatperson. She 'on't like anchors, her feet holdin' ground.

(*Rain stops. She puts down umbrella.*)

Whadja learn? School?
NIGGERCHINKNIGGERCHINKNIGGERCHINK

(Sudden fast-chatter of two Chinese women from outside.)

My grandfather the slave had but one kid I got no black cousins. Somewhere I got Chinese people. "Where my people?!" "They died," she says. My mother's parents dead, grandparents dead BUT. Still got people, Datong. North China. Fourth cousins, fifth, her uncles, great-aunts.

(Loud dripping, like a faucet leak. Agnes gets out of bed. Looks around for snoopers before speaking. A confidence:)

I got the key. Key locks everyone door. They can't get in. Can't get me. I ain't goin'.

(Women's hearty giggling from outside. Agnes hops back into bed.)

Daughter of my mother's mother's friend she finds out's here, Chinatown. My mother "Move!" Just for a while we come for a visit. Then they MOVE! I stay.

(A little corset falls from the ceiling, a cat-in-orgasm screech as it falls. As soon as it hits the floor, irregular, scratchy, eerie violin music. Agnes feels the newspaper with her palms, Ouija board–like. By feel, never looking at the paper, she stops moving her hands when she gets to the words set off in bold, says the words, no pause, then starts moving her hands again. The words are not stressed. She smiles, periodically laughs, as if these are all fond memories:)

I remember the time in the wagon crossin' Missoura **Eugene Debs** I remember the hot and the hot and the sun burnin' through the canvas I'm three **Ida B. Wells** remember him build me a rockin' horse.

(Rocking horse silently rocks forward, is still.)

Her dip me cool water pond I remember ice **fifty-nine lynchings** snow up to my five-year-old neck I remember her sing to me I remember her cousin write a letter **Theory of Relativity** her cousin my cousin write a letter "I'm comin'!" **Emperor Jones** cousin can't come The Exclusion Act *No Chinese* I remember crazy Miss Hong, Tacoma, we at the pump drinka water she come up mumblin' pick the invisible bugs off us **Prohibition** That man say ten years old Miss Hong see mother, father kicked, punched, dragged out, white men the cold rain, "Chinese must go!" marched to the expulsion train never seen again **Four thousand U.S. radicals arrested** Colorado Daddy the only black cowpoke, his birthday they give him a present **La Choy (in a** *can***!)** He open it. It's a noose **Twenty-five thousand black gather Madison Square Garden Marcus Garvey** the big toilet choice: "white only," "colored only," Daddy know what to do. Muuchin Mama and me look at each other

(Violin music abruptly stops.)

Earthquake: One hundred thousand North Chinese dead.

(Violin music abruptly starts.)

Middle a the night they wake me "MOVE!" "*WHY?*" I'm fifteen. "They comin'! *MOVE!*" I roll over. They throw water my face. I move.

(Two larger-than-life chopsticks fall to the floor with a big boom. Violin music gone. A low "aftershock" rumble continues under Agnes's speech.)

They ain't move me! They ain't move me! *(Secret:)* no one knows. They ain't heard me cough I stay here, keep it hid. Nosy neighbor seen me once, vomit the toilet. But I got it.

(She pulls out a key from her clothing.)

I go behind the desk the lobby, I find the extra key *no* one get in here! No one get in here They never find out. *(Slurring the third syllable)* Consumpt— Consumpt—

(Sudden bright sunlight floods in from the window. Hyperreal, as if the sun is right outside the window.)

No boat person here no cowboy no sanatorium. I stay.

(She swallows the key. Now starts to cough again. Begins small but becomes increasingly out of control. She tries to suppress it— with her hands, by pouring water out of her pitcher. Trying to drink it makes an enormous mess. Sound: footstep of a huge monster approaching from the corridor. In a panic she finally succeeds in stifling the cough. Another footstep. Another.)

Stay.

(Footsteps louder and more rapid.)

No! *My* room Don't touch it *my* room touch that door. Boundaries! Stay your boundaries *mine*! You can't touch it no KEY no KEY MINE this side the door MINE!

(Footsteps louder still, faster, now a run.)

DON'T BREAK IT DOWN! DOWN BREAK IT DOWN I'LL JESUS CHRIST ME! DON'T THINK I WON'T JESUS CHRIST NAIL MY HANDS MY FEET TO THIS STINKIN' BED *NOT MOVE!*

(Footsteps stop. A long stillness. Eventually Agnes looks around the room as if seeing it for the first time. Relief. Bit of a smile:)

Still.

(An exaggerated key-into-lock jiggling.
    The door slowly creaks open. Agnes turns to the door. Much daylight floods into the room.)

NEW

Constance Congdon

HIROKO *(To someone offstage)*: Kenny, I'm not sick anymore. I'll be all right.

(She staggers to a park bench and sits down, then lies down, feeling really bad. She wears high heels and a pastel-colored suit with a Nixon button and an "Honorary Delegate" ribbon.)

Uh-oh.

(*Lying down has made her more nauseous, so she sits up, noticing a pile of dirty clothes on the bench.*)

Ick! Ick!

(*She goes through a frenzy pushing the clothes on the ground and then examining the bench for any disgusting thing. She brushes herself off and sits, still afraid there might be some stray "ca-ca" on the bench somewhere. She burps.*)

'Cuse me.

(*Fear of eminent nausea makes her settle on the bench. She takes an elaborate cigarette pouch, out of her large, white purse. Then she digs around inside her purse and finds a huge silver ornamental lighter, the kind that used to sit on coffee tables. She looks at the lighter.*)

This isn't my lighter. (*Remembers where she got it*) Oh my gosh. Oh my gosh. This is from— Oh my god. (*Starting to lose control*) I stole a lighter! I stole a lighter! What am I coming to?

(*She starts to cry again and fumbles in her bag, takes out a Kleenex and blows her nose. Then lights a cigarette with the lighter, drops the lighter into her bag, and deeply enjoys the first drag of the cigarette.*
    She coughs a lot, drops the cigarette, then brushes her bodice clean of any stray cigarette ash. In doing this, she notices her Nixon button.)

Nixon, he lost! He lost! What's gonna happen? We have a Catholic in the White House! Kneel and stand up and kneel and stand up. Domino gloria, whatever the heck it is—he could be saying, "Kill the Japanese girl back there who's still sitting down. (*Speaks to someone she thinks she sees offstage—in the place where the light will later appear*) Ken? I'm not sick anymore.

(*No answer.*)

Is the bus here yet?

(No answer.)

Okayfine.

White boys—they are not gentlemen. Not gentlemen at all. Mom, you are right. Mom.

(Longs for her mom now and whimpers a little.)

Okay, you've been left, Hiroko. You, silly girl, have been left by a big stupid-head white boy in a park in the big, ugly city, filled with foreigners. Oh god oh god oh god. Fine. I'll get a taxicab or something. I'm an American girl and I can just get my own damn transportation.

(She takes off one of her shoes, removes a ten-dollar bill, and puts it in her bra.)

Just as soon as that light stop spinning. KENNNNNNNNNNNNNNNNEEEEEEEEE! I'm sorreeeeeeeeee!!

(From another corner of the square, a young "white" girl, Monica, enters, also dressed in a pastel-colored suit. She's also wearing Nixon buttons, but no "Honorary Delegate" ribbon. She see Hiroko.)

MONICA: Koko?

HIROKO: Monica?

MONICA *(Noticing their surroundings)*: This is some scuzzy place. This grass looks terrible. Who takes care of these places?

HIROKO: I wish I had a coke. Maybe Kenny can get me one.

MONICA: I thought I heard you shouting.

HIROKO: Just shouting for Kenny.

MONICA: I'm waiting on Dave—he's looking for some men's room that's supposed to be in this park somewhere. I loved your speech.

HIROKO: Nixon lost, anyway.

MONICA: But if your speech had been on television, he might have won.

HIROKO: Does anyone know we've been drinking? I didn't mean to, but Kenny brought it. He thought Nixon was going to win, so we drank to that. Then he didn't, but we kept drinking, anyway. I feel terrible. I never drink. I smoke, though. I just bought this case for my cigarettes.

MONICA (*About the cigarette case*): Pretty. I have one sort of like that. Dave picked it out. Where is he?

HIROKO: Maybe he and Kenny found each other.

MONICA: No one knows where anyone is. I think our sponsors are drunk, anyway. Mr. Buchanan went somewhere with Mrs. Stein and they can't find them.

(Monica see the clothes on the ground.)

EEEEyew. What are those?

HIROKO: They were on the bench. Be careful where you sit down.

(Monica looks at the bench and then catches the odor from it.)

MONICA: Get up! Get up! It's dirty.

(Hiroko gets up.)

HIROKO (*Woozy*): I stood up too quick. But where are we going to sit now? I can't stand up.

MONICA: The bus isn't here yet. And they kicked us out of the meeting hall. Some of the kids are in the lobby . . .

HIROKO: I'm not going back without Kenny.

MONICA: Dave will be back any minute.

(They're kind of hung up there, neither wanting to leave the bench area. They wait a few beats.)

I've got an idea.

(Monica takes a can of spray net out of her purse and sprays the bench. They both fan the bench with their purses to dry the spray net.)

HIROKO: Aqua Net will kill the germs.

(They sit. Automatically, they get combs out of their purses, take off their hats and tease their hair a bit and spray it, as Hiroko talks.)

I started in this because my debate coach, Mr. Nolte, said to. In debate, you're not supposed to care because that keeps you from arguing both sides really well. You "suspend judgment"—at least until debate season is over with. You know? Monica? But I really started to care about Vice President Nixon's platform.

MONICA: He was a debater. Nixon. I read that. He belonged to the same school club you and Dave and Ken do.

HIROKO: National Forensic League?

MONICA: Uh-huh. 'Course I really support Kennedy because my dad does, but he let me come on this trip, anyway, 'cause I wanted to go with Dave. Your dad supports Nixon?

HIROKO: My dad doesn't vote.

MONICA: Doesn't vote?

HIROKO: Something about the war. Something happened.

MONICA: What?

HIROKO: I don't know.

MONICA: He can't vote?

HIROKO: I don't know. He doesn't talk about it. When we left California, he stopped talking about much of anything. He works on the yard.

MONICA: You have the nicest yard. That's what my dad says. "The Japanese are natural gardeners."

HIROKO: I keep seeing a light over there.

MONICA: Maybe that's the door to the men's room.

HIROKO: I called for Kenny and he didn't come out.

MONICA: We'll go over . . . in a minute. I feel funny walking close to a men's room. You just never know what they do in there.

HIROKO: You wanted Kennedy all this time?

MONICA: Uh-huh.

HIROKO: You . . . a Catholic, Monica?

MONICA: No. We're Unitarian.

HIROKO: What's that?

MONICA (*Paraphrasing their dogma*): Oh, "all religions are good."

HIROKO: Do you have a . . . priest in this church?

MONICA (*Not sure about the facts*): Noooo. But I don't really know much about it. My dad doesn't make me go. There's that light again. What is it? Dave? Ken? Come ON. (*Beat*) Do you hate Catholics or something?

HIROKO: My mom.

MONICA: Why?

HIROKO: When I was little, we lived in this camp—my brother was born there—and anyway, the guy who ran it was Catholic and so was our Mayor who didn't help us. So Mom blamed them.

MONICA: Camp? What kind of camp?

HIROKO: A camp where they take all your money and your house.

MONICA: That's not right.

HIROKO: We don't talk about it.

MONICA: That's a stupid, wrong camp. In *America*?

HIROKO: We don't talk about it. Don't tell.

MONICA: I won't. *(Getting mad)* If my father had known about it—he would have—he would have— *(Still can't believe it)* In *America*?

(Hiroko is staring at the offstage light.)

I don't feel so good all of a sudden. Koko? Hiroko?

(Hiroko gets up and moves toward the offstage light.)

Hiroko? I'm sort of scared. Let's go to the hotel lobby and wait. *(Notices Hiroko moving)* What are you doing? The hotel is that— *(Pointing in the opposite direction)* —way!

(Hiroko comes to herself and faces Monica.)

HIROKO: I'm not going back there until I can go back with Ken. I don't want anyone to think I got stood up. I don't care if I have to wait until the sun comes up.

(Hiroko turns back to the light and watches it.)

MONICA: If that's the sun, you shouldn't watch it—it's bad for your eyes.

HIROKO: Feels like it's watching *us*.

MONICA: Could it be the sun?

HIROKO: Maybe—maybe in the city it's all misshapen and strange-looking because it has to fit through—

MONICA: —buildings and everything.

HIROKO: It is the sun! Oh, the sun's coming up, Monica!

(Monica joins Hiroko to look at the light.)

It's a new day!

MONICA: We're seniors!

HIROKO: We're feeling better!

MONICA: Good morning—
HIROKO: —morning, new world!

(The two young women are smiling at the light, when suddenly, it engulfs them, like blinding white light emanating from a huge door opening offstage. The light is accompanied by the cacophonous sounds of a zillion human voices shouting, singing, laughing and crying—all at once. The two women stare into what seems to be the source of the light, as if it were a doorway into the future where they can see people running and screaming, people protesting—all sorts of human drama and tragedy passing by the passageway. Hiroko puts her hand up to her mouth in shock, then silence and the light goes out.)

MONICA: What was that? Koko? What was that?

(Hiroko doesn't move for a moment, then turns to Monica. Hiroko opens her mouth to speak, but nothing comes out. She tries again, but nothing comes out.)

Are you hurt? Why can't you talk?

(Hiroko leans forward and blood comes out of her mouth. She catches some of it in her hand, and, as if to answer Monica's original question, "What was that?" meaning "What did you see?" Hiroko wipes the blood on her clothes.)

You're bleeding! What happened?!

(Monica's attention is pulled to Hiroko's eyes—she grabs Hiroko's face and looks into her eyes.)

What did we see?

(Gunshot.)

HIROKO *(In the voice of a black woman)*: MEDGAR! MEDGAR! NOOOOOOOOOOO! Oh nooooooo, my baby, *noooooooo!*

(Gunshot. A southern accent:)

Well, Mr. President, you can't say Dallas *doesn't love—*

(Gunshot. Gunshot.)

I have a *dream*—

(Gunshot.)

You see things and you say, "Why?" But I dream things that never were and I say, *"Why not?"*

My group herded men, women, children and babies into the center of the village, like a little island.

MONICA: Lieutenant Calley come over and said, "You know what to do with them, don't you?"

HIROKO: Lieutenant Calley come over and said, "You know what to do with them, don't you?"

MONICA: Don't you? And I said, "Yes."

HIROKO: "Yes." And he left and came back about ten minutes later, and said, "How come you ain't killed them yet?"

MONICA: Killed them yet? And I told him that I didn't think—

HIROKO: I didn't think he wanted us to kill them, that he just wanted us to guard them.

MONICA: He said, "No"—

HIROKO: "No, I want them dead." So he started shooting them. And he told me to start shooting. I poured about four clips into them—that's sixty-eight shots.

MONICA: So we started to gather more people, and we put them in the hut and then we dropped a hand grenade in there with them.

HIROKO: And then just outside the village there was this big pile of bodies. This really tiny kid—he had only a shirt on—

MONICA: —only a shirt on—

HIROKO: —nothing else—

MONICA: Nothing.

HIROKO: He came over to the pile—

MONICA: This really tiny kid.

HIROKO: He came over to the pile of bodies—

MONICA: This really tiny kid—

HIROKO: Only a shirt on—

MONICA: Nothing else.

HIROKO: He held the hand of one of the dead.

MONICA: And one of the GI's behind me dropped into a kneeling position—

HIROKO: —a kneeling position.

MONICA: And killed him with a single *shot*.

(The sound of "Miserere" by Arvo Pärt as the two women take off their suits and heels. They take the old stinky clothes out of the bag and put them on, methodically, until they both look like homeless bag people. They exit separately, carrying the plastic bags.

When the stage is empty, we hear applause and then Hiroko's voice, ending the speech she gave that Monica was so impressed with.)

HIROKO *(Voice-over)*: Thank you. But before I close, I want you to remember my name—Hiroko Kawase—because I am a young American. And although I have often wished I could see into the future, I know that's impossible; so, instead, I will look at all of you, and you look at me, and in our eyes you can see the future of America. It's 1960—the world is at peace—the future has come. *It's here.*

MY OLD HABIT PART 5

Mac Wellman

She has spied her shoes, and approaches slowly, in reverent disbelief. In a state of radiant happiness. She sweeps them up in her arms, turns them about to make sure, puts them on, and admires her very fine satin pumps.

Pause.

Quietly, members of the chorus gather about her, and begin the second chorus:

CHORUS:

    Dark; gloomy; dim
    Warm
    Sage; saint; sacred
    A festival

    To love; love; dear
    Small; slight; et cetera

    Opposite; to face
    To cover; a cover
    To extinguish; to put out

To scratch
Soul
Kind; affectionate

To pity; sympathize
Hungry
Stiffened, et cetera
Birth

Lamp; light
Burn; roast
Only; alone

Cheek; side of face

Candle
A wall
to light (a Lamp)
 Candle
 A wall
 To light (a lamp)
  Candle
  A wall
  To light (a lamp)

OLD WOMAN: My old habit of returning to places is the only thing
 I understand . . .

CRICKET

Alice Tuan

1.

CRICKET: *Cricket*

 (Pause.)

 Cricket

MR. FONG: What's that?

CRICKET: *Cricket Cricket*

MR. FONG: That teacher.

CRICKET: *Cricket*

MR. FONG: That foreign teacher. *(Crick)* The one who read me Dickinson.

CRICKET: *Crick*

MR. FONG: When we lived in Nanjing. *(Crick)* The one that brought me the broken watermelon. It had fallen off of her bicycle she said. Couldn't strap it on tight enough. She said "strap it on tight enough." *(Cricket)* The Americans. I thought: I will not go to a country where they cannot strap it on tight enough. And now, here I am.

2.

Ms. Moon measures sides of the square. Carlos tries to memorize poem.

CARLOS:

Teacher Fong!
One . . . seven . . . six . . . five
That . . . love . . . is . . . all . . . there . . . is
That love is all there is
That love is all there is
Is . . . all . . . we . . . know . . . of . . . love

That love is all there is
Is all we know of love

3.

CRICKET: *CRICKET CRICKET CRICKET*

MR. FONG: That was Nanjing. That foreign teacher. The one who read me Dickinson. Spare. Spare. The language worked as a Chinese quarter poem. "That love is all there is" . . . I read her Dickinson back . . . "is all we know of love."

CRICKET: *CRICKET CRICKET CRICKET CRICKET CRICKET!*

MR. FONG: No, the authorities were not pleased. The students watched our every move. The granny patrol reported us. We had to meet clandestinely on train platforms. Fifteen minutes at a time. A vision in white she was. Our shoulders brushed. Her vanilla scent intoxicated me. To sneak a peek into her crystalline eyes. We'd pour into a crowd just to be bunched up against each other. The last time.

CRICKET: *Cricket*

MR. FONG: The last time we met, she gave me her Dickinson. A blue bound book, the complete poems. Each turn of the page a whiff of her vanilla. I couldn't give her Dickinson back. The big mess came. A big mess they call, huh, Cultural Revolution . . . fucking hypocrites! It was devolution! Cultural devolution!

That foreign teacher sent back to the United States. I sent from Nanjing to the countryside. For twelve years. To learn from the peasants. Even though I'd learned from the foreign teacher. Especially because I had learned from the foreign teacher. I was to learn from the peasants how to blanken the slate. To blanken my slate.

CRICKET: *Crick*

MR. FONG: The day I arrived in the countryside . . . two days out of Nanjing by car . . . I planted acorns around my shack. Four sides of the shack. A line of Dickinson for each side I watered. One acorn at each corner. Two in between. A perfect twelve. A year. An hour. A meal. And Dickinson became clearer and clearer with each turn. It kept me alive. It was the feed. For twelve years. Each tree watered. Each word absorbed. Each kiss remembered.

4.

Ms. Moon marks the sides. Vardush, like Carlos, is memorizing her class assignment . . . though Vardush has it down, complete with meaning.

VARDUSH: 1765.

> That love is all there is
> Is all we know of Love;
> It is enough, the freight should be
> Proportioned to the groove.

(Jackhammer.)

5.

In darkness, a jackhammer of cricket sounds.
   Lights up on Mr. Fong, administering booze with an eyedropper to calm Cricket.
   Carlos enters.

CARLOS: Teacher Fong. Teacher Fong.

(Cricket cricket cricket.)

Teacher Fong?

(Crick-et crick-et crick.)

Teacher Fong?
MR. FONG: Carlos. My most diligent student.
CARLOS: How you say in English again?
MR. FONG: Cricket.
CARLOS: Cree-kee
MR. FONG: Cricket.
CARLOS: Cree-kee
MR. FONG: Cri- ih ih
CARLOS: Crih-ih-ih
MR. FONG: Ket
CARLOS: Keh. Crik-keh *(To box:)* Hey Crih keh crih keh. Hi crih keh crih keh. You fron da Cheena. Meester Fong breen you fron da Cheena. He fine you een tree of Miss Emily in da Cheena. Meester Fong lof you and lof you so much. Meesus crih-key.
MR. FONG: It was glooorious, Carlos, just glooooorious. The desert around my little shack grew into twelve mighty, swaying trees. In full square. My shack now a forest. And this cricket.
CARLOS: Cree-key
MR. FONG: She dwelled in the square of trees.
CARLOS: Cree-key
MR. FONG: She hopped the twelve, hopped to each corner I'd hear her.

(They "see" her hopping around the square.)

CARLOS: Cree-key cree-key cree-key
MR. FONG AND CARLOS: Cree-key. cree-key cree-key
CARLOS: Cree-key. cree-key cree-key

MR. FONG: 1104.

> The Crickets sang
> And set the sun
> And workmen finished one by one
> Their seam the Day upon

CARLOS: They seen the day come on
MR. FONG: Their seam the Day upon
CARLOS: They seen the day
MR. FONG: Their seam the Day upon
CARLOS: What mean this, Mr. Fong they see the day uhn ohn?

(Pause.)

MR. FONG: Remember it first. We will speak of meaning later.

(Jackhammer.)

6.

In darkness, a deafening jackhammer sound.
Mr. Fong sees the past. Cricket hopping from tree to imaginary tree around the present square.

MR. FONG: Singularly, I came to these states to find that foreign teacher.
CRICKET: *CRICK*
MR. FONG: Strapped my bags on tight . . . wandering . . . Seattle, Boston, Miami, Los Angeles . . . and points in between. I surrounded my world with English-learning mouths, teaching them to recite Dickinson . . . hoping these incantations would conjure you back to me. Now here, thirty years, you—foreign teacher, are still nowhere to be found. My foreign teacher: I can no longer endure as one, in this age of two. Two. Oh. Oh. Oh.

(Vardush enters, a vision in white. She sits beside him, out of breath. Mr. Fong is always enraptured with her speech.)

VARDUSH: I am HATE Hovic!
MR. FONG: Vardush!

VARDUSH: I am HATE HATER Hovic

MR. FONG: Vaaar-dooosh

VARDUSH: I am HATE hater HATEST Hovic

MR. FONG (*Beautifully intoxicated*): Vaaar-dooosh

VARDUSH: I say him, I say: I want go bookstore. He take me library. Okay. Okay. Book library . . . he no listen good. I say him: I want buy Miss Emily book. He say: no money. Pyuf! I say him: you go out and out drinking all money to stomach like country bump-kin DATOOMGALOOKH! You no drink two maybe three beer, you can have to buy Miss Emily book! Hovic say me: DOOON.

(*Mr. Fong stops Vardush's verbiage with a kiss on the mouth. The cricket chirps very rapidly. They cease.*)

I say Hovic: I want have book . . . no lend . . . HAVE . . . so I can have forever.

MR. FONG: Forever

(*Cricket cricket.*)

VARDUSH: So I come here to Diamond Square from library . . . so much more far than bookstore . . . so I have not fifteen . . . twelve minootes from Hovic pick me

MR. FONG: 1765

VARDUSH: Miss Emily?

(*Cricket.*)

MR. FONG: That . . . love is all there is . . . Is all we know of

VARDUSH: . . . . . . love . . . . is . . . is all . . . we know

MR. FONG: Love . . . it is enough . . .

VARDUSH: Love . . . . enough . . .

MR. FONG: The freight should be . . . proportional to the groove

VARDUSH: Proportional . . . Proportional . . . Proportional . . . groove.

(*Ms. Moon appears in full construction worker regalia, holds a jackhammer at first corner. 1880s and 1920s folk pass through.*)

I like the word. pro-por-tion-al because love is like proportional. Love make to the same size of the person spirit. Big spirit. Big love! You learn me good word Mr. Fong. Miss Emily make good make the word.

(Mr. Fong takes Vardush's hand and gently kisses it.
The jackhammeress begins.
She rounds the first corner, kinetically and violently bouncing.
Vardush and Mr. Fong are oblivious to the noise. Carlos rushes
in.)

CARLOS: HEY HEY HEY WHAT DOING? WHAT DOING?
I SAY STOP. STOP. STAHHHHHHHHHHHHHP!

(Ms. Moon stops.)

MS. MOON: You talkin' to me?

(She moves to the next corner.)

CARLOS: This . . . you . . . can't . . . it . . . this . . . you . . . why are you
changing the ground?
MR. FONG: I must ask you something, Vardush.
VARDUSH: What? What is it.

(Jackhammer. Jackhammer. Jack.)

Again Mr. Fong.

(Jackhammer. Jackhammer. Jack.)

Forever? Yes, Mr. Fong, yes.
MR. FONG: Glorious! Glorious! Vardush makes me two. One is mere
person, now two we are people.
VARDUSH: Yes we are.
CARLOS: But this is the ground for peoples. You cannot change it.
MS. MOON: I've got orders. Papers to prove it.
CARLOS: I can't believe it. Let me see.
VARDUSH: Can I see your box, Mr. Fong?

(Jackhammer Jackhammer Hack. Ms. Moon moves to the fourth
corner. Onlookers from the century gaze.)

Your cricket. It look dead but still make sound. Cri-ket. Cri-ket.
MR. FONG: That's it! That's it Vardush. Both dead and alive. It is
the age of two. Everyone will write two. The years begin with
two. 2000. 2001. 2002. Over and over again, we'll think of two.

Instead of one, it is the age of two. We can hold two opposite thoughts in our minds, all at once. No more minootes. I see you in class, Mr. Fong.

CARLOS: No! You cannot change my square. I practice here, one two three four, Miss Emily. No change. No change! I don't understand. Where is my square for to practice Miss Emily? Crick-ee, crick-ee, crick-ee.

MS. MOON: You with Mr. Fong?

CARLOS: Yes . . . Mr . . . Fong . . . Ms. Emily.

MS. MOON: Yes, I know. *(Beat)* Isn't it better to read, without sides. No stops. Fluid.

CARLOS: No more Diamond Square.

MS. MOON: But a new shape, a new shape to learn. A new shape to think, and resee. Soften the corners. Round out the lines. Now let it be: Moon Park.

CARLOS:

That love is all there is
Is all we know of Love;
That love is all there is
Is all we know of Love;

(A spoken Cricket duet—Vardush and Mr. Fong.)

That love is all there is
Is all we know of Love;

END OF PLAY

Bridget Carpenter writes for the stage and television. She was a resident playwright at the Royal National Theatre in London and has been nominated for numerous awards for her work on the TV series *Friday Night Lights*.

Ping Chong is a theatre director, choreographer, video and installation artist. Since 1972 he has created over fifty works for the stage, which have been presented at major venues all over the world.

Constance Congdon has received playwriting fellowships from the National Endowment for the Arts and the Rockefeller Guggenheim foundations. Congdon has been teaching playwriting at Amherst College for fifteen years.

Kia Corthron has received a Van Lier Fellowship, a Daryl Roth Creative Spirit Award and the Mark Taper Forum's Fadiman Award. Corthron's plays reflect her lifelong humanitarian efforts, which have taken her around the country and the world.

Maria Irene Fornes is a nine-time Obie Award-winner. She has directed numerous classical and contemporary plays and has mentored dozens of playwrights throughout her career.

Philip Kan Gotanda is a playwright and independent film maker. He has won fellowships from the National Endowment for the Arts and the Rockefeller and Guggenheim foundations.

Jessica Hagedorn is a novelist, poet and playwright. She is the recipient of a Guggenheim Foundation award and participated in the NEA/TCG Theatre Residency Program for Playwrights.

David Henry Hwang is a Tony Award-winning playwright and screenwriter. He serves on the council of the Dramatists Guild and has received fellowships from the Rockefeller and Guggenheim foundations and the National Endowment for the Arts.

Craig Lucas has written for the stage and the screen. He is the recipient of the Arts and Letters Award from the American Academy of Arts and Letters and two Obies, among numerous other awards.

Robert O'Hara is a playwright and director who also writes for film and television. He is the recipient of Center Theatre Group's Richard E. Sherwood Award and a Van Lier Fellowship.

Han Ong is the author of more than three dozen plays and is a performance artist and novelist. Ong is the recipient of fellowships from the MacArthur and Guggenheim foundations and the National Endowment for the Arts.

José Rivera studied with Gabriel Garcia Márquez at Sundance and was in residence at the Royal Court Theatre in London. Rivera has written several notable screenplays, including *The Motorcycle Diaries*.

Diana Son is an award-winning playwright, a writer/producer for television and a screenwriter. Son has won numerous awards and has taught playwriting to graduate students at the Yale School of Drama and the Dramatic Writing Program at New York University.

Alice Tuan was a participant of the NEA/TCG Residency Program for Playwrights and a recipient of a Beinecke Playwright Fellowship. Tuan is the head of Writing for Performance at California Institute of the Arts.

Mac Wellman is an Obie Award-winning playwright and the recipient of awards from the National Endowment for the Arts and the Rockefeller and Guggenheim foundations. He is a professor of playwriting at Brooklyn College.

Chay Yew is the recipient of the London Fringe award and a GLAAD Media Award. An alumnus of New Dramatists, he also works as a director and is the Artistic Director of Victory Gardens Theatre in Chicago.

Chay Yew's plays include *Porcelain*, *A Language of Their Own*, *Red*, *A Beautiful Country*, *Wonderland*, *Vivien and the Shadows*, *A Distant Shore* and *Visible Cities*. His other work includes the adaptations *A Winter People* (based on Chekhov's *The Cherry Orchard*) and Lorca's *The House of Bernarda Alba* and the musical *Long Season*. His work has been produced at the Public Theater, Royal Court Theatre (London), Mark Taper Forum, Manhattan Theatre Club, Wilma Theater, Long Wharf Theatre, La Jolla Playhouse, Fattore K (Naples), Intiman Theatre, Studio Theatre, Portland Center Stage, East West Players, Cornerstone Theater Company, Perseverance Theatre, La Mama (Melbourne), TheatreWorks (Singapore), among others. He is also the recipient of the London Fringe Award for Best Playwright and Best Play, George and Elisabeth Marton Playwriting Award, GLAAD Media Award, Made in America Award and Robert Chesley Award. His plays are published by Grove/Atlantic, Inc. He is an alumnus of New Dramatists.

He works as a director and was the Founding Director and Associate Artist of the Asian Theatre Workshop at the Mark Taper Forum where he produced and presented several seasons at the Mark Taper Forum's Taper Too.

In 2011 Chay Yew was named the Artistic Director of Victory Gardens Theatre in Chicago.